A MODERN GUIDE TO THE EUROPEAN PARLIAMENT

A MODERN GUIDE TO THE EUROPEAN PARLIAMENT

Martin Westlake

With a Preface by Sir Leon Brittan QC

PINTER
PUBLISHERS
LONDON AND NEW YORK

Distributed in the United States and Canada by St. Martin's Press

Pinter Publishers Ltd.
25 Floral Street, London WC2E 9DS, United Kingdom

First published in 1994

Distributed exclusively in the USA and Canada by St. Martin's Press, Inc., Room 400, 175 Fifth Avenue, New York, NY 10010, USA

British Library Cataloguing in Publication Data

A CIP catalogue record for this book is available from the British Library

ISBN 1 85567 200 6 (hb)
ISBN 1 85567 201 4 (pb)

Library of Congress Cataloging-in-Publication Data

Westlake, Martin.
   A modern guide to the European Parliament / Martin Westlake; with a preface by Sir Leon Brittan.
      p.   cm.
   Includes bibliographical references and index.
   ISBN 1–85567–200–6. – ISBN 1–85567–201–4 (pbk.)
   1. European Parliament.   I. Title.
JN36.W49   1994
341.24'24–dc20   94–29566
                                                               CIP

Typeset by Mayhew Typesetting, Rhayader, Powys
Printed and bound in Great Britain by Biddles Ltd., Guildford and King's Lynn

To Aldo, Edvard, Emma, Hannah, Laurence, Manon, Marguerite, Matthieu and Samuel. Tomorrow's democratic Europe is yours.

A Parliament is nothing less than a big meeting of more or less idle people. In proportion as you give it power it will inquire into everything, settle everything, meddle in everything. In an ordinary despotism, the powers of a despot are limited by his bodily capacity, and by the calls of pleasure; he is but one man; — there are but twelve hours in his day, and he is not disposed to employ more than a small part in dull business. . . But a Parliament is composed of a great number of men by no means at the top of the world. When you establish a predominant Parliament, you give over the rule of the country to a despot who has unlimited time, — who has unlimited vanity, — who has, or believes he has, unlimited comprehension, whose pleasure is in action, whose life is work. There is no limit to the curiosity of Parliament.

Walter Bagehot, *The English Constitution*, Oxford University Press, first published 1867 (1949 edition).

Contents

Preface

The European Parliament's evolution since it came into being in 1957 has been characterised by steady progress punctuated by sudden leaps forward. The Budget Treaties in the 1970s, the first direct elections in 1979, the 'Isoglucose' Court ruling of 1980 and the entry into force of the Single European Act in 1987 were all great leaps forward, but the entry into force of the Maastricht Treaty in November 1993 was undeniably the greatest leap of all. Although it was already a force to be reckoned with, the Parliament now sports a considerable expanded arsenal of powers, ranging from legislative assent through to the new 'co-decision' procedure, from consultation rights on trade agreements through to veto powers over accession and association agreements, from budgetary authority through to budgetary discharge, from the right to request initiatives through to the right to bring actions before the Court, from the new holding of committees of inquiry through to the powers of the new parliamentary ombudsman.

But I believe that the greatest change of all involves relations between those two quintessentially Community institutions, the Parliament and the Commission. From the outset, the European Parliament always had the right to sack the Commission, if it could muster a sufficient majority to pass a censure motion. Now, the Parliament has an important role to play in the appointment of the Commission. The President of the Commission is to be appointed after Parliament has been consulted, and the President-delegate, together with the other nominated members of the college, are to be subject to a parliamentary vote of approval. These provisions, together with the synchronisation of the mandates of the two institutions, must inevitably render the Commission more responsive and more accountable to the Parliament.

This tightening and clarification of the lines of accountability come at a time of great change for both institutions. The new Parliament has forty-nine more members than its 1979–94 predecessor, eighteen of them from the new German *Länder*, and it will have more when the applicant countries join the European Union. There are many new faces and, just as significantly, many of the old faces have gone, as the first direct-elections generation has given way to another. Above all, because the 1989–94 Parliament's mandate ended soon after the entry into force of the Maastricht Treaty, the new Parliament can genuinely claim to be the first European Parliament to enjoy the full range of its post-Maastricht powers.

The Commission that will begin its work in January 1995 will also be different to its predecessor in several important respects. As the first Commission appointed under the new Maastricht arrangements, it will have a five-, rather than the present four-, year mandate. It will also have a new President, the first for ten years, and there will also be many new faces. Like the Parliament, the new Commission will have to 'run in' the full range of the new Maastricht procedures.

Thus, at the same time as the relationship between them changes, there will be new faces and new roles for both institutions. The coming five years will be a period of learning and of experimentation but, perhaps above all, of political change. The 1995–2000 period will see at least one round of enlargements and perhaps two. There will be one inter-governmental conference in 1996 and further progress towards economic and monetary union.

Martin Westlake's *Modern Guide to the European Parliament* is thus a timely and welcome introduction to the way the Community listens to the voice of its citizens, through their directly elected representatives. He sees Parliament in its prescriptive and historical context and then describes how its idiosyncratic mixture of powers and prerogatives developed over time and how they work today.

The need for clear information about the Community's institutions, about the way they work and the powers they have, is universally recognised. This *Modern Guide* is both a readable description of what the European Parliament is and how it works and a valuable work of reference. I am very happy to commend it.

> The Right Honourable
> Sir Leon Brittan, QC,
> Vice-President of the
> Commission of the
> European Community

Introduction

The presumption of the title, a *'Modern' Guide*, stems mainly from the implementation of the Maastricht Treaty (and the decisions of subsequent European Councils) and the Parliament's accompanying rules changes. For, while direct elections and the provisions of the 1987 Single European Act have had undeniably profound consequences, there is good reason to suppose that the Maastricht Treaty has fundamentally changed the European Parliament's institutional position and role. That change has been fully absorbed in this text, which tries to portray the 'new' Parliament in all its different contexts: from the historical to the institutional, from the procedural to the political.

Some editorial comments are in order. I have spurned footnotes as much as possible, and I have tried to keep references to an absolute minimum. I have tried, as faithfully and as accurately as possible, to report Parliament's views as expressed through its reports and resolutions. These are listed in the bibliography in the chronological order of their adoption. Where references to these were unavoidable, I have cited the date of adoption in the text. Occasionally, I have translated ECU figures into pounds sterling. For simplicity's sake, I have used the January 1994 exchange rate and this may lead to differences with figures calculated earlier in 1993. For ease of reading, I have mostly referred to the Treaty on European Union as 'the Maastricht Treaty' and, when referring to new Treaty articles, I have used the abbreviation 'TEU'.

The views expressed and any errors in the text are entirely my own responsibility and do not in any way engage any other person or organisation. Nevertheless, I would like to thank the following friends and colleagues (in alphabetical order) for having either read and commented on parts of the text or for having provided valuable information and insights: Kieran St Cloud Bradley, Georges Caravelis, Richard Corbett, David Coyne, John Fitzmaurice, Philippe Godts, Geoff Harris, Francis Jacobs, David Lowe, Mike Shackleton, Saverio Solari. My thanks go to Robert Weaver for the occasional research tasks he so efficiently undertook. I would also like to thank my publisher, Nicola Viinikka, who first suggested I should write this book. Most of my research was undertaken in the libraries of the Commission and the Parliament in Brussels and of the Council of Europe in Strasbourg. My thanks go to the ever-helpful and efficient librarians of all three institutions.

Above all, I would like to thank my wife, Godelieve, who has been quietly supportive and cheerfully patient throughout the writing process.

Martin Westlake
Brussels
July 1994

1

The European Parliament in context

1.1 The paradigm of parliamentary democracy: decline, persistence and renewal

No student of modern democracy can fail to be struck by the ubiquity of parliamentary assemblies. They are indispensable to our vision of democracy, practical recognition of the basic tenet that the people and their differing views should be fed into, and hence reflected in, the political process. If ubiquity were the sole measure of the effectiveness of political institutions, then no other representative system could claim such overwhelming success. Every single modern democratic state has a parliament, as do many non-democratic systems. In some states (for example, Switzerland or the United States) the referendum is frequently used as a form of direct representation, though mainly at the regional or local level, while in others (for example, Denmark, France, Ireland, Italy and even the United Kingdom) a national referendum may occasionally be held on a matter considered to be of great constitutional importance. But even in these cases the referendum is only an adjunct to parliamentary representation. Parliaments are everywhere.

Decline?

And yet, say some, parliaments are in decline. Many reasons are cited for this. The rise of the political party and the need for party voting discipline snuffed out the independent parliamentarian who, it is argued, had previously acted in accordance with his conscience and his own best judgement. The rise of executive government, with its need for strictly marshalled governing majorities to confirm its legitimacy and pass its legislation, further contributed to the decline. (Though others point out that the mythical age of parliamentarianism was accompanied

1

by such undemocratic phenomena as the 'rotten borough' and limited suffrage.) Others cite the inexorable rise of the career politician — a world-wide phenomenon. Members come younger and younger to parliaments and stay for longer and longer. Critics of such a trend point out that it denies a parliament the vital richness of experience it needs both to represent properly the breadth of activities and interests in the country at large and to arrive at reasoned judgements. Professionalisation has been accompanied by specialisation, as the bulk of parliamentary scrutiny is increasingly exercised through committees with expertise relevant to the legislation in question. The rise of the specialist has marked the decline of the old-style, 'broad brush' parliamentarian devoted to debate of the major political issues of the day.

Abroad, the fractious and fragmented assembly of the French Fourth Republic led the draftsmen of the constitution of the Fifth Republic to favour a strong executive over a deliberately weakened parliament. Finland, with its particular history and strategic imperatives, has a comparably strong presidential regime. For historical reasons, the Norwegian Storting has a fixed four-year term to prevent abusive dissolutions but, although this may endanger a government's legislation, it has the curious effect of protecting the executive at the legislature's expense. The Swedish Riksdag has been weakened by almost half a century of Social Democratic ascendance. Austria's 'grand coalition' has also undermined its parliament's role. The *camera dei deputati* of the Italian First Republic was born relatively weak and was further weakened by the country's traditional resort to broad, fragile and frequently rejiggled governmental coalitions. The Belgian *chambre*'s relevance to the political process has been similarly undermined by the country's 'consociational' style of consensus politics and has further declined in line with the federalisation of the Belgian state, its competences increasingly devolved down to the councils of the regions and linguistic communities.

But the causes of the decline are not restricted to purely mechanical constitutional arrangements. They run deeper than that. Some argue that the rise of the modern state itself contained the seeds of parliamentary decay. Modern states are far more active and their responsibilities far broader than their counterparts of, say, the previous century. Many of these activities are highly technical and utterly impenetrable to the layman. Others are banal. Others require constant, immediate action (such as the day-to-day management of the exchange rate). Such activities do not lend themselves easily to the classic parliamentary methods of scrutiny and debate and, indeed, their impenetrability is an important explanatory factor in the rise of specialised parliamentary committees.

In the same context, some cite the post-war rise of economic planning. Encouraged by economists such as Keynes and Monnet and Beveridge, as well as by the conditions accompanying American economic assistance (particularly the Marshall Plan), states began to take a far more pro-active role in the management of their economies, whether to facilitate reconstruction or to level out the extremes of the classic recession/boom cycle. However, this increased role for the state was not necessarily accompanied by any corresponding extension of parliamentary oversight.

In some states, particularly Austria, Belgium, the Netherlands and Italy, a combination of pronounced social, religious, ethnic, linguistic and political differences has resulted in the evolution of quintessentially consensual systems ('consociational' democracy) where the need for pragmatic, equitable solutions has tended to undermine the centrality of parliament within the political process.

A more widespread phenomenon, thought to have profoundly undermined the *relevance* of parliaments (and governments), is that of corporatism, whereby economic and social actors increasingly bypass traditional political mechanisms, dealing directly with one another outside the classic political institutions and processes.

Last but not least, the world has become increasingly 'internationalised', both economically and politically. States are no longer truly independent actors. Their actions are limited by conventions, by international law, by international organisations, both governmental and non-governmental, and above all, by economic forces. The world is simultaneously more complex and more organised. Restraints on the independence of states have knock-on effects on the role and powers of parliaments. (A graphic example was provided in the mid-1970s by the conditions, principally unpopular spending cuts, externally imposed on the United Kingdom government when it sought an IMF loan after an extended run on the pound. Another graphic example was provided by the currency movements that resulted in sterling's withdrawal from the Exchange Rate Mechanism on 'Black Wednesday' in October 1992 and ultimately in the transformation of the ERM that occurred in August 1993.)

European integration, political and economic, has been identified as a prime factor in the erosion of parliamentary power. All Member States recognise the primacy of EC law which, in practice, means that laws adopted by the governments meeting together in Brussels (or rulings adopted by the Court of Justice in Luxembourg) hold sway over national legislation and legislatures. In other words, national parliaments are no longer pre-eminently sovereign. The process has been exacerbated by the fact that national parliaments traditionally do not have strong powers in international relations, and yet for a long time Community affairs were treated by many Member States as an aspect of international relations. Agricultural policy provides a good example of the transformation of politics from national to international level, with a transfer of decision-making from national capitals to Brussels and a corresponding weakening of national parliamentary scrutiny.

Thus, from all that has gone before, it can be seen that parliamentary decline has occurred in three different ways. First, there has been a decline in the independence and influence of parliaments and of their relevance to the political process. Second, there has been a decline, *de facto* and *de jure*, in the sovereignty of states and therefore in the powers of parliaments. They are no longer necessarily the ultimate legislators, and their decisions are vulnerable to international forces. Finally, there has been a decline in the role of parliaments as the only, or even the major, forums for national economic and political policy formation.

Persistence and renewal

Parliaments may have suffered relative decline, but they have persisted. Proof of their hardiness and attractiveness has come in the consequences of the political upheaval following the fall of the Berlin Wall and the collapse of the post-war consensus. The holding of free elections and through them the establishment of independent parliaments were the twin democratic talismans of the newly democratising Central and Eastern European countries. Youthful parliamentary democracies have grown up with vigour in Greece, Spain and Portugal, and in Spain an attempt to return to a more autocratic style of government was speedily and peremptorily rebuffed. In older democracies, despite the widespread discreditation of certain political classes as expressed at the polls, nobody has suggested doing away with the parliaments within which they worked. Parliaments are not only ubiquitous, they are perennial.

They are also adaptable and able to reassert themselves. The House of Commons has twice revamped its committee structure so as to be better able to follow the work of ministers and departments, and the House of Lords has developed a more pro-active role in the legislative process (significantly, the House of Lords' Select Committee on the European Communities was early to publish a report on the Lords' scrutiny of the inter-governmental pillars of the European Union). In Italy, the First Republic's discredited camera has given way to the "Second Republic"'s stronger and more relevant parliament. The introduction of a single chamber Riksdag and a revised electoral system in Sweden in 1971 has strengthened parliament's role as a policy-influencing assembly. The German Bundestag traditionally reviews its role in the legislative and political process every three or four years but recently unequivocally displayed its assertiveness in imposing conditions of parliamentary approval on the later stages of the economic and monetary union process established by the Maastricht Treaty. In France, President

Mitterrand's suggestion of the need to reinforce the assemblée's role has resulted in the Seguin reforms which, while modest, reversed an otherwise constant trend. In Belgium, the speaker of the chambre has sought ways of reasserting parliament's role in relation to the Community, particularly through inter-parliamentary cooperation. Above all, the quasi-executive powers of the Danish Folketing's Market Committee over Community-related affairs show how a parliament may use a potential source of erosion to strengthen its position.

However, one of the most encouraging signs of persistence and renewal is the growth in the role and powers of the European Parliament itself. Paradoxically, the development of the European Community has led to a relative decline in the relevance of the parliamentary democracy paradigm, but the Community, in the form of its Parliament, contains the best hope for an effective renewal of that paradigm. The remainder of this part of the study will seek to show how the European Parliament has developed from its very weak and unassuming beginnings and how it has successfully fought to win a place for itself in the Community's scheme of things. The key to understanding the role and powers of the European Parliament as they are currently constituted lies in the historical development of the European Economic Community and of the European Coal and Steel Community before it. Further sections show how the growth in the scope and competences of the European Community and of the Parliament within it have led to the need for cooperation between national parliaments and the European Parliament. A final section will show how the European Parliament's role is gradually unfolding in the broader European context.

1.2 The coalescence of European integration and the role of parliamentary assemblies

Beginnings: the Consultative Assembly of the Council of Europe

The first European parliamentary assembly to meet (on 10 August 1949) was that of the Council of Europe, an intergovernmental organisation that pre-dated the EEC by almost a decade. The Council of Europe grew out of an earlier defence agreement, the Brussels Treaty, which had been signed in the spring of 1948 by the five 'powers', Belgium, France, Luxembourg, the Netherlands and the United Kingdom. In October of the same year, the Brussels Treaty Consultative Council (its decision-making organ) decided to set up a committee to make recommendations on broader cooperation. The committee's recommendations were approved by the Consultative Council in January 1949, and invitations were sent out to Denmark, Ireland, Italy, Norway and Sweden in March

1949. The statute of the Council of Europe was signed by the foreign ministers of the ten countries at St James's Palace, London, on 5 May 1949. Significantly, the German Federal Republic, which came into existence on 24 May 1949, was only invited to join in the spring of 1950 and did not become a full Member State until May 1951 (that is, well after the accessions of Greece, Turkey and Iceland).

The Council of Europe was very much a child of its time. It was also the fruit of a protracted negotiating battle between the British, who were opposed to any form of autonomy, particularly for the parliamentary organ, and the French (led by Robert Schuman) and Belgians, who aspired to some supranationality. Composed of a Committee of Ministers and a Consultative Assembly (made up of nominated national parliamentarians), its primary aims, as set out in its statute, were to safeguard and realise 'the ideals and principles which are [the member states'] common heritage and [to facilitate] their economic and social progress'. In practice, these aims were to 'be pursued through the organs of the Council by discussion of questions of common concern and by agreements and common action in economic, social, cultural, scientific, legal and administrative matters . . .' Defence was expressly excluded. The Council of Europe's primary method was intergovernmental ('agreements and common action' could thus only be decided by unanimity). Although the first meetings of the Committee of Ministers were grand affairs, foreign ministers soon gave way to diplomats. Indeed, the Council of Europe has been likened to a standing diplomatic conference with a permanent secretariat. In the eyes of its Member States, it was predominantly viewed as a facet of foreign policy. As such, scrutiny and control were mostly to be conducted at the member-state (national parliament) level. The Consultative Assembly was perceived primarily as an additional debating chamber. It could not even decide its own agenda until May 1951 (prior to that, the Committee of Ministers decided what it could debate). As two European elder statesmen have put it, 'the assembly of the Council of Europe revealed itself to be above all a laboratory of ideas where eminent delegates sat. It discussed and launched many projects, but without succeeding in imposing them on governments' (Spierenburg and Poidevin, 1993, p.2).

For integrationists, the Council of Europe was a highly significant but also highly limited first step. As with another early attempt at European cooperation, the Organisation for European Economic Cooperation (OEEC — the forerunner of the OECD), a fundamental disappointment lay in the reassertion of the nation state resulting in the creation of what were essentially intergovernmental organisations, with unanimity mandatory. For some governments, led by the British, such developments merely amounted to a reassertion of the very independence of sovereign states for which the Allies had fought. For others, such developments were worrying reassertions of the very causes that led to the 1939–45 cataclysm. Moreover, by the end of the 1940s, many felt war might again be imminent.

The first step: the Common Assembly of the European Coal and Steel Community

Nowhere is the gloomy and pessimistic atmosphere of that time better captured than in Jean Monnet's *Memoirs*. Originally a wine merchant, and then a banker, with great international experience. Monnet was a sort of super-technocrat. He had worked as the French partner of an American bank before the war and had coordinated economic aid from London (as Chairman of the Franco–British Economic Coordination Committee) and Washington (British Supply Council) during it. He had not only observed the political and economic weight of a large federal state but had witnessed at first hand the benefits of economic planning in Roosevelt's New Deal and the American war economy. He was closely associated with the free French forces (he was a member of the French Committee of National Liberation) and, once the war was over, he was appointed to head a national plan (the national planning board, origin of French *dirigisme*) designed to revive and modernise the French economy. Horrified by the human material waste of the two great European wars he had witnessed, Monnet was a convinced European federalist, but by 1949 he feared the worst: 'if we do nothing, another war will be near. Germany will not be the cause, but she'll be at stake. She should cease to be at stake; she should become, on the contrary, a link' (Monnet, 1976, p.417).

The circumstances surrounding the particular origins of the ECSC, essentially a mixture of French and American strategic considerations, go a long way towards explaining the still weak and peculiar role of today's European Parliament, as well as the general configuration of the European Union's institutions and its constitutional arrangements. Monnet played an inspirational, central role in those origins.

Upon his return from a Swiss walking holiday in the spring of 1950, a depressed and apprehensive Monnet saw clearly that the solution could only come through a French initiative. The United Kingdom, with a disintegrating Empire and its own strategic considerations, was distracted by its special relationship with the United States. A victorious world power, it was not interested in the claimed advantages of supranational organisation — it had even balked at the idea of a payments union. The Labour government's Minister of Foreign Affairs, Ernest Bevin, was as fierce in his defence of United Kingdom sovereignty as Winston Churchill had been.

Monnet's particular concern, the traditional concern of French diplomacy to the present day, was the nature of the relationship between France and Germany. If the two were not to be at each others' throats again, they had somehow to be bound together. A gesture had to be made, and Monnet was clear in his mind that French diplomacy should make it. With equal clarity, he saw what that gesture could be.

Throughout the late 1940s, various ideas had been floated about the possible pooling of the two countries' coal and steel industries. Now Monnet seized on these ideas and linked them to geographical and political symbolism. As he put it, the Saar, the Rhine basin and Alsace-Lorraine were a naturally defined geographic area rich in mineral resources yet divided by artificial political barriers. The French coal and steel industries had traditionally been bedevilled by cheaper German production, with tensions rising whenever, as was frequently the case, the markets were squeezed (and surplus capacity was again imminent). Economic sovereignty had always been at the heart of Franco–German tensions. What better gesture, then, than a French government proposal that both states should give up their economic sovereignty over coal and steel production, ceding it to an independent, neutral, supranational authority? Such a gesture would have added poignancy because of the area principally affected and the industries involved. For centuries, the Rhine plain and the plateau of Lorraine had served as battlefields for warring tribes and nations (until finally restored in 1986, the façade of Strasbourg's cathedral still bore the scars of damage inflicted in the 1870 Franco–Prussian war). And what products were more central to the prosecution of modern warfare than the iron and steel used to build the tanks and guns of Sedan, Verdun and the blitzkrieg? (In terms of strategic importance, coal was to the Europeans then what Middle East oil is to the Americans now.)

Convinced by his own logic, Monnet invited two friends (Etienne Hirsch and Paul Reuter) to his country retreat and the three set about drafting a plausible, coherent proposal. The result was a simple, but wholly revolutionary, structure. The economic and political sovereignty ceded by the Member States would be vested in an independent High Authority (composed of a powerful president and nominees appointed by the Member State governments) which would be accountable, through an annual report and the power of censure, to a Common Assembly. (The model owed much to the business world, with the roles of the High Authority and the Common Assembly being similar to that of an executive board of directors and a shareholders' annual general meeting respectively.) Since the Council of Europe had an assembly, it would have been inconceivable for the envisaged coal and steel community not to have had one.[1] However, the point for Monnet was not the Assembly, but the High Authority. It would be a radical and fundamental departure, a truly supranational institution acting over and above national sovereignty. (None of the three original draftsmen were politicians or parliamentarians — Monnet came from the world of commerce, Hirsch was an engineer, Reuter a law professor — and it is therefore not surprising that they concentrated their thought on elaborating a convincing structure for what effectively amounted to a supranational industrial policy executive rather than mechanisms of ensuring democratic control over it.)

None of this took place in a vacuum. Monnet, who was to become renowned for combining fervent idealism with lucid pragmatism, was well aware that, on 10 May 1950, the French Foreign Minister, Robert Schuman, was scheduled to meet Ernest Bevin and Dean Acheson in London to discuss the future of Germany and the revision of the productivity thresholds that had been imposed upon it. Moreover, Monnet knew from his excellent Quai d'Orsay contacts that Schuman was casting around for ideas. Once Monnet had his plan, he set about selling it to the minister. The task, never likely to have been difficult given Schuman's progressive attitudes, was rendered easier by the fact (which Monnet had known all along) that Schuman was a native of Lorraine. Having first discreetly sounded out the Americans and the Germans (both of whom were enthusiastic — Monnet had never doubted that Acheson, whom he knew well from his Washington days, would be supportive), Schuman made his dramatic 9 May 1950 proposal 'that Franco–German coal and steel production should be placed under a common High Authority in an organisation open to the participation of the other countries of Europe'. In his *Memoirs*, Monnet wrote that he added the provision for the participation of other countries as a last-minute afterthought. In the event, Germany, Italy, Belgium, the Netherlands and Luxembourg all agreed to the principle (the United Kingdom declined), and then the negotiations began. Thus, contrary to the negotiations establishing the Council of Europe, the United Kingdom was not involved and Germany was. Significantly, the 'Schuman declaration' made no mention of an assembly.

Monnet's simple original blueprint was soon rendered more complicated. While Italy may at that stage have been a humbled and compliant state, the Benelux countries were intent on a robust defence of their interests. Belgium in particular feared the consequences of Franco–German hegemony for its own considerable coal and steel industries. At the insistence of the Benelux countries, a Council representing the Member State governments' interests was introduced to balance the power of the High Authority. Once the principle of exclusive supranationality had been lost, negotiations then concentrated on the relative powers of these two executive authorities, with Monnet doughtily defending the supranational High Authority's prerogatives.

Significantly, with the exception of Italy's Emilio Taviani, a young Christian Democrat politician, all of the negotiating states' representatives were diplomats or officials. Once again, it is not surprising, therefore, that the fight was not about the relative powers of the High Authority and the Common Assembly but about the relative powers of the High Authority and the Member State governments. (Indeed, it is striking just how little the Common Assembly is mentioned in Monnet's *Memoirs*.)

In a sense, it could be argued, the putative role of the Common Assembly suffered from the fact that it had already been proposed in Monnet's blueprint. Other institutions, in addition to the Council of Ministers, were added by the negotiators: for example, the High Authority was to be advised by a consultative committee composed of representatives of the coal and steel industries. Still wary of the proposed High Authority's independence, the negotiators insisted on an appeal mechanism against its decisions and so created a Court of Justice. And when discussions did turn to the Common Assembly, the main concern was the number of representatives for each Member State, rather than the Assembly's powers. Once again, this was a result of Benelux apprehensions of Franco–German dominance. Monnet's *Memoirs* cite the harsh opposition of the Belgian negotiator, Maximilien Suetens: 'Moreover, we do not accept that the organ of control should be a parliament drawn from national parliaments; political responsibility can only reside in the latter' (Monnet, 1976, p.473). Monnet had originally proposed that each of the larger Member States should have eighteen seats and that the Benelux countries should have eighteen seats among them. In the end, Belgium and the Netherlands each had ten and Luxembourg four. At that stage, it was imagined that the members of the Common Assembly would sit according to nationality (as they did in the Parliamentary Assembly of the Council of Europe), and Monnet was convinced that the Benelux countries were intent on creating a blocking minority. It was left to the individual Member States to decide how their members were to be appointed. In the end, all chose to nominate their members from within the membership of their national parliaments, but the Treaty's Article 21 specifically provided for the possibility of direct elections. The inclusion of this provision, although described by some as inconsequential window dressing, was a significant conceptual step.

The European Coal and Steel Community was established by the Treaty of Paris, signed on 18 April 1951. The Common Assembly met in Strasbourg for the first time from 10–13 September 1952. It immediately created an organisational committee to work out how it would operate and interact with the High Authority. Following this committee's recommendations, the second Assembly, which met in Strasbourg from 10–13 January 1953, created six specialised committees, ostensibly to follow the High Authority's activities (although one was more generally devoted to the political affairs and external relations of the Community).

The Common Assembly was the first international assembly in Europe with legally guaranteed powers. In retrospect, the Common Assembly seems a tame affair. It had no legislative powers. It could censure the High Authority but only on the basis of the Authority's annual report and only if such a motion were adopted by two-thirds of those voting, representing an absolute majority of its component members.

Nevertheless, as was stated at the outset of this section, many modern-day characteristics of the European Union, and particularly of the European Parliament, can be traced back directly to the arrangement agreed in 1951. There was a multi-roled High Authority (as Paul Reuter described it, it was simultaneously expert, banker, manager and referee); the Assembly had a lethal but unwieldy power over the High Authority (to this day the censure motion has never been used) but no powers over the Council of Ministers (whose members were and remain only individually beholden to the national parliaments); its legislative powers were non-existent (and are still comparatively weak); it sought to establish scrutiny and control powers through a specialised committee structure (the modern-day Parliament, like the United States' Congress, is a quintessentially committee-based parliament — see Chapter 4, Section 4.1). In terms of representatives, Germany was under-represented and the Benelux countries, particularly Luxembourg, were over-represented (and still are). These characteristics would be familiar to any modern student of the European Union.

Three other characteristics would also be familiar to modern-day students. The first was that in June 1953, six months after its inception, the members of the Assembly decided to sit according to political affiliation rather than nationality, a practice unhesitatingly taken over by the Parliamentary Assembly of the EEC and Euratom Treaties and by the European Parliament directly elected in 1979 (by contrast, political groups within the Council of Europe's Consultative Assembly were not recognised until 1956). The second was that, from the outset, relations between the Assembly and the High Authority, kindred supranational spirits, were good. As a member of that High Authority, Albert Coppé, put it: 'The High Authority understood straightaway how attractive an alliance with the Common Assembly could be, in order to ensure that the two institutions, which were genuinely *communautaire*, were on the same side' (Coppé, 1992). A third characteristic was that the Common Assembly, itself weak and frustrated by the limited integration achieved by the ECSC, almost immediately began to militate in favour of further steps towards European integration. This militant federalism had been foreseen by another European statesman, Alcide de Gasperi, and was to be taken up by a third, the Belgian Prime Minister, Paul-Henri Spaak.

A step back, but a conceptual advance: the European Defence Community

In June 1950, during the ECSC negotiations, war broke out in Korea, and the pessimistic international climate Monnet had described became even gloomier. Its military resources increasingly redirected, America insisted that Europe should shoulder more of the burden for its defence and, European countries having refused, began to argue for German rearmament. The American demands caused consternation and much agonising, particularly in Paris. Gradually, an idea first mooted by Konrad Adenauer in 1949 began to gather pace: a European Army. Once again, Jean Monnet was intimately involved in events. The French Prime Minister, Réné Pleven, laid a plan before the French Parliament on 24 October 1950. The 'Pleven Plan', as it became widely known, had been largely drafted by Monnet and led to broader discussion about the creation of a 'European Defence Community' (EDC). Again, the United Kingdom declined involvement. The six ECSC countries began protracted negotiations, ultimately resulting in the signature, in Paris, on 27 May 1952, of a Treaty Establishing a European Defence Community. It was a revolutionary document, going far beyond simple military cooperation. There was to be a common budget and common institutions. The detailed story of how the ill-fated treaty came to be vetoed by the French Assemblée on 30 August 1954 — a great blow to federalists — need not concern us here, but one aspect of the treaty was of great relevance to the development of the Assembly.

The treaty's Article 38, which had been inserted at the insistence of Italy's Prime Minister, Alcide de Gasperi, provided for a *directly elected* Common Assembly and for this Assembly to study ways of creating a federal organisation with a clear separation of powers and a bicameral parliament. The logic was clear: a Defence Community could not exist in a vacuum but would have to be balanced by a true political community. Because the EDC ratification process in the Member States promised to be lengthy, de Gasperi and Spaak suggested that the task of drawing up the blueprint should be conferred on the Common Assembly of the Coal and Steel Community. With imaginative dexterity, the ECSC Council of Ministers invited the ECSC Common Assembly, especially enlarged so it would have the same number of members as the projected EDC Assembly, to study and report back on the feasibility of a European Political Community. The Assembly was given six months to complete its work.

As we have seen, the ECSC Assembly met for the first time on 10 September 1952, and *the very next day* it set up a working party to draft proposals. Although encountering internal opposition from the left (the West German Social Democrats were totally opposed to German rearmament), the special Assembly was able to present a draft Treaty Establishing a Political Community by 10 March 1953. The draft treaty consisted of 117 articles, providing for an Executive Council, a Council of Ministers, a Court of Justice and, of course, a directly elected Parliament. (Federalists were nevertheless not entirely happy with the draft, which displayed some distinctly confederal characteristics.) Distracted by the debates surrounding ratification of the European Defence Community, the Member States never really focused their attention on the European Political Community and, the high-water mark of federalism in the 1950s, it died the day the French Assemblée voted against the EDC.

However, despite the disappointing end to the process, two important conceptual steps had been taken. The first was that, almost in passing, the six contracting governments of the ECSC had accepted the principle of a directly elected Common Assembly. The second was that, on only the second day of its life, the Common Assembly was invited to draft what amounted to a new European constitutional settlement. This experience has become inculcated in the European Parliament's collective memory. In its resolutions Parliament constantly calls on the heads of state and government of the Member States to confer upon it the task of acting as a constituent assembly in order to draft a European constitutional settlement. In February 1994, over forty years on, the Parliament unilaterally adopted a fresh suggested draft European constitution. It is the third full-blooded draft since 1979. Should the call ever come, no institution could be better prepared than the European Parliament.

The second step: the European Economic Community and the European Atomic Energy Community

Monnet's pragmatic theory of integration, as exemplified by the ECSC, was functional and sectoral in its approach. Full-frontal assaults on the sovereignty of the Member States faced insuperable odds. He reasoned that the benefits and simple operability of integration had first to be proven with a narrower start. Once the benefits of the integration of Europe's coal and steel industries had become obvious, integration would 'spill over' into other sectors, with states increasingly prepared to cede their sovereignty in other areas of economic activity. In this sense, the European Defence Community, particularly its Article 38, had been a deviation from the functionalist strategy, the opportunistic fruit of geo-political necessity. With its demise, Monnet urged a return to the sectoral approach, particularly in the fields of transport and energy and especially the then emerging field of nuclear energy. But the trouble with this approach was that the ECSC was not conspicuously successful at what it was supposed to do; though it had undeniably achieved results, the simple removal of tariffs had proved insufficient to remove distortions, and the High Authority's decisions were the subject of constant carping and even non-respect.

Perhaps teething problems were inevitable in such a revolutionary organisation. In any case, as the dust from the EDC débâcle began to settle, European politicians turned their attentions to a broader economic approach. On 1 and 2 June 1955, the foreign affairs ministers of the ECSC six met in Messina, in Italy, and agreed, in Monnet's words, to a 'relaunching [of] the European idea'. This was to be done through a mixture of Monnet's approach and the ideas contained in a Benelux memorandum proposing 'broad economic integration leading to a joint common market'. The Benelux memorandum was directly inspired by the Benelux organisation's own experience of trying to create a common market. Indeed, the three Benelux representatives, Paul-Henri Spaak, the Dutch Foreign Minister, Johan Willem Beyen, and the Luxembourg Prime Minister, Joseph Beck, had all been intimately involved in drawing up the plans for the Benelux Union while in exile in London during the war. Paul-Henri Spaak was appointed to head an intergovernmental committee. Its report was unveiled in March 1956 and approved by the foreign ministers, meeting in Venice, on 29 May 1956. Detailed negotiations began (with the United Kingdom once again declining to take part) and resulted in the signature, in Rome on 25 March 1957, of two treaties establishing a European Economic Community and a European Atomic Energy Community ('Euratom').

In many ways, the two treaties could be considered as a consolidation and extension of the ECSC method. This was particularly true of institutions: the equivalent of the old High Authority (renamed the 'Commission') was to work with a Council of Ministers, advised by an economic and social committee, overseen by a weak, 142-member Parliamentary Assembly, with a Court of Justice ruling in the case of disputes. (The Assembly, together with the Court, was common to the three Communities.) The weakness of the new Assembly, and in particular its lack of control over the Council of Ministers, was a great disappointment to the ECSC Assembly, which had been in close contact with the Spaak Committee's work. Nevertheless, in relation to both the powers and role of the Parliamentary Assembly there were a series of significant new provisions which were, ultimately, to have far-reaching consequences.

First, an article provided for direct elections to the Parliamentary Assembly. The Assembly itself was to 'draw up proposals for elections by direct universal suffrage in accordance with a uniform procedure in all Member States'. These would be submitted to the Council which, acting unanimously would lay down 'the appropriate provisions', which the Member States would then adopt 'in accordance with their respective constitutional requirements'. As has been seen, this was the fruit of the consensus reached in negotiations over the ill-fated EDC.

Second, the Parliamentary Assembly's right to censure the Commission was extended. Although the censure motion was still mentioned in the same context as the Commission's annual report, it was no longer the same treaty article. In other words, the Parliamentary Assembly was now free to censure the Commission in any context and in relation to any aspect of its activities. Implicitly, the Assembly's control powers were concomitantly extended to all of the Commission's activities.

Third, the Parliamentary Assembly gained significant, if weak, budgetary powers. (Although it should be pointed out that the ECSC's High Authority had enjoyed greater *supranational* budgetary power.) It became a twin arm of the budgetary authority, though it had only consultative powers and then only in very circumscribed areas of expenditure. As significantly, the Parliamentary Assembly was in future to grant the Commission retrospective discharge on its implementation of the annual budget (see Chapter 3, Section 3.3).

Fourth, several articles in both treaties introduced, through the consultation procedure, a formal right to parliamentary involvement in the Communities' legislative processes. In future, the Council had to consult Parliament on proposals made under those articles. (Hence the treaties spoke of Parliament's *advisory* and supervisory powers.) It was a very weak power, for the Council was not obliged to take any notice of the Assembly's opinions, but it was a significant beginning that would bear unexpected fruit in 1980.

Fifth, the treaties authorised the Parliamentary Assembly to establish its own rules of procedure. The full significance and potential of this provision was only to be realised after the 1979 direct elections.

Arguably until the implementation of the Maastricht Treaty in November 1993, and certainly until the implementation of the Single European Act in 1987, the basic configuration of institutions and powers set out in the Rome Treaties was to remain unchanged. And if this analysis has concentrated on these early years it is for that reason. Those wanting to know why the Community is as it is will find most of the answers in that seven-year period between the spring of 1950, when Monnet returned clear-headedly from his Swiss walking holiday, and the spring of 1957, when the EEC and Euratom Treaties were signed in Rome. Thereafter, changes and progress continued to be made but chiefly within the basic treaty structure. Other attempts were made to create a political community, particularly in the early 1960s, but the atmosphere had changed. Nineteen fifty-six had seen the invasion of Hungary and the ill-starred Anglo–French Suez expedition, and one highly consequential event was to occur just five months after the new treaties had entered into force. On 13 May 1958, the French Fourth Republic was threatened by a military *coup d'état* in Algeria. Charles de Gaulle, a champion of French national sovereignty, was brought back to power, the Fourth Republic dissolved and the Fifth Republic established.

Faux Pas *and* Petits Pas: *1958–78*

The 1958–78 period divides neatly into two very different decades. The first, a period characterised by set-backs and disappointments, broadly corresponded with de Gaulle's period in office, though not all problems could be laid at his door. Nevertheless, the second, a period characterised by small advances and hope, began soon after his abrupt resignation on 28 April 1969.

Officially, the ECSC 'Common Assembly' had become a 'Parliamentary Assembly', but the differing nationalities meeting in the European Parliamentary Assembly for the first time on 19 March 1958 apparently could not agree on what they would like to call their institution. The French and Italian members stuck to the language of the treaties, calling the institution l'Assemblée parlementaire européenne and Assemblea parlementare europea respectively. But the Germans called it the Europäisches Parlement, and the Dutch the Europees Parlement; literally, the 'European Parliament'. These different usages continued until 30 March 1962, when the French and Italian governments agreed to refer to the Parliamentary Assembly as, respectively, Parlement Européen and Parlamento Europeo. Nevertheless, the treaty language remained and in many official documents, particularly those emanating from the Council, continued to be used. Indeed, the treaties continued to refer to the 'Parliamentary Assembly' until the Single European Act, which officially changed the name to 'European Parliament', came into effect in July 1987. (The 1976 Act introducing European elections referred to it as the 'European Assembly'.) In choosing to call itself a 'parliament', the Assembly was not so much pretending to *be* a parliament as clearly pointing out that it *wanted* to become one. The same logic lay behind the name change in the Single European Act: the Member States were not so much declaring that the Assembly *was* a parliament as effectively recognising that it *should become* one. Some commentators think the 1958–62 name change was a mistake because it created the false reassurance that a parliament did exist. But, at the least, it was a powerful declaration of intent, a strong assertion that the Community should develop in accordance with the European parliamentary tradition. Perhaps it was also a conscious distancing from its weaker brother, the Consultative Assembly of the Council of Europe. In any case, the European Parliament was born and born frustrated.

It immediately asserted its independence by refusing to accept the Council of Ministers' preference that it should elect an Italian as its president (any Italian: the ministers were worried about the balance of nationalities among the presidencies of the various institutions and organisations), instead choosing by acclamation Robert Schuman. On the other hand, the Council early underlined the Parliament's weakness by creating, outside the treaty's provisions, a new institutional system of national administrators to whom much negotiating authority was delegated. The Committee of Permanent Representatives (universally known by its French acronym, 'Coreper') has grown into a vital part of the Community's decision-making machinery. Being outside the treaty structure, it lay completely beyond the Parliament's grasp or even its view.

Just as the ECSC Common Assembly had immediately become involved in moves to further integration so, once it had got its internal structures and procedures sorted out (it followed the ECSC Assembly in establishing committees and political groups), the European Parliament turned its thoughts to the next step. This was clearly mapped out in the treaties: the Parliament was to draft proposals for direct universal suffrage under a uniform electoral system and submit them to the Council of Ministers. In October 1958 it set up a working party to draft such proposals. The draft Convention ultimately adopted by the Parliament on 10 May 1960 was the result of intense and protracted debate and extensive consultation in national capitals. Unfortunately, it was forwarded to the Council (on 20 June 1960) just four days after the French Prime Minister, Michel Debré, had told the French national assembly that 'the essential thing in our view, as General de Gaulle has said . . . is the political association of states . . . through governmental cooperation . . . I do not see what direct elections by universal suffrage of a political assembly dealing with technical bodies or with higher civil servants can accomplish' (cited in Scalingi, 1980, p.59).

The French president was viscerally opposed to any supranational organisation. He grudgingly recognised the EEC, established as was seen just one year before the *coup d'état* in Algeria brought him to power, as a *fait accompli*, but he was determined to limit its power and influence and reduce these wherever he could. His preference was for a (preferably French-dominated) association of heads of state. (The six Member States had already agreed, at French insistence, to meet four times a year to discuss foreign policy issues.) In 1952, Debré had proposed a 'Pact for a Union of European States', and now de Gaulle and he were in the process of reviving the idea of a European confederation. (They proposed inter-state discussions aided by a Paris-based permanent secretariat and four commissions dealing with political, economic, defence and cultural matters.) Indeed, the Parliament's ill-timed suggestion of further federalist progress spurred de Gaulle on, as did Harold Macmillan's announcement that the United Kingdom government was 'rethinking' its position on the EEC. (British accession, de Gaulle reasoned, could only reduce French influence, and so he hoped his plan could be realised prior to that.)

So central was the French role in Europe that the other five Member States reluctantly went along with the French plans on the conditional (and ultimately mistaken) understanding that these would subsume and reinforce the Community institutions. In February 1961, at a first summit in Paris, the six announced the creation of an intergovernmental committee to study national cooperation and development of the Communities. In March, Parliament adopted a report grudgingly accepting the construction of Europe on 'two pillars'; progressive integration within the treaties and intergovernmental cooperation. (Ironically, and much to Parliament's chagrin, the French government successfully resurrected the 'pillars' idea thirty years later, during the Maastricht Intergovernmental Conference.) In June 1961, Parliament adopted a resolution conditionally accepting the idea of state summits. At the second such summit, in Bonn on 18 July 1961, the Member States decided to hold such meetings regularly, to examine Parliament's resolution on political cooperation and to set up a study committee, under the chairmanship of a French deputy, Christian Fouchet, to draft a treaty for the creation of a Union of States. On 31 July 1961, Harold Macmillan announced that the United Kingdom would apply for accession. Ireland and Denmark made similar announcements in August (Norway tabled its application in April 1962).

To federalists and those favouring the Community 'method' alike, it seemed as though there were grounds for optimism: moves to further integration were under review and enlargement seemed an imminent prospect. The Fouchet Plan, published in November 1961, came as a rude shock, above all to the Parliament. The Plan envisaged a Council of Heads of State, a European Political Commission made up of senior foreign affairs officials and a European Parliamentary Assembly, but there was no longer any provision for direct elections. The next month (December 1961), the European Parliament's Political Committee adopted a counter-report (the 'Pleven Report') which envisaged, *inter alia*, a directly elected Parliament which would be responsible for ratifying international treaties. (Both these ideas, it will be noted, have since come of age: elections in 1979 and treaty ratification, albeit limited in scope, with the Single European Act and the Maastricht Treaty.)

In the meantime, de Gaulle's prejudices about the 'Community method' were reinforced by the painful negotiations which resulted in the creation of the Common Agricultural Policy on 14 January 1962 (after 137 hours of discussion, a further 214 hours in sub-committee, 582,000 pages of documents and three heart attacks). On 16 January 1962, the French government shelved the Fouchet Plan, but on 18 January it published another. This second Fouchet Plan, which had been scrutinised and corrected by de Gaulle himself, was even more tough-nosed than the first (it is unclear whether de Gaulle intended this as a negotiating tactic). It shocked the other five Member States deeply. Negotiations continued, with further proposals and counter-proposals, until at Belgian and Dutch insistence further progress became entangled with the prospects for British accession, and the negotiations petered out. The atmosphere deteriorated further until in January 1963 matters reached their nadir when de Gaulle signed a bilateral Franco–German cooperation treaty and vetoed the British application for membership.

Throughout this period, all attention had been focused on de Gaulle's proposals and the Fouchet Plans. The Parliament's proposals for direct elections were at first sidelined, and then became outdated (the Convention had envisaged the holding of direct elections by 1962) and increasingly implausible. In a 27 June 1963 Resolution, Parliament urged the Council to act. The Council replied that 'the Councils must decide unanimously on provisions they recommend Member States to adopt. As this condition has not so far been fulfilled, the Councils are not in a position to say when they will be able to decide on the provision in question'. (Until the 1965 Merger Treaty there were three Councils: ECSC, EEC and Euratom.) By 1962 the Convention was effectively lost and hence also the integrationist impetus and momentum that the 'founding fathers' had intended. However, although the Convention itself was ill-fated, the drafting exercise had been a learning experience for the Parliament. It had confronted and examined all of the major problems — the number and distribution of seats, incompatibility of office, the possibility of more than one mandate and the uniform electoral system — and at least one of its proposals, for a five-year mandate, was ultimately to surface in the 1976 Act that led to the first, 1979, direct elections.

Two schools of thought about reform and elections overlapped within the young Parliament. One held that increased powers and importance would be a consequence of directly electing the Parliament. The other held the opposite view: the more powers the Parliament had, the more justification there would be for it to be directly elected. In truth, these views were not contradictory, and Parliament simultaneously adopted strategies appropriate to both. As we have seen, it swiftly fulfilled the treaty obligation of drafting a proposed Convention on direct elections. On the other hand, it also looked to rationalising, improving and extending its powers within the current treaty structure. In the latter context, two of its proposals were particularly successful.

The first, often repeated, was its demand for the Council to extend the practice of consultation (the Parliament's only, and very weak, legislative power) to more, then most, and ultimately all proposals it considered, regardless of the treaties' provisions. Because the Council was in no way obliged to take any account of Parliament's opinions, even where the treaties made consultation obligatory, such demands seemed relatively innocuous and their satisfaction relatively inconsequential. Thus, in a series of *ad hoc* undertakings made in 1960, 1964 and 1968, the Council agreed to consult the Parliament on virtually all legislative and non-legislative texts. The cumulative effect of these undertakings, long since consolidated by custom and convention, has been of great value to the Parliament; regardless of its particular role and powers. Parliament is now involved in everything that occurs in the Community. Though this seems straightforward now, it was anything but in the first five years of the young Parliament's life (in the very first year the Council adopted a budget while completely bypassing the Commission and the Parliament).

A second proposal, embodied in a Parliamentary resolution of October 1960, called for the different Councils and the two Commissions and High Authority of the three Communities to be merged. This was a self-evident rationalisation and was soon taken up by the Member States. The treaty establishing a single Council and a single Commission was signed on 8 April 1965 and entered into force on 1 July 1967. Parliament reasoned that it, as well as the cause of integration, stood to gain from such a move, since a single Commission, still beholden to Parliament, could only gain in authority. (A small additional bonus came with the extension of the *generalised* right of censure, previously restricted to the High Authority's annual report, to the ECSC. This extension will reach its logical conclusion in the year 2002, when the ECSC Treaty will expire and, if the Commission's recommendations are followed, its provisions absorbed into the European Community.)

Such developments, together with the integrationist enthusiasms of the German President of the Commission, Walter Hallstein, lulled the federalist and pro-Parliament camps into a false sense of optimism. In January 1965, de Gaulle and the new German Chancellor, Ludwig Erhard, were reported to have agreed to renew their discussions on political union. In December 1964, the six had hearteningly agreed to create a common agricultural system by 1 July 1967. Most significantly, the Council authorised the Commission to draw up proposals on how the common agricultural fund would be financed. The despondency accompanying the shock of the Fouchet plans and the collapse of talks on political union seemed to have evaporated. In retrospect, storm clouds had been quietly gathering: in March France had withdrawn from the military arm of NATO, and Hallstein, egged on by an enthusiastic Parliament, seemed dangerously transported beyond the bounds of pragmatic diplomacy. In the early hours of 1 July 1965, the French government quit the Council in high dudgeon and boycotted the Community altogether.

The 'empty chair' crisis represented a high-water mark of anti-supranationalism, effectively freezing the Community's development until the end of the decade. However, in the context of this study it is important to note that the Parliament's powers were at the heart of the controversy. The Commission had presented a complex package of proposals for financing the CAP. The controversy focused on the

Commission's proposal that the Community should have its 'own resources' (revenue raised from customs duties). Hallstein, explicitly following the logic of the maxim 'no taxation without representation' and enthusiastically following repeated parliamentary demands, proposed that the European Parliament should provide the necessary democratic oversight. For good measure, he opined that true democratic control would necessitate direct elections to the Parliament. All this was anathema to de Gaulle, who had previously dubbed the European Parliament 'that assembly of foreigners'.

The 1965 crisis was a grievous disaster, particularly for the Parliament. If, at least in theory, its proposals for direct elections had still been under discussion in the Council, they were now dead. Moves within two Member States for the unilateral introduction of direct elections — a possibility, it will be recalled, left open in the original ECSC Treaty — had also come to nothing. (On 20 May 1965, the German Bundestag rejected a bill introduced by the SPD principally on the grounds that elections would lose their significance if not held by all six states, and an idea debated by the Italian Camera dei Deputati to extend its membership to include its members of the European Parliament made no headway. A bill with similar intentions foundered in the French national assembly in the spring of 1968.) Its calls for budgetary powers had sunk with the French boycott, and the debate about 'own resources' and democratic control over them could not be revived until the transitional stage, decided in the wake of the 'Luxembourg compromise' that brought the French back to the Council table, ended in 1970. But some good came of the crisis nevertheless. In particular, once launched, ideas never entirely go away. Nor should it be forgotten that the Commission had not only wholeheartedly embraced the idea of granting the Parliament budgetary powers but had drafted proposals as to how this could be practically realised. Indeed, throughout the 1970s the budgetary powers envisaged by the Commission's 1965 proposals were to be rapidly consolidated, culminating in 1979 in Parliament's rejection of the 1980 budget.

In the autumn of 1969, with the end of the transitional period in view, the Commission drafted fresh proposals on the financing of the agricultural system, including proposals for 'own resources' and budgetary powers for the European Parliament. These led ultimately to the 22 April 1970 Luxembourg Treaty which, though falling far short of Parliament's wishes and the Commission's proposals, was a significant beginning. It allowed the Parliament to fix its own budget, and the Parliament was to have some authority over administrative expenditure, though operational expenditure — 96 per cent of the budget — was to remain exclusively in the purview of the Council. Own resources were to come into existence from 1 January 1975. In 1973, the Commission made fresh proposals which led ultimately to the far-reaching 22 July

1975 Brussels Treaty. To some extent obscured by contemporaneous moves to introduce direct elections (see below), the Brussels Treaty was a watershed for Parliament. It greatly extended Parliament's budgetary powers, giving it the right, albeit in circumscribed areas of expenditure and under stringent majority requirements, to amend the budget. Above all, the Treaty gave Parliament the right to reject the budget. Earlier in the same year (4 March 1975), a joint declaration of the Council, the Parliament and the Commission introduced a 'conciliation procedure' for the three institutions to facilitate agreement on proposals 'which have appreciable financial implications'. The declaration provided for the creation of a 'conciliation committee', consisting of representatives of the Council and the Parliament. For the first time, the Parliament was to be an interlocutor with the Council. By July 1975, Parliament had virtually all — discharge, rejection, amendment, conciliation — the budgetary powers it has today. Direct elections were to give it the courage to use those powers fully.

Direct elections and beyond

De Gaulle's 1969 departure encouraged the pro-federalists to speculate again. The European Parliament thought out loud about whether it might use a treaty power to take the Council to court for 'failure to act' on Parliament's June 1960 proposals but also recognised that the proposals were now so out of date as to be an unsuitable basis for a Council decision. The same year the Luxembourg, Italian, Dutch, French and Belgian parliaments all saw bills favouring the unilateral introduction of direct elections in individual Member States, but such demands were generally recognised to be impractical and incompatible, with the treaties' call for 'a uniform procedure in all Member States'. Pompidou remained implacable, Germany distracted. It became clear further moves would have to await the enlargement of the Community, when it was hoped that the United Kingdom, with its strong democratic and parliamentary tradition, would act as a counterweight to French intransigence. In the meantime, the Parliament resolved to prepare a new Convention. The first enlargement of the Community took place in 1973. (Ironically, by the time further progress was possible the pro-integration government of Edward Heath had been replaced by the more ambiguous government of Harold Wilson.) Nineteen seventy-four saw an upturn in the prospects for institutional reform, particularly in relation to the Parliament. On 14 May Helmut Schmidt replaced Willy Brandt as West German Chancellor. On 19 May Valéry Giscard d'Estaing was elected French president. The two new heads of state rapidly established a special relationship and a new understanding on the Franco–German alliance and the development of the Community.

A summit was held in Paris on 9 and 10 December 1974. The Member States issued a communiqué which promised that they would hold direct European elections 'at any time in or after 1978' and that they awaited 'with interest the proposals of the European Assembly on which they wish the Council to act in 1976' (although the British and Danish governments expressed reservations about the 1978 date). The Parliament, mindful of the desirability of keeping up the momentum, accelerated its deliberations on a fresh Convention, adopting new proposals on 14 January 1975. It reworked the number and distribution of seats and other provisions but was frank in its pragmatic prepared-ness to vote through an imperfect draft in order to get proposals before the Council as swiftly as possible. The 1 and 2 December 1975 Rome European Council (as summits were now known) examined a report on Parliament's Convention and announced that elections would be held 'on a single date in May or June 1978', but thereafter the timetable for elections became bound up with the British Labour government's problems with its increasingly fractious internal anti-Market critics and with a series of protracted arguments over the number and distribution of seats (see Butler and Marquand, 1981, pp.30–44). Compromise on size and seats was finally reached on 12 July 1976, the official Convention was signed on 20 September 1976 and sent to the individual Member States for ratification. The British problem then swung back into view. Labour Prime Minister James Callaghan, governing without a parliamentary majority, was a hostage to two diametrically opposed and equally vital groups: his anti-Market backbenchers and his pro-Market but also pro-proportional representation Liberal Party pact partners. The government finally kept its obligation, but the Boundary Committees' recommendations could not be made before the May 1978 deadline. European elections were eventually held on 7–10 June 1979. (A new clause was added to the act which stated that the Council could take a unanimous decision only after 'endeavouring to reach agreement with the European Parliament in a Conciliation Committee' — see Chapter 2, Section 2.4 and Chapter 3, Section 3.4.)

Turnout in some Member States was encouragingly high but in others, particularly the United Kingdom and Denmark, disappointingly low (see Chapter 2, Section 2.8). In most Member States, electoral campaigns remained obstinately devoted to domestic political issues, disappointing those who had campaigned so long for the introduction of direct elections. Furthermore apart from the immediate rejection of the budget (see Chapter 3, Section 3.3), there was no overnight transformation in the appearance and methods of the Community. The intergovernmental institutions, some of them 'extra-treaty' (Coreper, the European Council), had got a head start. There had been a generational change, too. Most of the personalities who had been so central to European integration — Monnet, Schuman, Adenauer, Spaak, Hallstein — were either dead or no longer politically influential. The new integrationists were somehow less fervent and more pragmatic, and it is perhaps no coincidence that the directly elected Parliament's first actions were in the budgetary field, where its right to involvement at the Community level was logically obvious.

Notwithstanding the apparent lack of immediate change, the introduction of direct elections had three important consequences or, rather, one important consequence with three different, inter-related aspects. That key consequence was independence. A first aspect was independence from national parliaments. Dual mandates were not outlawed and, in the case of some national contingents (for example, the French), were numerous, but the automatic direct linkage had gone. Whatever the previous practice, members of the European Parliament could no longer hold ministers to account except in so far as they were, through the presidency-in-office, representing the Council. It was for national parliaments to hold individual ministers to account. Thus, the Parliament's institutional role and position were clarified, being simultaneously both 'narrowed' and strengthened.

A second aspect was political independence. There could no longer be any confusion about representing nations or nationalities: European parliamentarians were elected to represent the European peoples. The European Parliament now had its own legitimacy, based on its account-ability and representatives. These qualities were to have an important implication in the eyes of the Court in a famous 1980 ruling, now universally referred to as the 'Isoglucose' case. In short, the Council had adopted an act where consultation of the Parliament was obligatory without waiting for Parliament to give its opinion. Acting in its quasi-constitutional mode, the Court found that

> The consultation provided for . . . is the means which allows the Parliament to play an actual part in the legislative process of the Community. Such power represents an essential factor in the institutional balance intended by the Treaty. Although limited, it reflects at Community level *the fundamental democratic principle that the peoples should take part in the exercise of power through the intermediary of a representative assembly.* Due consultation of the Parliament in cases provided for by the Treaty therefore constitutes an essential formality disregard of which means that the measure concerned is void. [My emphasis — see Table 1]

The third aspect was that direct elections had rendered the Parliament independent from the Commission and had indeed changed the whole nature of the relationship between these two supranational institutions. Prior to direct elections, the Parliament had relied upon the Commission to act as its interlocutor *vis-à-vis* the Council and in general to fight the good federalist fight. After direct elections, the Commission's role and legitimacy still sprang from the treaties, but the Parliament's now sprang from the European people. Precisely because of this, the Commission had always supported moves towards direct elections; increasingly it looked to the Parliament for the legitimation of its actions and proposals. But this led to a change in the relationship. Although the Parliament was still practically dependent on the Commission, the Commission was becoming politically dependent on the Parliament.

The period between the first direct elections in June 1979 and the implementation of the Single European Act in 1987 was characterised by a number of evolutionary developments. First, and above all, this period saw Parliament fully explore and consolidate its powers in the budget-ary field: budgets were rejected in 1979 and 1984 (and a supplementary budget in 1982); Parliament refused the Commission discharge in 1984; and on 30 June 1985, the Parliament, the Commission and the Council signed a joint declaration on various measures designed to improve the budget procedure (see Chapter 3, Section 3.3).

Second, building on the Court's ruling, Parliament explored the full extent of its limited theoretical role in the legislative process, imaginatively using its right to draft its own rules of procedure to create a mechanism for indefinite postponement of its opinion in formal consultation procedures in order to force concessions, particularly where the draft legislation was urgent (see Chapter 3, Section 3.4).

Third, the Parliament pursued its age-old strategy of seeking *'petits pas'* — small advances, either through the treaties or via concessions from the other institutions. For example, the Commission radically overhauled its procedures to ensure better representation to, and response in, the new Parliament. The joint declaration on the budgetary procedure was another example. But perhaps the most significant advance was the 19 June 1983 Stuttgart Council Solemn Declaration on European Union, which extended Parliament's powers in relation to foreign policy and — the first step in an evolutionary process culmi-nating in the Maastricht Treaty — granted it weak consultation rights in the Member States' nomination of the Commission President (the Council also undertook to reply to Parliament's questions, an obligation strangely omitted in the original treaties).

Fourth, the Parliament renewed its treaty obligation to draft proposals for a uniform electoral procedure. New proposals were made in March 1982 (a system of proportional representation in multi-member constitu-encies), but the Council was unable to agree on a system before the 1984 elections. A further attempt was made to draft a new set of proposals in the 1984–9 Parliament, but there was insufficient consensus to proceed to a plenary vote.

Finally, the Parliament pursued another age-old strategy, that of urging full-blooded federalist reform. The result, adopted in February 1984, was a 'Draft Treaty Establishing the European Union'. Although it came to nothing in itself, the Draft Treaty was a focal point for discussion about the constitutional mechanics of Union and was a direct ascendant of the Single European Act.

The Single European Act

By the early 1980s, the European Community was economically and politically stagnating. The conviction grew in business and political circles that it would be unable to retain its economic and political place in the world unless a new *rélance* could be brought about. A number of complementary forces combined: the desire of federalists to bring about further integration, most forcefully and comprehensively expressed in the Parliament's Draft Treaty Establishing the European Union; the desire of politicians for a more coherent and consistent external (foreign and trade) policy; the demands of the business community for deregulation (with eyes on the successful deregulation policy of Ronald Reagan) and the dismantlement of non-tariff barriers to trade; and, in 1985, the appointment of a new, dynamic Commission, including a former Thatcher minister, Lord Cockfield, steeped in the deregulatory spirit, and presided over by an ambitious, incisive and visionary president. A first result of these converging forces was the 25–6 June 1984 Fontainebleau European Council's decision to establish two intergovernmental committees, one to examine ways of advancing the concept of a 'people's Europe' and the other 'to make suggestions for the improvement of the operation of European cooperation in both the Community field and that of political, or any other, cooperation'. The second result, following the recommendations of these committees, and despite initial British, Danish and Greek objections, was the 28–9 June 1985 Milan European Council's decision to open an inter-governmental conference to discuss further reforms to the treaties. The ultimate result was the Single European Act (SEA), which entered into force in 1987.

In the Community, treaty reforms traditionally fall into two categories. There are those which involve the extension of practice and powers to new areas, and there are those which involve fundamental change. Thus, in a familiar pattern, the extension of the Community's competences was accompanied by a logical extension of the Parliament's competences (although the nature of the latter's involvement was not always to its liking). However, beyond these simple extensions, the SEA involved one radical departure which involved a fundamental new step for the Parliament. Although majority decision making in the Council had never been explicitly excluded, the 1966 Luxembourg Compromise effectively ruled it out. There were signs that this informal unanimity requirement was slowly crumbling, but the 1986 SEA expressly provided for majority decision making in a number of policy areas principally related to the establishment of the Internal Market (although it also explicitly provided for unanimity in some areas such as fiscal policy). Even the more sovereignty-consensus governments agreed that the broad raft of necessary legislation could never be adopted in time if the unanimity requirement remained intact.

Acceptance of majority decision making had clear constitutional consequences. Until then, it had been possible to argue that the lines of accountability to national parliaments were clear and absolute. But now a Member State minister could be outvoted in Council and a Member State government obliged to introduce legislation with which it had not agreed. Some constitutional counterweight to protect the rights of outvoted minorities was clearly necessary. Just as clearly, this counter-weight had to be at the Community level. Following this logic, the negotiators agreed to create a new, two-reading legislative procedure which, for the first time, gave Parliament the right to amend legislative proposals. The right was weak and carefully circumscribed by deadlines and majority requirements, and the draftsmen had deliberately built into the procedure dependencies between the three institutions concerned (Commission, Council and Parliament) — hence 'cooperation procedure' — but the principle was there. Where Parliament had previously had the dubious power of delay, it now had positive input into the legislative procedure (especially if the Commission 'protected' its amendments by taking them over).

The SEA contained a second radical departure for the Parliament. Since Parliament's inception, parliamentary reports on constitutional reform had argued for the Parliament to be granted the right to ratify international agreements. Like budgetary powers, the argument was based on competences. The Commission was the Community's principle negotiator on most trade issues and external agreements and, once finalised, agreements would be adopted by the Council. Once again, following this logic, the SEA negotiators introduced a new parlia-mentary assent procedure which was to apply to 'association agree-ments' as well as to applications for membership of the Community. The right to grant assent was a simple 'yes/no' right, and Parliament had to muster an absolute majority of its membership to grant assent, but the introduction of the principle of assent was to have far-reaching consequences in the context of the Maastricht Treaty.

Maastricht and beyond

The period between the implementation of the SEA and the Maastricht IGC was characterised by consolidation. Although Parliament had been frustrated by the SEA (which had fallen far short of its demands), it knew that future extensions of its powers would depend upon whether it was able to deal effectively with the powers it had been given. This was no simple task. The new procedures involved tight deadlines and absolute majorities, obliging Parliament to redraft its internal rules and change its practices. Despite apprehensions to the contrary, Parliament proved that it was both equal to the task and able to use its new powers responsibly (see Corbett, 1989 and Westlake, 1994b).

As far as Parliament's powers were concerned, the Maastricht intergovernmental process bore several similarities with the SEA IGC. First, where the Community's competences were extended, so were the competences of the Parliament. Again, Parliament did not always agree with the role and powers it had been given, but it *had* been given them. Second, principles granted previously were now extended and built upon and procedural restrictions relaxed. Thus, the cooperation procedure was extended to new policy areas, the majority requirement in the assent procedure was relaxed (though this did not necessarily enhance Parliament's powers) and the assent procedure itself extended to new policy areas outside external agreements.

Third, new principles were granted. One of the most significant was contained in a complicated new legislative procedure, the co-decision procedure, which involves up to three readings in Parliament and Council and a series of deadlines and majority requirements. The procedure puts Parliament on an almost equal footing with the Council. Ultimately, Parliament may veto legislation. A second highly significant new principle was a novel role for the Parliament in the appointment of the Commission President and a vote of approbation on the college as a whole. The full extent of the Maastricht Treaty's institutional provisions will be dealt with in Section 3 of this chapter (on the institutional context) and Chapter 3, Sections 3.1 and 3.4 (powers).

Perpetual struggle, steady advance

Earlier, it was claimed that the growth in the role and powers of the European Parliament was one of the most encouraging signs in the renewal of the European tradition of parliamentary democracy. As has been seen from the above account, the European Parliament was born hungry and frustrated and has developed into a habitual struggler. Where it has powers, it tries to exploit them as fully as possible and is always urging that these powers be extended. Where it has no powers, it is forever trying to exploit precedent, ambiguity and custom, applying a sort of creative accountancy to its rules of procedure and the treaties themselves. It militates constantly for new powers or new interpretations of old powers. And as the above account has shown, its powers and role have steadily grown; Parliament has come a long way from the relatively toothless Common Assembly of the European Coal and Steel

Community. Several other themes require elaboration before turning to the institutional context.

One theme, frequently neglected in text books, is that the Community is in a state of constant evolution; there is no fixed constitutional settlement. The European Parliament does not seek change within a fixed system but, rather, demands change as a function of change. This has led to a paradoxical situation in which the European Parliament wants change and yet is forever trying to stay abreast of it. The changes ultimately agreed by the Member States in all of the inter-governmental conferences to date have never gone as far as Parliament wanted but have always extended Parliament's role and powers in ways that have challenged its organisational capacities. To date, Parliament has always risen successfully to those changes, but its resources, and hence its resourcefulness, have been stretched (see, for example, Chapter 2, Section 2.11 and Chapter 4, Section 4.2 on the challenge and the consequences of majority requirements).

A second theme is that the Union/Community constitutional system is unique, *sui generis*. The foregoing account has shown how various institutions were introduced into the constitutional constellation — the Council, the European Council, Coreper — as a result of immediate pragmatic considerations in inter-governmental conferences. Despite all the many versions drafted by the Parliament or by the Commission's experts, IGCs have never referred to, let alone respected, a Philadelphia Convention-style blueprint. The result is not only an organically evolving, but a unique and idiosyncratic, system. It is tempting, but fundamentally misleading, to compare the European Union with federal states such as the United States, Switzerland, or Germany. Inevitably, the emerging European Union does share some structural characteristics with such federations, but the overall configuration of its institutions and their powers is very different. Accordingly, the European Parliament, which is far from being a parliament as far as that term would traditionally be understood in the Member States, has a *sui generis* role and a *sui generis* array of powers.

A third theme is the European Parliament's constitutional militancy, which extends far beyond its persistence in drafting, in line with its treaty obligations, conventions for uniform electoral systems. In the first place, the European Parliament is an instinctively federalist institution. As was seen, its predecessor, the ECSC Common Assembly, began to draw up a European Constitution on just the second day of its existence. The logic runs deep; by definition, whenever the Parliament demands new powers or extensions of its old powers it is acting as an agent of federalisation (see Westlake, 1994a for a study of this effect). Nor is it surprising that a relatively powerless institution militates in favour of constitutional reforms that will almost inevitably lead to an enhancement of its own powers. (Thus, to take but one example, the European

Parliament had both federalist and pragmatic reasons for demanding that the three Councils and the two Commissions and the High Authority be merged into two unified institutions.) The 'founding fathers' surely had this consoling consideration in mind when they were obliged to agree to a European Coal and Steel Community that fell far below their initial expectations. (Indeed, in his memoirs Jean Monnet writes admiringly — and altogether approvingly — about the newly born ECSC Common Assembly's 1952 decision to draft a European Constitution.) Thus, although the Parliament bobs on a sea where federal and confederal tides wash back and forth, there can be no mistaking the direction in which it wishes to go.

A fourth common theme discernible in the foregoing historical account is the European Parliament's consistency of behaviour. Two 'snapshots' of the European Parliament's major institutional initiatives, one taken in 1963, and the other taken thirty years on, in 1993–4, reveal few, if any, differences. In 1993 the European Parliament adopted a new Convention for the introduction of a uniform electoral system (see Chapter 2, Section 2.4) and has since been badgering the Council for action upon it (thirty years ago, the European Parliament was similarly urging the Council to act on its 1960 Convention). On 10 February 1994, the European Parliament adopted a full-scale suggested Draft Treaty for European Union (this was the sixth such draft adopted by the Parliament); its 1963 predecessor hovered between the revolutionary EPC draft and the far-reaching 1964 Furler report. Both the 1963 and the 1993–4 European Parliaments sought change through 'little steps', either through their rules or convention, and 'big steps', through treaty change (the 1993–4 Parliament linked its calls to treaty change to the enlargement of the Community). Both the 1963 and the 1993–4 European Parliaments sought more parliamentary involvement in the Community's legislative processes and in the adoption and implementation of its budget. If the Parliament has remained consistent, it is because the basic argument for parliamentary involvement has not changed.

Thus, a historical review of the Parliament's growth reveals great consistency in its views and its strategy. It has never faltered in its demands for direct and uniform elections, nor in its demands for further integration. At the strategic level, Parliament has consistently espoused a two-pronged approach, consisting of gradual advances within the current treaty framework ('little steps') and quantum leaps via treaty change. It has taken heart from the increasing pace of treaty reform, with inter-governmental conferences leading to the 1986 Single European Act and the 1991 Maastricht Treaty, and another inter-governmental conference foreseen for 1996. In its eyes, the biggest step of all would be to hold a constituent conference which would, once and for all, agree on a constitutional settlement for the Union. In its heart, it knows that, with a fresh round of enlargements already under way and perhaps more to come in the medium term, a constituent conference is not yet an imminent prospect. At the same time, the steady mapping out of the Union's constitutional mechanisms through an increasing number of inter-governmental conferences and inter-institutional agreements has made the prospect of such a constituent conference or, at the least, a more definitive constitutional settlement, less improbable.

The fifth, and perhaps most important theme in the context of this study is that, in seeking change, in seeking a greater role and more powers for itself, in (to use Bagehot's phrase) 'meddling' in everything, the European Parliament is also acting as an indispensable democratising agent within the Community system.

1.3   The institutional context: the Parliament's relations with the other Community institutions

At the European Union level (the Parliament's relations with national parliaments will be dealt with in the next section), the European Parliament forms part of a complex system of institutions, its relations with each of them being more or less (depending on the policy issue and procedure involved) inextricably intertwined. Some — the Committee of the Regions, the Court of Auditors (as an institution) — are very new. Others — the Council, the Commission — are as old as the Parliament itself. These relations, like the system itself, are organic and constantly evolving. This section describes the Parliament's relations with each institution in turn and attempts to give an overall impression.

The European Council

The heads of state or government of the Member States of the European Communities first met, at de Gaulle's behest, in the early 1960s. These meetings formed part of de Gaulle's vision of a confederal Europe of sovereign states and were intended as part-antidote, part-counterweight to the supranational, federalist Commission. De Gaulle felt passionately that the political direction of the Community then badly needed (particularly in regard to external relations) could only come from the states themselves.

The European Parliament greeted these meetings with profound ambivalence. On the negative side, the summits lay outside the treaty framework and were therefore beyond all European parliamentary oversight or influence (bypassing the Community system was, indeed, part of de Gaulle's intention). They constituted interference in and potential erosion of the Community system. Above all, they were the embodiment of state sovereignty. But, on the positive side, the European

31

Parliament saw reluctantly that there *was* need for political leadership of the Community. Moreover, it was clear (especially given the predominant position granted the French president in the new French Fifth Republic) that further institutional change — direct elections, for example — would necessarily depend on agreement at the level of the heads of state.

De Gaulle's initiative fell into abeyance with the 1965 'empty chair' crisis, but, as was earlier pointed out, once ideas have been launched, they rarely go away altogether. Community summitry was revived in the early 1970s and, at such a meeting on 9 and 10 December 1974 in Paris, was put on a regular basis (at the behest of another French president, Valéry Giscard d'Estaing). 'Recognising the need for an overall approach to the internal problems involved in achieving European unity and the external problems facing Europe,' the heads of state and government decided to meet three times a year. The 'European Council', as these meetings became called, was a response to two separate needs. The first was a need to overcome the arthritis of the Council of Ministers, which had been crippled by the unanimity requirement of the 'Luxembourg Compromise' and by its own fragmentation into sectoral Councils (which could disagree among themselves, making decision making even more fraught). The second was the Member States' recurring ambition to coordinate their foreign policies. Once again, and for the same reasons, the European Parliament met this development with ambivalence although by now tempered with pragmatism. Parliament could only approve of initiatives that might free the decision-making log-jam in the Council of Ministers; it could only encourage moves that might give the Community greater political weight on the world stage, but was opposed to the consolidation of an extra-treaty, national sovereignty-based institution lying beyond all (European) parliamentary control.

The Parliament's ambivalence was set out in an 18 December 1981 resolution. On the one hand, it implicitly recognised the European Council's role by calling upon it to inform Parliament fully of the content and outcome of its meetings. On the other hand, it insisted that the European Council should respect the 'institutional balance' intended by the treaties and, in particular, the Commission's role and the Parliament's control over it.

The European Council remained an *ad hoc* meeting, provided for by a simple political declaration rather than treaty provision, until the 1986 Single European Act brought it into the fold of the treaties, defining its membership and providing that it should meet at least twice a year but saying nothing about its functions or purpose. The Maastricht Treaty has further consolidated the European Council's position within the Community and European Union systems. For example, it now has the specific role of laying down economic guidelines for the Community (in the context of Economic and Monetary Union), a role it first performed in 1994, and it 'shall define the principles of and general guidelines for the Common Foreign and Security Policy' of the European Union. At the same time, the European Council's ambiguous status continues (it is not listed as a Community institution), and one article in the Maastricht Treaty (Article 109j) confuses matters further by referring to the Council 'meeting in the composition of the Heads of State or Government', implying that the European Council is an extension of the Council (of Ministers). In addition to the specific duties now laid out in the treaties, the overall functions of the European Council have been confirmed by practice and convention over the past two decades. Thus, it is simultaneously a high level forum, a policy initiator, and a decision maker.

In the simple terms of its own role and competences, the consolidation of the European Council has undermined the European Parliament's influence and oversight. Since 1981 (following Parliament's resolution), the practice has grown for the president of the European Council to report to the Parliament on the outcome of each summit, and the president of the European Parliament is now invited to attend and address the opening sessions of the European Council (the practice began in 1987, when the then President of Parliament, Lord Plumb, was invited to address the 29 and 30 June 1987 Brussels European Council). Though these concessions may have had some palliative effect, the European Parliament has nevertheless only a tangential influence on the European Council's deliberations and can only rarely claim to have had any direct influence on its decisions. Its influence is further weakened by the Council of Ministers' traditional deference to European Council decisions and, in particular, by the fact that the Council of Ministers dislikes amending legislation stemming from European Council decisions.

At the same time, with its traditional, pragmatic ambivalence, the European Parliament has not only grudgingly accepted the need for and existence of such a higher executive but constantly urges it to act and is quick to criticise it for inaction or lack of direction. (Some parliamentarians accept that the European Council has been a better friend to the European Parliament than the Council of Ministers). And now the Maastricht Treaty has left the European Parliament with no choice since, as has been seen, it grants the European Council specific and entirely legitimate roles in European economic and foreign policy. But the problem from the European Parliament's point of view is not only that the European Council exists but that the Parliament itself has no role, whether of influence or oversight, in relation to it. In other words, the European Parliament's objections are as much related to the practice as the principle.

However, there *is* a longer-term underlying problem of principle, bound up with the European Parliament's federalist vision. As will be seen in the next section, the Parliament holds that the legitimacy of the Union (present and future) emanates, or is dually derived, from the Member States and their citizens. In line with this logic, Union acts should be adopted by the Council (of Ministers), representing the states, and the European Parliament, representing the peoples, acting as co-legislators. The Commission, beholden to both, should be the executive. What role, then, should the European Council play?

In its latest suggested draft Constitution of the European Union (10.2.94), Parliament proposes that: 'The European Council shall impart to the Union the impetus necessary for its development and shall define, with the participation of the European Parliament, the general political guidelines of the Union.' There is only one other mention of the European Council in Parliament's draft. Its external relations' title takes up and builds on the language of the Maastricht Treaty, stating that: 'The European Council shall define the general principles and guidelines of the common foreign and security policy, including common defence policy and common defence.'

In part, this provision is a pragmatic recognition of the European Council's fundamental role in any foreign or defence policy initiatives, a role already enshrined in the Maastricht Treaty and unlikely to diminish. But the omissions in Parliament's draft Constitution are also instructive. For example, the European Council would no longer have another right enshrined in the Maastricht Treaty, that of laying down the economic guidelines for the European Union (hence unconsciously reflecting a fundamental difference in the two Fouchet plans of the early 1960s — the second placed economic policy, much to federalists' and the European Parliament's dismay, firmly under the tutelage of the envisaged Council of national leaders). And Parliament's draft Constitution is silent on how the European Council 'shall impart impetus' to the Union. These omissions and silences are bound up with the European Parliament's ambivalence towards the European Council. The roles the European Council informally and formally plays today, as 'super-executive', as *de facto* grand legislator, as *ad hoc* star chamber and legislative blockage-breaker to the Council, are not to the Parliament's longer-term liking and can have little place in its purist constitutional blueprint of the European Union which sees the European Commission alone as the Union's chief executive.

The Council of the European Union

A similar problem of principle, again bound up with the European Parliament's federalist vision, underlies its relations with the Council (since the implementation of the Maastricht Treaty, its formal title has been the 'Council of the European Union', but in everyday usage it is still referred to as 'the Council').

As was seen, the Council did not figure in Monnet's early blueprint for the European Coal and Steel Community, and was only introduced at the insistence of the Benelux states, primarily to protect the interests of such smaller states against Franco–German hegemony. The Common Assembly, which had been primarily conceived as a check and balance to the High Authority, had no power over the Council. On the contrary, the draftsmen granted the Council powers over the Assembly. Thus, the Assembly could be convened at the request of the Council to deliver opinions 'on such questions as may be put to it' (clearly, the draftsmen had further control over the High Authority in mind). Further, members of the Council could attend all meetings of the Assembly and could be heard at their request. The Assembly had no right to put questions to the Council, and the Council was under no obligation to respond to the Assembly. Control over the members of the Council would continue to be exercised by national parliaments. The High Authority was the interloper, and most thought was devoted to how *it* could be controlled. As was seen, the Paris Treaty did allow for the possibility of direct elections, but most commentators retro-spectively saw this as paying lip service to the democratic ideal ('democratic window dressing', as Scalingi put it, 1980, p.20) rather than the revelation of serious political intent. In particular, governments were fearful that direct elections would create a rival and antagonistic source of legitimacy.

The 1957 Rome Treaties were closely modelled on the Paris Treaty, particularly as far as institutional arrangements were concerned. But, in terms of relations between them, a subtle shift of power consolidated the Council's pre-eminent position and weakened that of the European Parliament. The Parliament was now expected to give its opinion on some legislative proposals (and hence the EEC and Euratom Treaties spoke of 'supervisory and *advisory*' powers, where the ECSC Treaty spoke of *supervisory* powers only), but the Council was not obliged to take notice of any opinions thus expressed, nor was it obliged to answer any questions addressed to it. Crucially, the decision to hold direct elections to the European Parliament lay ultimately with the Council. As we know, the Council did not decide until 1976 (and then following a 1974 decision in principle taken by the *European* Council), and the first direct elections were not held until 1979, more than two decades after the Treaties of Rome entered into force.

Proponents of the supranational approach had supposed that the intergovernmentalism of the Council would gradually wither as the advantages of the ECSC/EEC/Euratom supranational method became apparent. That this did not occur had something to do with de Gaulle's dominance and the resurgence, under his influence, of the sovereign state as the basic political actor. Moreover, it was Member State governments that had negotiated the Rome Treaties, and it is not surprising that they entrenched and consolidated their own dominant position within the decision-making machinery of the Communities. However, supranationalists placed their hopes in the provisions on direct elections. Improbable though it may seem in retrospect, supranationalists expected direct elections to be held in a matter of years after the entry into force of the Rome Treaties. Direct elections were to be the key, instilling popular legitimacy in the Community. When these did not occur the supranationalist cause and its expectations were set back.

Thus, in relation to one another, the 1960s saw consolidation of both the Council's predominant position and the European Parliament's relatively weak position. This differential had socio-anthropological consequences which are still of importance in understanding the relationship between the two institutions today. Glamorous, prestigious ministers (or worse, deputised ambassadors and civil servants) with busy agendas and wielding great power met hurriedly behind closed doors in intimate circumstances to take decisions potentially of great importance. In contrast, the less glamorous members of the European Parliament, many in political career backwaters and collectively wielding only the power of opinion, met occasionally as an adjunct to their full-time occupations as national parliamentarians to debate at great length and in full view of an uninterested public subjects over which they had little, if any, influence. Worse, the Council, in its failure to decide on direct elections, was seen to be responsible for this imbalance. Even today, relations between the two institutions are tinged by frustration, envy and resentment on Parliament's part and condescension on the part of the Council.

The 1970s saw the beginnings of a gradual, belated righting of the institutional imbalance. The first inroad was in the technocratic and relatively arcane sphere of the Community's finances. The Parliament and the Council are now 'twin arms of the budgetary authority'. As will be seen in Chapter 3, Section 3.3, Parliament may amend the Community budget (in the case of some categories of expenditure it has the last word), it may reject it and it exercises ever-increasing super-vision over the implementation of the budget. The budget cannot come into force without the signature of Parliament's president. These *real* powers not only obliged the Council to deal with the Parliament but to take it seriously. A 1975 joint declaration (of the Council, the Com-mission and the European Parliament) saw the creation of a 'conciliation procedure' for acts with 'appreciable financial implications' which, while it left the Council with the last word, involved a 'conciliation committee' in which Council and Parliament representatives met over the same table and sought agreement. The adoption of the budget itself increasingly involved the use of conciliation committees. Thus, in the budgetary field the Council and the Parliament were brought together, if not on equal terms, then at least on less unequal terms. The result, not surprisingly, has been a reduction in the sentiments described in the previous paragraph. Parliament is under no illusions about the imbalance in the relationship, but at least there *is* a relationship. Moreover, that relationship has instilled a measure of mutual respect. The Community's finances and the procedures involved are highly complex and surrounded in a miasma of technical jargon. Both sides speak the same technical language. The conciliation procedure frequently involves 'time outs', in which both sides meet separately to discuss their options before regrouping in the conciliation committee. In turn, these time-consuming practices frequently result in extended meetings carrying on well into the small hours in lonely buildings in Strasbourg, Luxembourg and Brussels. These practices have undoubtedly resulted in mutual respect and a sort of *esprit de corps* (though both sides would probably be loathe to admit it).

The Council has always had the legislative upper hand. From the inception of the Community, it has been virtually the sole Community legislator, and it was only with the introduction of the cooperation procedure in 1987 (through the Single European Act) that the European Parliament gained a positive input into the legislative process. The Maastricht Treaty introduced a fundamental new departure. In certain policy areas, legislation is adopted through a new co-decision procedure, consisting of a maximum of three readings by the Parliament and the Council. The procedure allows for conciliation procedures (similar to those involved in the budgetary process — see Chapter 3, Section 3.4) at both the second- and the third-reading stages. Ultimately, if the positions of the two sides cannot be brought sufficiently close together, Parliament may reject the legislative proposal in question. The co-decision procedure clearly builds on the twin experiences of the cooperation procedure and the budgetary (conciliation) procedure. It brings Parliament one step closer to its goal of equal co-legislator status with the Council.

Parliament has made considerable progress in one other area of its relations with the Council. The two now regularly meet, together with the Commission, in inter-institutional conferences. These may be devoted to particular topics (for example, inter-governmental conferences) or more general discussions of problems of common concern. This 'inter-institutional dialogue', as it is referred to, again puts the Parliament on more of a level footing with the Council. Increasingly, the Community institutions try to fill gaps in the provisions of the treaties with agreements among themselves. The Maastricht Treaty itself provides for two such inter-institutional agreements. Several more were agreed in the margins of the October 1993 Brussels European Council, and others are under negotiation. Once again, the net effect, both of negotiations and of the agreements, is to put the Parliament and the Council on more level terms.

The Maastricht Treaty has also put the Council and the Parliament on a more equal basis in one other highly important respect. EEC Article 152 states that 'The Council may request the Commission to . . . submit to it any appropriate proposals'. Of course, the Commission, which has the sole right of initiative, is under no obligation to make a proposal on the basis of a Council request, but, in practice, it has found it very difficult to refuse, especially given the Council's political weight. The result, in Parliament's eyes, has seemed close to a *de facto* right of initiative for the Council. For reasons of simple institutional balance Parliament found this *de facto* right difficult to accept, but there was also an underlying constitutional reason. In particular, as will be discussed in the next section, the European Parliament tends constantly to compare itself with the only comparable representative federal body in the world, the United States' Congress, which has a sole right of legislative initiative. That the Council should have a *de facto* right of initiative therefore jarred with the Parliament for purist constitutional reasons as well as for more straightforward reasons of inter-institutional rivalry. The Maastricht Treaty has redressed the balance directly by giving the Parliament the same right as the Council (New Article 138b states that 'The Parliament may, acting by a majority of its members, request the Commission to submit any appropriate proposal on matters on which it considers that a Community act is required for the purpose of implementing this Treaty'.) The Maastricht Treaty has also redressed the balance indirectly, as will be seen below, by giving the Parliament the necessary increased inter-institutional and political weight over the Commission for the theoretical right to request initiatives to be put into practice.

The Council is a hydra-headed beast; there is not one Council but many, with different groups of ministers meeting according to their different competences. The European Parliament has parliamentary committees with competences corresponding roughly with those of the specialised Councils but, at the political level, it is the European Parliament meeting in plenary which is the final political arbiter and most accurately corresponds with the institution of the Council. This can result in a sort of dissonance between the Parliament and its specialised committees, and certainly puts an onus on its specialised committees to build the broadest possible consensus within Parliament. This tendency is particularly apparent in the case of the Budgets Committee (special majorities are required for budgetary amendments), which has become extraordinarily adept at creating broad, cross-house coalitions within Parliament (see Chapter 4, Section 4.2).

The introduction, by the Single European Act, of qualified majority voting in the Council greatly accelerated the legislative pace, thereby diminishing what had previously been one of Parliament's most consistent complaints, that the combination of concentrated legislative power and the unanimity principle led to constant and lengthy blockage in Council. But, in the Parliament's eyes, the Council's working practices continue to effect the purity of the legislative process. There is a still strong instinct to achieve the greatest consensus possible, resulting frequently in concessions or derogations tending to dilute or undermine the legislation concerned. (Some critics in Parliament point out that, even under the cooperation procedure, unanimity remains axiomatic in the Council, since the Member States know that a unanimous Common Position is beyond parliamentary amendment — see Chapter 3, Section 3.4).

In addition to its different specialisations, the Council consists of a number of distinct hierarchical levels. Legislative proposals are first considered in working groups, composed of national civil servants (either flown in from national ministries or temporarily based in the permanent representations in Brussels). As proposals 'ripen' and problems are 'boiled off', they rise to the level of the ambassadors or their deputies, meeting together in an institution universally known by its French acronym, 'Coreper' (Comité de représentants permanents — committee of permanent representatives). Coreper was at first an informal arrangement but was brought into the treaties by the 1967 Merger Treaty. (Working parties continue to exist outside the treaties.) Even though the European Parliament has a burgeoning role in the Community's legislative process, it has an increasing problem in overseeing the legislative process in these other sub- or intra-Council bodies, where many, if not most, of the decisions of substance may be taken. As with the European Council, the Parliament has a multi-dimensioned problem. First, it must discover and attempt to influence the agendas and, second, it must attempt to discover and influence the deliberations of these bodies. At the same time, it can have no formal relationship with these bodies.

An often neglected aspect of inter-institutional relations is the attitude and actions of the secretariats of the institutions concerned. The European Parliament is assisted by a secretariat of convinced and mainly devout supranationalists, more generally described as a 'propulsive elite' (Pryce and Wessels, 1987, p.16). They act as an institutional memory (particularly important in a Parliament with high levels of membership turnover) and the administrative and legal champions of their institution. The Council secretariat-general plays a particularly important role in ensuring smooth transitions between Presidencies (see the next section). As with the Commission, the Council is on the defensive. Previously-established arrangements are constantly under attack from an institution which is, so to speak, constantly ambitious. Day-to-day relations are tinged (and can be poisoned) by such attitudes and considerations (see Chapter 4, Section 4.1).

In addition to its legislative functions, the Council also plays an important executive role. In principle, the Commission is the Community's executive, but in most policy areas the Commission is assisted in this task by committees made up of representatives of the Member States. There are three types of committee: advisory, management and regulatory. Under the advisory committee procedure, the Commission must take note of the committee's opinion about any set of draft measures but is not bound by it. Under the management committee procedure, the Council may, under certain circumscribed circumstances, take a different decision to that initially proposed by the Commission. Under the regulatory committee procedure, the Commission's proposals are more easily referred to the Council and can more easily be overthrown. The committee structure was streamlined as a consequence of the Single European Act, and it was hoped that the Council would have increasing recourse to the advisory committee procedure. In practice, the Council has rarely agreed to it.

The European Parliament objects to the Council's practice on committees (in the jargon, the whole subject is referred to as 'comitology') for three reasons. In the first place, management and regulatory committees can undermine the intent or scope of legislation. Metaphorically speaking, they allow the Member States (and national sovereignty) a second bite at the cherry. In the second place, the Parliament has no control over them. To the extent that it accepts the need, Parliament prefers advisory committees because the Commission alone retains executive responsibility, and hence the lines of accountability to the Parliament remain clear.

In the third place, and most profoundly, a Council exercising executive powers clashes with the Parliament's constitutional vision. Time and again in its draft Constitutions, the Parliament reasserts the twin sources of the Union's legislative legitimacy as the states represented in the Council, and the people, represented in the Parliament. Basing its vision on the classic division of powers, the Parliament sees the Commission as the sole executive. This consideration fundamentally colours the Parliament's attitude to the Council. There may be sibling rivalry, but the Parliament aspires one day to exactly the same status as the Council and therefore looks upon it as a future equal partner in the legislative process.

Latterly, however, the broader implications of the new co-decision procedure have blurred the purity of Parliament's constitutional vision. Basing itself on a Mohammed-to-the-mountain logic, Parliament has switched from an attack on the *principle* of management and regulatory committees to demanding the same powers as the Council within them (see Chapter 3, Section 3.8).

The Presidency

The Presidency of the European Union is not an institution as such, but it is an important factor in relations between the Council and the Parliament. The Presidency, which rotates among the Member States every six months, is responsible for arranging and chairing all Council meetings during its mandate. Its principle tasks (the treaties themselves are silent) involve advancing the Community's policy and legislative processes and representing the Council and the Union externally, *vis-à-vis* both third countries and the other institutions, including the Parliament. Status and prestige are principal considerations in the Presidency. A 'good' Presidency is generally judged to be one that gets things done or deals effectively with international events. Because the head of the state occupying the Presidency comes before Parliament to report on the European Council's meetings, Parliament has developed a self-styled role as 'judge' on each Presidency. It can compare a Presidency's declared intentions, as set out to Parliament at the beginning of the Presidency, with the results achieved when the six months are up.

Parliament's criticisms are generally of three types. The first consist of straightforward accusations of mismanagement. The second relate to the amount of Community 'spirit' displayed by a Presidency, particularly where Parliament feels that a Presidency has confused its own interests with those of the Community at the expense of the latter. Third, Parliament is very sensitive to the way in which a Presidency behaves towards the Parliament itself. On the one hand, Parliament expects to see the Presidency appropriately represented at important debates, and on the other it expects the Presidency to behave sympathetically towards it in any inter-institutional negotiations that may occur.

The Presidency is crippled in its relations with the Parliament by the simple fact that it can take few policy initiatives and express few policy views on behalf of the Council *per se*. It can express its own views, it can promise to represent Parliament's views back to the Council and it can remind Parliament of decisions taken by the Council, but it is nevertheless fundamentally inflexible. This is an important factor in overall Council–Parliament relations, since Parliament normally sees far more of the Presidency than it does of the Council. (Indeed, the Council in its 'pure' form of twelve ministers only meets the Parliament in conciliation committees and inter-institutional conferences.) Thus, relations between the Parliament and the Council can depend to a considerable extent on whether a Presidency 'gets on' with the Parliament. Since the Presidency is most frequently represented in Parliament by the foreign affairs minister or a deputy, much can depend in turn on personal and political chemistry.

The Commission

The Parliament and the Commission are kindred supranational institutions and share a federal vision of the European Union. They have always been institutional allies in the Community's cause. (It was the Commission's proposal, among other things, that the Parliament should have real budgetary powers that triggered off the 1965 'empty chair' crisis.) Moreover, the Parliament has always relied on the Commission's expertise and political understanding. (The Commission constantly championed the cause of direct elections and has always represented Parliament's point of view in inter-governmental conferences, from which the Parliament continues to be excluded.) However, this consensus and dependence sits ill with the theoretically 'adversarial', executive–legislative relationship envisaged by the treaties. (After all, the Parliament's first and for several years only significant power was to be able to throw the Commission out of office.)

Since the first direct elections were held in June 1979, the European Parliament has been steadily developing a more independent stance in relation to the Commission. Previously, it had only indirect legitimacy and was a part-time body. After direct elections, it had its own direct popular legitimacy (the Commission has none) and became a full-time institution. The Commission, which had always argued for direct elections, soon drew the consequences of this. Parliament continued to rely on the Commission for *practical* help (particularly the provision of information), but the Commission increasingly looked to the Parliament for the popular legitimation of its policy proposals, and the new legislative powers granted the Parliament by the Single European Act and the Maastricht Treaty have consolidated this trend (the co-decision procedure even deprives the Commission of its jealously defended absolute proprietorial right of initiative at the third-reading stage).

A good example of the Parliament's attempt to occupy what might be termed the high ground of popular legitimacy, and of the Commission's response, as well as the underlying tensions arising out of the Parliament's new confidence, came in a February 1994 debate on a proposal to limit the maximum power of large motorbikes. Contesting the Commission's belief that its proposal would enhance safety, Parliament wanted to reject the Commission's proposal, but the Commission felt it had good technical arguments on its side. Stung by parliamentary critics, the Commissioner responsible, Mr Bangemann, retorted:

> . . . it is true that I am not elected, but I am a member of a democratic system, and the Commission is an organ in a democratic institution, namely the European Union. We are playing our role — we are proposing something, and if there is a debate on whether or not it is democratic to accept or to reject our

own proposal, I have every right in the world to say to you . . . that it is a false argument to play on democracy in this context . . . I believe that the Commission is doing more to fulfil its role as a partner of Parliament in that dialogue by telling Parliament when it considers that Parliament is wrong, than by being silent or polite, by bowing to you and saying 'yes, you are elected'. I have also been elected . . . I am now a member of the Commission. But I am not a stranger to a democratic system — I am part of that democratic system and I am participating here in a democratic debate (European Parliament, *Verbatim Report of Proceedings*, 7 February 1994, p.25).

The Maastricht Treaty has introduced an even more fundamental change. From 1995 onwards, the mandates of the Parliament and the Commission will be synchronised. From 1994 onwards, the Member States must consult the European Parliament on their nominee for Commission President, and the whole Commission is subject to a vote of parliamentary approval before definitive appointment. The conse- quences of Parliament's new powers of appointment are dealt with in more detail in Chapter 3, Section 3.2, but most commentators agree that a primary consequence will be to render the Commission more responsive to the majority view within Parliament. In other words, the potential beginnings of a government–legislature-type arrangement are crystallising in the Parliament's evolving relationship with the Com- mission; Parliament is now involved in the Commission's appointment, and Parliament alone can dismiss it (though, under the provisions of EEC Article 160, the Court may, on application by the Council or the Commission, 'compulsorily retire' any member of the Commission who 'no longer fulfils the conditions required for the performance of his duties, or if he has been found guilty of serious misconduct').

Whatever the future constitutional development of the Union, the old bilateral relationship between the Commission and the Council ('the Commission proposes, the Council disposes', as it used to be said) has given way to a triangular relationship in which the Commission is increasingly accountable to the Parliament (Chapter 3 describes the Commission's procedural and policy accountability in more detail), as well as to the Council. Increasingly, the Commission has to navigate its policies between the representatives of the people and the represen- tatives of the states.

The Court of Justice

The European Court of Justice is the 'third man' of the Community's supranational institutions. A neglected subject outside specialist legal publications, the Parliament's relations with the Court are of fundamental importance, for it is no exaggeration to claim that, after inter-governmental conferences and the acts of the Parliament itself, the Court has been the most important factor in establishing and delimiting the Parliament's role and powers, 'in promoting a consistent conception of the European Parliament's role in the decision-making process' (Bradley, 1987, p.63). A possible explanation of this neglect is that, unlike Parliament–Commission or Parliament–Council relations (which are fundamentally *political*) relations with the Court are necessarily *legal*. But the Court's interpretations of the treaties have had far-reaching constitutional and political consequences.

Until the 1979 direct elections, the Parliament hardly existed as a legal entity. Under the treaties, staff cases had to be dealt with by the Court (they are now dealt with by a Court of First Instance). Apart from these, Parliament participated in legal proceedings just once, in 1963, and then at the invitation of the Court. In 1969 it considered introducing a case for 'failure to act' against the Council for failing to introduce direct, uniform elections, but ultimately decided against (see Chapter 3, Section 3.3). It was perhaps understandable that the old, nominated Parliament should have fought shy of litigation at the Community level, given that it was composed of delegated national law-makers.

The introduction of direct elections seemed to open the sluice gates, liberating Parliament, and in particular its Legal Affairs Committee and its gifted and ambitious legal service (although this was not formally created as a separate service until 1986). (The battle between the legal services of the different institutions is an important socio-political sub-text to their political relations — see Chapter 4, Section 4.1.) The result was a series of cases throughout the 1980s, brought by the Parliament and, reactively or in support, by the Commission, the Council and various Member States, which rapidly established a broad jurisprudence relating to the Parliament's place in the Community. Table 1 sets out the most important cases and rulings, together with the underlying issues and broader consequences, in chronological order. The result of this sudden flurry of activity in the Court was that, after a long period of isolation, the Parliament was swiftly integrated into the Community's legal system.

An early concern of the Member States, when the elected Parliament's activities first raised matters with potentially actionable consequences, was the Parliament's relationship to the rule of law. Was the Parliament, now elected by universal suffrage and hence with independent political legitimacy, beyond the law (as some of its supporters claimed), or subject to it (as the Member States fervently hoped)? The Court ruled consistently that the Community was a Community of law and that the Parliament was therefore subject to it and hence to the Court's rulings. (However, an apparent quid pro quo for the Parliament's submission to the rule of law has been the Court's consistent support for the Parliament's democratic role and prerogatives.) This basic attitude, and the underlying dialectic between the principle of Community law and the European Parliament as an expression of the democratic ideal (a role which the Court upholds), has sometimes rankled with the Parliament, as have the rulings, not always in favour of Parliament, based upon it.

In adopting such a stance, the court has consistently followed its primary vocation of ensuring respect for the treaties. As the 'Isoglucose' decisions made abundantly clear, it sees the Parliament as a democratic protagonist and is always tempted to give it a helping hand where it can. But the Court must also hold to the treaties. These state unequivocally that 'each institution shall act within the limits of the powers conferred upon it by this Treaty.' (TEU Article 4) The European Parliament, unlike most national parliaments, *is* limited by the treaties, its legislative role being particularly restricted. Further, its ability to act before the Court is, in comparison with the Commission and the Council, comparatively limited. Moreover, the Court strongly believes in (and in its rulings frequently refers to) the institutional balance foreseen in the treaties, and it is therefore at pains to protect the prerogatives of *each* institution. This, too, can rankle. (It is a moot point as to whether the Court is itself entirely beyond the Community's political system or, if only because of the political consequences of its rulings, part of what Pescatore (1989, p.208) has elegantly referred to as 'a parallelogram of multidimensional forces'.)

The Court's jurisprudence has not only sought to delineate the legal rights and obligations of the institutions but also to demarcate between the political and the juridical. The Court's 1986 ruling on the legality of the 1986 Budget and its 1988 ruling on the 'comitology' dispute have been particularly significant in this respect. In the former case, the Court found that Parliament's president had not validly declared the budget to be adopted because political differences still remained between 'the twin arms' of the budgetary authority (that is, the Council and the Parliament), and hence the Parliament's unilateral action was illegal. The Court refused to set itself up as a sort of 'third arm' of the budgetary authority and, indeed, fastidiously refused to become involved in the process leading to the adoption of the budget, ordering the Council and the Parliament to go away and reach political agreement, as foreseen by EEC Article 203. In the comitology case, the Court pointed out that:

the European Parliament is empowered, on the one hand, to exercise political control over the Commission . . . and on the other, to censure the Commission, where necessary, if the latter should fail properly to discharge that task. The European Parliament's political control is also exercised by means of the debates that it may organise on specific or general questions, which enable it to pass motions on the policy followed by the Council or the Commission.

In other words, while the Court was prepared to protect institutional prerogatives and the inter-institutional balance, it steadfastly refused to become involved in the political process, preferring to remind the Parliament of the array of political powers at its disposal.

The Maastricht Treaty effectively absorbed much of the Court's jurisprudence relating to the Parliament, consolidating its case-law position in the treaties. In particular, TEU Article 173 now explicitly provides for the Parliament to bring actions before the Court to protect its initiatives and, correspondingly, for 'acts of the European Parliament intended to produce legal effects *vis-à-vis* third parties' to be subject to review by the Court. Further, TEU Article 175 provides that an action for failure to act may be brought against the Parliament (as has always been the case with the other institutions). In addition, TEU Article 173 provides for 'acts adopted jointly by the European Council and the Parliament' (that is, acts adopted under the new co-decision procedure — see Chapter 3, Section 3.4) to be subject to review by the Court. These provisions are logical consequences of Parliament's new legislative role.

In its latest pronouncements (resolutions of 16.9.93, 9.2.94 and 10.2.94), the Parliament has argued: first, that the Court should be the sole arbiter of all Union constitutional conflicts; second, that the Parliament should be given exactly the same rights in relation to the Court and the judicial process as the Commission and the Council; and, third, that members of the Court should be elected by the European Parliament and the Council for one non-renewable term of nine years.

The first call is bound up in the debate over the Maastricht Treaty's particular mixture of the traditional 'Community method', where the Court has sole competence, and inter-governmental cooperation (on Justice, Home Affairs, and the Common Foreign and Security Policy), where the Court has none (see Chapter 3, Sections 3.5 and 3.7).

The second call is based on what the Parliament sees as continued discrimination against it, even after Maastricht. In particular, under the provisions of TEU Article 73, Member States, the Commission and the Council have broad-ranging rights to bring actions before the Court, whereas the Parliament may only bring actions 'for the purpose of protecting its prerogatives'. In practice, this means that the Parliament can only hope to rely on the Commission, pressuring it to pursue its general duties as 'guardian of the Treaties' (TEU Article 155) to bring cases on Parliament's behalf.

Third, the Parliament's call for elected members of the Court reflects the age-old debate about the virtues of independence versus democratic legitimacy. Former members of the Court tend to argue that the Court has done very well under present arrangements, whereby judges are nominated unanimously by the Member States for six-year renewable terms. Clearly, among its considerations is Parliament's desire that its own powers should match those of the Council. The American model of detailed, public Congressional hearings frequently surfaces in its debates. Confounding such a parallel, though, are the facts that Parliament (resolution of 16.9.93) expressly argues against public nomination hearings and that it recommends a nine-year, rather than life, term (though the nine-year term would be non-renewable). One further possible motivation in such demands is that the European Parliament is not the sole potential source of legitimation. For example, Thomas Goppel, the Bavarian Minister of European Affairs, has recently called for German members of the European Court of Justice to be elected by the Bundestag (*Agence Europe*, 6–7 December 1993). On the other hand, Parliament may simply be seeking consistency with its powers of consultation in relation to the Court of Auditors. (The Parliament recently debated this issue in February 1994. It adopted a gradualist approach, calling for at least formal consultation rights over appointments to the Court of Justice, and the then Greek Presidency-in-Office expressed sympathy with its arguments, specifically citing the imbalance with Parliament's rights *vis-à-vis* appointments to the Court of Auditors.)

The Court of Auditors

The Court of Auditors is in every sense the youngest of the Community institutions. It was established in 1975, when the separate audit boards of the EEC, Euratom and the ECSC were merged but was only elevated to the status of a Community institution in November 1993, when the Maastricht Treaty was implemented. The Court of Auditors was created in direct response to the European Parliament's arguments that such a body was necessary and should exist within the Community, and because of this the Parliament has always had a proprietorial, and almost paternal, attitude towards the Court. Composed of twelve members appointed for six-year renewable terms, its primary purpose is to audit the Community's finances and, in particular, 'whether all revenue has been received and all expenditure incurred in a lawful and regular manner and whether the financial management has been sound' (TEU Article 188c,2). To this end, it draws up an annual report which is part of the budgetary discharge procedure (see Chapter 3, Section 3.3). The Court of Auditors has the power to request all relevant information and documentation from the other Community institutions and the national audit bodies. In addition to its annual reports, it has the power to submit 'observations' on specific questions as it sees fit and to deliver opinions at the request of one of the other institutions of the Community (including the Parliament). Finally, TEU Article 188c,4 specifically provides that the Court should 'assist the European Parliament and the Council in exercising their powers of control over the implementation of the budget'.

As a result of these provisions, the Parliament's relations with the Court of Auditors take several forms. In the first place, Parliament is consulted on the candidatures for the Court, who are nominated by the Member State governments, then appointed unanimously by the Council. In practice, because (through a tacit gentlemen's agreement) the Member States trust in each others' judgement and refrain from questioning each others' nominations, Council unanimity is automatic. The Parliament's right to consultation (under TEU Article 188b,3) is apparently weak, since the Council is under no obligation to heed its opinion. *De facto*, Parliament practices what can be tantamount to a veto, since the refusal to countenance a nominee puts great political pressure on both that nominee and the proposing Member State to withdraw the candidature. Parliamentary refusal to countenance Member State nominees has so far occurred twice, in 1989 and 1993, with mixed results (see Chapter 3, Section 3.2). The logic is apparently ineluctable (how could an individual that Parliament has judged unacceptable help it in any useful way in exercising its powers?) but nevertheless escapable (not all members of the Court have necessarily to work with the Parliament). Because of this, Parliament has persistently called for it to be granted *assent* powers over the appointment of the members of the Court — that is, formal veto powers.

In the second place, the Court of Auditors' annual report includes separate sections on the finances of each of the Community institutions, including those of the Parliament. Thus the Parliament, an institution fiercely independent in spirit, must nevertheless submit its finances and all necessary documentation to the perusal of an appointed body. This arrangement has latterly led to some tension.

In the third place, the Court of Auditors enjoys a very close working relationship with Parliament's Budgetary Control Committee, which has particular responsibility for the discharge procedure. Members of the Court frequently appear before the committee, and the Court is frequently called upon to help it in its deliberations.

In the fourth place, the Court of Auditors' annual report is by convention submitted orally to Parliament by the Court's president, who subsequently takes a passive place in Parliament's debate on the discharge of the Community budget. Now that the Court is a fully fledged Community institution (the first discharge debate under these circumstances took place in November 1993), the Parliament must accord the Court and its president the respect of an equal. This can rankle.

In its latest report on relations with the Court of Auditors (11 March 1994), Parliament recognised that 'in recent years, relations between the Court of Auditors and Parliament have sometimes shown signs of strain. Those strains arise largely from the tension between Treaty provisions establishing the Court as an independent body but also as one with a duty to assist Parliament.' The Parliament goes on to insist that 'the Court and the Parliament have differing roles: the former is in the service of the taxpayer, the latter represents and is accountable to the taxpayer. The relations between the two institutions should reflect that distinction.' Parliament has enumerated a series of specific complaints: principally, the Court takes too long to respond to Parliament's requests for assistance; it is insufficiently pro-active in regard to its right to submit observations at any time; and it no longer confidentially transmits draft reports to the Budgetary Control Committee prior to their publication.

Nevertheless, the underlying theme is a familiar one: a long-frustrated European Parliament with hard-fought and hard-won powers and direct legitimacy finding it hard to come to terms with the relatively easily won independence of a new, appointed and quintessentially technocratic institution; the representative of the taxpayer bridling, as it were, at the independent spirit of the servant of the taxpayer. This attitude is borne out in the Parliament's latest draft Constitution, where the article on institutions would 'demote' the Court of Auditors from its current status as an institution to an organ which 'shall carry out specific tasks provided for by the Constitution'.

The Committee of the Regions

The 189-member Committee of the Regions was very recently created (by the Maastricht Treaty) and only first met in March 1994. The Committee is *not* an institution. The treaty describes its tasks as assisting the Council and the Commission by 'acting in an advisory capacity', but nevertheless has the autonomous powers of issuing opinions 'on its own initiative in cases in which it considers such action appropriate', and of meeting at its own initiative if it so desires. The European Parliament welcomed the establishment of the Committee as giving better expression to the complexity of the Union. Nevertheless, the creation of the Committee has given rise to profound misgivings within the Parliament. In the first place, Parliament has its own specialised Committee on Regional Affairs and Regional Policy, which has traditionally played a pre-eminent role in such matters as, for example, the distribution of the Community's structural and regional funds. In the second place, Parliament's membership itself contains regional representatives (obvious examples from the United Kingdom would include the Scottish and Welsh MEPs, and the three Northern Irish MEPs, John Hume, Ian Paisley and James Nicholson). In the third place, many MEPs have expressed misgivings at the potential independence of the new institution, particularly in relation to Parliament itself and in the context of the Community's constitutional development. As a result, the

Parliament and its specialised committee spent many hours debating what precisely it expected of the Committee of the Regions and what the relationship between the two could be.

Parliament's misgivings and ambivalence towards the Committee are neatly set out in a resolution adopted on 18 November 1993. On the one hand, Parliament welcomes 'the integration of the regional and local authorities into the Community's decision-making process' and, grouping the establishment of the Committee together with two other new developments in the Maastricht Treaty, European citizenship and the principle of subsidiarity, calls for the greatest possible decentralisation of Community policies. The resolution insists that all members of the Committee should be elected representatives, deriving 'direct democratic legitimacy from a regional or local assembly'.

But therein lies the rub: another Community-level body made up of elected representatives deriving direct democratic legitimacy, especially given the level of some of those representatives (in particular, regional ministers and high-ranking regional personalities from Belgium, Germany and Spain), could become a rival to Parliament itself. The resolution therefore goes on to declare Parliament's 'firm intention to establish direct and permanent contact with the Committee of the Regions, calls for the opinions of the Committee to be forwarded to Parliament officially and not sent only to the Council and the Commission' and 'recalls that the Committee of the Regions must not become an assembly participating in the drawing up of Community legislation as part of a bicameral system'. To this end, the resolution argues that the European Constitution 'should provide for a mechanism for the adoption of a provision defining the institutional role of the regions, when progress towards closer integration of the Union justifies it'. In Parliament's suggested draft Constitution (10 February 1994), the Committee of the Regions remains an advisory organ (on the same level as the Court of Auditors) to be consulted on all legislative initiatives concerning matters to be listed by an organic law.

Thus, while Parliament has both urged and welcomed the Committee of the Regions into the democratic fold, it has sought clear definitions of and limitations to its role. The Committee has been in existence for too short a period of time for it to have developed any definitive institutional stance of its own, but it seems almost certain to develop a higher profile than the organ whose secretariat it shares — the Economic and Social Committee.

The Economic and Social Committee

Like the Committee of the Regions, the Economic and Social Committee ('Ecosoc') is not an institution but an organ intended to assist the

Council and the Commission by 'acting in an advisory capacity' (TEU Article 4). Made up of 189 sectoral (industry, trades unions, agriculture, the professions) representatives, the Committee is designed to give expert, technical opinions on legislative proposals. Although slightly strengthened by the Maastricht Treaty, it remains a politically weak organ. It was modelled on the ECSC consultative committee, but probably owed its existence to the fact that five of the six founding Community Member States had similar institutions in their national political systems. Because of the integrationists' functional logic, it was thought that sectoral interests would be key participants in the Community's policy formation, and it was doubted whether the Parliamentary Assembly could be an effective forum for such interests.

The Economic and Social Committee has been weakened in many ways. Mandatory consultation of the Committee was limited to relatively few areas, and it has only had the right to 'own initiative' reports since 1972. Its opinions have to be given within tight deadlines (no 'Isoglucose'-type power of delay), and even here the Court has ruled that these are not indispensable, even where supposedly mandatory. The Economic and Social Committee was never the only channel open to sectoral interests, which have inevitably tended to group about the Commission, Council and Parliament, and its weak informal role as a forum for regional interests has been subsumed in the Committee of the Regions.

In its latest reflection on the Economic and Social Committee's institutional role (21 November 1991), the European Parliament recognised the Committee's value as a repository of specifically sectoral expertise and called for all the institutions (including the Parliament) to be able to consult it where they felt this to be necessary or useful (the Maastricht Treaty contains no such provision). The resolution also recognised the need to intensify cooperation between the Parliament and the Committee, particularly through the exchange of information and coordination of work, but such cooperation remains the exception rather than the rule. Fearful of the burgeoning role of the Committee of the Regions, some members of the Economic and Social Committee have suggested that the European Parliament might play a role in the nomination of the Committee's members, similar to or even stronger than Parliament's consultative role in the nomination of members of the Court of Auditors.

The European Investment Bank (and the European Bank for Reconstruction and Development)

The European Investment Bank (EIB) was established by the 1957 EEC Treaty. It is not an institution but a specialised organ. Its members, who hold its capital, are the Member States of the Community. Its tasks, as set out in EEC Article 130, are to contribute on a non-profit making basis via the granting of loans and the giving of guarantees to the 'balanced and steady development of the common market in the interest of the Community'. It is the largest provider of Community loan finance. Its total outstanding lending in 1992 amounted to some ECU 83,882 million (£62,911 million). Over 90 per cent of its loans are for projects within the Member States and the rest for projects outside.

In Parliament's view, the fact that the bank's operations overlap considerably with Community structural objectives, together with its non-profit making status, indicate clearly 'the underlying political motivation for its existence'. The bank quickly developed integral and complementary roles in the implementation of structural policy and as the Community's agent in lending and borrowing activities involving EC funds. Parliament's belief in the underlying political role of the bank was confirmed by the Maastricht Treaty, which made new provisions for the bank, including an explicit role in Community social and economic cohesion policy and an explicit role in coordinating the Community's financial instruments. The December 1992 Edinburgh European Council confirmed the EIB's integral role in economic and social cohesion and gave it a central place in the Community's new growth initiative.

The Parliament believes that the EIB's current role is only 'the embryo of a much wider policy function', with the bank effectively becoming 'a direct instrument of a more interventionist economic policy, forming part of an integrated political structure also including large parts of the Community budget and involving much Community legislation'. Parliament points to the bank's 'huge potential for growth' (under its statutes the bank may lend up to 250 per cent of its capital base — that is, almost twice its current book). For all of these reasons — the bank's status, *de facto* political role, and growth potential — the European Parliament argues that there is a strong case for a degree of democratic control over the EIB.

In addition to this basic political reasoning, the Parliament argues that there are good technical reasons for bringing the EIB under more democratic control, relating to the bank's activities as guarantor for loan operations involving both its own but also Community, general budget, monies.

In a recently adopted report (11 March 1994) Parliament set out these arguments and went on to point out that it, in tandem with the Court of Auditors, was far better placed than any other political body to exert control and to assess the EIB's application of Community policy. It therefore recommended the establishment of a new discharge procedure for the EIB based on the bank's annual report, a new strategy document to be published in advance of the relevant year, and a Court of Auditors report. It remains to be seen whether and how far these arguments are taken up by the Member States, but the gist of Parliament's concerns is clear as it seeks to assert political and budgetary control over an increasingly important economic actor.

Similar concerns underlie Parliament's desire, expressed in the same March 1994 resolution, to exert a degree of budgetary control over the activities of the European Bank for Reconstruction and Development. Here, Parliament is on much weaker ground. Although the individual Member States and the Community institutions are shareholders in the EBRD (51 per cent of its capital is held by Community institutions and the Member States), the bank is not a Community organ, and Parliament's arguments are based solely on the claim that it is better placed than any other institution to exercise control over its activities.

1.4 The European Parliament and the national parliaments

The European Parliament has never been the sole repository of direct democratic legitimacy in the Community. In particular, national parliaments play a crucial role through their powers over national ministers in rendering the Council accountable for its actions. Until fairly recently, there had been a tendency for the two parliamentary levels — national and European — to be considered in isolation. However, the provisions of the Maastricht Treaty and the treaty ratification process itself led to increased reflection about the level and nature of parliamentary accountability within the Community and the Union and to the degree of cooperation and balance of powers between them.

Constitutional revision

A basic distinction has to be made between parliamentary involvement in any revision of the treaties (that is, constitutional reform) and the more general involvement of parliaments in Community/Union activities. The mechanics of treaty revision are governed by Article N of the Maastricht Treaty. The European Parliament's formal role is restricted to non-binding consultation by the Council on the convening of inter-governmental conferences (IGCs). It cannot participate formally in IGCs, and resulting amendments do not require ratification by the Parliament. The European Parliament's informal role has grown substantially. It made its own proposals to the Maastricht IGC on both Economic and Monetary Union and Political Union, and these carried considerable weight. It got sympathetic Member States to lobby on its behalf. It engaged in a sustained dialogue with the IGC through such forums as inter-institutional conferences (involving both the Council and the Commission) and, though non-binding, its opinion on the resulting treaty was seen as an important political signal. Nevertheless, the European Parliament remained excluded from the formal IGC process, and its proposal to the Maastricht IGC that all future treaty amendments be subject to its assent was denied.

On the other hand, as the Maastricht ratification process has demonstrated, national parliaments are and will remain central to the revision mechanism. Article N stipulates that any treaty amendments shall only 'enter into force after being ratified by all Member States in accordance with their respective constitutional requirements.' In all twelve Member States these constitutional requirements include parliamentary ratification.

The European Parliament is painfully aware of this contrast, though it has always recognised national parliaments' prerogatives. The contrast was rendered all the more frustrating by the European Parliament's self-ordained role as a motor of integration and constitutional draftsman. (The Italian camera dei deputati and the Belgian Parliament's lower chamber, historically among the most sympathetic of national parliaments to the European Parliament's position, promised not to ratify the results of the Maastricht IGC if the European Parliament did not agree to it. However, the Parliament did agree to it; thus the promise was never put to the test. In any case, these parliament's promises could not substitute for a proper constitutional arrangement.)

In April 1994, in the context of the 1996 IGC, and in the wake of the row over blocking minorities and the Ioanima compromise agreement, the European Parliament managed to extract a potentially significant concession. A preparatory working group will be established in 1995 to commence the groundwork for the 1996 IGC. The working group will be composed of government representatives, but the Parliament is to be 'associated' with its work. However, such association will fall short of full participation in the group's deliberations, let alone full participation in the IGC itself.

From the 'European States General' to the assises

The European Parliament's recognition of shared legitimacy and of the strategic importance of national parliaments came in two resolutions adopted in 1988. The first resolution (16 May 1988) urged that 'a Treaty on European Union be adopted on a proposal from the European Parliament, duly mandated to this effect at its second re-election in June 1989' but also that 'a "European States General" of the parliamentarians of the twelve member countries of the Community and the European Parliament be convened in July 1989 to elect, in a joint Assembly, the President of the European Council and the President of the

Commission'. The second resolution (16 June 1988) urged the holding of a plebiscite on the political union of Europe and reminded the Council of its request 'to confer on the European Parliament the power to draw up a draft treaty on the Union to be submitted directly to the national parliaments for ratification'. None of these proposals was immediately realised, but some of the ideas they contained lingered and intermingled.

In particular, the idea of a 'European States General' was taken up in an October 1989 address to the European Parliament by President Mitterrand (European Parliamentary Debates OJ N° 3-382 25.10.89, p.163) who asked why it did not organise 'assises on the future of the Community in which, in addition to Parliament, delegations from the national parliaments and representatives of the Commission and the governments would also participate'. Within a month on 23 November, the Parliament had accepted 'the successive proposals of Felipe Gonzalez [on European citizenship] and François Mitterrand'. National parliaments were invited to this 'European Assises', which the Parliament described as 'an assembly of the parliaments of Europe', created 'to discuss the next stages in the implementation of the European Union'.

One of the Parliament's noted constitutionalists, Maurice Duverger, drew up a resolution on the mechanics of the Assises (adopted 12 July 1990), and preparatory meetings were held between the presidents, or speakers, of the national parliaments and the European Parliament and among the chairmen of those committees within national parliaments specialising in Community affairs. It was agreed that the Assises should be held in Rome on the eve of the Maastricht Intergovernmental Conference. The Duverger resolution spelt out the two basic aims of the Assises: to reduce 'the Community's democratic deficit by confirming the overwhelming support . . . for substantially strengthening the European Parliament's legislative powers and powers of democratic control'; and to prepare 'for the development of a constituent power in the Community in keeping with the principles of democracy, which are neglected by current procedures under which the European Parliament is excluded from Community reform'. Thus, although initially wary of any involvement of national parliaments, the European Parliament had nevertheless enunciated three objectives: organisation of the Assises was to be centralised through the Parliament; the Assises would be expressly restricted to consideration of constitutional reform; the Assises would be harnessed to the Parliament's reformist agenda.

The Assises was composed of 173 national parliamentarians and fifty-three members of the European Parliament. They sat in groups according to political affiliation and not in national contingents. All participating chambers were invited to submit their views (only the Spanish congresso did not do so), and a consensual thirty-two-point final declaration was adopted by a large majority (154 votes in favour, thirteen against: *EP Bulletin*, 30 November 1990). It considered *inter alia* that the procedure for the revision of the treaties must include, prior to ratification by the national parliaments, the European Parliament's assent.

From 'Congress' to Conference of the Parliaments

Within the Political Union IGC a proposed 'tree' model (extension of the Community method) had been supplanted by a three-pillar construction consisting of the traditional Community and two so-called inter-governmental 'pillars' (although provision is made for the association and involvement of both the Commission and the Parliament — see Chapter 3, Sections 3.5 and 3.7), one consisting of cooperation on a Common Foreign and Security Policy and the other consisting of Cooperation in the Fields of Justice and Home Affairs. Actions within the two 'inter-governmental' pillars could lie beyond formal European Parliament involvement and oversight, and the June 1990 Dublin European Council had already pointed out that 'a greater involvement of the national parliaments in the democratic process within the Union, in particular in areas where new competences will be transferred to the Union', should be considered (*EP Bulletin*, June 1990).

The French delegation favoured the creation of a new institution, the 'Congress' which, composed of delegates from national parliaments (later, half national parliamentarians and half MEPs), would be consulted on the Union's major policy options, notably in those areas falling outside the Community method and hence beyond traditional European parliamentary oversight. Reactions to the proposal were mixed. Some saw its justification in the issues of national sovereignty that would be involved. Others argued against the introduction of 'national' lobbies and the reintroduction of the dual mandate. The European Parliament itself was particularly wary. As the negotiations proceeded, the proposal was gradually transformed from a 'Congress' back into something more akin to the more familiar Assises, and provision for it slipped from an article in the treaty itself to a declaration annexed to the treaty.

The Conference invites the European Parliament and the national parliaments to meet as necessary as a Conference of the Parliaments (or 'assises').

The Conference of the Parliaments will be consulted on the main features of the European Union, without prejudice to the powers of the European Parliament and the rights of the national parliaments. The President of the European Council and the President of the Commission will report to each session of the Conference of the Parliaments on the state of the Union.

If the Conference was not, in the end, to be a fully fledged Community institution, it nevertheless represents a highly significant development. If the exact mechanics of its convocation remain unclear (logically, it can only be convened if all participating institutions agree), it nevertheless seems that the Conference of Parliaments will necessarily be consulted on the main features of the European Union as well as being informed on the state of the Union. Thus, national parliaments, together with the European Parliament, are now potentially jointly channelled into the treaty reform process both before the convocation of, and probably during, any IGC. This new role should be seen in conjunction with national parliaments' traditional oversight of governments and ministers, as well as their ratification powers. These arrangements should result in a much earlier, broader and interconnected parliamentary airing of the constitutional issues involved. (The convocation of the 1996 IGC, as provided for by the Maastricht Treaty, may provide a first occasion for the arrangements to be tested.)

Electoral College

The European Parliament's May 1988 call for a 'European States General' has already been mentioned. In its resolution of 26 May 1989, the European Parliament further proposed 'the creation of a "European Congress" composed of Members of the European Parliament and an equal number of members of the national parliaments'. The Parliament proposed that this Congress should elect 'the President of the Commission from a list of candidates put forward by the European Council, following a general policy debate'. However, in this context at least, the idea of a joint electoral college proved short lived.

By 23 November 1989 the Parliament was calling for 'amendments to the Treaties to confer on the European Parliament the . . . right to give its assent to the appointment of the Commission' and, by 14 March 1990, the 'right to elect the President of the Commission and to give its assent to the appointment of the Commission'. In the event, the Maastricht Treaty provides for the Member States to consult the European Parliament on the person they intend to appoint as president of the Commission, to consult the nominee on the other persons they intend to appoint as members of the Commission, and for the 'President and the other members of the Commission thus nominated' to 'be subject as a body to a vote of approval by the European Parliament' (see Chapter 3, Section 3.2). Thus, while the role of national parliaments remained unchanged, they retain the theoretical possibility (not used to date) to exercise influence, through national governments, on the choice of nominees.

Community legislation

A number of proposals have surfaced about ways of institutionalising the involvement of national parliaments in the Community legislative process at the Community level. In 1989, for example, Michael Heseltine proposed the creation of an upper house, or Senate, composed of national parliamentarians. More recently, amid the European Policy Forum's far-ranging 'Treaty for a Wider European Union' can be found the proposal for 'a two-chamber parliamentary review process with delegates of national parliaments introduced as a formal element into Union procedures for legislative review' (European Constitutional Group, 1993). The Speaker of the French national assembly, Philippe Seguin, argues that the European Parliament should become a senate, with a lower chamber composed of representatives from national parliaments (*La Tribune*, 25 April 1994). More recently still, Sir Leon Brittan has called for the creation of a 'Committee of Parliaments', composed of national parliament representatives and with specific rights and functions in regard to the enforcement of the subsidiarity principle, verification of the legal bases of proposals, scrutiny of all laws carrying the European Union into new legislative territory and of laws resulting from intergovernmental cooperation (Brittan, 1994, pp.226–30).

Some of these views may resurface in the context of the 1996 IGC, but the view that won out at Maastricht, a view consistently espoused by the European Parliament and the European Commission, was to retain the constitutionally pure and uncluttered lines of political accountability that had first been established by the 1957 Rome Treaties.

Thus, in its 12 July 1990 Duverger resolution, the European Parliament considered that 'it would not be useful to set up a new institution or "chamber of national parliaments" alongside the European Parliament as:

— experience of the European Parliament prior to direct elections shows the practical limitations of such a body;
— Community institutions already include a body representing Member States (the Council) and a body representing the electorate directly (the European Parliament);
— decision-taking would become even more complex and, therefore, less transparent.'

In its submission to the IGC, the Commission recalled that, in the Community system, 'it is national governments, sitting in the Council, that take the major decisions. Since national governments are accountable to national parliaments, it is for them to involve elected representatives in Community affairs in a manner which respects national traditions' (*EC Bulletin* Supplement, February 1991, p.79).

The British government shared these views and, in a submission to the IGC, set out three areas where improvements could be envisaged: the scrutiny of Community legislation by national parliaments; the transmission of information to national parliaments; and cooperation between the European Parliament and national parliaments. All of these concerns were echoed in a second declaration, annexed to the Maastricht Treaty, on the role of national parliaments in the European Union.

> The Conference considers that it is important to encourage greater involvement of national parliaments in the activities of the European Union.
>
> To this end, the exchange of information between national parliaments and the European Parliament should be stepped up. In this context, the governments of the Member States will ensure, *inter alia*, that national parliaments receive Commission proposals for legislation in good time for information or possible examination.
>
> Similarly, the Conference considers that it is important for contacts between the national parliaments and the European Parliament to be stepped up, in particular through the granting of appropriate reciprocal facilities and regular meetings between members of Parliament interested in the same issues.

These considerations were very much in line with a policy document adopted by the European Parliament's top management body (then known as the enlarged Bureau, now the Conference of Presidents) in September 1991. The document distinguished between two main structures: parliamentary committees and political groups. Timely information was identified as a key concern and an area where the European Parliament had a natural advantage. The overall theme was of closer cooperation with national parliaments on a pragmatic basis and within the framework of existing competences.

Inter-parliamentary cooperation

Cooperation between the directly elected European Parliament and national parliaments long pre-dated the Maastricht Treaty. Indeed, the European Parliament had already called for an intensification of such cooperation, which it considered 'imperative', in a 16 February 1989 resolution. Several distinct levels are discernible.

At the crown stands the Conference of Parliaments (Assises). Since it was decided that the Assises should not be 'institutionalised', the frequency of its convocation will probably depend to a large extent on the frequency of major constitutional developments within the Union.

An older, and more regular, form of cooperation is the Conference of Presidents (or Speakers) of the European Parliament and the national parliaments (upper and lower chambers). The Conference was first established in 1963, when Parliament's then President, Gaetano Martino, hosted a conference of the presidents, speakers and the secretaries-general of the national assemblies at a special conference in Rome (Scalingi, 1980, p.68). The Conference, which was re-launched in its present form in 1975 and therefore pre-dates direct elections, takes place every two years. (Every other year, a similar but far larger conference takes place between the presidents and speakers of the parliaments of the Member States of the Council of Europe.) The Conference has resulted in a series of practical conclusions and recommendations concentrated on two main concerns: enhanced parliamentary scrutiny of Community legislation and Union policies and enhanced inter-parliamentary cooperation.

The May 1989 Madrid Conference of Presidents unanimously decided to convoke a conference of those committees within the national parliaments specialising in Community affairs together with the European Parliament. The first such conference was held in Paris in November 1989, where it was decided that the conference should meet at least twice a year, once under each six-month presidency. The fourth such conference (Luxembourg, May 1991) adopted an official title (the Conference is generally known by its French acronym 'COSAC' — *'conférence des organes specialisés dans les Affaires communautaires'*) and its own rules of procedure. The sixth COSAC (Lisbon, May 1992) notably established a system of regular inter-parliamentary correspondence on European activities and affairs. COSAC's principle and enduring achievement has been to create and encourage sustained inter-parliamentary reflection on how best to overcome the 'democratic deficit'.

A fourth level of inter-parliamentary cooperation can be discerned in the frequent, if *ad hoc*, bilateral meetings between European and national parliamentary committees. Once again, this practice long pre-dated Maastricht (for example, in the late 1980s the European Parliament's Economic and Monetary Affairs Committee invited all of its counterparts in the national parliaments to visit Brussels individually in order to discuss the ramifications of the internal market legislative programme established by the SEA) but has been intensified by it. The European Parliament's Institutional Affairs Committee has held regular meetings with its national parliamentary counterparts, and exchanges between the European Parliament's Budget's Committee and the various national budgetary or finance committees are now well established.

The formula permits of many variations. To take but two recent examples: on 20 September 1993, the chairmen of all of the Committees of Foreign Affairs in the national parliaments came to Brussels at the invitation of the European Parliament's Foreign Affairs Committee Chairman, Enrique Baron Crespo, to meet with the President-in-Office of the Council, Willy Claes and the responsible Commissioner, Hans van

den Broek, in order to discuss such matters as the enlargement negotiations and the development of the European Economic Area. In another
example, in March 1993 the chairman of the European Parliament's
Committee on Civil Liberties and Internal Affairs organised a meeting
with his national homologues in order to discuss the most appropriate
ways of ensuring parliamentary oversight in the context of the third
Maastricht's 'pillar' of inter-governmental cooperation in the fields of
justice and home affairs.

Significantly, the European Parliament has established a unit within
its secretariat specifically devoted to the fostering and management of
relations with the national parliaments.

Political contacts between the European Parliament's political groups
and MEPs on the one hand and the national political parties and MPs
(including pan-European political parties) on the other clearly represent
a fifth level of interaction. The quality and quantity of such contacts vary
but can constitute an important underpinning to interaction at the inter-
institutional level.

Competition and culture

Away from the glare of the twin processes of the ratification and
implementation of the Maastricht Treaty, a quiet and perhaps inexorable
process is still unfolding. The process is underpinned by the conviction,
expressed by the November 1990 Assises, that 'Europe cannot be built
merely on the basis of discussions at governmental and diplomatic level,
but that the Parliaments of the European Community must be fully
involved in laying down the general direction it is to take'.

However, if the process portrayed here is inexorable, it would be
wrong to assume that developments have been smooth or free of
problems. As one commentator has put it, 'we have to face the fact that
the situation is in some ways one of built-in and almost guaranteed
rivalry' (Morgan, 1992). Beyond the vigorous defence of institutional
prerogatives, inter-parliamentary cooperation gives rise to a number of
questions at both the prescriptive and more purely practical levels. Who
is the chief interlocutor of the Community institutions in the parliamentary domain? If there is not to be a single interlocutor, then what
should be the division of roles and competences? Can such a division be
clear, or will competences necessarily overlap? Should mechanisms be
developed to govern the division of competences? For example, in its
second report on 'Europe after Maastricht', the House of Commons'
Foreign Affairs Committee declared:

> We do not believe national parliaments should become subordinate to the
> European Parliament. Nor do we wish to see a strict hierarchy of

responsibility established. We see greater merit in the development of a series of bilateral contacts between the European Parliament and each national parliament and the further development of national parliaments' pre-legislative role (cited in European Parliament, 19 May 1993).

Even simple bilateral contacts pose practical problems. For example, who is the interlocutor of the European Parliament, or of the other Community institutions, within the national parliaments? Specialised committees such as the Foreign Affairs Committee clearly have an overall interest, but what about the technical expertise of sectoral committees, particularly where potentially esoteric legislation is involved? It is clear that bilateral (let alone multilateral) cooperation depends very much on the approaches and mechanisms developed by the national parliaments to scrutinise and supervise Community (Union) activities. It is equally clear that these can be very different — from the considerable powers over ministers of the Danish folketing's market committee (or EC Committee, as it is now known), to the Italian camera dei deputati's traditional hands-off approach. There are similarly divergent approaches to the involvement of MEPs in the work of national parliaments. The German Bundestag's Committee on European Union (whose role has even been codified in the Basic Law, the German constitution) is composed of national parliamentarians and, in an advisory capacity, MEPs. Belgium's chambre, the Dutch Tweede Kamer and Denmark's folketing similarly involve MEPs in the national parliamentary scrutiny process. Other parliaments have no such provisions. (See Neunreither, 1994b, for a comprehensive discussion of these matters.)

Different parliamentary cultures and mechanisms give rise to similar problems at the multilateral level, whether political or practical. At the level of principle, for example, the Commons' Foreign Affairs committee is openly critical of the Conference of Parliaments/Assises as an 'unwieldy' and 'unprofitable' mechanism, and national parliaments cannot agree among themselves as to when the Assises should be convoked nor how it should sit (the European Parliament insists that MPs and MEPs should sit according to political affiliation). The speakers and presidents who make up the Conference of Presidents have greatly differing roles and powers. Clearly, their capacity to go beyond exchanges of information will be delimited by such differences, and a similar argument applies to COSAC.

Such problems are not insurmountable, but they do require flexibility and, inevitably, change. The Maastricht Treaty ratification process has provided a powerful impulse for just such change. For the European Parliament's part, it can be 'proud of its record in setting an ambitious agenda and its increasingly close cooperation with national parliaments offers a real chance that a new constitutional settlement can be worked out which satisfies the legitimacy of both the national and the supra-national parliamentary structures' (Harris, 1992).

1.5   The broader context

Western European Union

A major development in the Maastricht Treaty was the creation of a common foreign and security policy 'pillar' with provision for the development of a defence capacity. The Community does not itself have any defence capacity or competence, but an article in the treaty 'requests' the hitherto obscure Western European Union, which the treaty describes as 'an integral part of the development of the Union', to elaborate and implement any of the Union's decisions and actions having defence implications. A declaration by the nine members of the Western European Union (Greece is in the process of becoming a full member, Ireland and Denmark have observer status only) appended to the treaty sets out in some detail how the role of the WEU should be developed, both in relation to the European Union and in relation to the Atlantic Alliance.

The Western European Union's structure consists of a ministerial Council and a secretariat, now based in Brussels, and a Parliamentary Assembly. The Assembly is currently composed of 108 members (and 108 substitute members), all delegated from their national parliaments. (Delegates to the Western European Union assembly are drawn from within Member States' delegations to the Parliamentary Assembly of the Council of Europe. The big four, France, Germany, Italy and the United Kingdom, have eighteen members, Spain twelve, Belgium, the Nether-lands and Portugal seven and Luxembourg three.) The Assembly's functions are restricted to debate and the adoption of resolutions. The declaration annexed to the Maastricht Treaty expressly encourages closer cooperation between the Parliamentary Assembly of the Western Euro-pean Union and the European Parliament. The European Parliament traditionally sends a delegation of two of its members (drawn from the membership of its Foreign Affairs Committee) as observers to the Parliamentary Assembly's meetings.

The European Parliament sees its relations with the Western European Union and its Parliamentary Assembly in the broad context of the European Union's developing common foreign and security policy arrangements. At the moment these are inter-governmental, with unanimity in decision making, a shared right of initiative for the Commission and the Member States, and the Parliament's rights restricted to information and consultation (see Chapter 3, Section 3.5). In its constitutional blueprints for the Union (resolutions of 10 February

1994 and 24 February 1994), the Parliament envisages majority voting in the Council (after a transitional period) and a more pro-active right to make recommendations and to exercise control for the European Parliament. Defence policy would be entirely subsumed within the European Union, and hence there would be no need for any additional form of parliamentary involvement beyond the European Parliament itself and the national parliaments.

As to the mechanics, the treaty establishing the Western European Union was signed in 1948 for a fifty-year duration. The European Parliament argues that upon expiry of the treaty in 1998 the Western European Union should become an integral part of the European Union and that to this end all Member States of the European Union should by then have become full Members of the Western European Union. (It points to the 1996 inter-governmental conference scheduled by the Maastricht Treaty as an appropriate moment to introduce the necessary constitutional change.) The Parliament envisages the absorption of the WEU secretariat into the Community structure and the disbanding of the Parliamentary Assembly. Thus, the WEU Council's functions would be taken over by the Council of the European Union, and parliamentary scrutiny and control would be exercised by the European Parliament.

However, it seems unlikely that all Member States of the European Union will have been able to become full members of the Western European Union in such a short period of time, particularly if further enlargements take place as scheduled in 1995. Parliament's more pragmatic secondary line of argument is therefore that 'at the very least, the European Parliament's right to be consulted and informed should be extended to include the Western European Union Council if the WEU is to act on the Union's behalf', and it hopes that the 1996 inter-governmental conference (which is to review *inter alia* the Union's Common Foreign and Security Policy) will decide 'that the intergovern-mental procedures should gradually be replaced with Community procedures based primarily on majority voting in the Council, the legally binding nature of Council decisions, and the right of the European Parliament to a say and to exercise control' (24 February 1994, explanatory memorandum).

The North Atlantic Alliance and the North Atlantic Assembly

The North Atlantic Treaty Organisation, which groups together sixteen member countries, including eleven Member States of the European Union (Ireland is not a member; France is a treaty signatory but since 1966 has remained outside NATO's command structure), Canada and the United States of America, remains the lynchpin of the Western world's mutual security arrangements. At a NATO Summit meeting in

Rome in November 1991, NATO decided to establish a North Atlantic Cooperation Council which since March 1992 has grouped together the NATO member states with the newly democratising Central and Eastern European countries and some of the successor states to the Soviet Union. At a January 1994 NATO Summit meeting in Brussels, NATO decided to create a new form of associate membership, the 'partnership for peace', which was extended to all members of the North Atlantic Cooperation Council and the CSCE and has already been accepted in principal by a number of Eastern and Central European states.

The 1949 North Atlantic Treaty made no provision for any parliamentary involvement, but the member state parliaments increasingly felt that there should be some kind of organised parliamentary interest in and support for NATO, and in 1955 the North Atlantic Assembly was created. The Assembly is an inter-parliamentary organisation, with no formal role *vis-à-vis* NATO. Its primary purpose has been to act as a forum for legislators from the North American and West European member countries of the North Atlantic Alliance to meet together to consider issues of common interest and concern. Any policy input is exercised via the national parliaments. As NATO's role has evolved in the light of the recent political changes in the former Soviet Union and the Central and Eastern European countries, so the Assembly has broadened both its membership and its mandate.

The membership of the Assembly is composed of 188 delegated national parliamentarians from NATO member countries, with the size of national contingents varying from the United States' thirty-six senators and representatives, to the United Kingdom's eighteen delegates and Iceland and Luxembourg's three. In addition there are a further twelve five-member delegations from Central and Eastern European countries, stretching from Belarus, the Ukraine and the Russian Federation through the Baltic States to the Vysegrad countries. The Assembly meets in plenary session twice a year. Plenary sessions are normally devoted to set-piece debates on themes of current concern, with votes on policy recommendations prepared in the Assembly's five committees. The European Parliament sends a small delegation (typically three members drawn from its Foreign Affairs Committee) to the North Atlantic Assembly's plenary sessions.

The European Union has no formal role within the North Atlantic Alliance, but the declaration appended to the Maastricht Treaty on the Western European Union devotes a half-page to the WEU's relations with the Atlantic Alliance. 'The objective', the declaration states,

is to develop WEU as a means to strengthen the European pillar of the Atlantic Alliance. Accordingly WEU is prepared to develop further the close working links between WEU and the Alliance and to strengthen the role, responsibilities and contributions of WEU Member States in the Alliance. This

65

will be undertaken on the basis of the necessary transparency and complementarity between the emerging European security and defence identity and the Alliance.

The declaration goes on to specify how WEU Member States should intensify their coordination with the aim of introducing joint WEU positions into the process of consultation within the Alliance, synchronise meetings and harmonise working methods, and establish close cooperation between the NATO and WEU secretariats.

As with the WEU, the European Parliament considers NATO primarily in the broader context of the European Union's emerging Common Foreign and Security Policy. As seen in the previous section, Parliament envisages that all European Union Member States should become full members of the WEU and that the WEU and its structures should ultimately be fully absorbed into the European Union. It further hopes that 'the European Union will become part of the framework of the Atlantic Alliance by joining NATO as a "collective member", so that the Alliance may rest on two pillars of equal value'. Were such a development ever to take place, the Parliament's role would be assured through the powers it would hope to exercise over the Council of the European Union.

However, the whole concept is fraught with political problems. A first major problem, one that is being increasingly encountered by the European Union (particularly within the United Nations and its various specialised organs) as it steadily evolves into a political entity, is that of the position of a supranational organisation within an international organisation. Can the European Union (which does not have legal personality) join an organisation between states? A second, linked, problem concerns the status of the individual Member States. Would they no longer enjoy individual membership? If they continued to enjoy individual membership, could the other NATO members accept such 'double membership'? Behind such considerations is the European Parliament's acute consciousness that, for as long as the individual Member States of the European Union continue to retain their independence within NATO, parliamentary accountability will primarily be assured by the Member States' parliaments.

The Conference on Security and Cooperation in Europe

On 21 November 1990, the thirty-four-member Conference on Security and Cooperation in Europe met in Paris and signed up to a new Charter which created, *inter alia*, a new parliamentary assembly. The CSCE now has no less than fifty-three members and, in Parliament's words, 'acts as the Euro-Atlantic forum that monitors the observance of the principles of the Charter of Paris'. Prior to the Paris Charter, the Parliament relied on the good offices of the Presidency-in-Office of the Council to enable a parliamentary delegation to attend CSCE Review Conferences, allowing the Parliament to strike up contacts and pass on its own policy messages to a large number of the participants through meetings held in the margins of the conference itself.

In Parliament's eyes, the CSCE should, together with the Council of Europe (see below), form part of a 'system of European confederal cooperation' in which the European Union would play a central, dynamic role. To this end, Parliament argues that the European Union should join both the CSCE and the Council of Europe *in addition* to the Union's individual component Member States (20 January 1993). No action has yet resulted from Parliament's demands, and the concept seems set to remain theoretical in the immediate future. However, dual membership would again give rise to the problem of 'double represen-tation' referred to in the preceding section. At the level of the CSCE parliamentary assembly, the European Parliament's calls for an associate status through a parliamentary delegation, and for such a delegation to participate in the assembly's work, were rebuffed and, in the words of a recent report, 'the European Parliament still has to define its future role in the CSCE process'.

EFTA and the European Economic Area

The European Free Trade Association was originally formed as an alternative free-trading bloc for those European countries that could not countenance the degree of sovereignty sharing implied by membership of the EEC. However, the Community's successful internal market programme and the continuing convergence between the trade and foreign policy interests of the EFTA countries and the EEC gave several EFTA countries food for thought, and in the early nineties, following a 1989 speech by Jacques Delors, negotiations began to create a European Economic Area (EEA). After various delays, the EEA entered into force in January 1994 between the twelve EEC Member States and six of the seven EFTA states (Austria, Finland, Iceland, Liechtenstein, Norway and Sweden; Switzerland was forced to abstain from the EEA after a popular referendum result went against its membership). The European Parlia-ment gave its assent for this agreement. For the six EFTA countries, the agreement entails a commitment to transpose the Community's internal market legislation (the 'four freedoms') into national law and addition-ally involves some financial transfers. In return, the Community allows the six EFTA countries to participate fully in the internal market's economic and commercial cooperation, including the associated horizontal and flanking policies.

Operational decisions within the EEA are taken in an EEA Council, consisting of the members of the Council of the European Union, the EC Commission and one member from each EFTA country. The EEA Council is assisted by an executive EEA Joint Committee with executive and consultative functions. Parliamentary control is exercised in two ways. In the first place, the European Parliament is informed, and its opinion requested, on any 'EEA extension' to draft legislation. In the second place, the EEA agreement has created a new, sixty-six-member (thirty-three from each side) Joint Parliamentary Committee. The Joint Parliamentary Committee meets twice a year, alternating between a European Union and an EFTA Member State (it first met, in Brussels, on 9 February 1994). It can express its views in the form of reports or resolutions, but it has the duty of reporting on the EEA Joint Committee's Annual Report and may indeed call the president of the EEA Joint Committee to speak before it.

Prior to the EEA agreement, there were occasional contacts between specialised EFTA parliamentary committees and the European Parliament's own committees, and these occasional contacts have continued. But there is a third, partly transitional, way in which parliamentary contacts will be retained between the EFTA states and the European Parliament outside the EEA. Joint Parliamentary Committees have been set up between the European Parliament and the four applicant states (Austria, Finland, Norway and Sweden), and inter-parliamentary delegations exist with Iceland and Switzerland. (Switzerland's late withdrawal from the EEA resulted in a separate protocol. The result is a theoretical distinction between EFTA, including Switzerland, and the EFTA EEA countries, excluding Switzerland.) Thus, the initial fears expressed in the European Parliament about an erosion of democratic control have not been realized. If anything, the final institutional arrangements of the EEA have provided the potential for a reinforcement of parliamentary control.

The Council of Europe and the OECD

The institutional activity of the Council of Europe, which now has thirty-two full member countries and a further ten countries with observer or 'special guest' status, can be broken down into three component elements. The first is its primary activity of inter-governmental cooperation, with the drafting of conventions on matters stretching from cultural cooperation to the repatriation of people serving prison sentences in a state other than their own. The second, probably its most widely recognised activity, is the judicial work of its Commission and Court of Human Rights in interpreting the European Convention on

Human Rights. The third is the debates and recommendations of its Parliamentary Assembly, which has a purely consultative role.

In earlier years, the Council of Europe and the EEC were seen as rivals, the one championing intergovernmentalism, the other supranationalism. Until recently there was very little cooperation or coordination between the two organisations, and this was perhaps especially true of the Parliamentary Assembly and the European Parliament, particularly after the first direct elections in 1979 (until then, both bodies were similarly composed of delegated national parliamentarians). The Parliament's Rules of Procedure included a provision that it should draw up an annual report on its activities to be forwarded to the Council of Europe's Parliamentary Assembly, but this provision has long since fallen into neglect, although the rule still exists.

A significant step occurred when, in the mid-1980s, the European Parliament began to consider its relations with another Europe-based organisation, the Organisation for Economic Cooperation and Development (OECD). The OECD which, like NATO, counts non-European countries among its membership (for example, the United States, Canada, Japan) is a purely inter-governmental organisation, assisted by a secretariat. It has no parliamentary context but is obliged to submit an annual report on its activities to the Parliamentary Assembly of the Council of Europe. As part of a general process of self-assertion, the European Parliament sought input into this process, and it was ultimately agreed that the Parliament should send a delegation of its members to take part in the Parliamentary Assembly's debate on the OECD's annual report. Having won the right, the European Parliament has since tended to neglect it, but the experience served as an important reopening of political level contacts between the two institutions. Political events in Europe, with the creation of many issues of mutual concern, have led to more frequent contacts between the two parliamentary institutions, particularly between their specialised committees.

As a response to the Council of Europe's October 1993 Vienna Summit meeting (the organisation's first Summit at heads of state and government level), which fundamentally reassessed the role of the Council of Europe within a changing Europe, the European Parliament reconsidered the overall nature of the European Union's relations with the Council of Europe. In a 15 December 1993 resolution, the European Parliament reaffirmed the Council of Europe's 'unique role . . . in building new structures in Europe, particularly as regards the protection of human rights and fundamental freedoms, the promotion of Europe's cultural identity and the development and strengthening of democracy in the countries of Eastern and Central Europe'. It recognised that the entry into force of the Maastricht Treaty would lead to an overlapping of European Union and Council of Europe activities, particularly in the area of inter-governmental cooperation in judicial affairs. Parliament's resolution also emphasised the Council of Europe's informal role as a democratic 'anti-chamber' to membership of the European Union, describing it as 'the principal European organisation in which the Union and its Member States are able to participate and/or develop multilateral cooperation with the countries intending to apply for EC membership in the medium term'. Parliament further recognised that 'a new basis must be established for relations between the two institutions'.

In Parliament's view this new basis should be established in several ways but, once again, Parliament's general approach is coloured by its longer-term views on the development of the European Union's common foreign policy. First, the Commission should further develop joint and complementary action with the Council of Europe in such policy areas as economic and technical assistance to Central and Eastern European countries (for example, through the Community's PHARE and TACIS programmes, G-24 actions and the Council of Europe's own programmes).

Second, the European Union's Member States should better coordinate their activities in the Council of Europe, both through the adoption of common positions at ministerial level and more coordinated approaches to inter-governmental work.

Third, Parliament considers it 'both desirable and necessary that the Community should adhere to the European Convention on Human Rights so as to ensure that the rights of Community citizens are better protected, a vital aspect in the construction of European Union'. (Parliament adopted a resolution calling for Community accession to the Convention on 18 January 1994.) From its side, the Council of Europe's parliamentary Assembly has similarly invited the European Union to accede to the Convention.

Fourth, Parliament believes the European Union should itself accede to the Statute of the Council of Europe (such an idea would run into the same problems mentioned above in relation to the North Atlantic Alliance, but it should be pointed out that the European Community *per se* is already a signatory to a score of Council of Europe conventions). In the meantime, the Parliament feels that the European Union should be permanently represented through a standing delegation at the Council of Europe (the Council of Europe has long had a Brussels office for coordination with the European Community).

Fifth, Parliament expressed its conviction on 'the advisability of forging closer ties with the Parliamentary Assembly of the Council of Europe and of the exchange and accessibility of working documents and committee reports of the two institutions, so as to promote coordination and exchanges of opinion on matters of mutual interest'. Of all these recommendations, the last is the only one that lies entirely within the Parliament's own competences. (In February 1994, on the occasion of the annual meeting between the presidents of the European Parliament and the Parliamentary Assembly of the Council of Europe, these matters were discussed in great detail.)

Note

1. Some later commentaries imply that the Assembly was an addition, introduced at the insistence of the Dutch (see, e.g., Kapteyn, 1962), but contemporary documentation makes it clear that Monnet, and the French, always had an assembly in mind. For example, Paul Reuter recalls a 12 April 1950 meeting in Monnet's office: 'He'd clearly made his mind up: he had been looking for some time at such an approach and had been increasingly trying out the ideas that had been running through his head. "What do you think of a Franco–German Parliament?" he asked. I grimaced. To do what? Didn't we already have one in the Council of Europe?' (Reuter, 1980, p.19).

2
The electoral link

2.1 European citizenship

This chapter examines the most formal and fundamental expression of any parliamentary democracy: the relationship, through the ballot box, between electors and elected. In this context, the Maastricht Treaty introduced a radical new departure, establishing the concept of European citizenship ('citizenship of the Union') and asserting that the right to vote in European elections was one of the principal rights and expressions of that citizenship. In its modern form, the concept of citizenship as consisting of both duties *and rights* with regard to the state goes back to Rousseau. Indeed, if there have been hesitations about the concept at European level (for example, the concerns voiced in Denmark during the protracted debates accompanying the ratification of the Maastricht Treaty), it is precisely because of the implicit recognition of something akin to a state at European level.

Long a dream of federalists, concrete expression of the concept of European citizenship is a relatively recent phenomenon. The preamble to the ECSC Treaty spoke of 'a broader and deeper community among peoples long divided by bloody conflicts'. By 1957, memory of those conflicts was far enough away for the preamble to the EEC Treaty to declare determination 'to lay the foundations of an ever-closer union among the peoples of Europe'. But it was not until the watershed of the 1974 Paris Summit that the concept of citizenship, and then citizenship of the Member States, first entered the equation. The summit entrusted a Belgian politician, Leo Tindemans, with the task of consulting with the Member States and the Community institutions and reporting back to them on 'an overall concept of European Union'. The 1975 Tindemans report was primarily concerned with proposals for political and institutional reform, but it also recommended a series of actions to protect citizens' rights and raise citizens' consciousness of Europe. Although the Tindemans report did trigger off detailed discussions, these soon petered out, and the 1976 Hague Summit simply noted its 'great interest'. Political attention and energy was thereafter chiefly focused on arrangements for the first direct elections to the Parliament.

Interest in citizenship was rekindled by the June 1984 Fontainebleau Council, which established two *ad hoc* committees, one to consider further political and institutional reform and another to address the specific subject of the peoples' Europe. The Adonnino Committee drew up two reports, in March and June 1985. The March 1985 Milan European Council approved the proposals of the *ad hoc* committee. The ensuing Single European Act's preamble spoke of the Member States' determination 'to work together to promote democracy on the basis of the fundamental rights recognised in the constitutions and laws of the Member States'. A separate paragraph spoke of 'the wishes of the democratic peoples of Europe, for whom the European Parliament, elected by universal suffrage, is an indispensable means of expression', thus taking on board the language of the Court of Justice in its 1980 'Isoglucose' ruling. But in its concrete provisions, the Single European Act took account of none of the recommendations of the Adonnino Committee. Nevertheless, as has so frequently occurred in the development of the European Union, some of the Adonnino proposals were later to be taken on board, in this case by the Maastricht Treaty.

In 1990, when the Member States had decided to hold an inter-governmental conference on political union, the Spanish government and its Prime Minister, Felipe Gonzalez, proposed that the future treaty should include provisions concerning European citizenship *per se* and, in particular, the right to vote and to stand as a candidate in European Parliament elections in the Member State of residence. The November 1990 Assises of national parliaments and the European Parliament (see Chapter 1, Section 1.4 above) similarly agreed that the inter-governmental conference should consider making such proposals, and the December 1990 Rome European Council welcomed the Spanish government's initiative and called on the inter-governmental conference *inter alia* to examine to what extent certain civic rights, including the right to vote in European elections, could be enshrined in the treaty.

In a quantum leap, the Maastricht Treaty established citizenship of the European Union. Article 8 states that 'every person holding the nationality of a Member State shall be a citizen of the Union', and that 'citizens of the Union shall enjoy the rights conferred by this Treaty'. Thus, for example, in third countries where their own Member State is not represented, Union citizens have the right to protection by the diplomatic or consular authorities of *any* Member State, on exactly the same conditions as the nationals of that state. Union citizens have the right to petition the European Parliament and apply to its Ombudsman (see Chapter 3, Section 3.8). Every citizen of the Union has the right to move and reside freely within the territory of the Member States and, as a natural corollary of this, TEU Article 8b states that 'every citizen of the

Union residing in a Member State of which he is not a national shall have the right to vote and to stand as a candidate in elections to the European Parliament in the Member State in which he resides, under the same conditions as nationals of that state'.

2.2 The right to vote and to stand as a candidate

Given that the pre-direct elections European Parliament was composed of delegated national parliamentarians, it could be argued that the citizens of the Member States always enjoyed some sort of electoral linkage, however tenuous, with the Parliament, but most commentators see June 1979 as the belated beginning of the relationship between the European voter and the European Parliament. The EEC and Euratom Treaties had always contained provisions both for direct elections to the Parliament and for the establishment of a uniform electoral system, but uniformity has so far eluded the Union. Indeed, as the next section will describe, the introduction of direct elections was only ultimately achieved by separating off and postponing debate over a uniform system.

Because of this lack of uniformity, the September 1976 Community Act 'concerning the election of the representatives of the European Parliament by direct universal suffrage' is laconic about the nature of electors and candidates. A catch-all phrase states that, 'pending the entry into force of a uniform electoral procedure and subject to the other provisions of this Act, the electoral procedure shall be governed in each Member State by its national provisions'. Voters get one more mention: 'No one,' a separate article bluntly states, 'may vote more than once in any election of representatives to the European Parliament'. The Act says nothing about candidates, although it expressly permits dual mandates (of national parliaments and the European Parliament) and expressly rules a number of other offices and activities (principally of the other Community institutions) as being incompatible with the office of MEP. Thus, to this day, it is *national* legislation in the separate Member States that governs who may vote and stand and under what conditions.

Conditions in the United Kingdom are governed by the 5 May 1978 European Assembly Elections Act. British and Irish citizens resident in the United Kingdom aged eighteen years or over are entitled to vote. Contrary to the practice in national elections, members of the House of Lords may vote. British citizens resident outside the country may vote if they are government officials or members of the armed forces or if their names appeared on an electoral register in the United Kingdom in the twenty years preceding the election. Candidates must be at least twenty-one years of age. Members of the House of Lords and clergymen may also stand for election. Candidates need not be nominated by a political party, but must be endorsed by thirty electors. A £1,000 deposit must be paid and is forfeited if the candidate fails to obtain one-fifth of the votes cast. The conditions for voters and candidates in the other Member States are summarised in Section 2.5 of this chapter.

The Maastricht Treaty (and a subsequent December 1993 Directive adopted by the Council) has now dealt with an anomaly arising out of an increasingly prevalent phenomenon. As the frontiers between Member States crumble, and as the trade in goods and services between them increases, so the numbers of Europeans going abroad to study and work has increased. Some five million people now live in a Member State other than the Member State of their origin. Within the Community, 630,000 Irish and 400,000 Britons live abroad, and the number of resident citizens of other Member States stands at approximately 62,000 in Ireland and 880,000 in the United Kingdom (1993 figures).

In its first, 1960, draft Convention on election by direct universal suffrage, the European Parliament had first proposed that Europeans resident abroad should nevertheless be able to vote in elections to the European Parliament, either in their country of origin or in their country of residence. Since Member States failed to agree on the introduction of direct elections, the problem about voting rights was to remain theoretical until 1979. In a 1977 resolution on voting rights in the forthcoming direct elections, the European Parliament repeated its call for citizens to be able to vote 'in loco' in their country of residence, and some preliminary work was undertaken in the Council. The Parliament repeated its calls in various resolutions, and notably in 1982, 1988 and 1991. The call was not ultimately heeded until the 1992 Maastricht Treaty.

Resident Union citizens may now vote and stand in European elections in their Member State of residence if they so wish (they must make an express declaration to that effect to the electoral authority of their Member State of residence). The December 1993 Directive is effectively based on the principal of mutual recognition; if a resident Union citizen satisfies the criteria that would apply to a citizen of the Member State of residence, then he or she may vote or stand as a candidate in the Member State of residence under exactly the same conditions. Similarly, if a resident citizen would not satisfy the conditions necessary to stand as a candidate in his or her Member State of origin (for example, a disqualification), then he or she is unable to stand in the Member State of residence. (On the other hand, the Directive leaves it up to the authorities in the Member State of residence whether to disqualify a resident *voter* disqualified in his or her Member State of origin.) The Directive's other provisions are concerned principally with the avoidance of double-voting and double candi- datures. Because of the very high number of non-national residents it hosts, Luxembourg has been granted a special derogation whereby residents must satisfy a minimum residence requirement before being able to stand as candidates. Thus, thirty-four years after the European Parliament first proposed such measures, European citizens may at last, since June 1994, vote and stand in European elections in their country of residence.

2.3 Direct elections

As was seen in Chapter 1, Section 1.2, the nature of appointment of delegates to the ECSC Common Assembly was left up to the individual Member States, but direct election was already acknowledged as a possibility. ECSC Article 21 stated that 'The Assembly shall consist of delegates whom the parliaments of each of the Member States shall be called upon to appoint once a year from among their own membership, or who shall be elected by direct universal suffrage, according to the procedure determined by each High Contracting Party'. By the time of the signature of the 1957 EEC and Euratom Treaties, the Member States were apparently all committed to *direct* elections to the European Assembly. Moreover, they wished to see a *uniform* system instituted. EEC Article 138(3) stated that 'The Assembly shall draw up proposals for elections by direct universal suffrage in accordance with a uniform procedure in all Member States. The Council shall, acting unanimously, lay down the appropriate provisions, which it shall recommend to Member States for adoption in accordance with their respective constitutional requirements.'

As was also seen above, Parliament's 1960 draft Convention introducing elections to the European Parliament by direct universal suffrage, drafted in fulfilment of Parliament's obligations under Article 138(3), ran into the implacable opposition of the French government and was effectively shelved until de Gaulle's departure in 1968. In March of the next year, 1969, the Parliament adopted a resolution reminding the Council that it had fulfilled its treaty obligations and that the Council ought in turn to fulfil its own obligations in the matter. In closing, the resolution made an oblique reference to EEC Article 175, which states that 'Should the Council or the Commission, in infringement of this Treaty, fail to act, the Member States and the other institutions of the Community may bring an action before the Court of Justice to have the infringement established'.

It seemed that the Parliament might *prima facie* have a good case. The Council was jolted into action. In order to evade the threat of legal action, it instructed Coreper to study the matter. Although the ambassadors could not reach agreement on any of the main items in Parliament's draft Convention (which included a complicated proposal for a transitional arrangement), the December 1969 Hague European Council stated that 'The question of direct elections shall be given further consideration by the Council'. Thereafter, the issue bumped along in Council working groups and parliamentary committees, without any great progress ever being made, until the change in French policy following Valéry Giscard d'Estaing's election as French president. (Other contributory factors were the entry into the Community of the United Kingdom and Denmark, with strong parliamentary traditions, and the increases in Parliament's budgetary powers.)

In the meantime, the Parliament had been reassessing its strategy. The 1960 draft Convention had long since been overtaken by events, and a consensus grew that Parliament could and should supersede it with fresh proposals. At the same time, various consultations with national parliaments, particularly those where unilateral attempts had been made to introduce direct elections, had underlined an almost complete lack of consensus as to what a uniform system could be. In June 1973, the Parliament decided to draw up a new report, appointing a Dutch Socialist, Schelto Patijn, as rapporteur. In retrospect, Patijn's report was a masterpiece of pragmatism. Patijn separated the issue of *uniformity* from the relatively more consensual matter of *direct elections*, proposing that each Member State should determine the electoral system it would use for the first direct elections, while the European Parliament would draw up a proposal for a common electoral system for subsequent elections. His report, ultimately adopted by Parliament in January 1975, set a target date of the first Sunday in May 1978 for the first direct elections to be held. While Parliament was considering his report, the December 1974 Paris Summit met and, with a weather eye to Patijn's recommendations, noted 'that the election of the European Assembly by direct universal suffrage, one of the objectives laid down in the Treaty, should be achieved as soon as possible. In this connection, [the Heads of State and Government] await with interest the proposals of the European Assembly, on which they wish the Council to act in 1976. On this assumption elections by direct universal suffrage could take place at any time in or after 1978.'

By July 1975, when the Italian government took over the Presidency, doubts about the United Kingdom's continued membership had been resolved by a favourable result in the June 1975 referendum. A Council working party on direct elections was rapidly established and soon hard at work. As in the preceding parliamentary debates, two of the most contested issues were the number and distribution of members, and the question as to whether the dual mandate should be allowed, or even, as the Danish government wished, be made compulsory. The jockeying over the number of seats for Member States was strongly reminiscent of the similar jockeying which had occurred in the negotiations preceding the signing of the Rome Treaties. Agreement slowly emerged until, at the July 1976 Brussels European Council, final agreement was announced.

The last outstanding problems had been the linked matters of the number and distribution of seats. There were to be 410 seats altogether, with eighty-one for France, Germany, Italy and the United Kingdom, twenty-five for the Netherlands, twenty-four for Belgium, sixteen for Denmark, fifteen for Ireland and six for Luxembourg. The Member States' political agreement was followed up by the September 1976 Act Concerning the Election of the Representatives of the Assembly by Direct Universal Suffrage. The accompanying Council decision included an announcement of the Council's intention 'to give effect to the conclusions that the election of the Assembly should be held on a single date within the period May–June 1978'. But it proved impossible to respect this deadline.

One of the chief reasons was the British Labour government's domestic political problems. The 1975 referendum had resolved the issue of membership but had badly split the Labour Party. A third of the cabinet were opposed to direct elections and the government, which had no parliamentary majority, had to tread carefully. In February 1976, the government had published a Green Paper on *Direct Elections to the European Assembly* which had conspicuously refrained from discussing alternative electoral systems. A Commons Select Committee was subsequently appointed and in August 1976 reported back in favour of the traditional United Kingdom first-past-the-post electoral system. Slow to act, the government published a White Paper ('with green edges') in April 1977, leaving open the choice of electoral systems among a Regional List approach, the single transferable vote and first-past-the-post, although the Cabinet itself had already decided in favour of a Regional List system. Meanwhile, in March 1977, the government had staved off defeat in the Commons by agreeing to a 'Lib–Lab pact' with the Liberal Party, and one of the conditions for Liberal support was a government promise that the legislation on direct elections should be put to Parliament that summer, with a free vote on proportional representation.

Despite the government's endeavours, delaying tactics from the opponents of direct elections meant that the Bill was not to receive Royal Assent until May 1978. On 13 December 1977, the House voted by 319 to 222 in favour of the first-past-the-post system though, because of its particular political circumstances and a desire to see all the main political tendencies represented, the Single Transferable Vote (STV) in a single three-member constituency was preferred for Northern Ireland. In April 1978, the Copenhagen European Council recognised the impossibility of the original 1978 date (the Netherlands, too, was late in adopting its legislation), and fixed a new date, the four-day period of 7–10 June 1979.

Thus, after years of stagnation, the log-jam had at last been broken. In retrospect, Parliament's own proposals, in the form of the Patijn report, were crucial. Patijn had taken over the 1960 draft's idea of a transitional period and had linked this to a distinction between the principle of direct elections and the more complicated principle of uniformity. Tactically, too, the idea of a target date had enabled Member State governments to decide upon and thereafter focus their efforts on a realistic objective. But, fifteen years after the first direct elections were held, the next step, the introduction of a uniform system, has so far proved insurmountable.

2.4 Uniform elections

In retrospect, Parliament's first (in 1960) draft Convention was a complicated affair, though it was driven by exactly the same pragmatic reasoning as the Patijn resolution. A major complication was the introduction of a provision whereby during a transitional period only two-thirds of members would be directly elected, with the other third continuing to be nominated by the Member State legislatures from among their ranks. This provision was expressly intended to 'preserve firm links with the national parliaments' and to avoid the election of a Parliament of unknowns (it being reasoned that big domestic names would be unwilling to sit in the European Parliament alone). The decision as to when the transitional period should end was left to the European Parliament itself. A second departure from strict respect for the language of the treaty was that directly elected members would be elected according to differing national systems. This followed from the transitional arrangements, since a uniform system could only be instituted at the end of these. Indeed, the 1960 draft Convention over-came the thorny problem of uniformity by postponing it, proposing instead that an 'interim advisory committee', composed of Council (EEC, Euratom and ECSC) and European Parliament delegates should decide on such a system by a two-thirds majority vote. (Though the Convention was itself ill-fated, the proposal for some sort of joint Council–Parliament drafting party ultimately found its way into the 1976 Act establishing direct elections which provides for a Council–Parliament conciliation committee — see Chapter 3, Section 3.4).

In drafting its Convention, the Parliament contended with all of the recurring major issues involved and, as will be seen from the following list, most of these have since been 'boiled off' over the past three decades: the number and distribution of members (see next section); voter and candidate age (now determined by national arrangements); the dates of elections (now held over a four-day, Thursday to Sunday, period, a compromise between those Member States that traditionally hold their elections on a Thursday — for example, the United Kingdom — and those that traditionally hold their elections on a Sunday — for example, Italy); the duration of the mandate (it is now, as the 1960 Convention had proposed, five years); 'adequate preparation of the electorate' (money is now provided to launch information campaigns); the replacement of members (currently according to national arrangements); the compatibility of other offices (now set out in the 1976 Act) and of the dual mandate (the 1976 Act allows it, but three Member States, Belgium, Greece and Spain, apparently in breach of the Act, forbid it). Only the thorniest problem of all, that of uniformity, still remains.

In the meantime, four additional factors have now entered into the equation. The first, following British accession, is the idiosyncratic, constituency-based, first-past-the-post United Kingdom electoral system. All eleven other Member States have relatively pure proportional systems (see Table 2). After several intellectually complicated attempts to square the circle, it is now generally recognised on all sides that agreement could only be reached if the United Kingdom in particular were to accept some form, however attenuated, of the principle of proportionality, with all that this might be held to imply for its domestic elections (though some point out that the principle has already been accepted for European elections in Northern Ireland). The second factor is the still-reverberating post-Maastricht debate about the principle of subsidiarity, which all Community institutions, including the European Parliament, have taken to heart. As much a state of mind as a legal concept, the principle of subsidiarity has latterly led Parliament to rethink its stance over the provisions of the treaties on uniform elections. In particular, Parliament no longer considers *uniformity* to be synonymous with *identicality*, and there is more understanding of the deep-rootedness of cultural differences and traditions. The third factor is Italy's decision, following a national referendum, to change its national electoral system away from pure proportionality towards a system containing elements of the British system. This impeccably popular decision has undermined the absolutist moral position of proponents of proportional representation. The fourth important factor is that the Maastricht Treaty has amended the third paragraph of TEU Article 138 so as to require the assent (by absolute majority vote) of the European Parliament for the adoption of a uniform procedure (that is, in addition to the previously required unanimity in Council and adoption in the Member States 'in accordance with their respective constitutional requirements'). Thus, the old irony of the Parliament having only weak consultation powers in regard to the system that would be used to elect it has been brought to an end. In this context at least, the Parliament now has a major say in its own destiny. (A fifth factor, shortly to enter into the equation, will be further enlargements.)

Since the 1979 direct elections, Parliament has made three separate attempts to draft a uniform system in accordance with its obligations under Article 138. In March 1982, after a series of reverse votes in committee, Parliament adopted the Seitlinger report (Jean Seitlinger was a French Christian Democrat from Lorraine), which called for proportional representation in multi-member constituencies of between three and fifteen seats. The d'Hondt system of proportional representation was recommended, but there was an option for single-list preferential voting. The Parliament had its sights set on the next round of European elections in 1984. The Council duly established a working party to consider Parliament's proposals but was unable to reach agreement in time (the British electoral system was a major stumbling block). After the 1984 elections, the Parliament decided to draw up another report. The rapporteur, Reinhold Bocklet (a German CSU member), based his report on Seitlinger's proposals but adopted a more cautious and flexible approach. However, his proposals became the subject of intense and divided debate, both in committee and, later, in a special parliamentary working group. In the end, Parliament was unable to adopt fresh proposals before the 1989 European elections.

The Parliament elected in 1989 resolved on a fresh approach, this time illuminated by the debate over the principle of subsidiarity. A Belgian Liberal, Karel de Gucht, was appointed rapporteur. An interim report was first published in May 1991 (adopted 10 October 1991). Following an opinion from Parliament's Legal Affairs Committee on the implications of the principle of subsidiarity, the report boldly ruled out the adoption of an identical electoral procedure in the twelve Member States, preferring the 'establishment of common criteria on certain essential aspects of the electoral procedure'. A second de Gucht report, adopted on 10 June 1992, was principally concerned with the number and distribution of seats and will be considered in detail in Section 2.6 of this chapter.

In January 1993, the British Liberal Democrat party, which believed itself to have been consistently denied seats in the European Parliament because of the British electoral system, brought an action against the European Parliament, under EEC Article 175, before the European Court of Justice, arguing that the Parliament had failed to fulfil its obligation of proposing a uniform electoral system. Although the Court's Advocate General ruled the case inadmissible on the grounds that a single political party did not have sufficient legal interest to bring a case, the prospect of a Court case had already jolted the Parliament into action. In March 1993, the Parliament adopted a third de Gucht report by a large majority which included all the major political groupings within Parliament. The report reaffirmed the principle of proportional representation. Voting was to be 'based on lists drawn up either for the whole territory of a Member State or for regions or multi-member constituencies'. One or more preferential votes could be cast where elections were based on lists. Member States could, if they so wished, institute a minimum threshold for the distribution of seats, set at between three and five per cent of the votes cast. These proposals were pragmatically designed to pose as few problems as possible to most Member States.

Parliament tackled the 'British problem' with characteristic ingenuity, separating off two distinct problems: the single-member constituency link on the one hand and the principle of proportionality on the other. A separate clause in the resolution provides that 'if a Member State uses a single-member constituency system, not more than two-thirds of the seats assigned to this Member State may be distributed in these constituencies; the remainder of the seats assigned to the Member State shall be distributed by means of lists in such a way as to ensure that the distribution of all the seats of this Member State corresponds to the proportions of the total votes cast'. In other words, of the United Kingdom's then eighty-one members, fifty-four would continue to be directly elected by single-member constituencies and the other twenty-seven members would be used to 'top up' the share of those parties (principally the Liberal Democrats) discriminated against by the first-past-the-post system. Moreover, another separate clause in the resolution provided that 'Member States may make limited special arrangements in order to take account of regional features'. This clause was of obvious relevance to the case of the United Kingdom, where Scotland, Wales and Northern Ireland are traditionally over-represented in the distribution of constituencies. In Karel de Gucht's words, 'I have tried to make it as difficult as possible for Britain to say no.'

The de Gucht resolution was forwarded to the Council during the Danish Presidency (first half of 1993), which was distracted by its own political problems bound up with the ratification of the Maastricht Treaty. The succeeding Belgian Presidency, perhaps initially discouraged by the fears expressed by some legal experts that the de Gucht resolution might not satisfy the requirements of Article 138 (in particular, did it propose a uniform system?), decided to pursue the related matter of voting rights and European citizenship discussed above, and was able to bring that matter to a successful conclusion in December 1993, in time for implementation before the 1994 European elections. Thus, the Council, as opposed to the Presidency, has not yet been formally in receipt of the de Gucht proposals, and the 1994 European elections were therefore conducted under the diversity described below. Pragmatically accepting the special political circumstances surrounding the ratification and implementation of the Maastricht Treaty, the European Parliament has not seemed unduly concerned by this. However, speaking in April 1993 at a London Conference, de Gucht stated his belief that the European Parliament would seriously consider bringing legal action against the Council for failure to act if implementation looked like being delayed beyond the 1999 European elections.

It is pointless to speculate as to whether the de Gucht proposals, or something similar to them, will be implemented. (Some commentators point out that the further enlargements scheduled for 1995 will further cloud the picture by introducing new Member States with their own distinctive electoral systems. Others point out that Italy's recent decision to change its domestic electoral system has weakened the case of the proponents of proportional representation.)

The United Kingdom Conservative government has refrained from any detailed comment. John Major has said that 'we are ready to discuss the issue in Council when the Presidency decides to table the report. If the Council were to reach a consensus, which remains to be seen, it would certainly need to respect different national traditions. We acknowledge the attempt made by the de Gucht report to take these considerations into account' (HC Deb 24/5/93 c370W). The Labour Party's *Report of the Working Party on Electoral Systems 1993* (the 'Plant Report') proposed a regional-list system for European elections, with eleven multi-member, regionally defined constituencies. This would be compatible with the de Gucht resolution. The Liberal Democrat Party has consistently supported the principal of proportionality and would stand to gain most from the introduction of a PR system.

The chief arguments of those favouring the introduction of proportional representation are as follows. First, representativeness takes on special importance for the European Parliament, and distortions (for example, the over-representation of the Conservatives in 1979, or the under-representation of the Greens in 1989 — see Section 2.8 below) are particularly regrettable. Second, European elections are clearly distinct from national general elections, and the introduction of PR for the former would not necessarily act as a 'thin end of the wedge'. Third, a traditional argument against PR, that it creates weak coalition governments, is irrelevant to European elections, which involve no government formation. Fourth, PR has worked perfectly satisfactorily in Northern Ireland (and has not acted as a 'thin end of the wedge' either). Fifth, the de Gucht proposals would specifically enable the United Kingdom to continue with its traditional single-member constituency link. Sixth, the constituency link is in any case necessarily weaker in constituencies composed of an average of half a million voters. Seventh, the first-past-the-post system has so far produced disproportionately large swings in the share of seats between the Conservative and Labour Parties which has had important internal consequences for the Parliament (see Section 2.8 below). Finally, the introduction of a uniform system is a legal obligation derived from a treaty to which the United Kingdom has subscribed.

Opponents of proportional representation argue that the choice of electoral system is necessarily rooted in a country's culture and history and cannot be imposed through an objective political decision, however noble the ideal. Unless real benefits accrue, the expense and upheaval caused by the introduction of a new system cannot be justified. (Proponents of the de Gucht proposals point out that they are specifically designed to minimise such upheaval and to maintain as far as possible national electoral cultures.)

2.5 The current diversity

The 1994 European elections were fought under circumstances of considerable diversity. Thirteen different systems are in use (the United Kingdom uses two; first-past-the-post for England, Scotland and Wales, and STV for Northern Ireland). These systems are not necessarily the same as the systems used in national elections. For example, France uses a single constituency PR system with a five per cent threshold for European elections, as opposed to the more familiar two-round elections to single-member constituencies it employs for elections to the national assembly. Only the Netherlands uses roughly the same system and the same constituency. Two countries employ particular distinctive systems: the United Kingdom (first-past-the-post) and the Irish Republic (STV).

Six Member States (Denmark, France, Greece, Luxembourg, the Netherlands and Portugal) use a single constituency corresponding to their national territory, the others have divided their territories into varying numbers of constituencies, from three in Belgium, to eighty-five in the United Kingdom (eighty-seven members, but Northern Ireland forms one three-member constituency).

Some Member States (Denmark, Germany, Greece, Italy and the Netherlands) favour candidates presented by political parties. In Greece, only political parties or alliances between political parties may present candidates. In four other states independent candidates have to produce differing numbers of signatures in support of their candidature (6,200 in Denmark, 4,000 (at the federal level) or 2,000 (at the *Land* level) in Germany, 30,000 in Italy) or pay a deposit (18,000 Dutch florins in the Netherlands). Four Member States require differing numbers of signatures from all candidates — 5,000 in Belgium, 15,000 voters (or fifty deputies) in Spain, twenty-five in Luxembourg, and thirty in the United Kingdom. In Ireland one person may present his or her own candidature. Three Member States require payment of a deposit (in France, 100,000 French francs per list, in Ireland £1,000, and in the United Kingdom £1,000 sterling). In Italy and the Netherlands there is a minimum age of twenty-five for candidatures and in France of twenty-three; in Belgium, Greece, Ireland, Luxembourg and the United Kingdom the minimum age is twenty-one but in Denmark and Germany eighteen.

In five Member States (France, Germany, Greece, Portugal and Spain) voters have no influence on the lists presented by the political parties. In Belgium, Denmark, Italy and the Netherlands, voters can alter the order of candidates on the list of their chosen political party. In Luxembourg, voters can vote for candidates on different party lists. In the United Kingdom and Ireland voters vote for individual candidates. In Denmark, Ireland, the Netherlands and the United Kingdom voters go to the polls on the Thursday, and in the other eight states on the Sunday. In eight states the right to vote is optional, whereas in Belgium, Greece, Italy (where it is a 'civic duty') and Luxembourg it is obligatory (following the post-Maastricht changes, the obligation applies equally to other Member State citizens who are resident, and have indicated their preference to vote, in these four states), though enforcement of the obligation varies. In all Member States the minimum voting age is eighteen.

Five states (Belgium, Denmark, France, the Netherlands and Spain) count and distribute votes proportionally on the basis of the d'Hondt system. Luxembourg uses a variation on this, the 'Hagenbach–Bischoff' system. Germany uses the 'Hare–Niemeyer' procedure. Ireland and Northern Ireland use the Single Transferable Vote system, whereas Greece uses a 'reinforced' proportional representation system. In all Member States counting begins at the close of the last polling booth on the Sunday evening of the voting period.

The rules concerning finance vary considerably. In some Member States (for example, Germany and Greece), state financing is made available as a proportionate function of the political parties' representation. In Denmark there is no state financing. In other Member States (Italy, Luxembourg) certain expenses are reimbursed.

There are also important differences concerning the official opening of the campaign, if any. In Denmark, Germany, Greece, Ireland, Luxembourg and the Netherlands there is no official opening of the campaign. In Belgium, the campaign opens forty days before polling day, in Italy thirty days before, in the United Kingdom one calendar month before, in Spain twenty days before, in France fifteen days before and in Portugal just twelve days before.

There are similarly broad differences about opinion polling. In Italy, there is no limit, whereas in Portugal opinion polls are forbidden for the duration of the campaign. In Belgium and Luxembourg polls are forbidden during the last month of the campaign. In Greece, polls are not allowed on television and, by convention, press polls are not published during the last three to four weeks of the campaign. In France polls are forbidden during the last week, in Spain during the last five days. In Denmark, Germany, Ireland and the Netherlands the publication of polls is forbidden on polling day.

Media access and coverage is also the subject of greatly differing provisions, with some countries imposing constitutional rules on proportionality of coverage and others concluding informal arrangements among the political parties. To take two extremes, in Portugal television time is divided among all lists, whereas in France television time is primarily divided among parties represented in the national assembly or senate.

Europe's cultural and electoral diversity is perhaps nowhere better illustrated than in a comparison of the hours of opening of the polling booths. Only three Member States have the same hours (Denmark, Portugal and Spain, 09.00–20.00); all the others are different, some remarkably so (Greece, 05.00–19.30 — sunrise to sunset, Italy, 06.00–22.00, Belgium, 08.00–13.00, Luxembourg, 08.00–14.00, Netherlands, 08.00–19.00, France, 08.00–20.00, Germany, 08.00–21.00, the United Kingdom, 08.00–23.00, and Ireland, 09.00–21.00); a Belgian voter has just five hours in which to vote, whereas a British voter has fifteen and an Italian sixteen.

In Belgium the 1994 elections coincided with elections for the Council of the Brussels Region, in Germany with local elections in seven *Länder*, and in the United Kingdom with five by-elections. In Italy, three national referenda were held simultaneously, and in Luxembourg the General Election was once again held on the same day.

2.6 The numbers and distribution of members

A striking feature of the history of the European Parliament is the amount of time that has been spent in debating the number and distribution of members. Until the December 1992 Edinburgh European Council, the basic balance was established on the basis of an agreement reached between Jean Monnet and Konrad Adenauer in Bonn in April 1951. During a discreet visit to Bonn, Monnet told Adenauer, 'I have been authorised to propose to you that relations between Germany and France within the Community should be governed by the principal of equality, in the Council as in the Assembly and all the other Community institutions, whether France enters alone or with the French Union, whether Germany is the West alone or reunited' (Monnet, 1976, p.516). At the time, it should be recalled, it was France that had the upper hand and Monnet's offer was intended and recognised as a magnanimous act. Adenauer gave his 'full agreement', reminding Monnet 'how much I am attached to equal rights for my country in the future'.

Monnet's initial proposal was for a sixty-two-member Assembly, with eighteen seats each for France, Germany and Italy, and a further eighteen seats for the Benelux countries. Believing that members would naturally sit according to nationality, and apprehensive about Franco–German hegemony, the Benelux countries held out for a larger share of the seats, and the resulting political agreement, enshrined in the Paris Treaty, was a seventy-eight-member ECSC Assembly, with four seats for Luxembourg, ten each for Belgium and the Netherlands, and eighteen each for France, Germany, and Italy. The big three redressed the balance *vis-à-vis* the Benelux countries in the 1957 Rome Treaties. Each had thirty-six members in the European Assembly (a figure arrived at by simply doubling their entitlement under the ECSC Treaty). The Benelux countries' entitlements were also increased but by less. Belgium and the Netherlands retained their parity, with fourteen seats each, and Luxembourg received six. This 142-member arrangement, with adjustments for enlargements, was to last until 1979. (In the 1973 round of enlargements, the United Kingdom was awarded thirty-six seats, and Denmark and Ireland ten each).

The Parliament first considered the matter of the number of its members in its 1960 draft Convention on direct elections. It proposed simply tripling the actual number of members, giving the big three 108 seats each, and tiny Luxembourg the extraordinary number of eighteen! Parliament's next consideration of the matter, the 1975 Patijn report, was far more empirical in its approach. Using a regressive proportional formula based on Member State population, Patijn proposed a 355-member Parliament. Germany was to have seventy-one seats, the United Kingdom sixty-seven, Italy sixty-six and France sixty-five. The Netherlands would have twenty-seven seats, Belgium twenty-three, Denmark seventeen, Ireland thirteen, and Luxembourg six. Thus, French–German (and Belgian–Dutch, and Irish–Danish) parity would have been broken, as indeed is the case today. Although the Patijn recommendations themselves were never taken up, they were also the precursor to two other developments. The first was the use of a regressive proportional formula based on population. The second was the acknowledgement that over-represented Luxembourg's quota of six seats should serve as the point of departure of any calculation.

In the Council, positions were divided between the larger Member States, who favoured a proportional system based on population (since they stood to gain from it), and the smaller Member States, who favoured a more discriminatory approach. In rapid succession the Council considered French, Irish and Belgian plans before finally reaching a political settlement at the July 1976 Brussels European Council. The directly elected Parliament was to consist of 410 members. Britain, France, Germany and Italy were to have eighty-one each. The Netherlands was to have twenty-five members, Belgium twenty-four, Denmark sixteen, Ireland fifteen and Luxembourg six. (Interestingly, the Belgian Presidency relinquished its country's parity with the Netherlands in the search for unanimity, giving one of its seats to Denmark, which promptly earmarked the extra seat for Greenland. Following a referendum, Greenland withdrew from the Community in

1982, but Denmark retained the seat. Ultimately, Belgium gained an extra seat in the December 1992 settlement, but the Netherlands was awarded a further six seats in the same round.) The 1976 agreement was to last, with adjustments for enlargements, until 1992 (Greece was awarded twenty-four seats in 1981, and Portugal and Spain received twenty-four and sixty respectively in 1986).

The *ad hoc* 1951 Monnet–Adenauer agreement finally came to be questioned after the fall of the Berlin Wall in the autumn of 1989 and the subsequent unification of the two Germanies in October 1990. It was inconceivable that the five new *Länder* should not be represented in the European Parliament; yet, from Parliament's point of view, it was equally inconceivable that representation of the eleven western *Länder* should be diminished in any way. At the same time, further enlargements of the Community seemed increasingly likely. Agreement on increasing Germany's membership was almost reached at the Maastricht European Council. With a view to these developments, and as part of its exercise in drafting fresh proposals for a uniform electoral system, the Parliament adopted a report in May 1992 setting out its views on the number and distribution of members. The de Gucht report used a regressive proportional method based on population similar to Patijn's 1975 calculations and similarly accepted Luxembourg's current six members as the point of departure. Finally, at the December 1992 Edinburgh European Council, the Member States agreed to increase the number of members and their distribution in line with the European Parliament's proposals, as set out in the de Gucht report. Germany was to have ninety-nine members; the United Kingdom, like France and Italy, was to gain six extra members, raising its total membership to eighty-seven.

Thus, since June 1994, the European Parliament has been composed of 567 members: Germany has ninety-nine members; France, Italy and the United Kingdom eighty-seven; Spain sixty-four; the Netherlands thirty-one; Belgium, Greece and Portugal twenty-five; Denmark sixteen; Ireland fifteen; and Luxembourg six. In December 1993, the Brussels European Council decided to follow the de Gucht proposals once more in relation to the forthcoming enlargements of the Union. Should Austria, Finland, Norway and Sweden accede to the Union in the near future, as seems most likely, then the 1999 European elections will elect a 639-member Parliament. All of these numerical permutations are set out in Table 3.

2.7 Constituency boundaries in the United Kingdom

The provisions of the 1976 Council Act (at the Community level) establishing direct elections to the European Parliament were eventually introduced into United Kingdom law by the 1978 European Assembly Elections Act, which provided for the distribution of the United Kingdom's entitlement of eighty-one seats among its component parts, giving sixty-six to England, eight to Scotland, four to Wales and three (in one multi-member constituency) to Northern Ireland. The United Kingdom's traditional Boundary Commissions (for England, Wales and Scotland) were then given the task of drawing up the seventy-eight mainland constituencies. Though the timetable was very tight, their task was relatively simple. The statutory criteria for European parliamentary constituencies required that Scotland, Wales and England be divided up into the allotted number of constituencies. Each constituency was to consist of 'two or more whole [Westminster] parliamentary constituencies and having an electorate as near the electoral quota as is reasonably practicable'. The electoral quota was to be established by dividing the total parliamentary electorate by the total number of allocated seats. In other words, they were to build European constituencies out of the building blocks of Westminster constituencies, aiming to create units of about 500,000 voters.

The Boundary Commissions were expected to review the boundaries as required (as they duly did in 1983–4, 1988 and 1991) and, in the normal run of things, they would have been expected to review the boundaries so as to incorporate the six new seats arising out of the 1992 Edinburgh European Council's decision (see above). However, the Boundary Commissions were busy with a review of Westminster constituencies. The potential difficulty of achieving the necessary adjustments in time for June 1994 led some commentators, particularly those in or close to the Liberal Democrat camp, to suggest that some form of PR could be used to allocate the 'loose' six seats. Karel de Gucht suggested that they should be awarded to the best losers (in other words, the Liberal Democrats) as a step towards Parliament's recommendations. The government maintained that the six extra seats would be accommodated by redrawing the boundaries.

The European Parliamentary Elections Bill was published in June 1993. It allocated five of the six extra seats to England, one to Wales and, in order to overcome the problem of the Boundary Commissions' unavailability, provided for the creation of two *ad-hoc* European Parliamentary Constituency Committees, one for England and one for Wales. Though legally perfectly above board, the use of *ad hoc* committees attracted some criticism, since it did not allow for the normal procedures of provisional recommendations and local enquiries used by the Westminster Boundary Commissions.

The two *ad hoc* committees published their provisional recommendations in September 1993. With minor adjustments, these were voted through the House of Commons in February 1994. An immediate anomaly in their recommendations was that, because of the urgency of their work, they could not take account of the contemporaneous work of the traditional Westminster Boundary Commissions. In other words, they were obliged to employ basic building blocks (the old Westminster constituencies) that would be out of date just as soon as the Westminster Boundary Commissions reported their recommendations. This has raised the criticism that the MEPs elected in 1994 face the prospect of redistributed constituencies before the next elections in 1999.

Only twenty-four of the existing eighty-one seats were unaffected. Outside London, only seven of the fifty-six seats remained unchanged. This had the immediate effect of necessitating reselection procedures in a large number of constituencies.

Nevertheless, the most striking feature about the new boundary proposals was how slight their effects were reckoned to be, given the massive changes involved. In general, marginal seats were reckoned to have been rendered less marginal and, where big changes occurred, they more or less cancelled each other out, and this apparent 'neutrality' certainly made the proposed changes more acceptable to the big parties.

2.8 Results to date

1979

Because they were the very first, the 7 and 10 June 1979 European elections were the focus of great attention and great expectations. Of the 180 million voters in the nine Member States, almost 111 million did turn out and vote (an average of 65.9 per cent). The result was a general swing to the centre and right, but the elections were predominantly fought out in terms of national politics, and there was little sense anywhere of history in the making.

In the case of the *United Kingdom*, the elections came barely a month after the 3 May General Election. The lacklustre campaign, in which the only nationally known candidate was Barbara Castle, was limited to barely a fortnight, and politicians' witty epithets summed up the atmosphere. The Conservative Party's Deputy Leader, Willie Whitelaw, spoke about the stirring up of apathy and Labour's Roy Hattersley about 'profound superficiality'. A demoralised Labour Party, which had only just lost office after a lengthy struggle to govern without an overall majority, ran a low-key and confused campaign. An anti-Market trend was in the ascendant within the Labour Party, which had further reduced its potential profile by banning dual mandates. Polls showed that potential Labour voters had stayed at home, and the result, on a very low turnout of under 32 per cent, was a Conservative landslide.

The Tories took sixty seats to Labour's seventeen. The doughty and indefatigable Winifred Ewing won the only other mainland seat for the SNP. (Her constituency, the Highlands and Islands, was larger in area than the whole of Belgium!)

Italy held a General Election on 3 June so that the European electoral campaign ran for just one week and became caught up in the political parties' manoeuvrings to form a new government coalition. The chief significant feature was the PCI's (Communists) double loss (in both General and European Elections), which led to introspection about the party's former cooperative approach with the Christian Democrats. Despite the proximity of the General Election, turnout was remarkably high at 90 per cent, though this was attributed more to Italy's political culture (voting is still technically obligatory) and general enthusiasm for all things European than a high profile campaign.

Luxembourg held a General Election on the same day, 10 June, as the European elections, and the principal political question was the survival of then Prime Minister Gastorn Thorn's left–centre coalition. In the event, a swing to the right forced the coalition out of office.

In *France*, the elections were seen on the right as a dress rehearsal for the 1981 presidential elections, with President Giscard d'Estaing and Jacques Chirac vying for the nomination. At the time Giscard was generally reckoned to have contained Chirac's ambitions. With Simone Veil, his popular Minister of Health, heading the list, the Giscardians won almost 28 per cent, as opposed to the Chiracian RPR's 16 per cent. Jean-Marie Le Pen's extreme right 'Euro-droite' alliance was forced to withdraw from the campaign through lack of funds. On the left, the Socialists won 23.5 per cent and Marchais' Communists 20.5 per cent. The Socialist Party's campaign was similarly marked by pre-presidential manoeuvring. Marchais' nineteen MEPs swelled the Communist group within the European Parliament to over a tenth of the total membership.

In *Ireland* the European elections served principally as a mid-term referendum on Jack Lynch's increasingly unpopular Fianna Fail government. In the event, Fianna Fail took just five of the fifteen seats on offer and won its lowest number of first-preference votes since the party's formation in 1926. Fine Gael and the Irish Labour Party took four seats each, but the great surprise was the success of two independents, 'T.J.' Maher in Munster and Neil Blaney in Connacht Ulster, both of whom sat in the Parliament until 1994.

In *Denmark* a coalition of anti-membership parties succeeded in mounting a rerun of the 1972 referendum on accession to the Communities, but they did not win the argument, returning just six of Denmark's sixteen MEPs. (In *Greenland* the campaign was dominated by the sole issue of separatism.)

In *West Germany* the European elections were seen principally as a portent for the next year's General Election, with jockeying for position on the right. Turnout, at 66 per cent, was disappointing. Despite Willy Brandt's active list leadership, the SDP lost ground to the Christian Democrats (39 per cent) and their Bavarian stable mates, the CSU (10 per cent).

In the *Netherlands* all points of the political compass were agreed on the benefits of membership, and this consensus was generally believed to have contributed to a low-profile campaign and surprisingly low turnout (57.8 per cent). The governing coalition parties (Christian Democrats and Liberals) took fourteen of the twenty-five seats.

In increasingly fragmented *Belgium*, the most striking feature was the winning performance of Leo Tindemans, a former Prime Minister. He headed the Flemish Christian Democrat list, which won seven of Flanders' thirteen Euro-seats.

In overall terms, representatives of some fifty-two political parties were elected, forming themselves into seven political groups. Despite the British Labour Party's poor showing, the Socialist group was easily the largest within the Parliament and was the only group composed of members from all nine Member States, though it was easily out-numbered by a centre–right, Christian Democrat–Liberal, coalition. The hard core of anti-marketeers within the British Labour contingent created much friction within the Socialist group.

Because of the freak result, British Conservatives became a force in their own right, temporarily displacing the Liberal group as the traditional third force in the European Parliament. In turn, the Liberal group had suffered from the absence of British Liberal Members, and British Liberals were swift to point out that, under PR, they would have won about ten seats and the Tories about forty.

1984

With the now familiar exception of *Denmark*, the issues in the 1984 European elections remained obstinately national and domestic and, with novelty value now spent, turnout was lower in several Member States.

In the *United Kingdom* the campaign focused solely on domestic political issues, from the abolition of the Greater London Council to the miners' strike (then twelve weeks old). An exit poll indicated that more than half of those who voted did so to express views on domestic political issues, 19 per cent voted because they always did so and only 29 per cent voted because they regarded European issues as important. The only European angle concerned the festering British budgetary rebate problem, which was to be resolved less than two weeks after the elections at the Fontainebleau Council. The Conservatives had known they would have to lose some of their seats resulting from the freak 1979 result. In the event they lost fifteen (and Labour won the same amount), but with 41 per cent of the vote they still remained the largest political party. Labour, which had begun to withdraw from its former anti-Market stance, saw its support up three points on 1979 to 36.5 per cent. The Labour Party was also happy to have reasserted itself in its role as chief opposition for, despite a spectacular win for the SDP at the Portsmouth by-election held on the same day, and despite registering 19.5 per cent of the national vote, the Liberal–SDP Alliance failed to win a single seat.

In *Belgium*, the only issue was the government's austerity programme. The results were marked by the disappearance of the regionalists and the appearance of the Greens in Wallonia, while in Flanders the Christian Democrats lost ground to the Socialists and Ecologists on the left and the Liberals and Vlaams Blok on the right. In a new departure, national legislation was passed to enable resident Member State nationals to vote in the Belgian European elections. In the event, only 377 of the estimated 20,000-strong Anglo–Irish expatriate community actually availed themselves of the possibility.

In *Denmark* turnout was up by four points over 1979 (52 per cent). The campaign was a rerun of the 1979 pro- versus anti-Market debate but the Popular Movement against the EC only increased its share of the vote slightly, retaining its four seats. The clear loser was the anti-tax Progress Party. Its vote slumped disastrously and it lost its only seat. The clear winner was the major governing coalition party, the Conservative People's Party, which doubled its share of seats from two to four, and the three other centre–right coalition parties saw slight increases in their support.

The elections in *France* produced several shocks. The first was the success of Jean-Marie Le Pen's Front National, which took 11 per cent of the vote (it had never won more than 2 per cent in a national election), entitling it to ten seats in the European Parliament. This was the extreme right's best electoral performance since the Poujadists in 1956 and put it on the same level as the Communists. This was a second shock. The Communists' share of the vote was 4 per cent down on the 1981 presidential elections and represented only half of its 1979 vote. The Communists had been collaborating in the Socialist-led government since 1981, and their disastrous result was widely interpreted as a consequence of this. The Socialist vote, which traditionally benefited from any decline in Communist support, did not benefit on this occasion and was down to only 21 per cent. In what was clearly a plebiscite on the government, the total left-wing vote was reduced to 36 per cent (from 56 per cent in the 1981 parliamentary elections). But the traditional opposition parties did not see any increase in their share of the vote. The single UDF/RPR list led by Simone Veil obtained 1 per cent less of the vote than the two parties had won separately in 1979. These results led to much political introspection. The Communists questioned the benefits of participation in government, and the traditional parties of the centre–right had to work out how to respond to the challenge from their right. The third shock was the low turnout which, at 57 per cent, was a record low for any national or local election. Indeed, the Communists attributed their failure in part to differential turnout.

The results in *Germany*, where turnout was also poor (57 per cent compared to 67.5 per cent in 1979) displayed a similar pattern. The campaign itself dwelt chiefly on the government's domestic record, fifteen months on from the General Election. Both the Christian Democratic sister parties, Kohl's CDU and the Bavarian CSU, saw their shares of the vote decline in comparison with 1979, when the parties had been in opposition (from 39 to 37.5 per cent and 10 to 8.5 per cent respectively), while their junior coalition partners, the Free Democrats, saw their share of the vote slip under the 5 per cent threshold (the first time the party had been eliminated since the founding of the FRG) and they lost all of their seats at Strasbourg. At the same time, the opposition SPD were unable to capitalise on the government's slide in popularity and saw its own share of the vote decline from 41 per cent in 1979 to 37.5 per cent in 1984. The clear winners were the Greens, who won their highest ever share of the national vote (8.2 per cent) and seven Strasbourg seats.

The second round of European elections in *Greece* to be held in the space of three years (the first were held in conjunction with a General Election in October 1981) were fought entirely on national issues, with Papandreou's governing PASOK remaining ahead but losing ground (13.5 per cent down from 1981) and a disappointed New Democracy making only modest gains, thereby preventing it from pressing its case for a new round of national elections to be held.

In *Ireland* a steep decline in turnout, down from 63 per cent in 1979 to 48 per cent in 1984, was interpreted as an indication of disaffection and apathy. Typically, the campaign concentrated on domestic issues and was characterised by rivalry between the governing Fine Gael/Labour coalition and Charles Haughey's Fianna Fail opposition. While it did win an overall majority of the votes cast, Fianna Fail did less well than it had expected. The principal loser was the junior coalition partner, the Labour Party, which lost all four of its Strasbourg seats, leaving Ireland as the only Member State not to send left-wing representation to the European Parliament.

The 1984 European elections in *Italy* were memorable chiefly for the fact that the Communist Party (PCI) overtook the Christian Democrats as the country's single largest party. Some attributed the PCI's success to a wave of sympathy following the recent death of its popular Secretary General, Enrico Berlinguer, and most saw the result as being of psychological importance rather than political weight. Indeed, the PCI's *sorpasso* obscured the main aspects of the election which were that the larger parties, both the PCI and the Christian Democrats, had consolidated their positions and that the smaller parties, and particularly Prime Minister Craxi's Socialists (who had hoped that their performance in government would win them votes at the expense of the perpetually excluded PCI), fared disappointingly.

For the second time, *Luxembourg* held a General Election at the same time as the European elections. A sharp swing to the left was interpreted as a consequence of the recession, although the opposition Christian Democrats kept their three MEPs, and the chief result was to undermine the ruling Socialist–Liberal coalition.

The 1984 European elections in the *Netherlands* produced the lowest turnout on record for a national election (50.5 per cent compared with 58 per cent in 1979). A much-publicised poll taken a few months before the elections had shown that only 30 per cent of the population were aware elections were to be held, and only 10 per cent identified them as European. The campaign itself was overshadowed by the governing Christian Democrat/Liberal coalition's decision on cruise missiles, culminating in a parliamentary debate on the eve of polling day. Although the Labour Party was the overall winner, the Christian Democrat vote was thought to have performed well under the circumstances (down 5 per cent on 1979, losing two seats), and the Liberal Party actually won one more seat. A new Green Progressive Alliance won two seats.

1989

The 1989 European election in the *United Kingdom* was the first (and last) time Margaret Thatcher 'lost' a national election. The Conservative vote was six percentage points down on its 1984 vote (from 41 to 35 per cent), the party lost thirteen seats and was completely wiped out in Scotland and Wales. The Labour Party enjoyed an 8.5 per cent swing in its favour, winning 40 per cent of the vote (its highest share since 1970) and thirteen more Strasbourg seats. The Conservative campaign was marred by an open row over the party's European policy between Thatcher and former Prime Minister Edward Heath and was undermined by an ill-judged publicity campaign. But poll evidence suggested the electorate were using the opportunity of a mid-term plebiscite to punish the government for a number of unpopular policies, principally the poll tax, the health service, interest rates and the standard of drinking water. The Conservative splits and unpopularity, plus the success of Neil Kinnock's steadily advancing policy review, enabled the

Labour Party to present a comparatively unified, positive and higher profile. Labour's performance was widely interpreted as an indicator for the next General Election, but many pointed out that a similar result in a General Election would have given Labour only a very small working majority. The 1989 elections were also notable for two other phenomena. The first was the decline of the traditional third party. The Social and Liberal Democrats won just 6.2 per cent of the vote, less than the Liberals' worst-ever result thirty-five years previously. And David Owen's 'rump' SDP could only fight sixteen seats and took just 0.5 per cent of the vote. The second, related, phenomenon was the spectacular success of the Green Party which, having never previously saved a deposit, won 15 per cent of the vote. This was more than green parties won in any other Member State, yet the electoral system denied the British Greens any seats.

In *Belgium* the 1989 European elections confirmed the eighth governing coalition of Wilfred Martens and were otherwise chiefly notable for the strong showing by the ecologists in both Flanders and Wallonia, and the success of the extreme-right Vlaams Blok, which won 4 per cent of the poll and a Strasbourg seat.

In *Denmark,* turnout was down to just 46 per cent (from 52 per cent in 1984) and, although the question of membership was still an issue (the Popular Movement against the EC retained its four seats), the chief themes were domestic, with Prime Minister Poul Schlüter's Conservative People's Party losing two seats and the coalition Liberals winning an extra seat.

The 1989 European elections in *France* were the seventh set of elections in fifteen months and, at 49 per cent, the turnout reflected this. Once again, the principal themes of the campaign remained domestic. There was much jockeying on the traditional right, resulting in two separate lists, one led by Giscard d'Estaing, and another by Simone Veil. The overall results showed a considerable loss: thirty-three seats altogether (the single list had won forty-one in 1984), and the centre–right's share of the vote down by over 6 per cent. The Socialists saw their share of the vote go up three points, and they picked up two more Strasbourg seats. But the French Communists saw their apparently inexorable decline continue, with 8 per cent of the vote and seven seats (11 per cent and ten seats in 1984). Front National support remained stable at the 11 per cent mark. The great winners were the French Greens, who took 11 per cent of the vote and won nine seats.

The 1989 European elections in *Germany* were held in the shadow of the impending 1990 General Election and barely touched on European issues. Occurring a few months before the Berlin Wall fell, they revealed a certain disillusionment among the electorate and a desire for Germany to reassert itself, both in the EC and in NATO. Turnout was slightly up (62 per cent), but support for most of the traditional parties (the CDU and the CSU but also the SDP) was down. Only the FDP, which managed to scrape back over the 5 per cent threshold and thus won four seats, had reason for cheer. On the other hand, the sudden success of the new extreme right Republikaner Party, which won 7 per cent of the vote and six seats, gave great cause for concern.

In *Greece* the European elections were entirely overshadowed by a simultaneously held General Election which saw Papandreou's PASOK lose to New Democracy (although, in the European Parliament, there was only a one-seat difference between the two parties' shares).

In *Ireland* the European elections were similarly swamped by an unexpected General Election which had been called for the same day just three weeks in advance. The only issues were domestic, and the prime question was whether Haughey's Fianna Fail should and could win a working majority. In the end, a swing to the left forced Fianna Fail back into coalition.

In *Italy*, the country's forty-eighth postwar government collapsed just one month before the European elections, and the campaign was dominated by the parties' jockeying for position in the next coalition. The Communist Party saw its share fall back from its 1984 high, while the Christian Democrat share remained stable, but the big winner was Craxi's Socialist Party, which saw its representation strengthened from nine to twelve seats. Other notable features were the success of a Green alliance, which won five seats, and a proliferation of regional parties.

In *Luxembourg* a General Election was once more held on the same day. Party representation in the European Parliament remained the same.

In the *Netherlands* Ruud Lubbers was heading a caretaker government after his centre–right coalition had collapsed, and the campaign issues remained solidly domestic. His Christian Democrats emerged from the election with their support slightly strengthened and two more Strasbourg seats, while their junior coalition partners were apparently punished with the loss of two seats for precipitating the collapse.

In *Portugal*, turnout was down hugely (from 72 per cent to 51 per cent) from its first, 1987 European elections, but the latter had coincided with a national election. The elections were seen as a mid-term referendum on the two-year-old Social Democrat (centre–right) government, which lost one seat, while the Socialist opposition won two seats.

In *Spain*, Felipe Gonzalez's Socialists were considered to have done well in losing just one seat, retaining their majority share of the vote. But both of the principal opposition parties similarly lost ground. The principal beneficiaries, and a major characteristic of the Spanish elections, were a profusion of regional parties.

The results of the 1994 elections are set out in Annex 1.

2.9 'Second-order national elections' or European elections?

In the run up to the first direct European elections in June 1979, a number of predictions were made about the likely nature and consequences of European elections. Some expected the rapid formation of European-level political parties, doing familiar ideological battle along traditional party political divisions but at the European level. Some predicted a new ideological division between the supporters of supranationality and national sovereignty. Most commentators felt that, whatever the pertinence of ideological differences, the creation of European elections would rapidly lead to the identification of specifically European level issues. Yet, as the forgoing analysis of three sets of European elections has shown, European election campaigns in all of the Member States have remained stubbornly domestic in substance. Further, although the three largest traditional European political families, the Christian Democrats, the Socialists, and the Liberals, have all now created European political parties with European electoral manifestos, future European election campaigns in the Member States are likely to continue to be dominated by national political issues for a long time to come. It is easy to see why.

A German political scientist has argued forcefully that European elections should be considered as 'second-order national elections' (Reif, 1980 and 1985). He defines first-order elections as national presidential or parliamentary elections. They are primarily concerned with power distribution and government formation and are characterised by a high level of electoral participation and high-profile campaigns. Second-order elections are all the rest. They do not involve national power distribution or government formation, turnout tends to be lower, and campaigns tend to be lower key (party organisations attach less importance and devote less resources to them, and the national media are less interested). Because no national level power is at stake, voters feel 'liberated'. In addition to lower turnout, this liberation manifests itself in two ways. First, smaller, less traditional and more extreme parties tend to benefit. Second, depending on the stage in the national electoral cycle, governing parties will tend to perform less well, as electorates register mid-term disaffection. The forgoing accounts of the 1979, 1984 and 1989 elections have provided excellent examples of all these phenomena. (Table 4 shows turnout in the three elections.)

According to this theory, it is precisely because no national (or superior) power is at stake, and because results depend on the stage in the various national electoral cycles and on domestic political circumstances, that European elections must be classed as second-order *national* elections and must be considered as being subordinate to first-order national elections. Whether European elections were innately sub-ordinate to national elections or not, it is clear that they would necessarily have always to interact with national electoral cycles; they cannot be held in a timeless vacuum. Where European elections are held at the same time as national elections they will necessarily be over-shadowed, if not swamped, by domestic considerations. And where elections, whether European or other, are held soon after national elections, they are likely to suffer from the phenomenon of 'electoral fatigue'. On the other hand, where other elections, whether European or other (for example, local elections), are held away from national elections, they are likely to be used by the electorate to make mid-term judgements on government (although, as the above accounts have shown, support withdrawn from governing parties is not necessarily invested in traditional opposition parties).

An obvious conclusion is that, for as long as the European Parliament is 'subordinate' to national political processes, the substance of European electoral campaigns will continue to be determined primarily by national political issues. At the same time, a number of observations are in order.

First, a common theme in the predictions made about the Parliament's evolution and development is that the timetables rather than the substance tend to be exaggerated. While, with new enlargements and a 1996 IGC in the immediate offing, there is reason to believe that the pace of institutional and political change within the Union may pick up, the Parliament is unlikely to throw off its 'subordinate' status for some time to come (after all, leaving aside the 'new democracies' of Greece, Portugal and Spain, even the constitutionally youngest Member States, Italy, Germany and France, have seen many more general elections than the European Parliament's four to date).

However, second, there are already clear signs of political and constitutional evolution. At the political level, common issues and results are gradually becoming discernable. In the 1984 European elections, for example, the siting of cruise missiles was an important theme in several Member States, and particularly in Italy and the Netherlands. Environmental issues (for example, water and air quality) were a clear common theme in the 1989 European elections, with the Greens or ecology parties doing well in Belgium, France, Germany, Italy, the Netherlands and the United Kingdom. Other common phenomena have included the rise of small extreme right parties in Belgium, France, Greece, Italy and Germany, and the rise of regional or single-issue 'splinter' parties.

At the constitutional level, the Maastricht Treaty has already granted the Parliament an important new *de facto* power of appointment over the Commission and its President. This new provision, tested for the first time in the autumn of 1994 (the appointment of the 1995–2000 Commission) is considered in more detail in Chapter 3, Section 3.2.

Suffice it to note here that, for the first time, a clear linkage exists between European elections and the appointment of the European executive. Given the organic nature of the Union's constitutional development, this linkage can be expected to evolve steadily into something altogether less subordinate.

A third observation is that criticisms related to the current apparent 'non-Europeanness' of European elections are partly based on a false premiss. The 'Europeanness' of the elections relates not only to the substance of the political debate but also to their simultaneity and the common institution involved.

Fourth, those who predict a future European Parliament ideologically divided along supranational and national sovereignty lines forget the nature of the current mechanism for constitutional change within the Union. As was explained in Chapter 1, Section 1.4, the European Parliament remains excluded from the process, which remains resolutely focused on national ratification procedures and therefore on national parliaments. Much as many MEPs would like their institution to become a constituent assembly, it seems unlikely it will ever fulfil such a role. And, although opposition to further integration remains a live issue in some Member States, a vast majority of Parliament's membership enjoys broad consensus on the whole matter of European integration.

Fifth, comparison with the political systems in the Member States may lead to a misunderstanding about the likely nature of European political parties. These will never be collections of universally recognised genial polyglots with compendious knowledge about local issues throughout the Union, from the Shetlands to the Canaries. On the contrary, a far more appropriate parallel is to be found in the United States' model, where political parties are never more than loose and temporary electoral coalitions. (In the same context, it could be pointed out that the vast majority of American citizens had no idea who Bill Clinton was one year before his election to the Presidency and, in Europe, Jacques Delors became universally known because he was President of the Commission, and not the other way around.)

Finally, the current lack of any linkage between European elections and government formation or the distribution of power puts particular emphasis on the representativeness of the European Parliament. The normative side of this will be considered in more detail in the next section, but it should be pointed out that the current nature of European elections poses a number of potential problems in this context. In the first place, the 'liberated' nature of European elections, when combined with proportional systems, can give rise to exaggerated swings in support, particularly for what might be termed 'non-governmental' parties, the traditional repositories of 'protest' votes. Second, system-based distortions in results have been of particular concern to the European Parliament. The United Kingdom's first-past-the-post system has been a frequent villain: whether the freak over-representation of the British Conservatives in 1979, the denial of any seat to the Greens in 1989 or the denial until 1994 of any seat to the Liberals/Liberal Democrats. Prior to the third de Gucht report (see above), the European Parliament had frequently debated the desirability of thresholds, with a view to the French and German rules, which deny seats to any party receiving less than respectively 3 or 5 per cent of the national vote. (Ironically, in Germany in 1984 it was a 'mainstream' traditional party, the Free Democrats, which fell foul of this rule, while the extreme right Republikaner Party and the non-traditional Greens both won seats.) In line with its now more pragmatic approach, Parliament's most recent recommendation left decisions about thresholds up to the Member States.

2.10 Candidates and careers

Who are the members of the European Parliament? Where do they come from? How are they selected? Do they follow careers within the Parliament and, if so, what do these look like?

In 1979, when the first direct elections to the European Parliament were to take place, many party political and national authorities were concerned that the new Parliament should not completely or immediately lose all its expertise and links with its past; it needed a sprinkling of 'old hands' during a 'running in' period. Some were additionally afraid that the new Parliament would be born into obscurity; it needed some national political figures to keep it in the public eye, at least at the outset. These concerns had several consequences. A first was the existence of a large number of dual mandates (that is, MEPs who were simultaneously members of their national parliaments), including many who had been members of the pre-1979 appointed European Parliament. A second was the existence of a large number of political personalities who had made their name in their domestic political systems and brought their reputations to the Strasbourg assembly. Both these phenomena tended to diminish or obscure the creation of new or distinct patterns. MPs and domestic political personalities would naturally tend to see their activities in the European Parliament as an adjunct rather than their *raison d'être*, and both had to divide their time between their different activities. Attendance was subsequently selective. After fifteen years of existence, the directly elected Parliament is firmly bedded down in the Union's political and constitutional system, and the number of dual mandates has diminished greatly.

On the other hand, the European Parliament's membership continues to sport a number of political 'personalities'. Some of these are in frequent attendance and are highly active in the Parliament. A good current example is the former Belgian Prime Minister Leo Tindemans who, as leader of the Christian Democratic group in the Parliament, the European People's Party until 1994, has been both highly active and highly influential. But others attend only occasionally and seem to take little active interest in the Parliament. Their membership has much to do with proportional representation and in particular with the traditional continental list system. Party leaders and major politicians frequently put their names at the head of their parties' lists as a gesture both of commitment and of support. For example, the leader of the French Socialist Party, Michel Rocard, headed the French Socialist Party list for the 1994 European elections (as did François Mitterrand in 1979 and Laurent Fabius in 1984 and 1989). This has much to do with the primarily domestic nature of European election campaigns which, as we have seen, are still fought primarily on national political issues and along national political divisions. Sometimes, such 'list leaders' resign their seats immediately after the elections (as Mitterrand did in 1979), ceding their place to the next candidate on the list. But sometimes they stay on (as Fabius did in 1984), content to have an additional, if occasional, political platform.

One other factor explains the presence of political 'personalities' in the Parliament. This is that it can provide an alternative electoral platform for national politicians currently out of power or temporarily out of domestic electoral office. This role is enhanced by the fact, examined above, that the European Parliament's fixed-term electoral cycle is generally out of synchronisation with national electoral political cycles. Centralised list systems lend themselves to this practice, precisely because winning positions on the list are decided by the central party authorities, rather than any local selection procedure.

Another marked phenomenon of the European Parliament's membership is the generally low level of participation. Absenteeism has been a problem from the Parliament's earliest days. A 1962 study of the ECSC Common Assembly devoted an annex to the subject (Kapteyn, 1962, pp. 255–7), discovering that those who had to travel furthest attended least. On only two occasions during a five-year mandate, when the Parliament elects its president for the next two and a half years, will roughly full attendance in plenary sessions be achieved. Attendance is significantly higher where particular majorities are required as, for example, is the case with the adoption of the budget, and the Parliament has traditionally mustered large majorities when voting the annual agricultural prices package. Since the enactment of the Single European Act in 1987, absolute majorities have been required in the cooperation and assent procedures. So poor was parliamentary attendance that some commentators feared the new procedures could not work. In the event, Parliament was obliged (and still is) to set aside one afternoon in the month for voting on Single European Act procedures in order to be sure of the required majorities, but it still sometimes fails to muster a sufficient proportion of its members. (It should be noted in passing that the new co-decision procedure introduced by the Maastricht Treaty, which also requires absolute majorities, has exacerbated this potential problem.)

The poor general levels of attendance in the Parliament can be attributed to a number of different factors. Some commentators point primarily to party political patronage, facilitated by list systems. According to these critics, safe positions on party lists are frequently given to candidates as rewards for loyalty and service to the party, rather than for any ability to carry out the duties of an MEP or, indeed, any enthusiasm about the job. Such beneficiaries of party political patronage have little incentive to attend the Parliament zealously, since they know that their positions on the lists depend on their relationships with their respective central party organisations, rather than their attendance records in Parliament. Whatever the scale of this problem anecdotes abound within the Parliament of conscientious MEPs being fielded low down on their parties' lists or, alternatively, scarcely seen MEPs being fielded high up.

Such loyal servants of political parties are likely to be older and are hence more likely to be discouraged by the large amounts of travel involved in doing the job of an MEP, particularly those representing the more peripheral parts of the Union. This argument applies to a greater or lesser extent to all members of the European Parliament and is frequently cited by those MEPs who would prefer the Parliament to have a single place of work. It certainly helps to explain why attendance at Parliament's week-long plenary sessions peaks steeply in the middle of the week, since MEPs are naturally anxious to leave as late and return as early as possible to their homes, offices and constituencies.

A more fundamental explanation for the low attendance levels at Parliament's plenary sessions is the lack of governmental, or oppositional, incentive. No government stands or falls on a European Parliament vote. On rare occasions (for example, censure motions, rejecting the budget, refusing discharge, assent on enlargement, appointment of the Commission's President), parliamentary votes can be of great political importance, although even then the importance will always tend to be measured in inter-institutional, rather than the more familiar party political, terms. Because of the absence of any direct linkage to government and the Parliament's relatively small legislative role, party discipline is necessarily much looser. Moreover, as the next section will show, the Parliament is innately consensual in character and practice, and this also dilutes the party political incentive that would normally be more prevalent in a national parliament.

Another underlying explanatory factor is the background political culture of the Member State concerned which explains why little of what has gone before applies to UK MEPs. In fact, UK MEPs have a very good attendance record, and very few of them correspond to the model of the prominent political personality outlined above. The reasons for this are bound up in two factors: the electoral system and political culture. All three major political parties establish centrally approved lists of potential candidates, but the selection process itself is decentralised to the respective party organisations at European constituency level. Although the central party organisations can and sometimes do put pressure on Euro-constituency organisations to select certain candidates, the strategy is as likely to backfire, and there were some spectacular examples of just such failures during the selection procedures for the first directly elected Parliament in 1979. For obvious reasons, Euro-constituency organisations tend to prefer candidates with local links, and the result has been a less well-known, but highly accountable, overall membership. The accountability comes not from the elections themselves, since a large proportion of Euro-constituencies are normally safe seats for one party or the other, but from this selection procedure, combined with strongly ingrained political culture. Repeated surveys have shown that, no matter how large their majority, UK MEPs genuinely feel accountable to and responsible for their constituencies and as part of this, and despite a comparatively low level of media attention, they are conscientious attenders.

In this context, the outgoing 1989–94 Parliament scored a significant public relations *coup* in May 1994 in its vote on the principle of the accession to the Union of Austria, Finland, Norway and Sweden. Despite forecasts that the Parliament would find it very hard to muster the required absolute majorities (260 votes), no less than 480 members (of Parliament's total membership of 518) were present in Strasbourg for the vote.

Another striking aspect of the European Parliament's membership is the very high level of turnover. Only about half of the MEPs elected in 1989 had been members of the outgoing Parliament. Of these, only eighty-three had been members since 1979. The average span of membership per MEP has been calculated at just three and a half years (Jacobs and Corbett, 1990, p.43) which is worryingly short, particularly for a young institution (Westlake, 1994a). However, there are distinct variations among different Member States' contingents and, once again, these differences can perhaps best be explained by reference to electoral systems and political culture.

The United Kingdom contingent, for example, has shown the lowest level of turnover. Of the eighty-one MEPs first elected in 1979, thirty-two (40 per cent) still remained in 1993 (although two of these had lost their original seats and were later re-elected elsewhere). This phenomenon has much to do with the single-member constituency system and the fact, stated above, that a majority of constituencies are safe for the incumbent.

Moreover, unlike the list system, the rigidities of the constituency system make it more difficult (though far from impossible) for MEPs to switch to their national political systems. On the other hand, the element of political culture is well illustrated by the fact that twenty-six (32 per cent) of the eighty-one German MEPs first elected in 1979 were still MEPs in 1993. Indeed, fifty-six of the eighty-three MEPs who had been in the Parliament since 1979 came from the United Kingdom and Germany alone. At the other extreme, only six (7.5 per cent) Italian MEPs had served since 1979, and the average length of service of an Italian MEP is just two years (Jacobs and Corbett, 1990, p.44).

The overall effect of these high levels of turnover and low levels of participation has been to reduce the number of 'active' members, and it is to them that we shall now turn. An immediate observation is that the European Parliament has not escaped from the phenomenon, generalised in Western parliamentary democracies, of professionalisation. Politicians tend to come to the Parliament at a younger age and thus are generally less experienced in other walks of life (the presence of prominent personalities offsets this trend to some extent). Their previous professions will tend to have been linked with their political careers. Thus, many MEPs have come to the Parliament via local or regional political office or local political activity. Indeed, for many regionally based politicians, membership of the European Parliament is an extension of their regional political activity. Another sign of professionalisation is the large number of MEPs drawn from the writing and talking professions — teachers, university lecturers, lawyers, writers, journalists, broadcasters: people with vital experience of communication and argument.

One phenomenon, connected with turnover levels, is the use of membership of the European Parliament as a 'stepping stone' to membership of the national parliaments. The phenomenon has been particularly pronounced among UK MEPs; twenty-six of the eighty-one UK MEPs elected in 1979 have since attempted to get selected and elected to Westminster, seventeen of them successfully. However, detailed study of these cases reveals that the phenomenon is less widespread and more difficult than might be thought. Many UK MEPs get selected and elected to the European Parliament because they have been active and are well known in local politics. They get invited to try for selection to Westminster seats for the same reason; of those who were successfully selected by a Westminster constituency, fourteen were selected to a Westminster constituency within their Euro-constituencies. There is little proof that MEPs got themselves elected to Strasbourg as a way of moving on to Westminster. On the other hand, being an MEP, with all the party political privileges and constituency expertise that entails, clearly does help in getting a Westminster selection (see Westlake, 1994a).

There are more women in the European Parliament (about 25 per cent) than in most Member State parliaments, although there are considerable variations among national contingents. As will be seen in Chapter 4, Section 4.3, women's rights are one of the causes championed by the Parliament. At the practical level, this has resulted in the provision of basic facilities (for example, crêches) designed to avoid any potential hindrance of women MEPs' activities. At the political level, women MEPs enjoy strictly equal opportunities. The first president of the directly elected European Parliament, Simone Veil, was a woman, women MEPs regularly occupy many of the most important positions in the Parliament (vice-presidencies, committee chairmanships) and many female members are former ministers or have since gone on to become national ministers. The only limit on the number of female MEPs is imposed by the selection and election procedures within the individual Member States. Here, progress is slowly being made. For example, the French Socialist Party's list for the 1994 European elections was divided on a strictly fifty-fifty basis, with male and female candidates alternating on the list.

Is it possible to follow a political career within the European Parliament? The answer is 'probably, yes', but careers in the Parliament are very different from, say, typical Westminster careers. Parliament's internal rules provide for equitable representation of all groups and nationalities within the institution. In practice, this means that the occupation of most hierarchical positions is the result of careful, consensual calculation among the political groups and among the national contingents within them. Moreover, occupation of such positions is rotated every two and a half years, to provide maximal opportunities during each Parliament's five-year mandate. Typical careers within the European Parliament are thus made by judicious movement from one post to another, always assuming that the necessary political backing is available. A good example of this is provided by Lord Plumb. As Sir Henry Plumb, he was elected to the European Parliament in 1979 as the Conservative MEP for the Cotswolds. As a former President of the National Union of Farmers, he was championed by the British Conservatives and elected Chairman of the European Parliament's Agriculture Committee. A few years later, he was elected President of the European Democratic Group (largely composed of British Conservative members). In 1987, he was elected President of the Parliament.

2.11 The European Parliament and the 'democratic deficit'

It is impossible to study the European Parliament and the electoral link without reference to its vital role in redressing what has become popularly known as the 'democratic deficit'. Opinions vary greatly as to the exact nature and extent of the democratic deficit, and hence as to how it can best be eliminated, but the broad outlines of the problem are clear, and few doubt that the European Parliament has a major role to play in this context.

As was seen in Chapter 1, Section 1.2, the chief normative value of the earliest attempts at European integration was not the promulgation of democracy but the avoidance of war and the guarantee of economic prosperity and social well being. Indeed, one commentator has argued that, ultimately, the ECSC was only acceptable to the Member State governments *because* it was essentially undemocratic (Boyce, 1993, p.468). If not exactly an afterthought, the Common Assembly was considered to be a minor accessory, with its powers restricted to something akin to those of an annual general assembly of shareholders. Democracy at the Community level was in any case largely an irrelevance, since it was still considered to reside primarily in the component units of the Community, the Member States, and through them in their democratically elected parliaments and governments and hence in the Council of Ministers.

At the Member State level, governments and their ministers could be held accountable for their actions to the national parliaments. However, as the process of European integration advanced, the level of decision making in an increasing number of policy areas shifted up to the level of the Community, and thus increasing numbers of decisions were taken away from the traditional national policy-making processes. Government representatives negotiated decisions behind closed doors in the Council. These non-negotiable decisions were then handed down to the national parliaments for scrutiny and approval. Because the Council worked on a basis of unanimity, ministers could still theoretically be held to account, but in 1987 and 1993 the Single European Act and the Maastricht Treaty introduced qualified majority voting to an increasing number of policy areas, so that national representatives could be outvoted. It was no longer sufficient simply to hold individual ministers to account.

In effect, the Council of Ministers has evolved into the Union's primary legislature, but it is unlike traditional legislatures in two important and intimately related respects. Most commentators agree that the fundamental democratic deficit in the European Union is that the Union's primary legislature is neither transparent nor accountable. Laws which were once passed openly in the Member State parliaments are now increasingly passed behind closed doors in the Council, an institution which, as an institution, is accountable to nobody. (Precisely the same argument applies *mutatis mutandis* to the European Council.)

Democratic reformists argue that a first step must be to render the Council's dealings more transparent, and there are gradual moves in this direction. For example, since the October 1992 Birmingham European Council, Council meetings have been preceded by a public session, since the December 1992 Edinburgh European Council the results of certain votes in the Council have been published, and other traditionally secretive Council devices, such as statements in the minutes, are increasingly, if selectively, published.

The European Parliament sees Council transparency as a necessary but insufficient condition for democracy at the Union level. It argues that the Council must be held to account for its decisions. It accepts that greater transparency will make it easier for national parliaments to hold their ministers to account for their part in Council decisions but argues that this can only be part of the equation. As was seen in Chapter 1, Section 1.4, it does not believe that national parliaments can hold the Council to account at Union level. It accepts that ministers meeting in the Council are the legitimate representatives of the Member States, but argues that the Union is derived from a dual legitimacy: that of the states and that of the people. It concludes that the democratic deficit can only be remedied at the level of the Union itself and in particular by a redistribution of powers between the Council and the Parliament. Ultimately, in Parliament's view, this particular aspect of the democratic deficit will not be entirely remedied until the Parliament enjoys full co-legislative powers with the Council, and the co-decision procedure introduced by the Maastricht Treaty is seen therefore as an important step in this direction.

However, in Parliament's view the democratic deficit is not only a matter of the *legislative* powers of the Union's institutions. A further aspect, already mentioned in Chapter 1, Section 1.4, is the Council's idiosyncratic mixture of both legislative and *executive* powers. The European Parliament feels that the Council's continued exercise of such executive powers is undesirable, if not undemocratic, for four principle reasons. In the first place, in a democratic constitutional system of checks and balances, the mixture of legislative and executive powers represents a constitutionally undesirable concentration of power in one institution. Second, in its executive mode, the Council is largely unaccountable whereas, were executive power to reside solely in the Commission (as, the Parliament would argue, the treaties intended), lines of political accountability to the European Parliament would be clear. In the third place, the Parliament would not itself want to hold the Council to account, even if it could do so, for Parliament sees the Council as a future equal co-legislator, and in its view it would be an aberration for one arm of the legislative authority to hold the other to account. (A fourth reason, already touched upon in an earlier analysis and of less relevance here, is that Parliament sees the Council's exercise of executive power through management and consultative committees as a 'back door' reassertion of national sovereignty.)

As was seen above, the broader implications of the new co-decision procedure have led Parliament to shift its position from constitutional purism to a more pragmatic desire for equal executive rights with the Council, but it is perhaps too early to discern any new underlying constitutional logic.

Another important aspect of the democratic deficit concerns the power and accountability of the Commission. The European Parliament has never questioned the treaty-ordained nature of the Commission's powers but has always argued that these were inappropriate in an appointed body. As will be seen in Chapter 3, Section 3.2, successive political decisions and conventions have gradually recognised the logic of this argument. The provisions of the Maastricht Treaty represent a significant step in this direction. As to accountability, the European Parliament has been gradually tightening its control over the Commission over the broad range of its competences, from budgetary discharge through to, say, committees of inquiry, and this trend can be expected to continue, both through changes to the treaties and political convention. It will be recalled that, in Parliament's latest suggested constitutional blueprint for the Union, the Commission would become as accountable as any national executive.

Two other important aspects of the democratic deficit concern the Community's budgetary arrangements and the economic and monetary union process established by the Maastricht Treaty. These aspects will be dealt with in more detail in the next chapter. On the budgetary side, Parliament argues that the Community's revenue should be separate, transparent and fully accountable to the European Parliament rather than, as is currently the case, being subsumed in national budgets and therefore mostly invisible and unaccountable. Furthermore, the Parliament has persistently called for its full powers to be extended across the whole range of Community expenditure. While it accepts the need for an independent Central Bank, the Parliament's chief apprehension with regard to economic and monetary union is what it sees as a lack of parliamentary accountability in the fixing of the Community's economic policy.

Other, less frequently argued, sources of the Union's democratic deficit have included the progressive constitutional role played by the European Court of Justice, the historically elitist nature of European integration and the growth of corporatism at the European level. In all of these cases the Parliament claims or seeks important counterbalancing roles. For example, the Parliament has called for the power to appoint, together with the Council, judges to the Court (see Chapter 1, Section 1.4); Parliament sees itself as the popular linkage with the Union's political elites; and Parliament itself has become the focus of Washington-style lobbying by corporatist interests (see Chapter 4, Section 4.2).

However, there is another, more conceptual, way of considering democratic arrangements in the Union, and the rest of this section is devoted to a brief examination of these fundamental concepts. In modern, populous, complex democratic states, interests are necessarily aggregated. The largest aggregate interests tend to hold sway over smaller interests, although minorities' rights are frequently entrenched. The exact mechanisms for aggregating interests and governing the relationships between larger and smaller interests depends very much on the political and constitutional culture of the state involved. For example, where political representation is determined by a system involving proportional representation, government is frequently by coalition. Such coalitions tend to exaggerate the power of the smaller coalition partner(s) and, in any case, may change fairly frequently. The result is that minorities are frequently involved in the exercise of power, and only politically extreme minorities are continuously excluded. Other political systems enjoy similar levels of legitimacy and popular acceptance while regularly excluding large minorities, and even numerical majorities, from political power. The classic example is the United Kingdom's first-past-the-post electoral system which, notwithstanding its regular exclusion of significant minorities, has never been the object of popular disapproval. The key to the United Kingdom system's legitimacy is its popular acceptance, and this, in turn, is based on a stable political culture with deep historical roots (and particularly strong attachment to the ideas of constituency linkage and strong government).

The European Union is vast, and its political institutions are very young. Its size and youth result in a number of political consequences. The first is that aggregated interests tend to be looser. This could be seen, for example, in the 1994 European manifestos of the two largest traditional European political families, the Socialists and the Christian Democrats, which were necessarily drafted in very general, consensual terms. The second is that minorities are both more numerous and less easily excluded. (This goes a long way towards explaining the proliferation of representative bodies in the Union: the states in the Council, the people in the Parliament, the national parliaments and the European Parliament in the Assises and the COSAC, the regions in the Committee of Regions, the social partners in the Economic and Social Committee and industrial interests in the ECSC's Consultative Committee, to mention only the more well known.) The third, related, consequence is that the Union is an inherently consensual entity; inclusion will always be preferred to exclusion, and consensus will always be preferred to confrontation.

The desire for consensus runs very deep and is indeed entrenched in the treaties. The Parliament, for example, is obliged to muster absolute majorities in the cooperation, codecision and certain assent procedures and even larger majorities for certain budgetary amendments (Table 5 sets out the different majority requirements in the Parliament). Even where simple majorities would be sufficient, the Parliament makes great efforts to muster large, cross-party majorities, and its political and constitutional resolutions are considered weak and ineffectual unless they command such big, and broad, majorities.

Running counter to the proliferation of representative bodies and of levels of popular participation and the constant search for the greatest possible consensus is the efficiency argument. Efficient political systems need clear political messages; multiple levels and institutions may well result in different, perhaps contradictory, and weaker messages (as its critics have gleefully pointed out, the European Parliament has on occasion proved itself capable of adopting contradictory resolutions). Moreover, efficient political systems need relatively strong political institutions whose powers are neither too diluted nor too distorted through the need to share important functions with other institutions. This differential between the imperatives of maximal consensus on the one hand and decision-making efficiency on the other is one of the major fault-lines running through the Union's institutional structure. For example, the decision-making efficiency involved in the Council's constant search for maximal consensus has been a primary explanatory factor in the growth in the role of the European Council.

Such considerations lead in turn to the underlying debate about the constitutional structure of the European Union and hence the roles of the different institutions within it. For a long time, those who were opposed to further European integration were also opposed to the democratisation of the European Community because as was seen in Chapter 1, Section 1.2, it was felt that the creation of a directly elected Parliament would be tantamount to the creation of an institution constantly militating in favour of further centralising integration. Similarly, the pro-integrationists, the European Parliament among them, thought mainly in terms of the gradual creation of a Community of federal type, with increasing powers being exercised at central level. As one commentator has put it, 'the argument over national sovereignty in the Community tended to obscure the conflict between state sovereignty and parliamentary sovereignty' (Shackleton, 1993b, pp.3–4).

In recent years, the debate has moved beyond this simplistic dichotomy. On the one hand, there has been a pragmatic recognition that certain powers and policy making have shifted to the level of the Union and that the European Parliament is better placed than national parliaments to exercise democratic control at that level. With the principle of subsidiarity now enshrined in the treaties (and hence justiciable before the Court of Justice), as well as the subject of several political agreements among the Union institutions, those against an over-centralisation of powers have been more prepared to distinguish between the problem of centralisation and the conceptually distinct, albeit related, problem of democratic control. At the same time, the European Parliament's approach to integration has become more nuanced. Through political debates such as those accompanying the principle of subsidiarity and the creation of the Committee of the Regions, it has not only come to recognise that limits to centralisation are democratically desirable but has itself sought to establish where such limits might lie. Moreover, as was seen in Chapter 1, Section 1.4, the European Parliament has come to accept that parliamentary control cannot be exclusively exercised at the Union level and that cooperation with national parliaments is both necessary and desirable.

As Shackleton has put it, 'the argument over the democratic deficit cannot be separated from the broader debate about whether the [Union] offers a new autonomous level of governance of federal type, whether it remains fundamentally a forum for cooperation between sovereign nation states or whether it offers a new domain for its citizens to participate in the political process' (Shackleton, 1993b, p.1). The Parliament's rhetorical response, repeated at regular intervals, is that the Union needs a once-and-for-all constitutional settlement, in which a constituent assembly (preferably the Parliament itself but at the least involving it) would, Philadelphia Convention-style, adopt a fully worked out constitution which would thereafter govern relations between the component parts and institutions of the Union. Even supposing that at any one time there were basic political agreement among the Member States as to the appropriate degree of integration, such an approach begs a large number of questions about the constitutional structure of the Union.

At the same time, the European Parliament is pragmatically aware of the organic nature of the Union's political and constitutional evolution, a process reliant on occasional inter-governmental conferences in which powers are gained incrementally and never suddenly and in which the ideal almost invariably falls prey to the politically possible. In this perspective, a number of associated trends are discernible. The first is that the European Parliament *is* steadily gaining both more power and new powers and, in the legislative sphere in particular, the Maastricht Treaty has already granted it limited co-legislative rights. The second is that the Council *is* gradually becoming more transparent and more responsive in its dealings with the European Parliament. And, as will be seen in the next section, the new procedures introduced by the Maastricht Treaty oblige the two institutions to work more closely together. The third trend is that the Commission *is* becoming more accountable to the Parliament. (Some interpret this, when taken in conjunction with the Commission's collegiate nature, as an indication that any future Union government is more likely to be along cabinet, rather than presidential lines.) The fourth is that, as was seen in Chapter

1, Section 1.4, Member State parliaments are becoming more involved in scrutinising the Union policy-making process and that parliamentary cooperation in general is increasing. A further inter-governmental conference is foreseen for 1996, and none of these trends is likely to be reversed then.

3

The powers of the European Parliament

3.1   The power of dismissal (the censure motion)

Parliament's oldest power is its strongest, yet paradoxically it has never been used. Under certain conditions, carefully laid down in the treaties and in its own internal Rules of Procedure, Parliament may dismiss the whole Commission. A censure motion must be tabled by one-tenth (fifty-seven) or more of Parliament's membership. The treaties impose a three-day period between the tabling of a censure motion and the vote thereon. The vote must be open and, successfully to dismiss the Commission, Parliament must approve the motion by a two-thirds majority of the votes cast *and* an absolute majority of its full membership. Only seven censure motions have ever been tabled and only three have been tabled since 1979. Five of these were defeated, and two were withdrawn (see Westlake, 1994b, p.30).

As was explained in Chapter 1, Section 1.2, the censure motion was initially conceived as a power that could only be exercised once annually, as a potential sanction of the ECSC's High Authority by the Common Assembly, based on the High Authority's Annual Report. Later, the 1957 EEC and Euratom Treaties and the 1965 Merger Treaty generalised the power, so that ultimately the Parliament could censure the Commission at any moment and on any aspect of its activities. As the power was extended, so Parliament tightened up its own rules, making it increasingly difficult for minorities or maverick coalitions to table censure motions.

Despite, or perhaps because of, the fact that it has never been used, the censure motion lies at the heart of relations between the Commission and the Parliament. Although the successful adoption of a censure motion remains improbable, the Commission is highly sensitive to any suggestion that the power might be used and swift to respond to any underlying complaints. Even casual parliamentary discussion of the possible use of the power is seen as a sanction of sorts. The censure motion has been likened to a nuclear weapon and, to extend this Cold War metaphor, the seven censure motions tabled to date have been a little like the ritual sorties of cruise missiles: proof that the weapon exists rather than of any serious intention to use it.

Despite its apparent power, the censure motion has been criticised for being weak and unwieldy. Some argued that the Council could simply reinstate a censured college, but this avenue, always supposing the Council could have found unanimity for such a controversial move, has since been closed off by the Maastricht Treaty's new provisions on the involvement of the Parliament in the appointment of the Commission (see the next section).

Some argue that the power is so blunt as to be unusable, since Parliament is far more likely to be unhappy with the Commission's behaviour in a particular policy sector rather than with the college as a whole. However, there is nothing to prevent Parliament from adopting critical resolutions on particular policies or sectors (and by implication the Commission member responsible for them), and it is in any case very rare for significantly large numbers of MEPs to be so unsatisfied. More fundamentally, Parliament has fought shy of the concept of sanctions on individual members of the Commission because this would undermine the institution's cabinet-style collegiality and thus prejudice the Union's constitutional development.

Another criticism of the censure motion is that it is misdirected at the Commission, rather than at the Parliament's traditional institutional foe, the Council, and that use of a censure motion against the Commission as a way of sanctioning the Council is constitutionally unclear. (Even the Court's jurisprudence seems to suggest that the Parliament may use the censure of the Commission as an explicit rebuke to the Council.) However, given Parliament's desire to become an equal co-legislator with Council, it is doubtful whether Parliament would wish to go as far as censuring the Council, even were that possibility open to it.

The new provisions of the Maastricht Treaty have greatly enhanced the potential role of the censure motion. In a number of ways, the Commission has been rendered more accountable to the Parliament, and so the ever-present threat of potential sanction is likely to become more relevant. The censure motion is still a long way from the more familiar and much-loved tool of traditional parliamentary oppositions, the vote of confidence, but it will continue to play a central role in the Union's political and constitutional development.

3.2 The power of appointment (consultation)

The Commission and its President

It is no exaggeration to assert that the Maastricht Treaty has fundamentally changed the nature of the relationship between the Commission and the Parliament. As from January 1995, the Commission's mandate will be extended from four to five years and synchronised with that of the Parliament. As from the autumn of 1994, the Member States will continue, unanimously, to nominate the President of the Commission, but they will have to consult the Parliament on their nominee. Moreover, the other members of the Commission will be appointed in consultation with the presidential nominee. Most fundamentally, the nominated Commission and its President will be subject as a body to a vote of approval by the Parliament and only then appointed (unanimously) by the Member States.

This is a very new power, yet to be exercised, and it is impossible to predict exactly how it will unfold in practice. However, Parliament's new Rules of Procedure, adopted in September 1993, and a resolution on the matter adopted 21 April 1994, give a clear indication as to its thinking on the matter. The Council's presidential nominee will be invited before the Parliament and requested to make a policy statement. The statement will be followed by a debate, and by a roll-call vote. Presumably, Parliament will look at the candidate's thinking on the major issues confronting the Union and some indication of his or her plans for the next five years, as well as seeking a substantial echo of its own concerns and policy priorities. The Maastricht Treaty says nothing about the consequences of a negative parliamentary opinion at this stage, but it would clearly be politically difficult, if not impossible, for the Council to proceed to the nomination of the other members of the Commission if Parliament had already rejected the presidential nominee. (The real strength of Parliament's consultative power is more likely to be implicit, inasmuch as the Council and the individual Member States will avoid proposing candidates who are likely to encounter problems; the Parliament may develop informal mechanisms for making its 'pre-consultation' views clear.)

Though not mentioned in the treaty, from Parliament's point of view, the second stage in the procedure will be the debate and adoption of its own policy priorities, which it will then use to influence the policy goals of the nominated Commission.

According to Parliament's rules, individual proposed candidates would then be invited to appear before the parliamentary committee matching their prospective field of responsibility. These provisions are likely to cause considerable difficulty, since the distribution of portfolios among the seventeen members of the Commission has traditionally been one of the most fraught and complex tasks of the President-designate, normally accomplished only at the eleventh hour. Parliament's thinking is that individual nominees should be put forward as a function of their specialities and that the distribution of portfolios among Commission members (and, by implication, among Member States) should take place at a much earlier stage in the nomination procedure. Parliament may even try to force the President-designate's hand by inviting individual nominees to appear before one committee rather than another. As to the individual hearings in committee, Parliament would appear to have modelled its proceedings on the 'confirmation hearings' of the United States' Congress, with two basic levels of inquiry: the qualifications, probity and appropriateness of the candidate, and the candidate's policy outlook.

The final step would be for the President-designate to present the programme of the designated Commission to the Parliament, followed by a debate and a vote. Parliament's intentions throughout this procedure are clear: it will seek to have the maximum possible policy input into the new Commission's plans at the outset and will thereafter seek to hold the Commission to them. As one notable commentator, for twenty-eight years Secretary General of the Commission, has put it:

> This group of measures considerably increases the Parliament's ability to exercise political control over the work of the Commission: the part played by the Parliament in the appointment of the Commissioners will . . . be made on the basis of a legislative programme which will in turn give full significance to any possible motion of censure. These measures will lead also and perhaps especially to the accentuation of the political character of the Commission. Very soon the preliminary approval of its membership by the Parliament will be the decisive factor; the final appointment by the governments will retain only a formal character (Noël, 1992b, p.115).

Noël's analysis has been confirmed by one of the European Parliament's most distinguished constitutionalists, Sir Christopher Prout:

> . . . it is no exaggeration to say that the extension of the term of office of the Commission from four to five years and the acquisition by Parliament of a veto over the appointment of the new Commission have transformed the constitutional balance of power between Parliament and the Commission. If we have the political courage to use this new weapon — and we have drafted a pre-appointment advice and consent procedure in [our] Rules — it should in future be impossible for the European Council to pursue a legislative programme which does not reflect the will of Parliament. Moreover, the political complexion of a new Parliament should be reflected in the composition of the Commission (European Parliamentary Debates OJ N 3-434, 14 September 1993, pp.39–40).

117

Thus, although it is a technical inaccuracy to talk about the Parliament's powers as those of appointment (rather than approval), in practice Parliament will in future have a powerful say in the appointment of individuals and the college as a whole. In the longer term, the way lies open for Parliament to make its own proposals about suitable candidates. Some MEPs have already argued that the political groups should field their own candidates for the Presidency of the Commission during the European elections and others that all candidates should be drawn from among Parliament's membership (most Commissions to date have sported a sprinkling of former members of the European Parliament). Either of these steps would represent a significant move towards the traditional party political, government–parliament model.

The members of the Court of Auditors

After repeated calls from the Parliament, the Court of Auditors was brought into being in 1975, and became a fully fledged Union institution with the entry into force of the Maastricht Treaty in November 1993. The Court's twelve members are appointed unanimously by the Council on the basis of recommendations from the Member States and after having consulted the Parliament. On the face of it, Parliament's consultative rights are very weak since, like all other consultation procedures, the Council is not obliged juridically to take any account of the opinion expressed by the Parliament. In practice, however, Parliament may on occasion have a strong say in the appointment of the Court's members, depending on the sensibilities of particular Member States.

In November 1989, when Parliament was consulted on the appointment or reappointment of six candidates, it felt 'unable to give a favourable opinion' in respect of two of them, the French and Greek candidates. Much to the Parliament's satisfaction, the French government withdrew and replaced its candidate. The Greek government, which was in the middle of a political crisis, claimed it was unable to find a more suitable candidate. Parliament let the Greek candidature stand, but it felt that an important precedent had been set. In December 1993, Parliament was again requested by the Council to give its opinion on the appointment or reappointment of six candidates. It approved four and, more boldly than in 1989, expressly did not approve two of the candidatures. However, on this occasion the governments concerned (Italian and Portugese) did not withdraw their candidates, and all six appointments were confirmed by the Council. The behaviour of the two governments concerned was a disappointment to the Parliament, since the French government's action in 1989 had led it to believe that it had acquired a *de facto* veto power over such appointments. However, the

Member States and the Council acted entirely within their prerogatives, and the Parliament could do little more than regret that its opinion had on this occasion been discounted.

As with its other appointment procedures, Parliament's 'confirmation hearings' of candidates for the Court of Auditors loosely follow the American model. Candidates are invited to appear before Parliament's specialised Budgetary Control Committee, meeting in special session. Candidates are then questioned about their qualifications and experience, and their appropriateness is ascertained. As with all other 'confirmation hearings', save that of the Parliamentary Ombudsman, Parliament's procedures are based on a simple logic. Candidates are under no obligation to accept Parliament's invitations to appear before it, but a candidate who refused to appear would stand very little chance of winning parliamentary approval. Thus, an apparently weak power was rapidly transformed into a potentially strong power. However, as was seen in Chapter 1, Section 1.3, the Parliament strongly believes and will continue to insist that it should have assent powers ('confirmation powers') over such appointments, and its most recent experiences, where Member States ignored its opinions, have confirmed that belief.

The President of the European Monetary Institute

Following the entry into force of the Maastricht Treaty, Stage II of the process of Economic and Monetary Union began on 1 January 1994 (see Section 3.6 of this chapter). Measures for Stage II included the establishment of a European Monetary Institute, which has as its principal duties to coordinate monetary policies and prepare the Union for the transition to Stage III. In reality, it is generally seen as the forerunner of the European Central Bank which will be created the day Economic and Monetary Union comes into being.

In a fresh departure, the treaty provided that the President of the EMI should be appointed unanimously by the European Council (that is, the heads of state and government), on a recommendation from the central bank governors, after consulting the European Parliament and the Council. Although it soon became clear that the European Council's decision would be little more than a formality, based on the Council's recommendation (that is, the 'ECOFIN' Council, made up of the ministers of economics and finance), the treaty significantly granted the Parliament equal consultative rights with the Council.

The central bank governors' recommended candidate, nominated in October 1993, was a deeply experienced, highly respected and widely admired Belgian banker, Baron Alexandre Lamfalussy, and there was never any doubt about his appropriateness for the position. There was thus some political pressure on the Parliament to give rapid approval to his candidature. The specialised parliamentary committee in this case, the Committee for Economic and Monetary Affairs and Industrial Policy, together with its Sub-Committee on Monetary Affairs, refused to bow to the pressure, and an appropriate hearing procedure was carefully elaborated. This time the Parliament modelled itself directly on the United States Senate's confirmation hearing for the nominee to the position of Chairman of the Federal Reserve. (A fact-finding mission to Washington by the Monetary Sub-Committee's Chairwoman, Frau Randzio-Plath, had enabled her and an accompanying member of the Sub-Committee's secretariat to study the matter in detail.) The candidate was sent a written questionnaire and invited to respond. He was then invited to a formal hearing in committee where he, and his responses, were subjected to further questioning. The Committee then voted a positive recommendation which, in November 1993, was confirmed by the Parliament as a whole.

The EMI is a transitional body, and so it is unlikely that Parliament will again be invited to pronounce on an EMI presidential nominee, but the importance of the parliamentary procedure lies in the precedent it sets for appointments to the Executive Board of the future European Central Bank. These will be made by the European Council, acting on a recommendation from the Council, after it has consulted the Central Bank's Governing Council (made up of the governors of the Member States' Central Banks) and the European Parliament. In taking the appointment of the EMI presidential nominee so seriously, Parliament was setting out its role and an important line of accountability in the future Economic and Monetary Union.

The Parliamentary Ombudsman

The Maastricht Treaty has granted the European Parliament significant appointment power in one other area of its activities. The European Parliament alone has the power to appoint an Ombudsman who is empowered to receive complaints from any citizen of the Union or any resident natural or legal person concerning instances of maladministration in the activities of the Community institutions or bodies (see Section 3.8 of this chapter). The creation of an Ombudsman is an important step in the establishment of European citizenship, and the Parliament's appointment power is a natural corollary of its closeness, through European elections, to the European people.

The Maastricht Treaty (Article 138e) provides that the European Parliament shall appoint the Ombudsman, that he (or she) 'shall be appointed after each election of the European Parliament for the duration of its term of office' and that he (or she) 'may be dismissed by the Court of Justice at the request of the European Parliament'. These bare bones were fleshed out in an October 1993 agreement between the Parliament and the other institutions, but the Parliament alone will remain responsible for the Ombudsman's appointment.

3.3 Budgetary powers

Amending and enacting the budget

In one important respect, the European Parliament is far from being a true parliament in the traditionally recognised sense of that term, although it does nevertheless have considerable budgetary powers. The discrepancy is bound up in the particular way in which the Union budget is decided.

In the first place, historically based sayings such as 'no taxation without representation' and 'the power of the purse strings' suggest that parliaments have a primary role to play in authorising and scrutinising the level and the method of government revenue and hence of expenditure. In the case of the United Kingdom, for example, the granting of parliamentary powers and budgetary control were a *quid pro quo*, a concession made by the Crown in return for the right to raise revenue in addition to its own. But for much of the European Community's early life its expenditure was decided by Member States' ministers meeting, without any direct reference to Parliament, in the Council. Similarly, until 1970, the Community's revenue consisted of contributions drawn from the Member States' national budgets, again without any parliamentary control on the overall amounts involved. Since 1970 the European Parliament has gained increasing power over expenditure, but the European Union's revenue has remained largely beyond its grasp.

In the second place, traditional budgetary processes in the Member States look first to available revenue before deciding on the distribution of expenditure, the chief constraint on revenue-raising in modern democracies being the unpopularity of increasing taxes. But in the European Union the traditional relationship between revenue and expenditure is reversed; expenditure is first decided and revenue is then made available as a function of it. This reverse system has probably failed to attract popular criticism for a number of reasons, but principally because the amounts involved are relatively small, and even smaller when split up between the Member States. In addition, the Union's own resources, made up as they are of customs duties, agricultural levies and a percentage of the VAT base, are innately obscure.

On the expenditure side, the European Parliament's role is only partial. There is an obvious reason for this: the vast bulk of taxation and

121

expenditure within the Union (including defence, education, health and social welfare) is still conducted at the level of the Member States and is therefore subject to the authorisation and scrutiny of the Member State parliaments. In addition, many of the Union's activities (particularly legislation) do not in themselves involve much expenditure or, if they do, require such expenditure at the level of the Member States rather than the Union itself.

The European Union's budget, as a percentage of the Union's total GDP (that is, the sum total of the GDPs of the twelve Member States), amounts to just 1.22 per cent (1.24 per cent forecast for 1994). This can be compared with the United States' federal budget, which stands at roughly 2 per cent. In 1977, a report commissioned by the EC Commission (MacDougall, 1975) recommended that the EC Budget should be increased to about 2.5 per cent of EC GDP. It was thought such a level would have a snowball effect on the pace of integration of the EC, as such a level would necessarily entail large-scale Community-level policies and redistribution programmes. The traditional fiscal conservatism of Member State governments aside, a powerful reason for the small size of the Union's budget at Union level has precisely been the fear shared by certain Member States that increases in the Union's budget would encourage the integration/federalisation process. Indeed, the tension between devolved expenditure and proposals for further centralisation is a constant dynamic within the Union's political process. On the one side are ranged arguments about sovereignty, subsidiarity, fiscal orthodoxy and the danger of relaxed levels of public expenditure and on the other arguments about efficiency and, above all, economies of scale. An important knock-on effect of the small size of the Union budget is that the European Parliament's relatively limited powers apply to only a very small proportion of total revenue and expenditure within the European Union. In turn, an important consequence of this, as will be seen below, is that the Parliament has a vested interest in militating in favour of a larger Union budget and hence the transfer of resources from the Member State governments to the Union.

As was seen in Chapter 1, Section 1.2, the European Parliament first acquired significant budgetary powers with the creation of the Community's 'own resources' in 1970 (the Union's own resources are now made up of customs duties and agricultural levies on imports from outside the Union, together with a proportion of national VAT receipts and a 'fourth resource', created in 1988, similar to national contri-butions). Although the Member States determined the upper limit of the own resources, the resources belonged solely to the Community, which had thus gained an independent source of revenue. Until then, democratic control had been exercised exclusively by the Member State parliaments. The creation of financial resources flowing directly to the Community by-passed this control which could logically only be replaced by the granting of similar powers to the European Parliament (a similar logic had lain behind the Commission's 1965 proposals which had so infuriated de Gaulle). Parliament's budgetary powers were consolidated by further treaties (1975, 1977) and by decisions or agreements between the institutions (1972, 1975, 1982, 1985, 1988 and 1993). Today, the Parliament and the Council, respectively representing the people and the states, constitute the twin arms of the budgetary authority. Only the European Parliament's president may sign the Union budget into law, a power confirmed by the European Court of Justice's jurisprudence. Nevertheless, there are significant limitations on Parliament's budgetary role and a great imbalance as between the powers of the two institutions.

The most important limitation derives from a basic distinction between 'compulsory' and 'non-compulsory' Union expenditure. 'Compulsory' expenditure is defined as all expenditure necessarily resulting from the treaties or from acts adopted in accordance with the treaties and broadly includes all agricultural expenditure, refunds to Member States and expenditure arising from international agreements with third countries. 'Non-compulsory' expenditure is all the rest, including the structural funds. The distinction exists chiefly because, at the time when the first budgetary reforms were enacted in 1970, the French government was not prepared to grant the European Parliament strong budgetary powers in a policy area (agriculture) which it considered, as it still does today, a vital national interest. The distinction imposes a double limitation on the Parliament.

The first restriction is what the European Parliament has always seen as a largely arbitrary differentiation between 'compulsory' expenditure, where the Parliament has little power, and 'non-compulsory' expenditure, where is has far greater powers — indeed, the last word — to amend and direct expenditure. The second, quantitative limitation is that 'compulsory' expenditure, and above all agricultural expenditure, has always taken a lion's share of the budget. Thus, Parliament has only ever had significant powers over a fraction of the Union's budget, as Table 6 illustrates.

Historically, this stark fact has had three consequences. The first has been that, arguments about centralism and devolution aside, Parliament has had a vested interest in encouraging increases in overall expenditure since, if such increases were not in themselves linked to increases in non-compulsory expenditure, they would at least offset the inexorable annual increases in compulsory expenditure and above all the financing of the Common Agricultural Policy. The second consequence has been increasing pressure within Parliament to somehow limit the apparently uncontrollable increases in compulsory expenditure and hence, gradually, increasing acceptance of the need for reform of the Common Agricultural Policy so as to leave breathing space for other policies and activities, and particularly those the Parliament itself has championed (see Chapter 4, Section 4.3). The third logical consequence has been repeated attacks by the Parliament on the distinction between compulsory and non-compulsory expenditure, with attempts to reduce the potential scope of compulsory expenditure or at least to blur the distinction. As will be seen, in all three areas Parliament's efforts have met with only mixed success.

The process by which the Union draws up its budget, as provided for by the treaties, is a complicated procedure involving at least two readings in the Council and the Parliament, with differentiated powers and majority requirements as a function of the reading stage and the category of expenditure involved. A series of treaty amendments and inter-institutional agreements smoothed out many of the problems involved, but the procedure remained fraught with difficulties and inter-institutional clashes until 1988, when a revolutionary inter-institutional agreement radically altered the budgetary procedure (see Westlake, 1994b, p.34). Nevertheless, to understand how the Parliament has tried, with mixed results, to extend its budgetary powers, it is necessary to go back briefly to the pre-1988 budgetary process.

The treaties provide for the establishment of two separate ceilings on expenditure: the overall amount of own resources and (with regard to non-compulsory expenditure only) an annual maximum rate, with the latter theoretically falling within and beneath the former. Until 1988, the size of the Community's budget on the compulsory expenditure side was self-determined, as a consequence of the conjunction of the Council's decisions on support prices for agricultural products and world market prices for the same products. On the non-compulsory side the treaties specified, as they still do, that expenditure can increase from one year to the next by no more than what is called *the maximum rate of increase*. This maximum rate is calculated by the Commission on a statistical basis, taking account of standard indicators such as economic growth, government expenditure and the rate of inflation. Parliament has the right to draft entries into the budget up to an amount equal to half of the maximum rate. In practice, this has amounted to amounts of the order of 300 to 400 million ECUs (£225m to £300m at January 1994 exchange rates) which, although relatively small in comparison with the overall budget, represents a significant economic influence, especially if viewed cumulatively.

However, Parliament was aware that its economic influence could be increased if the maximum rate of increase itself could be increased, as the treaties allow for the Council and the Parliament so to do, by common agreement and if certain, relatively easy, conditions are met (qualified majority in Council, absolute majority and three-fifths of the votes cast in the Parliament). These conditions contrast starkly with the far 'heavier' conditions required to increase the overall amount of own resources (ratification in the twelve Member States and unanimity in the Council). The result was that the Parliament spent much of the 1980s up to 1988 trying to convince the Council to agree to an increase in the maximum rate. The Council found it difficult to accede to such requests, not only because of its traditional fiscal conservatism, heightened by economic depression and monetary problems in many Member States, but also because compulsory expenditure, chiefly in the shape of agricultural expenditure, was spiralling upwards, apparently beyond control. This led on several occasions to situations where the Community budget scraped against the upper limit of overall own resources. Inter-institutional tension reached a peak in 1985, when Parliament's president deliberately signed a budget that unilaterally went more than 600 million ECUs beyond the previously established maximum rate figure. The Parliament argued that the Council had failed to provide adequate finance, with Spain and Portugal shortly to join the Community and a build-up of payment commitments from previous years. The Council took the Parliament to Court and won, with the Court ruling that any new maximum rate had to be explicitly agreed between the two arms (Council and Parliament) of the budgetary authority (see Table 1). Parliament was to take the lessons of this experience to heart, lessons which led directly to the 1988 and 1993 inter-institutional agreements.

The 1988 inter-institutional agreement, which devolved from and relied upon a series of decisions taken at the level of the European Council, radically changed the nature of the budgetary process in a number of fundamental ways. In effect, the heads of state and government agreed to a new framework for Community financing which allowed for a major expansion in the revenue available to the Community, while imposing restraints on the expansion of certain types of expenditure and in particular on agricultural expenditure. The inter-institutional agreement set out 'financial perspectives' until 1992. It provided for a doubling of the structural funds by 1992 and, since such increases took the non-compulsory element of the budget way beyond the maximum rate, was tantamount to a prior agreement between the twin arms of the budgetary authority to increase the maximum rate. The inter-institutional agreement set out expenditure, and maximum annual increases in non-compulsory expenditure, by category. Above all, the inter-institutional agreement was predicated on reform of the Common Agricultural Policy.

As is effectively the case with all inter-institutional agreements, the individual institutions made substantial concessions in return for perceived substantial advantages yet, because of the relatively long time-span involved and the notorious difficulty in calculating the Community's basic statistics, an element of gambling was involved by both the Council and the Parliament.

The Parliament made two significant concessions. First, it was impossible to calculate with any certainty what the true maximum rate of increase might be in future years. By tying itself in to previously established maximum rates of increase for five years, the Parliament was potentially forgoing the full extent of its possible powers on the non-compulsory expenditure side. Second, because the inter-institutional agreement established expenditure patterns by *category* of expenditure, Parliament could no longer move money around from category to category on the non-compulsory expenditure side as would have been possible previously.

The Council also made two chief concessions. The first, a mirror-image of the Parliament's calculation, was to tie itself in to previously established increases in the maximum rate which might in reality, far outstrip what would otherwise have been the case. The second was to agree to constraints on the rate of increase of compulsory expenditure. (There was some irony in this: the Council had originally sought to ring fence the Common Agricultural Policy against any increase in Parliament's powers, and now the Parliament sought to ring fence the Common Agricultural Policy precisely in order to increase its powers.)

Both sides made substantial gains. The greatest was mutual budgetary peace, which both recognised as a necessary condition if the 1992 programme on the realisation of a true internal market (a shared aim but particularly dear to the Council) and a series of flanking policies were to be realised on time. Both the ultimate doubling of the structural funds and the constraints on agricultural expenditure were clear gains for the Parliament. Increases in structural fund expenditure had been a consistent policy aim of the Parliament and, it will be recalled, such expenditure was non-compulsory and hence subject to more extensive parliamentary control. Constraints on agricultural expenditure would meanwhile leave more headroom for non-compulsory expenditure, again increasing Parliament's role and facilitating expenditure on its own policy priorities.

So successful and mutually acceptable was the 1988–92 prototype inter-institutional agreement that a new inter-institutional agreement was signed to cover the 1993–9 period. The agreement is based on the same principle as the 1988 agreement: that is, the mutual agreement of financial perspectives by category of expenditure, entailing prior acceptance by both arms of the budgetary authority of the annual maximum rates of increase for non-compulsory expenditure within each category. A major hiccough in the 1988 agreement occurred as a result of German unification in 1990 which resulted in a large amount of unforeseen, and therefore unagreed, expenditure. The 1993 agreement overcame such potential problems through a series of built-in conditional revision clauses. The financial framework will be reviewed in the event of enlargement, and the whole content of the agreement will be re-examined at the 1996 inter-governmental conference (as foreseen by the Maastricht Treaty). In addition, after its installation in January 1995, the new Commission (over which the Parliament hopes to exercise greatly increased influence) may also propose a revision of the agreement and the financial perspectives. All of these possibilities are in addition to the workings of a mutually agreed annual mechanism for the revision of the financial perspectives.

The 1993–9 inter-institutional agreement will almost certainly be replaced by another, and so there is good reason to believe that the old-style Council–Parliament battles about increases in the maximum rate, with spectacular rejections and occasional spillovers into the Court, have given way to a more subtle (and probably more obscure) but ultimately more effective strategy of slow but constant advance.

How successful has the Parliament been in realising its strategic objectives? In the first place, and despite the reluctance of some Member State governments, there have been considerable increases in the overall size of the Union budget, the most striking increases occurring as an integral part of the 1988 and 1993 inter-institutional agreements. However, it is impossible to calculate whether the increases in the annual maximum rates for non-compulsory expenditure foreseen in the inter-institutional agreements amount to more than Parliament might otherwise have been able to achieve in a traditional, annual budgetary procedure. (But this, as pointed out, was part of Parliament's 'gamble'.)

In the second place, Parliament has had some success in increasing non-compulsory expenditure and in decreasing compulsory expenditure as overall proportions of the budget. Once again, though, the inter-institutional agreements have played a vital role in this process. As Table 6 shows, the percentage of compulsory expenditure (though not the absolute amounts involved) as a proportion of overall expenditure had decreased regularly since 1988 (at the same time the absolute amounts of non-compulsory expenditure doubled in the 1988–91 period). Thus, the consensual approach of the inter-institutional agreement has been far more effective than Parliament's previous unilateral and essentially adversarial attempts to increase non-compulsory expenditure. This is not to imply that these previous attempts were entirely without success. Under the treaties, if the Parliament proposes an amendment which involves a decrease in expenditure, or an increase which is compensated for by a decrease elsewhere, the Council needs to muster a qualified majority to reject it (in contrast with proposals to increase expenditure, which fall unless approved by a qualified majority in the Council). Parliament had some success in creating new budgetary 'lines' and in favouring its preferred policies but has now at least temporarily foresworn the full scope of these powers by signing up to the inter-institutional agreement. Moreover, now that the argument is no longer about the principal of agricultural reform but more about the degree, Parliament will hope to see continued declines in the proportions of compulsory expenditure, and in this context the protagonists of its budgetary strategy have taken heart from the Blair House agreement between the European Union and the United States and the inclusion of agriculture in the successfully concluded GATT Uruguay Round.

Parliament has also seen gradual progress in reducing the scope, and blurring the distinction, of compulsory expenditure. It has repeatedly pointed out the inconsistencies in the basic distinction, and from a parliamentary perspective it has frequently seemed that the Council was defending the distinction on inter-institutional grounds rather than with reference to a coherent principle. Once again, the inter-institutional agreements and the linked agricultural reforms have been of great importance. A key to the 1988 agreement was the acceptance of constraint on compulsory expenditure. As a function of the 1993 inter-institutional agreement, the Council agreed that all structural fund and internal policy expenditure constituted non-compulsory expenditure. And as a function of the division of expenditure into non-transitive categories with separate upper limits, the distinction has become less relevant and the difference in Parliament's powers less stark. Parliament has persistently called upon the Council to renounce the distinction and has hopes of progress in this direction at the 1996 inter-governmental conference (see Chapter 4, Section 4.4).

Another area of Council–Parliament tension in the budgetary field concerns the nature of the relationship between legislative activity and budgetary provision. Where Parliament's legislative powers are limited or non-existent, it has sought to achieve a pseudo-legislative role via the budget. When Parliament was first granted budgetary powers, it argued that where money had been entered in the budget by the budgetary authority this had to be implemented by the Commission. But the Council argued that the budget alone was not a sufficient legal base and that the Commission could only act within an established legislative framework (with the Council having almost exclusive legislative powers). In 1982, the three institutions signed a joint declaration which specified that a legislative base was required for 'significant new Community actions', and the institutions agreed to use their best endeavours to establish an appropriate legislative framework by May of the financial year concerned. But the agreement was ambiguous. The two key terms, 'significant' and 'new', were open to conflicting interpretations, and it frequently proved impossible to establish an appropriate legislative framework in good time. On the other side of the budgetary coin, as agricultural expenditure spiralled, it seemed that the amounts provided in the budget could be exceeded if the legislation adopted by the Council made extra budgetary provision necessary. Under persistent parliamentary pressure the Council ultimately agreed that, where the financial provision for a legislative act was not available, the policy could only be implemented once the budget had been suitably amended (and hence once Parliament had had its say). The primacy of budgetary decisions over the financial implications of legislative decisions has now been firmly enshrined in budgetary orthodoxy via the 1988 and 1993 inter-institutional agreements. Moreover, the Maastricht Treaty has introduced a provision whereby 'with a view to maintaining budgetary discipline, the Commission shall not make any proposal for a Community act, or alter its proposals, or adopt any implementing measure which is likely to have appreciable implications for the budget without providing the assurance that that proposal or that measure is capable of being financed within the limit of the Community's own resources'. To some extent, Parliament's concern to establish pseudo-legislative powers through the budget was a function of its lack of true legislative powers. Since it has gained some legislative power, and particularly since the implementation of the Single European Act in 1987, Parliament has placed less emphasis on this use of its budgetary powers. However, it will continue to argue for a more equitable, and more democratic, distribution of powers between itself and the Council.

In fact, as was pointed in Chapter 2, Section 2.1, Parliament sees the whole issue of its budgetary powers as an important (if complex and frequently arcane) aspect of the European Union's democratic deficit. It sees its exclusion from proper control over a majority of expenditure on the basis of an inconsistent distinction as undemocratic, and consistently calls for its powers to be extended to cover all expenditure.

However, Parliament sees the revenue side as the fundamental root of the problem. It recognises that the European public is largely unaware of the Union's budgetary process but sees this as a direct result of the fact that the Union's revenue is linked to and calculated on the basis of national budgets; in other words, there is no direct link with the taxpayer, who is also for the most part the voter.

In Parliament's view, the self-evident way to overcome this lack of popular linkage would be to create a Union tax, levied directly by the Union, so that the voter/tax payer could see exactly how much the Union was costing and might begin to want to have a say, expressed via his parliamentary representative, as to *how* that money should be spent. This is why, despite the opacity of the jargon involved and inherent complexity and obscurity, many parliamentary insiders see Parliament's budgetary strategy as a primary long-term key to giving European elections true popular political significance.

The European Parliament had hoped that the Commission might propose such a 'fifth resource' (in the jargon) in the context of the budgetary reforms accompanying the implementation of the Maastricht Treaty (a carbon tax was mentioned as a possibility). In the event, the Commission's reforms, though far-reaching, did not go so far. In its reaction to this disappointment and the implementation of the

Maastricht Treaty, the Parliament decided to propose an inter-institutional conference in the course of 1994 to consider the whole system of the Union's resources with a view to the 1996 inter-governmental conference. The Council has agreed to participate in this conference, which may well result in embryonic proposals for reform.

Rejecting the budget

Until relatively recently, any account of Parliament's budgetary powers would probably have begun with its power to reject the draft budget (together with any supplementary budgets). Yet today parliamentary rejection of the budget has become, if anything, a more distant prospect than a motion of censure. The treaties provide that the Parliament may reject the budget (by a majority of its members and two-thirds of the votes cast) if there are 'important reasons'. The old, appointed Parliament eschewed this right, but the directly elected Parliament rejected the budget in the first year of its existence (1979), rejected a supplementary budget in 1982 and rejected the whole draft budget again in 1984. The Community seemed set fair for further budgetary storms for the rest of the century, but since 1984 Parliament has never again come near to rejecting the budget.

The chief reasons for this are derived from the ambiguity of the treaties, which describe how Parliament may reject the budget but do not really explain what should happen next. In practice, parliamentary rejections have always pushed the budgetary procedure beyond the end of the current budgetary year. If a budget has not been adopted by the beginning of the relevant financial year, the treaties provide that the Union should enter into a system of 'provisional twelfths', whereby 'a sum equivalent to not more than one-twelfth of the budget appro-priations for the preceding financial year may be spent each month'.

This system effectively penalised Parliament in two ways. In the first place, it meant that all of its first- and second-reading amendments to the draft budget fell with the rejection of that budget, so that the envisaged payments were at best delayed and at worst diminished or lost. In the second place, the system of 'provisional twelfths' applied to all sections of the budget, including the section devoted to Parliament's own, internal budget. This could have awkward consequences for a young and ambitious institution with an expanding staff.

Again, because of the treaties' ambiguities, the advantages of rejection for the Parliament were not particularly evident. The precise treaty wording seems to suggest that the whole budgetary cycle of draft budget and first and second readings should begin again. In practice, the institutions agreed to a sort of third reading, based on a new Commission draft designed to reconcile the positions of the two arms of the budgetary authority. A new budget could only ever be agreed through the mutual consent of the Council and the Parliament, and this meant that the Parliament would ultimately always be obliged to negotiate. Negotiations inevitably entailed concessions and movement away from initial bargaining positions. Moreover, the Council was in practice better placed than the Parliament to 'sit out' any budgetary crisis caused by parliamentary rejection. And so it gradually became apparent to Parliament that, although there was some institutional kudos and valuable publicity to be had in rejecting the budget, the policy advantages were undermined by the provisional twelfths system and the ultimate need to arrive at a compromise.

Since the signing of the first inter-institutional agreement in 1988, parliamentary rejection of the budget has been rendered even more improbable, although both arms of the budgetary authorities have underlined that their treaty-based budgetary rights remain unchanged. The improbability derives from the wording of the treaties, which speak of 'important reasons' for rejection. Indeed, for as long as the Parliament is voluntarily engaged in and bound to a consensual inter-institutional agreement, it is difficult to see what might constitute a sufficiently important reason for rejection.

For the time being, at least, the power to reject the budget has become a reserve power, like the censure motion. Unlike the censure motion, Parliament has proved that it is prepared to use the power, if necessary, but that necessity currently seems remote.

Implementation and scrutiny

Once the two arms of the budgetary authority have agreed the Community's budget, and once the president of Parliament has signed it into existence, the Commission alone becomes responsible for implementing the vast bulk of the operational budget (the treaties stipulate 'on its own responsibility and within the limits of the appropriations, having regard to the principles of sound management') but with the Parliament exercising constant scrutiny. This it does in a number of ways.

First, should it prove necessary to transfer money during the budgetary year the Commission must ask the permission of the budgetary authority, with the Parliament having the last word where non-compulsory expenditure is concerned. In practice, the need for such transfers often occurs, and the Commission is therefore frequently called upon to justify its requests before the specialised parliamentary committee on budgets. On occasion, Parliament uses its powers to block or delay expenditure.

Second, in approving the budget, Parliament may put money into a 'reserve' from whence it can only be liberated with the agreement of the budgetary authority. Again, Parliament has the last word where non-compulsory expenditure is concerned. Parliament frequently uses the reserve as a bargaining device, exacting concessions from the Commission as to precisely how money will be spent in return for the release of that money. Parliament may also use the reserve where it does not wish to block expenditure but is uncertain about the levels proposed. This can happen, for example, in regard to proposed staffing levels, with Parliament releasing money from the reserve only when it is convinced that the extra staff are required.

Third, in adopting the budget Parliament has the power to amend the 'remarks' accompanying each line of expenditure. These remarks specify the use to which the money is to be put. Parliament regards these as binding and is at pains to check that the Commission fully respects them.

Fourth, Parliament has always followed the implementation of the budget as part of its preparations for the following year's budget. Until the 1988 inter-institutional agreement, each autumn saw a detailed debate, on the basis of a Commission statement, about the implementation of the current budget (the procedure is known as the 'Notenboom procedure', after the Dutch MEP, Harry Notenboom, who first proposed it). The purpose of this procedure is to enable Parliament to see where money earmarked for particular purposes has not been fully spent and to establish why. (Since expenditure can not be carried over from one year to the next, unspent money is effectively lost.)

Fifth, Parliament's scrutiny of the implementation of the budget has taken on fresh importance since the signing of the 1988 and 1993 inter-institutional agreements. The Notenboom procedure has now effectively been extended into a year-round exercise. The Commission forwards monthly reports to the Parliament on the implementation of the budget, and it also forwards 'early warning' reports on agricultural expenditure. The reason for this is clear: the Parliament wants the earliest possible warning if compulsory expenditure seems likely to exceed its previously agreed financial envelope so that corrective action can be taken and, if necessary, revision of the envelope made to prevent any encroachment on the non-compulsory financial envelopes within each spending category.

Sixth, Parliament has expressed consistent concern about fraud, both for moral reasons and also because large-scale fraud has been identified as a significant element in agricultural expenditure and hence is an aspect of the problem of control over compulsory expenditure.

Discharge

The most formal aspect of Parliament's scrutiny of the implementation of the budget is its power of discharge, which has been significantly reinforced by the Maastricht Treaty. The treaties provide that the Parliament, acting on a recommendation from the Council (acting by a qualified majority), 'shall give a discharge to the Commission in respect of the implementation of the budget'. Each year the Commission submits to the Council and the Parliament the accounts of the preceding year relating to the implementation of the budget. The Court of Auditors, which has a general obligation to 'assist the European Parliament and the Council in exercising their powers of control over the implementation of the budget', plays a particularly important role in the process. It has to examine the accounts and, in the form of an annual report, certify 'whether all revenue has been received and all expenditure incurred in a lawful and regular manner and whether the financial management has been sound'.

The Parliament bases its decision on whether to grant discharge on the Commission's accounts and the report of the Court of Auditors but also on any further information the Parliament may request from the Commission. Parliament has a specialised committee, the Committee on Budgetary Control, whose primary purpose is to scrutinise the accounts and recommend discharge, and the Commission's specialised services are now engaged in a constant policy dialogue within this committee.

The discharge has been described as 'the political endorsement of the Commission's stewardship of the Communities' budget', and 'the necessary final act in adopting the Communities' accounts' (Jacobs and Corbett, 1990, p.206). It assures 'financial probity and managerial efficiency through the retrospective scrutiny of the Commission's accounts' (Westlake, 1994b, p.31).

Until the implementation of the Maastricht Treaty, Parliament's discharge power was an all-or-nothing affair; either discharge was granted, or it was not. Again, as with rejection of the budget, the treaties are ambiguous about what should occur should Parliament refuse to grant discharge. In the early days of the directly elected Parliament, it was thought that refusal to grant discharge would be tantamount to a motion of censure and that the Commission should resign. In November 1984, for the first and to date last time, the European Parliament refused to grant discharge, but the Commission, whose mandate ended in December 1984 (as Parliament well knew), did not resign, so that the experience did little to clarify the matter. Refusal to grant discharge in the middle of a mandate would create a very different situation, and some constitutionalists within Parliament have argued that, were the Commission to fail to resign, Parliament should automatically resort to a censure motion. Whatever the *constitutional* obligations, the Commission would clearly see refusal to grant discharge as a grave *political* matter.

Parliament sought to introduce some flexibility and more subtle political content into the procedure by occasionally deferring discharge.

This may happen through a simple lack of time (as occurred, because of the direct elections, in 1979), but Parliament may request further documentation from the Commission (as it did in 1980 and 1985) or it may use deferral as an expression of discontent on a linked issue (this occurred in 1992, when Parliament wished to express its disappointment at the Commission's failure to make a proposal on a 'fifth resource' and in 1994, over concerns about the provisions of measures to combat fraud).

The principal shortcoming of the discharge procedure remains the matter of timing. Typically, the Parliament will grant discharge on a budget which is two years' old. In other words, the 1994–9 Parliament will not begin to grant the accompanying 1995–2000 Commission discharge until 1997 (with regard to the 1995 budget), and from 1997 onwards the Commission's budgets will be discharged by the 1999–2004 Parliament!

Nevertheless, the Maastricht Treaty has enhanced the procedure and Parliament's power by introducing a new, intermediate form of sanction on the Commission. The treaties now provide that 'the Commission shall take all appropriate steps to act on the observations in the decisions giving discharge and on other observations by the European Parliament relating to the execution of expenditure' and, at the request of the Parliament, 'the Commission shall report on the measures taken in the light of these observations'. The European Parliament adopted new internal Rules of Procedure in September 1993 which link these powers with Parliament's generalised power to bring actions before the Court for failure to act. Under the treaties, an institution whose failure to act has been declared by the Court is legally required to take the necessary measures to comply. Thus, Parliament has armed itself with a new weapon, less of a blunderbuss than refusal to grant discharge, which it could use to force a recalcitrant Commission to comply with its policy preferences. The exact extent of these powers will be established gradually and most probably through the Court's jurisprudence. Nevertheless, in the area of discharge the Maastricht Treaty has enhanced both Parliament's scrutiny function and its potential powers of policy leverage.

3.4 Legislative powers

Consultation

Although the consultation procedure is always described as a legislative power of the Parliament, the description is misleading. If consultation enables Parliament to influence legislation this can only be done obliquely, through delay, and thanks to a series of undertakings by the other institutions and an open-ended Court ruling. Indeed, Parliament's legislative influence under the consultation procedure is better described as an ingenious response to its lack of true legislative powers.

The ECSC Common Assembly had no consultative role. As a weak response to the granting of broader legislative powers to the EEC and Euratom, the Rome Treaties provided for the European Assembly and the Economic and Social Committee to be consulted in a number of (mainly overlapping) policy areas. There was one apparently insignificant difference in the consultative rights of the two bodies. A treaty article provided that the Council or the Commission could set a time limit for the submission of the Economic and Social Committee's opinion. There was no similar article applying to the Parliamentary Assembly, although another article did enable the Council or the Commission to request an 'extraordinary session' of the Assembly. The Parliamentary Assembly's initial frustrations concerned the scope of consultation (the pace of legislation, and hence of consultations, in the early years of the Community was extremely limited in comparison with the legislative activity of the Union today). Throughout the 1960s, the Council gradually gave in to the Parliament's pressure, extending the practice of consultation of the Parliament to all important problems in 1960, all legislative proposals in 1964, to most non-legislative texts in 1968 and to all proposals of any kind in 1973. Ironically, the Council's magnanimity was based on the very weakness of the procedure, for neither the Council nor the Commission was under any compulsion to take notice of Parliament's opinions. Moreover, these voluntary, or *facultative*, consultations were purely conventional and did not result from any treaty obligation. The Community's legislative procedures remained essentially a dialogue between the Commission as draftsman and the Council as legislator.

Parliament's role in the formal consultation procedure was first enhanced in 1973, when the Council and the Commission gave a series of undertakings about the timing and nature of its consultations. The Council and the Commission agreed that the Parliament should be reconsulted whenever significant changes were made to the text on which the Parliament had given its opinion. This undertaking at least ensured that Parliament's opinions remained relevant, although there was great ambiguity and scope for differing interpretations in the term 'significant'. A Commission undertaking about justifying its position on parliamentary draft amendments before Parliament led to much greater parliamentary involvement, albeit largely passive, throughout the legislative process. And the Commission also gave an undertaking that it would alter its proposal in line with the parliamentary amendments it had accepted. This was highly important. Under the formal consultation procedure, the Commission forwards its draft proposals to the Council, and the Council then consults the Parliament. However, until the

Council has reached a decision, the Commission retains proprietorial rights over its proposal. It can change it at any time and, if it so decides, can withdraw it. Using its limited influence over the Commission, the Parliament now hoped to be able to pressure it into absorbing parliamentary amendments into an altered proposal, which might then pass through the Council, over whom the Parliament had no influence whatsoever.

However, Parliament's position was constantly weakened by its lack of any persuasive weapon (short of the unthinkable use of a censure motion) until 1980, when an unexpected ruling of the Court gave it something of what it lacked. The now famous 'Isoglucose' ruling, cited more fully in Chapter 1, Section 1.2 and Table 1, declared the 'due consultation of the Parliament in the cases provided for by the Treaty' to be 'an essential formality'. Parliament's unexpected success revolved around a technicality. The gist of the case against the Council was that it had not exhausted all the possibilities open to it for getting Parliament's opinion and, in particular, it had not requested an extraordinary parliamentary session, as it had the right to do. The ruling was open-ended because the Court chose not to spell out what its ruling would have been if the Council had made such a request and Parliament had still failed to deliver an opinion. (Neither the Council nor the Parliament has sought clarification from the Court on this point, although several suitable potential cases have occurred.)

Encouraged by the Court's more general pronouncements about its democratic role in the Community, the Parliament saw in this ruling a *de facto* power of delay, for under the formal consultation procedure the Council could not now adopt a decision until Parliament had delivered its opinion. (There is no similar jurisprudence relating to voluntary consultations, but since these are not treaty obligations, Parliament's *prima facie* case would appear to be much weaker.) With some ingenuity, Parliament redrafted its internal Rules of Procedure to allow for an indefinite referral back to committee of its draft opinions. This power of delay went some way towards giving the Parliament the bargaining tool it had previously lacked, but only some way.

In practice, before moving to a final vote on its opinion, the Parliament asks the Commission to express its position on Parliament's amendments. If the Parliament is not satisfied, it may decide to refer its opinion back to the competent committee, ostensibly for 'reconsideration', in reality in order to delay giving its opinion and thus force concessions from the Commission and the Council. (The Court's judgment confirmed the Parliament's right to be consulted but did not explicitly refer to any power of delay.)

There are many weaknesses in the consultation procedure as it has evolved. The most important remain that the Council is not in any way directly obliged to take notice of Parliament's opinions (or amendments), that the Parliament only participates in the legislative procedure at one pace removed (through the Commission), that the power of delay is in itself negative (and the Parliament may be hurting its own best interests by delaying legislation) and that delay can only force concessions where decisions are relatively urgent. Last and not least, Parliament is acutely aware that, despite frequent Council undertakings to the contrary, Council working groups frequently reach technical agreement long before Parliament's opinion has been delivered. Under those circumstances, and particularly where the Council decides unanimously, Parliament's amendments stand very little chance of being accepted and further delay serves little purpose.

Despite all of these weaknesses, the formal consultation procedure has been of great use to the Parliament and, together with an enthusiastic and cooperative Commission, has been particularly effective in tying the Parliament into the legislative procedure, however passively. Indeed, from a historical perspective, Parliament's consultation powers have acted as a sort of constitutional anti-chamber to the true legislative powers later introduced by the 1987 Single European Act and the 1993 Maastricht Treaty.

Finally, in one important and distinct area of consultation, the powers of appointment of the Commission President considered above, Parliament's opinions must obviously be awaited and are clearly of potential consequence. It is highly unlikely that Member State governments or the Council would proceed with a particular nominee if Parliament had expressed a negative opinion although, in the interests of diplomacy, Parliament is likely to make the likely outcome known before the vote takes place, thus sparing the candidate the ignominy of a negative vote.

Cooperation

For the European Parliament, the introduction of the cooperation procedure by the Single European Act in 1987 was as much of a watershed as the first direct elections in 1979 or the granting of budgetary powers in 1970. It marked the end of the old, bipolar, Commission–Council legislative procedure and the beginning of a new, triangular relationship in which the Parliament enjoyed true, if limited, legislative input and could hope for further increases in its role and powers. In the Parliament's eyes, it marked out the beginning of a path which it hopes will ultimately lead to full legislative co-decision powers with the Council.

Much as, in 1970, Parliament had been granted budgetary powers to balance the shift of budgetary revenue from Member State to Community level, so the cooperation procedure was seen as a sort of constitutional *quid pro quo* for the introduction of qualified majority voting in certain policy areas in the Council. In theory, the Community was to move to a system of qualified majority decision making in the Council as early as 1966, but the fruit of Charles de Gaulle's insistence on a right of veto had led to a generalised 'veto culture' which, in turn, had led to a constant, and paralysing, unanimity requirement in Council. The SEA's explicit provisions for qualified majority decision making in the Council were pragmatic political recognition that the policy goals set out in the SEA and, above all, the realisation of the internal market by the declared date of 1992, would be impossible unless decision making was liberated from the constraint of total unanimity.

For as long as unanimity reigned, Member State parliaments had retained theoretical control over the legislative activity of the governments' representatives in the Council but, once a majority system was installed, there was a clear possibility that a government (and by implication the wishes of the national parliament to which it was responsible) could be outvoted. Parliamentary control, it was argued, could only be reasserted at the Community level, through the European Parliament.

The European Parliament, whose militant calls for institutional reform had been a major factor in the decision to hold the inter-governmental conference that resulted in the SEA, was frankly disappointed with its new powers. These were complex, carefully circumscribed, left the Council with the legislative upper hand and were far from the genuine co-decision the Parliament had sought. At the same time, the cooperation procedure was a new power, and the Parliament immediately recognised that its effective and responsible use would be the key to the future granting of any new powers. Put another way, Parliament's hopes of any future extension of its powers would be dashed if the cooperation procedure proved unworkable, particularly if that breakdown could be attributed to the inter-institutional conflicts some feared (with the budgetary militancy of the European Parliament in the early 1980s still fresh in their minds).

Similar apprehensions had coloured the work of the SEA's draftsmen, and the cooperation procedure is aptly named. The procedure involves two stages. The first reading is almost the same as the consultation procedure, with the Council consulting the Parliament on the basis of a Commission proposal. There are no time limits involved, so that the Parliament enjoys exactly the same *de facto* power of delay as it would do under the consultation procedure. The Parliament adopts amendments (the treaty, sticking to the formal language of consultation, speaks of Parliament's *opinion*) and forwards these to the Council. The Council then adopts a 'common position', which is returned to Parliament for a second reading. (The bare bones of the procedure are very similar to the legislative *navette* between the French Assembly and Senate.) The Council may adopt its common position by a qualified majority, although nothing prevents it adopting common positions by a greater majority or even by unanimity (which, as will be seen below, greatly erodes Parliament's power). Once the Council has forwarded its common position to the Parliament, a three-month time limit comes into force (though this may be extended by one month if the two institutions agree), representing the beginning of the second reading stage. Parliament has three possibilities.

If, within the three months, Parliament unconditionally approves the common position or fails to take a decision, the Council adopts the common position, which then becomes law.

If, always within the three months, Parliament can muster an absolute majority of its members to reject the common position, the Council can only overturn the decision by unanimity (it has a further three months in which to do this). In most cases, rejection is an unattractive option for the Parliament, since Parliament more usually finds itself persuading a reluctant Council to act and, in terms of public opinion, rejection inevitably risks casting Parliament in a negative role. At the same time, the Council is unlikely to dismiss lightly the risk of losing draft legislation at the second reading stage.

In practice, Parliament's power has been greatly undermined by the Council's ingrained, consensual instinct to decide unanimously where at all possible. Clearly, if Parliament knows the Council has reached unanimity at the first reading stage, rejection at the second reading stage becomes a purely symbolic gesture. But, looked at another way, Parliament need only find one sympathetic Member State to put real political muscle into its power to reject.

Theoretically, the Commission retains its proprietorial right to withdraw its proposal at any stage, and it has been argued that, where Parliament has rejected a common position unanimously adopted by the Council, political pressure could be put on the Commission to bow to Parliament's wishes and withdraw its proposal. However, the Commission, which has steadfastly refused any obligation automatically to withdraw under such circumstances, insists that it will always act on its own judgement, which may not necessarily coincide with the Parliament's. For example, it may prefer the adoption of an imperfect law, which could later be adapted, to the absence of any law. (Indeed, Parliament's power to win concessions through the menace of rejection is stronger where a failure to adopt legislation would result in a legal vacuum.)

The Parliament has so far used its power to reject extremely sparingly — just four times in seven years. In 1988, the Parliament rejected a common position on the protection of workers against carcinogens on the grounds of insufficient provision of consultation with and information for workers. The Council was unable to reach unanimity, and the proposal lapsed. In May 1992, Parliament rejected a common position on sweeteners in foodstuffs because of what it saw as potentially protectionist elements in the proposal. The Commission resorted to what was referred to as a 'technical withdrawal'. In July 1992, Parliament rejected a common position related to the energy consumption of domestic appliances. On this particular occasion, Parliament's objections concerned the arcane field of arrangements for delegated powers. The Council was able to overturn unanimously Parliament's rejection, and the Parliament did not press its case with the Commission.

Most recently, in October 1993, Parliament rejected a common position related to the maximum power of motorbikes. Parliament objected to what it saw as an unjustified and mistargeted attempt by the Commission to limit the engine size of very big motorbikes on safety grounds. Consideration of this proposal gave the Parliament a largely unexpected opportunity to create close links with its grassroots on what turned out to be a very popular issue, as Parliament was effectively lobbied by occasionally leather-clad but always well-organised bikers. Parliament's hand was greatly strengthened by the knowledge that at least one Member State could not agree to the common position. In the event, the steam went out of the affair when the Maastricht Treaty came into force before the three-month period had expired, and the proposal then became subject to the new co-decision procedure (and hence a third reading).

The third possibility open to the European Parliament at the second reading stage is by far the most constructive. Parliament may propose amendments by an absolute majority of its members. These are forwarded to the Commission which must, within one month, re-examine its original proposal, together with the Council's common position and Parliament's amendments, and then forward its re-examined proposal to the Council. The Council can only modify the Commission's re-examined proposal, which may incorporate parliamentary amendments, by unanimity, whereas a qualified majority is sufficient to adopt it as it is. The Council may adopt parliamentary amendments not supported by the Commission by unanimity. One way or another, the Council has to decide within three months (which may be extended to four months if the Council and the Parliament agree), otherwise the proposal falls.

For the Parliament, the cooperation procedure was simultaneously a disappointment and a challenge. At the practical level, it could only exploit its powers to reject or amend common positions at the second reading stage if it could regularly and reliably muster absolute majorities yet, as described in Chapter 2, Section 2.10, the Parliament traditionally suffers from poor attendance. To overcome this purely mechanical problem, Parliament decided to group all of its SEA votes together in the middle of each plenary week (usually early on the Wednesday evening), and this measure has proved largely successful.

At the institutional level, the implementation of the cooperation procedure was the subject of much inter-institutional dialogue and reflection, especially between the Parliament and the Commission. Both institutions saw that the legislative blockages were a major risk of the new procedure, particularly since much of the legislation involved concerned the realisation of the internal market, which both the Commission and the Parliament favoured and where the SEA had introduced an ambitious deadline (31 December 1992). As the 'motor' of integration and principal architect of the 1992 programme, the Commission had a particularly vested interest in seeing that its legislative proposals did not stall in the complexities of the new procedure and, in addition to its enthusiasm for the concrete integrationist progress the internal market would represent, the Parliament had a vested interest in proving that it could contribute effectively and positively to the legislative process through the new procedure.

For their different reasons, but with mutual understanding, both the Parliament and the Commission saw the first-reading stage as the key to the success of the procedure. From the Commission's point of view, there was much less risk of blockage at this more flexible stage. The Commission's role was also less fraught then, since there was much less pressure on it to make hard political choices between the potentially conflicting desires of the Parliament and the Council.

The relative advantages to the Parliament of the first-reading stage were clear. There was no majority requirement and no deadline and, if the Council 'played the game' by awaiting the Parliament's opinion before reaching political agreement (as it had repeatedly promised to do), the Parliament could still hope to have some influence on its deliberations. A major shortcoming in the procedure as provided for by the treaty was that there was nothing to stop Parliament tabling new, and perhaps more numerous amendments at the second-reading stage. Overwhelming waves of amendments at that point risked strangling the legislative process in exactly the way both the Parliament and the Commission feared. To avoid this dilution of its powers the Parliament, under the skilled tutelage of one of its noted constitutionalists, Sir Christopher Prout, unilaterally introduced a provision in its internal Rules of Procedure whereby amendments at the second-reading stage would only be admissible if they sought to restore Parliament's first-reading position, were the result of a compromise agreement between the Council and the Parliament or sought to amend a part of the common position which differed substantially from the text on which Parliament had been originally consulted. The best proof of the value of the logic of this self-denying ordinance is that representatives of the Council and the Commission still sometimes inadvertently hold the

European Parliament to account for these undertakings as though they were obligations flowing from the treaties (as logically, perhaps, they ought to have been).

Quantitative proof of the relative flexibility of the first-reading stage is provided in Table 7. Since the procedure came into force in 1987, the Council has accepted almost 43 per cent of Parliament's amendments at the first-reading stage, as opposed to only 23.5 per cent at the second-reading stage. The Commission's greater openness at the earlier stage is also clear, as is Parliament's overall input into the legislative process (see Westlake, 1994b, p.38). However, these raw statistics can give no indication of the Parliament's qualitative legislative influence. As some commentators have pointed out, the Council may 'buy off' the Parliament (that is, discourage it from rejection) by accepting high proportions of less consequential parliamentary amendments, creating a quantitative impression of success while rejecting high proportions of Parliament's more important amendments.

The cooperation procedure had a number of knock-on institutional consequences. One was to underline the importance, as far as the Parliament was concerned, of the Commission's initial choice of legal basis for its draft legislative proposals, since the legal basis would determine whether the Parliament had a weak consultative or a strong cooperation-procedure role. A direct consequence of this was the reinforcement of Parliament's scrutiny, through its Legal Affairs Committee, of the Commission's chosen legal bases, with recourse to the Court of Justice as an ultimate weapon. In practice, there have been surprisingly few differences of opinion. In 1988, Parliament took the Council to Court over the choice of legal base in a decision on the maximum permitted levels of radioactivity in foodstuffs following the Chernobyl disaster (see Table 1). The Commission had proposed as legal base an article from the Euratom Treaty which gave the Parliament only weak consultative rights. The Parliament argued for an article that would entail the cooperation procedure, and hence two parliamentary readings, but the Court ruled in favour of the Council. (While the Parliament was unhappy with the ruling on the substance, the Court confirmed the Parliament's right to bring such cases in the defence of its prerogatives.) However, in a 1991 ruling ('Titanium Dioxyde'), the Court annulled a Council directive, arguing that the legal basis used should have been different, granting Parliament two readings. In its ruling, the Court explicitly underlined the democratic importance of the Parliament's participation in the legislative process.

Another consequence of the procedure was to increase greatly the degree of substantial inter-institutional dialogue. This was partly because of the imperatives of the new procedure, particularly as far as the Commission was concerned. But increased dialogue was also necessitated because of the way in which the SEA was drafted. In particular, there were a number of ambiguities and silences that could have undermined the practical functioning of the procedure. To overcome these difficulties, the institutions were obliged to come to a number of understandings and 'gentlemen's agreements', culminating in a 1990 'code of conduct' mutually agreed by the Commission and the Parliament. (A very similar process of 'filling out' the provisions of the treaties through constitutional convention and inter-institutional agreement occurred after the 1970 and 1975 Budgets Treaties and is occurring again now with the implementation of the Maastricht Treaty.)

Substantial inter-institutional dialogue bore its own fruit of greatly enhanced mutual understanding. Above all, the cooperation procedure induced a great change of attitudes towards the Parliament and the Commission and, perhaps more reluctantly, in the Council. It should be recalled that, prior to the implementation of the SEA, Parliament's only true power lay in the budgetary field; and the specialised Directorates-General in the Commission and the Council, who were engaged in constant dialogue and political process with Parliament and its Budgets Committee, were used to working constructively with the institution and held it in respect. Because of the vertical organisation of the Commission and the Council, these attitudes did not spread throughout the other services of the organisations. The SEA and the cooperation procedure changed all that. Few parts of the Commission and the Council have not had to deal with the Parliament in its new legislative guise, and the Parliament now has to be taken seriously not only for moral reasons but also for very practical ones. As pointed out before, the cooperation procedure is aptly named, encouraging cooperative attitudes on all sides, as was underlined by the heads of state and government meeting at the December 1992 Edinburgh European Council who paid 'tribute to the vital role played by the Commission . . . and to the constructive cooperation . . . between the Council and the Parliament' (Conclusions of the Edinburgh European Council, 1992, *EC Bulletin* 12).

The SEA had one further, in-built consequence for the Parliament. Because the cooperation procedure was principally linked to the achievement of the internal market, Parliament's new power was greatly dependent on a finite legislative programme. The successful completion of the internal market would necessarily entail a slow-down in the pace of legislation (as has indeed been the case). Thus, for an ambitious Parliament having tasted true legislative influence for the first time, a consolidation of its powers would be insufficient. They would have to be extended, and effectively this was what occurred with the implementation of the Maastricht Treaty. Not only was the cooperation procedure extended to new fields of application but, just as the consultation procedure could be described as a sort of anti-chamber to the cooperation procedure, so the cooperation procedure could be described as a form of anti-chamber to the co-decision procedure introduced by the Maastricht Treaty.

Co-decision

The draftsmen of the Maastricht Treaty coyly refrained from using the word 'co-decision', but that is how the new procedure introduced by the treaty is universally described. In many cases, the new procedure has replaced the cooperation procedure (in some cases it applies to limited parts of new areas of Union competences, such as culture and health) and in all applies to about a dozen articles of the treaty, including such matters as the free movement of workers, the right of establishment and the internal market.

The European Parliament has greeted the new procedure with some ambivalence. On the one hand, it has undoubtedly won its long-declared aim of co-legislative status with the Council and can now hope to consolidate and extend its new powers as it successfully managed to do with the cooperation procedure. On the other hand, the procedure itself is opaquely complex (consisting of three readings where Parliament would have preferred two, resulting in a total maximum time span for the second and third readings of fifteen months) and, in Parliament's view, is still unfairly balanced in favour of the Council.

In the first-reading stage, the Commission drafts its proposals and submits it to the Parliament and the Council. This represents a small but significant and equitable streamlining of previous arrangements, since under the consultation and cooperation procedures the Commission submits its proposals to the Council alone which then consults the Parliament. As with the consultation and cooperation procedures, the Commission may modify its proposal in the light of Parliament's amendments. The Council adopts a common position, by qualified majority, and communicates it to the Parliament.

Four possibilities are open to the Parliament at the second-reading stage. If, within three months, the Parliament approves the common position, then the Council definitively adopts the act 'in accordance with the common position'. If Parliament fails to take a decision within three months, then the Council may also adopt the act 'in accordance with the common position'.

If, within the three months, the Parliament indicates by an absolute majority that it intends to reject the common position, the Council may convene a conciliation committee to explain its position. If Parliament thereafter confirms its rejection of the common position by an absolute majority, then the proposed act shall be 'deemed not to have been adopted'. On the other hand, Parliament may decide to table amendments, in which case it comes back to the fourth possibility.

The fourth possibility at the second-reading stage is that Parliament proposes (by an absolute majority) amendments, which it then forwards to the Council and the Commission, with the Commission being obliged to deliver an opinion on the amendments. Two possibilities are then open to the Council.

The first is that it can approve, within three months, all the parliamentary amendments, in which case it amends the common position accordingly and adopts the act. The Council only needs a qualified majority to approve those amendments where the Commission has delivered a positive opinion, but it can only approve by unanimity amendments on which the Commission has delivered a negative opinion.

The second possibility open to the Council is that it does not approve the act within the three months. In this case, the presidents of the Parliament and the Council convene a conciliation committee. Two possibilities are then open to the committee. The conciliation committee may, within six weeks, reach agreement on a joint text. The Council must act by a qualified majority and Parliament by a majority of its representatives in the committee (a majority currently would be seven out of twelve). The two institutions then have a further six weeks, with the Council acting by qualified majority and the Parliament by absolute majority, in which to adopt the act in accordance with the joint text. If one (or both) of the institutions fails to approve the act within the six weeks, it is deemed not to have been adopted.

On the other hand, the conciliation committee may be unable to approve a joint text within the six weeks. Two further possibilities are then open to the Council. If the Council does not act within six more weeks, then the act is deemed not to have been adopted. If, within those six weeks, the Council (acting by qualified majority) is able to confirm its common position, possibly with amendments proposed by Parliament, then two further possibilities are open to the Parliament. If Parliament does not act within six weeks then the act is finally adopted. However, if within those six weeks Parliament is able to reject the text by an absolute majority, then the act is deemed not to have been adopted.

The potential risks and dangers of the procedure are clear, particularly in the later stages. The procedure is potentially lengthy and highly complex, requiring a far higher degree of practical and political coordination among the three institutions, and it is not linked to a mutually attractive raft of legislation, as was the 1992 programme. In addition, the Commission has expressed apprehension about the withdrawal of its traditional proprietorial rights over draft legislation — which it has always argued are an important aspect of the overall institutional balance of power — at the third-reading stage, though the Commission plays an active role in the conciliation committee and is ordered by the treaty to 'take all the necessary initiatives with a view to reconciling the positions of the European Parliament and the Council'. (Indeed, the Commission's role is akin to that which it plays in the budgetary procedure.) For its part, Parliament is apprehensive about what it sees as an increasingly negative role at the third-reading stage. However, some parliamentarians argue that the Parliament will in any case have to be discriminating in resorting to the conciliation procedure, and others are optimistic that the conciliation committee will generally be able to reach effective compromises.

As with the cooperation procedure, the Parliament and the Commission have, for their different reasons, identified the earlier readings as the key to the success of the procedure. The Commission still has ownership over draft legislation and is intimately involved in the legislative process. And, as with the cooperation procedure, the Parliament has far more hope of seeing its amendments taken on board and can still pressure the Commission into modifying its initial proposal. (In its initial reaction to the Maastricht Treaty, Parliament tried unsuccessfully to pressure the Commission into giving an undertaking to withdraw its proposals automatically where the conciliation committee had been unable to agree a joint text.)

Whatever its potential shortcomings, the co-decision procedure is a remarkable step forward for the European Parliament. For the first time it has true co-legislative powers with the Council. If the conciliation committee is successful, then the result is a jointly agreed text and, regardless of the stage in the procedure at which an act may be adopted, the treaties now refer to 'regulations, directives and decisions adopted jointly by the European Parliament and the Council'. Moreover, acts adopted under the procedure are jointly signed into law by the presidents of the two institutions.

With rights come responsibilities. In particular, acts adopted jointly by the Parliament and the Council are subject to the review powers of the Court of Justice, and the treaties now provide for the possibility of actions against the Parliament for failure to act.

Conciliation

Conciliation is not a separate legislative procedure but is an integral part of certain types of legislative procedure. Confusingly, there are four different types of conciliation procedure. Two of them — the conciliation procedure within the budgetary procedure (to confuse matters further, there are two variations) and conciliation on the uniform electoral procedure — are not part of a legislative procedure but are included for simplicity's sake in the following analysis. It should be noted that Parliament frequently makes unilateral provision for conciliation procedures (see 'legislative assent' below), but such provisions have had mixed success, since they rely on the willingness of the other institutions, and particularly the Council, to 'play ball'.

The 1975 conciliation procedure
The original conciliation procedure can be traced back to the ongoing dispute between the Council and the Parliament, recounted above, about the budgetary consequences of legislative proposals. In the 1970s, it will be recalled, Parliament tried to use its budgetary powers to limit or influence the Council's legislative activity, where it had no direct power at all. In order to avoid the risk of conflict, the Council agreed to sign up to a joint declaration (to which the Commission and the Parliament also put their names) establishing a conciliation procedure.

The procedure was to be used for 'Community acts of general application which have appreciable financial implications'. In submitting a proposal, the Commission was to indicate whether it thought the act could be subject to the procedure. The procedure itself could be triggered by a request from either the Parliament or the Council where the Council intended to depart from the opinion adopted by the European Parliament.

The aim of the procedure was 'to seek an agreement between the European Parliament and the Council'. The two sides were to meet in a conciliation committee, consisting of the Council (that is, representatives of all twelve Member States rather than the presidency) and representatives of the European Parliament. The procedure would normally not take longer than three months, with the joint declaration providing that 'when the positions of the two institutions are sufficiently close, the European Parliament may give a new opinion, after which the Council shall take definitive action'.

The Parliament soon became disillusioned with the new procedure. It was sparingly used — just five times between 1975 and 1981 — and the Parliament lacked any real or immediate power to force concessions from the Council. But it enjoyed a renaissance in the mid-1980s, when the procedure was more frequently used and Parliament won significant concessions on a number of draft regulations. Moreover, liberal interpretation of the conditions in the joint declaration has led to the use of the procedure where proposals do not necessarily have 'appreciable financial implications.' Latterly, the Parliament and the Council (together with the Commission) have occasionally resorted to exploratory or negotiating meetings on important political issues, and these have been tantamount to informal conciliation procedures. Such meetings took place, for example, in the context of the first stage of economic and monetary union (Jacobs, 1991), and the urgent legislative process preceding German unification (Westlake, 1991).

In retrospect, the 1975 conciliation procedure can be seen as the forerunner of the conciliation procedure within the co-decision procedure introduced by the Maastricht Treaty. Indeed, the primary advantage of the conciliation procedure was that it formally provided one of the few circumstances in which the Parliament could meet directly with the Council *per se*. Most other procedures involved go-betweens and/or filtering of some sort between the two institutions: for example, lawyers before the Court, the Commission on parliamentary amendments, the Council's presidency. But the conciliation procedure involves direct encounters between the representatives of the Member States and the representatives of the people and is thus at the very least an important 'getting to know you' exercise.

Budgetary conciliation
Two variations on the conciliation procedure take place within the annual budgetary procedure. Early on in the cycle, the Council and the Parliament meet in a conciliation committee to discuss the preliminary draft budget. Typically, this meeting takes place in Strasbourg and, once it is over, the Council adopts its draft budget. Technically, the meeting is not a conciliation meeting, nor is its purpose to reconcile the two institutions. Rather, it enables them to identify major differences. Nevertheless, the format is similar, and it provides another rare occasion for the Parliament and the Council to meet together. Council and Parliament representatives meet again in the budgetary cycle, just before the Council adopts its second reading of the budget. The purpose of this second conciliation committee is more precisely to reconcile the two sides (see Westlake, 1994b, p.32). The budgetary conciliation procedure was probably inspired by the 'reconciliation procedure' between the two houses of Congress at the first-reading stage of the United States' federal budget.

Conciliation (and assent) on a uniform electoral procedure
As was pointed out in Chapter 2, Section 2.4, the 1976 Community act introducing direct elections to the European Parliament made a new provision whereby:

> ... the Council acting unanimously on a proposal from the European Parliament after consulting the Commission, shall adopt such measures after endeavouring to reach agreement with the European Parliament in a conciliation committee consisting of the Council and representatives of the European Parliament.

The provision was originally weak, inasmuch as the Council only had to *endeavour* to reach agreement with the Parliament, but the Maastricht Treaty has now reinforced Parliament's role by granting it the final say, through assent and by an absolute majority of its members. However, having itself so far made three full-scale proposals for a uniform system, Parliament is under no illusions that the real stumbling block remains the unanimity requirement in Council.

Conciliation within co-decision

Two conciliation committees are foreseen within the co-decision procedure. The first may occur early on in the procedure, if the Parliament has indicated its intention to reject the Council's common position. Under these circumstances, the Council 'may convene a meeting of the conciliation committee . . . to explain further its position'. Thereafter, the Parliament may either confirm its rejection or decide to table amendments. This first conciliation committee seems to have been at least partly modelled on the first conciliation committee in the budgetary process. However, the text of the treaty implies that the Parliament might be persuaded not to resort to the extreme of rejection, so that the committee is clearly intended to exercise some reconciling function, bound up in the Council's further explanation of its position. By the same logic, although the treaty does not oblige the Council to convene a conciliation committee at this stage, it is difficult to imagine the circumstances where it would not wish to do so. Above all, Parliament has drafted its rules in such a way that a failure by the Council to convoke the conciliation committee would automatically lead to rejection. Where Parliament is successfully dissuaded from rejection, the procedure swings back into the third reading.

It is at that third-reading stage that the more important of the two conciliation committees may be convoked, if the Council is unable to accept all Parliament's amendments. The purpose of the second conciliation committee is to achieve a joint text or at the worst to establish the impossibility of agreeing to one. The Maastricht Treaty laid out only the barest bones of the new procedure, and in October 1993, shortly after the treaty had entered into force, the Council, Parliament and Commission adopted an inter-institutional agreement to flesh out the procedure by setting out how conciliation would work in practice.

Conciliation committees are composed of the twelve members of the Council and an equal number of representatives of the Parliament. The inter-institutional agreement is based on the principles of equality and alternance between the Council and the Parliament. Thus, the committees are alternatively chaired by the president of the Parliament and the Council presidency and meet alternately in the Parliament and in the Council. The secretariat of the committees is provided jointly by the General Secretariats of the Council and the Parliament.

Parliament held lengthy internal debates as to how it should be represented in the conciliation committee. It had to balance continuity (as to procedure) with expertise (on the particular matter in question) and equitable representation of its component political groups, all within a total membership of twelve. Ultimately, in November 1993, the Conference of Presidents opted for a mixed method. Seats in the conciliation committee were first divided proportionally among the larger political groups, with the Party of European Socialists taking five, the European People's Party four and the Liberal Group one, the two remaining seats being shared between the other political groups within the Parliament, with the exception of the extreme-right European Right. Continuity on procedure is provided by three 'permanent' members, two from the Party of European Socialists and one from the European People's Party, though the other political groups could decide to appoint a permanent member among themselves if they so wish. Expertise on the particular subject matter under negotiation is provided from within the different political groups' 'non-permanent' members, so that, if the legislation concerns, say, the environment, efforts will be made by the larger political groups to ensure that the competent committee chairman, or a vice-chairman, is among their delegation, together with the rapporteur on the report in question.

Parliament's early experiences of the procedure have been revealing. In the first place, in the Parliament's eyes there has been a generalised 'de-mystification' of the Council much as had previously occurred with Parliament's budgetary specialists. The Council, its procedures, its secretariat, its personalities and even its buildings are no longer 'off limits' to Parliament. The Council is becoming more familiar and is held less in awe; MEPs are now entitled to stalk its corridors and sit at its tables in search of compromise and concession. In the second place, the Parliament rapidly realised that, on the substance of issues subject to the procedure, Parliament could only hope to 'do serious business' if it sent delegations that could winningly combine expertise, experience and good tacticians. In the third place, from the Council's point of view, the procedure has been little less than a revolution and, although in a sense conciliation could be reduced to systematic bluff-calling, the stakes are very high (see 'comitology' in Section 3.8 of this chapter). In the fourth place, and more generally, the procedure has already been subject to *ad hoc* refinements. The most important of these is the introduction of informal conciliation meetings, typically between a reduced number of parliamentarians and the Council Presidency, in the search for the basis of a compromise solution before issues are subject to the formal procedure itself. It has been said that the Commission is like a 'thirteenth Member State' at the Council table; the co-decision procedure has clearly added a fourteenth actor.

'Legislative assent'

As will be seen below in the discussion of Parliament's external economic powers, the 1987 Single European Act introduced a new sort of parliamentary power: assent, by an absolute majority of Parliament's members, to association agreements and the accession of new Member States. The Maastricht Treaty extended this power in two ways. First, the assent procedure has been extended beyond the traditional external relations field into the legislative sphere. Parliamentary assent is now required for measures facilitating the right of residence and freedom of movement within the Union, and the definition of tasks and objectives and the coordination of the structural funds. (The assent procedure also applies for the uniform procedure for direct elections, the creation of the cohesion fund, amendments to the European System of Central Banks and the entrusting of special tasks to the future European Central Bank.) Second, the previous absolute majority requirement has been largely relaxed — in most cases a simply majority in Parliament is now sufficient.

Parliament's power of seemingly indefinite delay in the consultation procedure effectively depends on the absence of a Court ruling, but in the case of the assent procedure Parliament's power of delay is open-ended, clear-cut and beyond doubt; either the Parliament grants its assent or it doesn't. Once again, as with the rejection of the budget or refusal to grant discharge, the treaties are silent as to what should occur if the Parliament *does* refuse assent. In practice, in the external relations field, Parliament's refusal has never led to the complete withdrawal of a proposal. A period of time has been allowed to lapse, during which the Commission may make or seek concessions (and pressure may be brought to bear on the Parliament), and then the Council brings the proposal back before Parliament with a renewed request for assent.

Parliament sees assent in the legislative field as a blunt instrument where, unlike an internationally negotiated agreement, it may wish to see proposals amended. When changing its rules in September 1993, the Parliament therefore tried to introduce some flexibility and more legislative influence into the procedure. The rules now distinguish between assent to international agreements and legislative assent. In the case of legislative assent procedures, the competent parliamentary committee may now decide to draft an 'interim report', which may include 'recommendations for modification or implementation of the proposal' — that is, draft amendments by another name. Where such amendments are adopted by Parliament, its president must automatically request the opening of a conciliation procedure, with the competent committee making a final recommendation on whether or not assent should be granted 'in the light of the outcome of conciliation with the Council'.

Thus, Parliament hopes to bring pressure to bear on the Council to accept legislative changes by threatening the refusal or postponement of assent. The power is clearly greater where legislation is urgent. Although not mentioned in its rules, Parliament has a reserve power to which it may resort should the Council refuse to 'play ball'. Since the Commission may modify or withdraw its proposal at any stage in the procedure for as long as the Council has not acted, Parliament will look to the Commission to cooperate constructively with it.

However, Parliament's legislative assent powers are potentially undermined by a number of factors. First, the Council may refuse conciliation, particularly since this is a unilateral provision of Parliament's rules rather than a treaty requirement. Second, many parliamentarians feel the assent procedure in general has been weakened by the relaxation of the absolute majority requirement, which makes the lobbying task facing the other institutions far less daunting. Third, although the power is enhanced where legislative proposals are urgent, the power is correspondingly weaker where there is no urgency. Fourth, in many cases Parliament's own resolve will be undermined by its basic desire to see legislation passed. Finally, although granting assent is a positive act, the real power in the procedure lies in the withholding of assent — which is negative and puts the Parliament in the potentially dangerous position of having to justify its refusal.

The right to request initiatives

From the outset, the EEC Treaty provided that 'the Council may request the Commission to undertake any studies the Council considers desirable for the attainment of the common objectives, and to submit to it any appropriate proposals'. Although the treaty put the Commission under no obligation to accede to the Council's requests, in practice the Commission found it difficult to refuse and in earlier years was frequently happy to draft proposals and become active in new policy areas at the behest of the Member States themselves. The Parliament grew increasingly irked by what it saw as the Council's almost automatic right of initiative. At the same time, the Parliament frequently saw its calls for action and requests for proposals (as expressed through its 'own initiative' reports) largely spurned.

The Maastricht Treaty introduced a new, similar provision whereby the European Parliament may now, 'acting by an absolute majority of its members, request the Commission to submit any appropriate proposal on matters on which it considers that a Community act is required for the purpose of implementing this Treaty'. The granting of the right to request initiatives can be seen as yet another move in a gradual balancing of the rights of the Parliament and the Council. The Parliament immediately called upon the Commission to accept automaticity, but the Commission refused while emphasising that such a legislative initiative from the Parliament would be read as 'a very strong political signal' (Westlake, 1994b, pp.98–9).

Parliament saw that the power would have to be used responsibly and very sparingly if it were not to become diluted, and so introduced a series of conditional mechanisms into its internal Rules of Procedure. Thus, in addition to the treaty's absolute majority requirement, such requests must be formulated by a parliamentary committee through an 'own-initiative' report, with the prior authorisation of the Conference of Presidents, and can only be made where the Commission has failed to respond to any earlier request (adopted by a simple majority). The competent committee has to be sure that a similar proposal is not in the Commission's Annual Legislative Programme, that the Commission is not in the process of preparing legislation on the matter or that such preparations haven't been delayed for some justifiable reason. Proposals that have financial implications must indicate how sufficient financial resources can be found (here Parliament is consciously echoing its strictures to the Council and the new provision of the Maastricht Treaty on the maintenance of budgetary discipline). Parliament's resolution must indicate the appropriate legal base (and thus Parliament's own powers in the legislative process that might follow), and be accompanied 'by detailed recommendations as to the content of the required proposals'. Last, and by no means least, the proposal must respect the principle of subsidiarity and the fundamental rights of citizens.

Taken together, these conditions will make Parliament's use of its right to request initiatives a rare occurrence, especially since Parliament has created the possibility for the Commission to draft its own proposal, thus avoiding the awkwardness of a detailed request. Above all, Parliament's increased, and ever earlier involvement in the Union's legislative planning should render the need to request initiatives largely unnecessary.

Legislative planning

In the Community's early life, the pace of legislative activity was relatively slow, and hence the demands on the *de facto* legislature, the Council, were relatively slight. As the Parliament became more involved in the legislative process, the other institutions had perhaps to coordinate their activities slightly more to slot in with the Parliament's monthly plenary sessions (coordination over timetables had taken place in the budgetary procedure since the introduction of the Parliament's budgetary powers in 1970). But a fresh departure came in 1987, with the entry into force of the SEA. At one level, the SEA involved the adoption of a huge raft of legislation in relation to the creation of the internal market, with much legislation subsequently flowing from earlier framework legislation. At another level, the SEA involved the Parliament intimately in the legislative process and, at a third level, the cooperation procedure introduced a complicated legislative procedure with built-in and sometimes tight deadlines. (In the context of the realisation of the internal market, the loss of a piece of legislation would have been considered particularly grave.)

The result was a sudden need for the institutions to coordinate their legislative activity, both internally and among themselves. For example, the Council and the Commission introduced a 'rolling programme' of legislation to coordinate the activities of succeeding Presidencies, and the Commission had clearly established its own internal coordination to ensure that it could produce the vast amount of legislation involved. In addition, the Commission, spiritually closer to the Parliament, was particularly concerned that the legislative process should keep pace with the '1992' deadline and thus engaged in a mutual legislative planning exercise with the Parliament. From the Commission's point of view, annual legislative planning exercises would help the Parliament to schedule its precious plenary time and generally bind it into the legislative programme. Indeed, having proved its practical worth, the planning exercise has now become an institutionalised process, and an indispensable mechanism for the Commission, since the programmes establish which plenary is scheduled to adopt a report, which committee is responsible for the report and the timetable for that committee.

The Parliament had its own interests, explained above, for ensuring a relatively smooth and efficient legislative process, but it had an additional interpretation of the planning exercise. In the Parliament's view, the general exercise of legislative planning gave it new input into and influence over the policy-formation process. In the longer term, the Parliament envisages a Union-level policy process in which the legislative activity of the executive (the Commission) will respond to the policy preferences of the legislature (the Parliament and the Council). Parliament's post-Maastricht rule changes on the appointment of the Commission have introduced an additional element, since the designated Commission will be expected to announce its (five-year) programme during the investiture debate, and the Parliament clearly expects that initial outline to reflect its own policy preferences. The Parliament will thereafter hold the Commission to the overall programme through the annual legislative planning process. However the legislative planning exercise ultimately evolves, Parliament's role within and influence over it seems certain to grow.

3.5 External powers

Assent to accession

Prior to the Single European Act, the enlargement of the Union was a matter purely for the Member States and, through their ratification processes, the national parliaments to decide. In a new departure, the Single European Act granted the European Parliament assent power, whereby no state could become a member of the Community unless the Parliament had given its assent by an absolute majority of its members. However, at the time of the SEA's entry into force, 1987, further enlargement of the Community was considered a distant prospect, and the impending realisation of the internal market merely encouraged EFTA states to seek to share some of its benefits through the creation of a European Economic Area (which ultimately came into force on 1 January 1994). The fall of the Berlin Wall in the autumn of 1989 radically altered the European political map. The former DDR was rapidly absorbed into the German Federal Republic, and other former Iron Curtain countries such as Poland, Hungary and the then Czechoslovakia spoke openly of their hopes of rapidly becoming members of the European Community. This precipitated fresh reflection within the EFTA states and ultimately four of them, Austria, Finland, Norway and Sweden, decided to apply for membership of the Community. At the June 1992 Lisbon European Council, the heads of state and government decided that accession negotiations could only be considered once the Maastricht Treaty had been ratified; but by the December 1992 Edinburgh European Council they had decided that accession negotiations could go ahead, with accession itself conditional on the ratification of the Maastricht Treaty, the provisions of which the applicant states would be expected to take wholly on board. Thus, with the entry into force of the Maastricht Treaty in November 1993, the Parliament's theoretical assent powers in relation to enlargement became a real and imminent prospect.

Many of the European Parliament's constitutionalists argued that these assent powers gave it a powerful weapon for forcing further institutional reform within the Union. In the beginning, there were suggestions that Parliament might be able to withhold assent in order to force concessions across a broad range of institutional arrangements, including such matters as the extension of Parliament's legislative powers. Such initial arguments later gave way to more pragmatic assertions that the Parliament could at the least insist on changes to those institutional arrangements within the Union where enlargement would in any case necessitate change, if only mechanical extrapolations. Such matters included the number of members of the European Parliament and of the Commission but, above all, the weighting of the votes of the individual Member States in the Council, where the Parliament was afraid that a mechanical extension of weighting might create new forms of blocking minorities (for example, neutral states or small states) which could slow down the pace of integration, particularly in the field of the Common Foreign and Security Policy.

The Parliament's demands about the size of its own membership were largely pre-empted by the December 1992 Edinburgh and December 1993 Brussels European Councils' decisions to take on board Parliament's own proposals (see Chapter 2, Section 2.6). Most of the Parliament's other demands were effectively rejected by the heads of state and government at the December 1993 Brussels European Council (in other words, long before Parliament was actually called upon to grant its assent) who decided on a simple mechanical extension of the number of members of the Commission and of the weighting of the votes of Member States in the Council. (The vexed question of size of a qualified majority was handed on to the Council to decide in the context of the enlargement negotiations themselves.) Virtually all substantial discussion of institutional reform was thereby postponed to the 1996 inter-governmental conference.

In a resolution on the results of the December 1993 European Council, the Parliament regretted the postponement of 'any genuine institutional reform', expressed concern 'that the European Council has not proposed, in the institutional field, anything other than a purely mechanical transposition of existing rules' and reiterated its 'intention to link its assent to achievement of the conditions necessary to ensure the viability of the Union and its decision-making capacity' (15 December 1993). However, since it unequivocally favoured further enlargement, there was never any doubt that Parliament would ultimately give its assent, though it might delay giving its decision. Its acceptance of the European Council's decisions was implicit recognition of the political realities of enlargement and, in particular, the insistence of the applicant states that the Union should not 'shift the goalposts' on institutional arrangements before the new states were themselves able to participate in the decision-making machinery that would affect such changes. In effect, the Parliament's attempt to use its assent powers to force institutional change failed before it had begun. But a number of parliamentarians doubted whether the Parliament would ever have had the resolve to use its powers in that way: big political and historical issues, such as German unification and enlargement, might simply be too big for such tactics too succeed.

Two developments renewed debate within the Parliament about the possibility of withholding, or at least postponing, its assent for enlargement. The first was that the enlargement negotiations took longer than had been hoped. Since the overall target was accession on 1 January 1995, it was felt that the Parliament would have to give its assent before its last pre-elections session in May 1994. But as the negotiations spilled over into the spring of 1994 it seemed as though the Parliament might have insufficient time for its deliberations. The second development was the row with the British government over the size of the blocking minority — the decision passed on by the December 1993 European Council. In addition to delaying the conclusion of the negotiations still further, the row angered the Parliament, which saw the Ioaninna compromise between the Member States as a dangerous development.

Debate raged on in Parliament for three weeks. Should Parliament give its assent in May, or pass the decision on to the new Parliament, which would first meet in July? The media asked another question: would the Parliament be able to muster the absolute majorities required? In the event, on 4 May 1994, the Parliament confounded its critics by decisively rejecting any postponement and approving accession by overwhelming majorities.

On the matter of enlargement, the Parliament's assent comes fairly late in the process. The Commission is first to give its opinion on a state's application, which is followed by a Council decision to begin negotiations. The negotiations are conducted by the Council, aided by the Commission. The concluded agreement is then put to the Parliament for its assent, and then 'submitted for ratification by all the Contracting States in accordance with their respective constitutional requirements', which in all cases include ratification by the national parliaments. Given these arrangements, it is difficult to imagine the circumstances in which fundamental differences of opinion could arise among the institutions.

Both Malta and Cyprus have since applied for membership of the Community, and their applications are actively under consideration. In the longer term, the prospect of eventual membership has been explicitly extended to the Vysegrad countries — Poland, Hungary, and the Czech and Slovak Republics — some of these have already applied. In short, Parliament will be called upon to exercise its assent powers far more frequently than could ever have been imagined in 1985, when the SEA was negotiated, or even 1987, when the SEA entered into force.

Assent to association

In addition to accession, the 1987 Single European Act granted the European Parliament assent powers in relation to the conclusion of all association agreements (that is, agreements extending beyond trade to political-level arrangements 'involving reciprocal rights and obligations, common action and special procedures'). It soon became apparent that Parliament's assent powers applied not only to association agreements themselves but to any revision or addition to such agreements and thus went further than the SEA draftsmen had perhaps intended. Parliament's assent powers were further enhanced by the consequences of the collapse of the Communist regimes in Eastern Europe which soon led to the conclusion of 'European Agreements' with Poland, Hungary, and the Czech and Slovak Republics, with agreements with other Central and East European states in the offing. In all, between the entry into force of the Single European Act and the entry into force of the Maastricht Treaty, the Parliament was called upon to grant assent on some fifty-four acts. Outright rejection of any act was very rare; indeed, it happened just twice. More frequently, Parliament failed to muster the required absolute majority in favour, although this too only happened just six times (see Westlake, 1994b, p.30).

The assent procedure, particularly on financial protocols, gave Parliament an important lever, both *vis-à-vis* the Union's trade negotiator, the Commission, and with regard to the third state(s) involved. Large financial programmes had to be postponed on several occasions, as the Parliament sought political commitments and concessions on the human rights records of the states involved. A perhaps unintended nuance arose within the procedure when it soon became apparent to the Parliament that the absence of an absolute majority was sufficient to bring about delay, whatever the relative size of any simple majority. The Maastricht Treaty did away with this nuance by relaxing the absolute majority requirement and thus, in the eyes of many parliamentarians, weakened its assent powers (in the United States Senate, by contrast, a two-thirds majority is required for advice-and-assent before the president can ratify any treaty).

However, the Maastricht Treaty also extended the scope of Parliament's assent powers to other agreements establishing a specific institutional framework by organising cooperation procedures, agreements having important budgetary implications for the Community and agreements entailing amendment of an act adopted under the co-decision procedure. The logic of the last provision is clear: Parliament now has the right to grant or withhold its assent to any agreement affecting an act which it jointly adopted with the Council. The extension of the procedure to agreements having budgetary implications for the Community is also a significant advance for the Parliament.

Consultation and information on trade agreements

Nevertheless, the European Parliament's principal frustration in the external trade field lies in the limited scope of its assent powers and its weak influence on the negotiating process. On this subject, Parliament looks constantly across the Atlantic to the United States, where Congress has the power 'to regulate commerce with foreign nations' and has a formidable armoury of political weapons to exert influence on negotiations and even negotiate agreements. As was apparent in the negotiations over the GATT Uruguay Round, the European Union's Member States present a common (and powerful) face to the external world on all trade and commerce matters, with the Commission acting as the Union's chief negotiator, on the authorisation of the Council. And yet, an aggrieved Parliament constantly points out, the treaties grant the European Parliament no role in the negotiation or conclusion of the majority of the Union's trade and commercial agreements. (Here all comparisons with the United States Congress were particularly galling, since the deadlines to which the negotiators had to work were imposed by the Congress.) Moreover, the Maastricht Treaty did nothing to change this perceived neglect.

Parliament has further pointed out the inconsistencies in the distribution of its current assent powers, whereby it may be called upon to give its assent to a relatively minor and uncontroversial technical amendment to an association agreement and yet may have no say in the conclusion of a major and far-reaching trade agreement. The Parliament has also argued that the definitions of exactly what constitutes an association agreement, or not, can be inconsistent (although these complaints became temporarily muted when, allaying Parliament's suspicions, all the 'Europe agreements' with the newly democratised countries of Central and Eastern Europe were submitted to the European Parliament for its assent). Parliament closely monitors the negotiations of all trade agreements (such agreements would normally be listed in the annual legislative programme) and would almost certainly use its powers before the Court to defend its prerogatives in this area.

Despite its relative formal weakness, the European Parliament has gained significant rights to consultation and information on external trade matters. A principal development has been that the Community has increasingly entered into agreements which go beyond straightforward commercial agreements and yet fall short of a full-blown association agreement. Until the Maastricht Treaty, these agreements, dubbed 'cooperation agreements', were based on a catch-all article which provides that where 'this Treaty has not provided the necessary powers, the Council shall, acting unanimously on a proposal from the Commission and after consulting the European Parliament, take the appropriate measures'.

In June 1983, at the Stuttgart European Council, it was agreed that Parliament would be consulted on all 'significant' international agreements. Although Parliament unilaterally sought a liberal interpretation of the word 'significant' through its own Rules of Procedure, in practice it was left to the Council to determine the significance of agreements and hence Parliament's rights.

The Maastricht Treaty has both rationalised and consolidated Parliament's consultation rights. In addition to its assent powers, the treaty now expressly provides for the Parliament to be consulted on 'agreements between the Community and one or more states or international organisations' except proposals for implementing the common commercial policy. However, the Maastricht Treaty also weakens Parliament's traditional power of delay by providing that the Council may lay down a deadline and act in the absence of Parliament's opinion if not adopted within that deadline.

The European Parliament's rights to information have been considerably enhanced and extended by a series of political conventions, known collectively as the 'Luns–Westerterp' procedures (after two Dutch foreign ministers). Where more important agreements are concerned, the Commission and the Council now generally participate in a parliamentary debate before negotiations begin, and thereafter the Commission keeps the Parliament informed (mainly through Parliament's Committee on External Economic Relations) of the state of negotiations. Confidential briefings on the content of negotiating mandates and the outcome of negotiations may take place, and the Commission and the Council will generally take part in parliamentary debate once an agreement has been concluded. Whatever its formal powers, Parliament is well informed on trade matters and therefore well placed to exert pressure on the Commission and the Council through its powers of questioning and debate.

Consultation on the Common Foreign and Security Policy

Since its earliest days, the European Parliament has pushed for the European Community to match its economic muscle with the political machinery that would enable it to take its place on the world stage. In its view, progress towards a Common Foreign and Security Policy (CFSP) has been painfully slow, with the consequences of the absence of a CFSP being thrown into uncomfortably sharp relief by recent events such as the Gulf War and the wars in the former Yugoslavia.

After the significant first step of the SEA's provision on European cooperation in the sphere of foreign policy, the Maastricht Treaty finally established an embryonic CFSP. The CFSP is fundamentally inter-governmental in nature and lies outside the EC Treaty, in a separate title (commonly described as an inter-governmental 'pillar'). Nevertheless, it does involve three Community institutions — the Council (and the

European Council and the Presidency), the Commission and the Parliament — provides for the establishment of common positions and joint actions and has a built-in review clause, linked to the 1996 intergovernmental conference.

The Parliament's response to the CFSP provisions was correspondingly ambivalent. In a 7 April 1992 resolution, it drew attention to the 'major shortcoming' in the treaty that 'leaves the common foreign and security policy outside the European Community Treaty (with, therefore, a lesser role for the Commission and the Parliament and no possibility for legal redress at the Court of Justice)'. At the same time, it recognised the 'commitment to a common foreign and security policy' as a 'positive element'.

Despite its misgivings, the European Parliament has important rights to information and consultation, as well as explicit power to ask questions and make recommendations. Specifically, the Maastricht Treaty provides that 'the Presidency shall consult the European Parliament on the main aspects and the basic choices of the common foreign and security policy and shall ensure that the views of the European Parliament are duly taken into consideration'; that 'the European Parliament shall be kept regularly informed by the Presidency and the Commission of the development of the Union's foreign and security policy'; that 'the European Parliament may ask questions of the Council or make recommendations to it'; and that 'it shall hold an annual debate on progress in implementing the common foreign and security policy'.

The Commission also has an important and independent role to play in the formulation of the CFSP. In general, 'it shall be fully associated with the work carried out', but it has a specific right to refer to the Council any question relating to the CFSP and may submit proposals to the Council. The Maastricht Treaty charges the Commission with the duty to keep the European Parliament regularly informed of the development of the Union's CFSP.

The Parliament has been at pains to establish mechanisms that make the most of its various powers of information and consultation. In January 1992, Parliament transformed its Political Affairs Committee into a Foreign Affairs Committee and appointed a heavyweight political figure (Enrique Baron Crespo, an outgoing President of Parliament and former Spanish minister) as its chairman. Parliament's September 1993 rules changes make the committee expressly responsible for ensuring the due consultation of Parliament and that Parliament's views are subsequently taken into account. The committee is also primarily responsible for the drafting of recommendations to the Council.

The Parliament is closely following debates within the Council as to how the CFSP and its actions will be financed. In particular, should the Council opt for the Community budget, then Parliament will seek to exercise influence and control through its more general prerogatives as a twin arm of the Community's budgetary authority.

The Maastricht Treaty's CFSP provisions are a good example of an area where the Parliament is becoming less narrowly linked to the Commission and where the Council is becoming more broadly involved with the Parliament. Using its tried-and-tested method of tying the institutions into mutually agreed conventions, the Parliament hopes to flesh out and concretise the Maastricht provisions. (For example, how regular is 'regularly'? And what should the Council do with Parliament's recommendations?) Early indications are that the Council will resist any such tendency towards a formal agreement (with its concomitant consequence of 'Communitarising' an inter-governmental pillar), but inter-institutional talks on the subject nevertheless continue. In the meantime, the Parliament will continue to seek to 'overcome' the pillar structure by encouraging the Commission, an institution more open, sympathetic and accountable to the Parliament, to develop its role in foreign policy to the full.

Joint parliamentary committees and interparliamentary delegations

As a consequence of its internal budgetary and organisational autonomy, the European Parliament has been able to establish inter-parliamentary delegations to a number of countries, in addition to the joint parliamentary committees established in the context of association agreements. Altogether, there are currently twenty-nine inter-parliamentary delegations and joint parliamentary committees, and one delegation to the EC–European Economic Area Joint Committee. The discussions of joint parliamentary committees generally concentrate on matters of pertinence to the associate state's ultimate accession to the Union. Inter-parliamentary delegations have a broader brief, involving direct trade and foreign-policy discussions with parliamentarians from the countries concerned, together with wider debates of common political issues. Delegations meet alternatively in the third country and in the Union and are regularly briefed by the Commission and by other authorities. Thus, although not technically speaking a power, inter-parliamentary delegations serve as an additional source of information and influence for the Parliament. Some inter-parliamentary delegations are of particular importance. For example, the 42nd inter-parliamentary meeting between the European Parliament and the United States Congress took place in Athens just three days after the January 1994 NATO Summit and just two days after the Transatlantic Summit between President Clinton, President Delors, and President-in-office Papandreou. Subjects discussed included the 'partnership for peace' offer made by NATO to the Eastern European countries, the continued crisis in the former Yugoslavia, the Middle East peace process, the GATT Uruguay Round, the North Atlantic Free Trade Association and a series of bilateral economic problems.

The power of expression — the European Parliament in the world

Whatever the European Parliament's objective constitutional status, and whatever the 'real' extent of its powers, such gradations and distinctions are frequently of much less importance when viewed from outside the European Union. The European Parliament is the European Union's *only* representative parliamentary body and, because of this, its pronouncements are taken seriously. In similar vein, when dignitaries and heads of state (from President Reagan to President Yeltsin, from the Queen of the United Kingdom to Yasser Arafat) visit the European Union, the European Parliament seems the natural forum for them to address. A measure of importance attached to the Parliament's pronouncements can be gleaned from the fact that the United States' embassy in Brussels has a parliamentary attaché whose job includes following the Parliament's work (in Brussels and Strasbourg) and, where necessary, discreetly lobbying its members. Debates in the European Parliament that concern a third country are usually well covered by the media of that country, and parliamentary criticisms can provoke considerable controversy abroad. In itself this is a weak power, but a power none the less and, perhaps because it symbolises European democracy, Parliament's criticisms create particular sensitivities in the field of human rights.

3.6 Economic and Monetary Union

Stage one — July 1990–December 1993

The history of the Community has been punctuated by attempts to bring about closer economic and monetary cooperation with a view to ultimate union. As early as 1960, a Short Term Economic Policy Committee, composed of representatives of the Commission and the Member States was established, and in 1964 a Committee of Governors of Central Banks and a Budgetary Policy Committee were set up, together with a Medium Term Economic Policy Committee. These early attempts never got beyond forecasting. However, in 1969 Raymond Barre, then a Vice-President of the Commission, drafted a report calling for full economic and monetary union, and this was followed by a commitment to such a union by the heads of state and government at the December 1969 Hague Summit. A committee under the chairmanship of the Luxembourg Prime Minister, Pierre Werner, reported back to the Member States with concrete proposals, and in February 1971 the Council adopted a staged programme for the adoption of full economic and monetary union by 1980. However, following the first oil crisis, dollar convertibility ended in August 1971, and the Werner plan was blown off course by the ensuring monetary crisis, coupled with the strains on individual currencies consequent upon enlargement.

By 1977, all that remained was a forlorn 'snake' of seven cooperating currencies, including two non-Member States (Norway and Sweden). In October of that year Roy Jenkins, then President of the Commission, called for renewed efforts, and in 1978 Valéry Giscard d'Estaing and Helmut Schmidt responded with a proposal for a new European Monetary System (EMS), which came into existence in December 1978, at the Brussels European Council. The new European Monetary System consisted of a more flexible 'snake' arrangement and was accompanied by the creation of a new European Currency Unit (ECU) whose value was determined through a 'basket' of national currencies. Despite theoretical and political misgivings about the value of such a system, the EMS proved a relative success and seemed to encourage high levels of exchange-rate stability for its member currencies. The 1987 Single European Act noted the success of the EMS, introduced a new treaty article designed to encourage further cooperation between Member States and their monetary authorities and provided for the possibility of further institutional changes.

The gradual achievement of the internal market was thought to contain its own functionalist dynamic. In particular, it became clear that the benefits of an internal market would be undermined if intra-Community trade continued to be subject to the uncertainties of currency fluctuation and the burden of currency transaction costs. Thus, less than a year after the entry into force of the Single European Act, the June 1988 Hanover European Council created a committee composed of central bank governors and chaired by the President of the Commission, Jacques Delors, to study how the Community might progress to economic and monetary union. The Delors Committee reported back in April 1989, proposing a three-stage plan for progress to full economic and monetary union. The June 1989 Madrid European Council agreed that the first stage of the economic and monetary union process should begin on 1 July 1990.

The Commission soon tabled proposals related to the strengthening of the role of the Committee of Governors of the Member States' Central Banks and the Economic Policy Committee as integral parts of the first stage of economic and monetary union. The European Parliament had only relatively weak consultative powers in relation to these proposals but, voicing concern about ensuring proper accountability, was able to wield its powers of delay in conjunction with the Madrid Council's set date for the beginning of the first stage in order to force some concessions from the Commission related to the consultative and information rights of the Parliament itself.

The Commission's draft proposals included a Council decision (adopted in March 1990) on the attainment of progressive convergence of the economic policies and performance of the Member States. This decision resulted in half-yearly multilateral surveillance exercises whose purpose was to obtain reciprocal commitments from individual Member States leading to self-enforced policy coordination. The process was reinforced by the voluntary presentation of convergence programmes by each Member State which were specifically aimed at addressing the main sources of difficulty in terms of convergence, and in particular divergent inflationary and budgetary trends. Parliament's Economic and Monetary Committee (and latterly its Sub-Committee on Monetary Affairs) was intimately involved in this process, as such programmes were presented to the committee by the Member State governments as part of the process.

Stage two — January 1994–December 1996 or 1998

The fall of the Berlin Wall in November 1989 precipitated the collapse of most of the Central and Eastern European Communist regimes and, with these events as its background, the December 1989 Strasbourg European Council agreed to establish an inter-governmental conference on economic and monetary union at the end of 1990. A special October 1990 Rome European Council agreed that the second stage of economic and monetary union should begin on 1 January 1994, and the economic and monetary union inter-governmental conference (together with another on political union) was opened at a second Rome European Council in December 1990. The resulting draft treaty amendments were ultimately adopted at the Maastricht European Council in December 1991.

In January 1992, with a view to the implementation of the treaty, the European Parliament created a Sub-Committee on Monetary Affairs, which was thereafter to monitor the process of economic and monetary union and is Parliament's principal interlocutor with the European Monetary Institute (as it was with the Committee of Central Bank Governors).

The Maastricht Treaty itself entered into force on 1 November 1993, and the Commission again immediately tabled the necessary secondary legislation related to the realisation of the second stage, including such matters as the excessive deficit procedure, prohibition of privileged access by public institutions to financial institutions, and the determination of the financial key for the European Monetary Institute which was to be created at the outset of the second stage. There were six measures altogether. Four were subject to the consultation procedure and two to the cooperation procedure. Anxious to see the timetable for economic and monetary union respected, the Parliament engaged in a polite fiction, whereby the consultation process began, on the basis of informal proposals, long before the Maastricht Treaty came into force. Thus formal adoption of its opinions and second readings took place in November, leaving sufficient time for the measures to enter into force at the beginning of the second stage in January 1994.

The first stage of economic and monetary union consisted of enhanced monetary cooperation and concerted attempts ('learning by doing', multilateral surveillance) to bring about the convergence of the Member States' economies, with enhanced roles for the Committee of Central Bank Governors, the Economic and Monetary Policy Committees and the specialised ECOFIN Council. The Parliament, and particularly its Sub-Committee on Monetary Affairs, concentrated a great deal of effort on keeping Parliament fully abreast of developments. This it did through regular exchanges of views, some of them behind closed doors, with the responsible commissioner (Henning Christophersen) and high-ranking Commission officials, with the ECOFIN Presidency and occasionally other ministers, with the President of the Committee of Central Bank Governors and occasionally other Central Bank Governors, with experts and officials from the Economic and Monetary Policy Committees and with a broad array of experts from the monetary field (for example, the former German Chancellor Helmut Schmidt came before the sub-committee). The recurrent crises besetting the Exchange Rate Mechanism in the autumn of 1992 and the summer of 1993 enhanced the importance of these frequent exchanges.

Thus, in addition to consultation on some paving legislation, Parliament's main powers in the first stage were mostly concentrated on gleaning detailed, up-to-date, and 'inside' information *as of right*. Parliament could claim some success, and the cooperation of key figures such as the president of the Bundesbank and the general openness of the Community's monetary policy-making circles set good precedents for the next stages.

In contrast to the essentially informational approach of the first stage, the second stage involved the creation of the European Monetary Institute, to which the Maastricht Treaty gave a series of specific responsibilities, ranging from strengthening central bank cooperation to the preparation of the third stage. It granted the Parliament a series of specific powers, divided into four categories. First, as was seen above, it had consultative powers, including some falling under the cooperation procedure in relation to the legislation paving the way for the second stage, and will be entitled to consultation on any further legislation conferring other powers on the European Monetary Institute in relation to the preparation of the third stage. (In this context, Jacques Delors has repeatedly stated that the EMI should be given more responsibility.)

Second, as was also seen above, it has consultative powers in relation to the nomination of the president of the European Monetary Institute. Third, the European Monetary Institute must address an annual report on its activities, together with its annual accounts, to the European Parliament, together with the European Council, the Council and the Commission, and the same article (in a protocol to the treaty) provides that 'the President of the EMI may, at the request of the European Parliament or on his own initiative, be heard by the competent Committees of the European Parliament'. (In fact, in his 'confirmation hearing' before the Parliament, the current president, Baron Alexandre Lamfalussy, promised close collaboration with and full information of the Parliament.) Parliament has introduced a specific rule enabling the president of the European Monetary Institute (and ultimately the president of the future European Central Bank) to present his annual report to Parliament meeting in plenary session. (It is an indication of the office's importance that only the president of the Court of Auditors enjoys a similar right to present his institution's annual report.)

Fourth, the Parliament has consultative powers in relation to the mechanism for the transition from the second to the third stages. The treaty provides that, by December 1996, the European Council (acting by a qualified majority) must: decide whether a majority of the Member States fulfil the necessary conditions for the adoption of a single currency; decide whether it is 'appropriate' for the Community to enter the third stage; and set the date for the beginning of the third stage. The European Council will base its decisions on convergence reports adopted by the Council. The European Parliament will be consulted on these, with its opinion going straight to the European Council.

If the date for the beginning of the third stage has not been set by the end of 1997, the treaty provides that it will start on 1 January 1999, with the European Council deciding which Member States fulfil the conditions for transition to a single currency. Again, the European Council will base its decision on the Council's reports and Parliament's opinions on them.

Those Member States not fulfilling the conditions at the time of the shift to the third stage will be granted derogations. When appropriate, but minimally every two years, the Council will decide which Member States with a derogation have fulfilled the necessary conditions and accordingly abrogate the derogations. The treaty provides that the Council's decisions should be based on a discussion in the European Council after consultation with the Parliament.

Stage three — January 1997 or 1999 onwards

At the beginning of the third stage, those Member States fulfilling the necessary conditions will give up their national currencies and move to a single, shared currency. The Maastricht Treaty's blueprint for economic and monetary union rests on two bases. The first is the enhanced coordination of the Member States' economic policies, backed up by constant monitoring and potential sanctions in the case of persistent destabilising policies. The second is an independent European Central Bank, crowning a European System of independent Central Banks. The treaty sets out specific rights and powers for the Parliament in regard to both the economic and monetary aspects of the union.

The broad guidelines of economic policy within the Union would then be 'discussed' by the European Council and adopted in the form of a recommendation by the Council. The Council must then inform the Parliament of its recommendations. In order to ensure closer economic coordination and sustained convergence, the Council has a constant watching brief to monitor economic developments within each of the Member States as well as to assess the consistency of Member States' economic policies with the broad guidelines set by the European Council and the Council. Where a Member State's policies are considered inconsistent, the Council may make 'recommendations' to the state concerned and may further decide to make its decisions public. Both the president of the Council and the president of the Commission report to the European Parliament on the results of multilateral surveillance and, if the Council should decide to make its recommendations public, the president of the Council may be invited to appear before the competent parliamentary committee. The treaty provides that any rules the Council adopts to govern the multilateral surveillance procedure must be subject to the cooperation procedure, which grants Parliament two readings.

The treaty provides the Parliament with a number of accompanying and occasional powers, mostly of information or consultation. Where a Member State experiences severe difficulties caused by exceptional circumstances beyond its control, the Council may decide to grant financial assistance, and in such cases the president of the Council must inform the Parliament of the decision taken.

Where a Member State persists in running an excessive deficit, a number of sanctions are open to the Council, ultimately including compulsory repayment and the imposition of fines. Again, in such circumstances the president of the Council must inform the Parliament of the decision taken. The criteria for assessing the scale of a Member State's deficit are set out in a protocol to the treaty. These will ultimately be replaced by definitive provisions, with the Council acting unanimously after having consulted the Parliament.

If the Council decides to confer specific tasks on the European Central Bank relating to the prudential supervision of credit institutions, it must seek the assent of the Parliament. If the Council decides to amend certain articles of the Statute of the European System of Central Banks, it must seek the assent of the Parliament, and it must consult the Parliament when adopting the detailed provisions set out in the ESCB Statute. On the monetary side, the Council must consult the Parliament when concluding arrangements for an exchange-rate system for the ECU in relation to third-country currencies, and the president of the Council must inform the Parliament of the adoption, adjustment or abandonment of the ECU central rates. The president, vice-president and four other members of the Executive Board of the European Central Bank are to be appointed by the European Council, on the basis of a Council recommendation. The Council must consult the Parliament (and the ECB's Governing Council) on its recommendation.

The European Central Bank has to draft two annual reports, one on the activities of the European System of Central Banks and another on the current and previous year's monetary policy, and these reports will be addressed to the European Parliament, the European Council, the Council and the Commission. The president of the European Central Bank will present the report to the Council and the Parliament, and the Parliament may then hold 'a general debate on that basis'. The treaty further provides that 'the President of the ECB and the other members of the Executive Board may, at the request of the European Parliament or their own initiative, be heard by the competent Committees of the European Parliament'. Finally, the president of the Council will inform the European Parliament on its decision laying down detailed provisions concerning the composition of the Economic and Financial Committee which is to be established at the beginning of the third stage.

Parliament's criticisms

As in so many other areas, the European Parliament greeted the Maastricht Treaty's provisions on EMU with ambivalence. It had long called for moves towards economic and monetary union and had indeed drafted its own report on the subject in the run-up to the inter-governmental conference, and so it unequivocally welcomed 'the historic decision taken by the Maastricht European Council to introduce a single currency' (7 April 1992). At the same time, the Parliament drafted a list of shortcomings, some political, some technical and some more purely constitutional.

Potentially the largest political debate had been won early on, inasmuch as a large majority within Parliament accepted the need for the European Central Bank and the national central banks making up the European System of Central Banks to be independent in the conduct of their duties. The Parliament thus rallied to a widespread consensus within the Community institutions, it being generally acknowledged that the German government could not sign up to the creation of a central bank that would be less independent than its own Bundesbank. In fact, so enthusiastically did the Parliament support the concept of an independent Central Bank that its resolution 'deplored' the envisaged management structure of its forerunner, the European Monetary Institute, which Parliament considered insufficient to ensure its independence *vis-à-vis* the current central banks and national governments. More recently, Parliament has adopted an 'own initiative' report urging all Member States to render their central banks truly independent. (In the early spring of 1994, the adoption of a series of own-initiative reports relating to the status and independence of the EMU institutions seemed to rekindle debates within Parliament about accountability, but the basic provision of the Maastricht Treaty was not itself questioned.)

As to the Central Bank's mandate, Parliament expressed regret at the treaty's 'exclusive' concentration on the Bundesbank's prime concern, price stability, to the detriment of other socio-economic considerations. Indeed, future economic policy debate in the Union, as is currently the case in the Member States, will inevitably revolve to some extent around the conflict between the advantages of anti-inflationary policies and the disadvantages of those same, deflationary, policies, particularly at times of economic recession.

Parliament greeted the consequences of the monetary turbulence of autumn 1992 and summer 1993 with a jaundiced eye, for in its recommendations, and indeed in its own draft treaty amendments, on economic and monetary union, it had repeatedly stressed the dangers of a long transitional period, pointing in particular to the risk of providing the exchange markets with easy targets for speculation. Thus, Parliament felt vindicated, sadly rather than gloatingly, that the ERM's narrow bands had to be relaxed in August 1993. In its own eyes, perhaps more profoundly, the experience provided proof that Parliament was able to give good technical as well as political advice.

However, the Parliament's major concerns were, and remain, constitutional, particularly with regard to economic policy. Its April 1992 resolution deplored:

> the fact that, when economic policy-making takes effect, the scope for parliamentary influence will suffer at national and European level, since national parliaments will lose their ability to discipline national governments because the Council will act by a qualified majority, while the European Parliament will be notified after the event.

The resolution went on to list a number of areas where 'the blueprint for economic policy outlined in the Treaty makes redundant the democratic control exercised hitherto by the national parliaments'. In other words, on economic and monetary union as in other areas, the European Parliament sees as its vocation to try and reassert parliamentary control at Union level. In its eyes, the treaty's provisions, welcome though they are in terms of the commitment to economic and monetary union, aggravate the Union's democratic deficit.

Parliament has resolved on a three-pronged strategy to overcome these shortcomings. The first approach is fully to exploit and consolidate its treaty-based powers. In this context, the Parliament has been much encouraged by the generally open and cooperative attitudes of the president of the European Monetary Institute, the Commission and the Council Presidency. The second approach, as with CFSP, is to seek consensual inter-institutional agreement on exactly how the mechanics — of consultation, of information — are to be realised. However, as with the many other inter-institutional agreements now in existence, Parliament tends to seek elements that go beyond the treaty's provisions. Again, as with CFSP, early indications suggest that the Council is reluctant to enter into such an agreement, although mutually acceptable practical arrangements will in any case have to be agreed in some areas.

Parliament's third approach will be to seek amendments to the treaty at the 1996 inter-governmental conference. The European Parliament will seek to reassert the control it feels national parliaments have lost in such areas as safeguard measures *vis-à-vis* third countries, financial assistance from one Member State to another, the right to make certain recommendations (as the treaty stands, a Member State has to ask the Commission to make such recommendations), penalties on Member States with persistent budget deficits, international monetary or foreign exchange agreements, the assessment of convergence programmes and so on. More generally, the Parliament will seek a rationalisation of its rights, which it feels are scattered inconsistently through the treaty, and the reinforcement or extension of its powers (for example, transforming information into consultation, or consultation into cooperation, co-decision or assent).

Above all, the European Parliament will seek more pro-active involvement in the establishment of the Union's broad economic policy guidelines. As matters currently stand, these are drafted by the Commission, adopted by the Council, discussed by the European Council and then transformed into recommendations by the Council. Parliament's only right is to be informed about the recommendations, after the event, by the Council. The Parliament has already used its untrammelled right of expression to force the Commission and the Council into political debate preceding the drafting of economic guidelines, and the Commission has been at particular pains to keep the Parliament informed of its work in this field, but the Parliament wants a more constructive and influential role in the process in formal treaty terms. In its initial response to the Maastricht Treaty, the European Parliament regretted that the treaty had failed 'to provide any economic policy authority with adequate democratic legitimacy to counterbalance the autonomous monetary policy authority of the European Central Bank', and one of its primary aims at the 1996 inter-governmental conference will be to try and correct this perceived imbalance. (One possibility would be for Parliament to insist on provisions for a greater role under the detailed rules for the multilateral surveillance procedure which the Council is obliged to adopt, via the cooperation procedure, by Article 103.5.)

3.7   Justice and home affairs

A separate title in the Maastricht Treaty set out detailed provisions for cooperation among the Member States in the fields of justice and home affairs. After the provisions on the Common Foreign and Security Policy, this was described as the second inter-governmental 'pillar' within the treaty, but the description is not entirely accurate. The treaty sets out nine areas of 'common interest' to the Member States from asylum and immigration policy through to judicial and police cooperation. In these areas, the Member States 'inform and consult one another within the Council with a view to coordinating their action' and to that end have established collaboration between the relevant departments of their administrations. A Coordinating Committee of senior officials has been set up to prepare the Council's work. Under the new provisions, in addition to general coordination, the Council may adopt joint positions and promote further cooperation, adopt joint actions and draw up conventions.

However, the Community institutions are intimately involved in the cooperation process. The Commission has a right of initiative in all areas concerned with asylum, immigration, entry, movement and residence of third-country nationals, combating drug addiction, combating fraud and judicial cooperation in civil matters. Moreover, the Commission is 'fully associated with the work in the areas referred to in this Title'. The Council (in its guise as a meeting of the 'High Contracting Parties') may include provision within any conventions that it adopts that the Court of Justice should have jurisdiction to interpret provisions and rule on any disputes, and it may decide that operational expenditure related to any of the provisions under the whole title should be charged to the budget of the European Community, in which case the budgetary procedure laid down in the treaties would be applicable.

Both the Presidency and the Commission are charged with the duty of regularly informing the European Parliament of all discussions in the areas covered by the title. The Presidency has to consult the European Parliament on the principal aspects of activities in the areas referred to in the title, and has to 'ensure that the views of the European Parliament are duly taken into consideration'. The treaty also provides that the

Parliament may ask questions of the Council or make recommendations to it and that it should hold an annual debate on progress made in the areas referred to in the title.

From all of the foregoing it can be seen that the Union's justice and home affairs cooperation, as established by the Maastricht Treaty, is not purely inter-governmental; the Community's institutions are all involved to some extent, with the Commission being particularly involved in all activities. But nor does such cooperation fall under the traditional 'Community method'. In effect, justice and home affairs cooperation is a hybrid process, straddling the more purely inter-governmental convention-drafting activities of the Council of Europe and the Community's legislative method. The Maastricht Treaty's draftsmen clearly saw these provisions as being transitional, designed to encourage the closer and regular cooperation which would bring about in due course a sufficient degree of mutual confidence for these policy areas to be subsumed into the Community proper. Nowhere are the draftsmen's intentions more evident than in the last article in the title, which provides that the Council, acting unanimously on the initiative of the Commission or a Member State, may decide to bring action in specified areas within the treaty (and a corresponding article within the treaty allows for such areas to be thus brought in). Commonly referred to as the *passerelle* (bridge), this provision would ultimately enable the Commission and the Member States to bring all areas where the Commission has an initiative fully under the treaty.

Once again, the Parliament greeted these provisions with ambivalence. It saw the 'pillar' structure as a general shortcoming of the Maastricht Treaty which, as it put it; '. . . leaves cooperation in the spheres of justice and home affairs outside the European Community Treaty thus escaping effective parliamentary and judicial control in an area in which citizens' rights are directly affected with no democratic procedures for decision-taking in this matter'. As with the Common Foreign and Security Policy provisions, Parliament is resolved on generally seeking to overcome the pillar structure by encouraging the Commission to develop its role within justice and home affairs cooperation to the full. (Clearly, in the medium- to longer-term, it will encourage the Commission to use the *passerelle* as much as possible.)

In January 1992, with a view to the Maastricht Treaty's provisions, the Parliament created a new Committee on Civil Liberties and Internal Affairs with an explicit brief to monitor the Council's activities in this field, as well as to draft recommendations and in general to create a parliamentary forum to 'shadow' inter-governmental cooperation. The new committee soon saw the importance of cooperating closely with national parliaments so that in this area, perhaps more than in any other, the European Parliament is collaborating closely with national parliaments in order to assert maximal democratic control.

173

3.8 Parliament's other scrutiny and supervisory powers

Questions

Written questions

In addition to the powers outlined above, the European Parliament also possesses a small arsenal of traditional parliamentary powers for scrutinising the activities of, and holding to account, the other Community institutions. One of these is the right to ask questions. The original EEC Treaty distinguished between the Commission and the Council in this regard. It provided that the Commission 'shall reply orally or in writing to questions put to it by the European Parliament or its members'. There was no similar provision for the Council, and it was not until the 1983 Stuttgart European Council that the Council gave an undertaking to answer all of Parliament's questions. Though in practice it makes little difference, the Council's undertaking remains a political convention rather than a treaty obligation.

Parliament has evolved three types of question, and each has come to serve a very different purpose. All members of the Parliament have the right to table written questions to the Commission and the Council. These are generally short written requests which are forwarded to the institution concerned and although they may be political in intent or content are primarily designed to elicit information. The number of such questions is large and steadily increasing (3,281 in 1991, 3,526 in 1992, 4,111 in 1993), with the vast majority (on average about 90 per cent — 3,051 in 1992, 3,588 in 1993) addressed to the Commission. The reasons for this high proportion are bound up in the nature of the Commission's functions, particularly as policy and budgetary executive, its extensive contacts with national authorities and its traditional openness to the Parliament. The downside of the high number of questions tabled is the typically lengthy periods involved in drafting responses. The Parliament has introduced mechanisms to prioritise written questions requiring no detailed research, unilateral deadlines and the optional transformation of written questions into questions in committee. For its part, the Commission has repeatedly undertaken to cut down delay and to this end has introduced internal mechanisms to speed up replies, although it cannot accept Parliament's unilaterally imposed deadlines. These phenomena, increasing quantities of questions and unavoidable delays in replies, have led to a degree of frustration in Parliament which has chiefly found its outlet in two alternatives: personal correspondence with a commissioner (commissioners' parliamentary postbags are growing exponentially) and question time. The disadvantage of a letter is that it will not have the formal and official status of a reply published in the *Official Journal* (the Community's official gazette). The disadvantage of question time is that it requires the presence of the member at an awkward hour on the Wednesday evening in Strasbourg.

Oral questions

In the Parliament's early life, when its legislative and budgetary powers were few and weak, oral questions were considered an important power. They were far from having the government-defeating potential of the dreaded *interpellation* of the French Fourth Republic, but they did enable the Parliament to follow up the institution's response with a debate and (unlike the French Fifth Republic's *questions au gouvernement* or adjournment debates in the House of Commons) the adoption of a resolution, and hence a vote. However, as Parliament's legislative and budgetary powers have grown in number and importance, and as plenary time has been increasingly occupied by such business, the oral question has diminished in relative importance.

Over the years, the oral question has also been subject to a process of stylisation and formalisation, so that it now provides a very particular role in the European Parliament's activities. In the first place, the varieties of oral question (oral question with debate, without debate etc.) that used to exist have been gradually whittled down to just one sort. Second, the conditions governing the tabling of oral questions have been gradually tightened up, with the power of decision lying chiefly with the leaders of the major political groups. Under current practice, oral questions may only be tabled by a committee, a political group or at least twenty-three members (this used to be seven members and, before that, five). Moreover, it is the Conference of Presidents, which is made up of the leaders of the political groups (with votes weighted according to the size of the group), which decides whether questions will be placed on Parliament's plenary agenda. In the third place, the practice has grown of including oral questions as 'footnotes' to other debates on related subjects. This practice has evolved directly out of the pressure on plenary time. Fourth, it is common for similar questions to be tabled to the Commission and the Council, thus involving both in the reply process.

The result of all these developments has been to transform the oral question into an exclusive tool of the political groups and committees, used principally in the organisation of set-piece debates for the evocation of specific information on important political topics, culminating in the adoption of a resolution. As such, the formalised oral question serves several purposes. It is a device for signalling political concern. It is a device for eliciting political information from the institution concerned, thus holding it to account. It is a device for involving the other institutions in political debate on topical political issues. But, equally, it is a device for Parliament to express itself.

Question time

The European Parliament's question time is a much-maligned and much misunderstood procedure. It was introduced soon after the United Kingdom first sent a contingent to the Parliament in 1973 and as a direct response to a memorandum from the then leader of the Conservative delegation, the late Peter Kirk, who sought ways to enliven the Parliament's proceedings. Kirk had the highly stylised model of the House of Commons' Prime Minister's Question Time in mind, but this could never work in a culturally diverse Parliament where debates had to be interpreted through earphones, where there was no government and opposition and, above all, where there was no prime minister.

The European Parliament's question time also suffered from the same decline in relative importance suffered by oral questions, and for a long time its efficiency was further diminished by its being shuffled around at very short notice to make way for more important business. Latterly, the procedure has been granted a fixed 'slot', but this is at the awkward time of nine until midnight on the Wednesday evening in Strasbourg, and attendance has suffered as a result. This has had the knock-on effect of making those patiently waiting for their question to be taken anxious that all other questions preceding it be dispatched as rapidly as possible. Presidents in the chair are therefore under constant pressure to interpret the rules strictly, ruling out more than a certain number of supplementary questions even where a promising line of questioning appears to be opening up. (On more than one such occasion this author has heard presidents in the chair apologising for there having been a debate!)

Until Parliament's September 1993 post-Maastricht rules-change package was adopted, a parliamentarian was guaranteed a written answer to a question if it was not reached or if absent from the chamber when it was called. This led to the use of the procedure by some members as a form of express answering service, further diminishing its intended purpose. The procedure has been further undermined by the nature of the institutions involved. The Council is represented by the Presidency, but the nature of the Presidency makes it virtually impossible for ministers representing the Presidency to take a creative, pro-active part in the proceedings. The Commission's role in the proceedings, on the other hand, is hampered by its collegiate nature and the frequent unavailability of the commissioner responsible for any particular subject. Parliament has sought to overcome this problem by providing for question times to the president and individual members of the Commission, but because it sees the principal of collegiality as a deontological part of the Community's inter-institutional balance, the Commission has refused to be bound by such distinctions.

Despite all of these shortcomings, the procedure has survived, largely unchanged, for twenty years. A powerful reason for this is that question time remains one of the very few areas of Parliament's activities where the backbencher may enjoy direct, formal interaction and debate with a commissioner or a minister. A second, linked, reason is that those MEPs elected to constituencies (particularly the British and the Irish) can use the procedure to raise matters of particular concern to their constituencies. A third reason is that MEPs can win commitments, particularly from commissioners, to look into or report back on particular matters, and as these commitments are minuted, commissioners can be held to account. Finally, the procedure does work as intended, if only occasionally, in getting commissioners and ministers to spell out particular aspects of policy, to enter into debate (however truncated) and in generally asserting Parliament's right to control (see Westlake, 1990).

Sir Christopher Prout, one of Parliament's noted constitutionalists, has argued that Parliament generally neglects its supervisory powers to its own detriment. The question time procedure is one area where those powers have been invested with fresh significance by the Maastricht Treaty because of the greatly increased number of obligations on the Council and the Commission to inform, consult and report to the Parliament. Thus, the question time procedure may be neglected currently, but if, as some predict, Parliament's legislative load declines (post-1992) and its plenary time expands (see Fitzmaurice, 1994), and as it seeks to exploit fully its powers to hold the other institutions to account, the procedure may yet enjoy a modest renaissance.

Follow-up to the Commission's undertakings

The Commission has introduced an internal mechanism to ensure that, where a commissioner has accepted parliamentary amendments during the legislative process, its proposals are accordingly modified (in fact, the commissioner is normally authorised — in the jargon, 'habilitated' — by the college in advance). The Commission prepares a monthly report to Parliament which sets out all of the Commission's legislative undertakings and its action upon them and, although a rare occurrence, the Parliament may ask questions as a function of this. A current practical shortcoming in this procedure (known as *'suites données'*) is that it is held after question time just before midnight on Wednesday evenings in Strasbourg. The procedure is currently under review.

In addition, the Commission compiles a list of all of the undertakings it has given in relation to Parliament's non-legislative reports. The responsible committees are automatically informed of the Commission's follow-up on particular measures and a bi-annual compilation of all of the Commission's undertakings and the action it has subsequently taken is forwarded to the Parliament. This particular aspect of Parliament's scrutiny powers may take on new significance in the context of its own Rules of Procedure with regard to requests for legislative initiatives.

Implementing powers (comitology)

As was seen in Chapter 1, Section 1.3, the Commission is frequently assisted in its executive functions (that is, in the management, supervision and implementation of Community policies) by advisory, management or regulatory committees composed of representatives of the Member States. A primary reason for the Parliament's aversion to management and regulatory committees is that it has no direct control over their work, and it has only indirect control over advisory committees. However, the Parliament can exercise a form of indirect scrutiny over their work through access to the working documents the Commission drafts for these committees. Since 1988, the Commission has undertaken to send copies of all such documents to the Parliament at the same time as they are sent out to the committee members. Parliament's internal rules provide for such documents to be scrutinised by the responsible committee. In practice, the vast bulk of such documentation is subject to scrutiny only at the level of Parliament's officials. However, on occasion the Parliament may decide to revive political-level scrutiny, as occurred during the process leading up to German unification.

The co-decision procedure has given the subject of implementing powers a new twist, since Parliament is now a co-legislator under the procedure and is therefore not only resolved on refusing to countenance the introduction of management and regulatory committees in draft legislation, but in a 15 December 1993 resolution called for a new mechanism of joint Council–Parliament political supervision over implementing acts. In effect, Parliament is in the process of changing its position from its previous constitutional formalism to a more pragmatic search for a similarly active role in implementation. The Council, the Commission and the Parliament are currently involved in talks to create an inter-institutional agreement with regard to the new position but, at the time of writing, the Parliament seems intent on holding to this view and to its corresponding amendments even at the risk of jeopardising otherwise positive outcomes to third-reading conciliation procedures.

Committees of inquiry

A specialised form of supervisory power exists in the form of parliamentary committees of inquiry. Prior to the Maastricht Treaty, the authority of these committees was derived solely from Parliament's internal Rules of Procedure, and a perceived weakness of such committees was that they had to rely on the cooperation of the other Community institutions and national authorities and had no legal recourse or persuasive legal tools, although for the most part such cooperation was forthcoming. The Maastricht Treaty introduced a provision whereby, at the request of a quarter (currently 142) of its members, the European Parliament may 'set up a temporary Committee of Inquiry to investigate, without prejudice to the powers conferred by this Treaty on other institutions or bodies, alleged contraventions or maladministration in the implementation of Community law' (the Maastricht inter-governmental conference took over the exact wording of Parliament's internal rule). The treaty further provided that the detailed provisions governing the exercise of the right of inquiry had to be determined by the common accord of the Parliament, the Council, and the Commission. Negotiations of this inter-institutional agreement have been protracted, as the Parliament has sought maximal powers of access to the documents and the officials of the Council and, where necessary, the Member State governments and their administrations. Nevertheless, Parliament's power to launch inquiries now has the authority of a treaty basis and is a significant addition to its arsenal of supervisory powers.

Petitions

From its earliest days, the Parliament unilaterally granted nationals of the Member States the right to petition it, but the process took on fresh importance with the advent of direct elections, when the provision for the right to petition was recognised as an important way of forging links with the European electorate. The right to petition also became increasingly associated with the Parliament's campaign to enshrine the concept of European citizenship in the treaties and to give the concept concrete dimensions of significance to the citizen (see Chapter 2, Section 2.1).

The directly elected Parliament set up a separate Committee on Petitions in 1987, and in a 1989 inter-institutional agreement the Commission and the Council agreed to cooperate fully with the Parliament in the implementation of its internal policy. The Maastricht Treaty recognised the success of the procedure by providing that: 'Any citizen of the Union, and any natural or legal person residing or having his registered office in a Member State, shall have the right to address, individually or in association with other citizens or persons, a petition to the European Parliament on a matter which comes within the Community's fields of activity and which affects him directly.' In practice, the Parliament relies heavily on the Commission, since many petitions require further information or the Commission's opinion before the Parliament can decide (for example, of the 536 petitions Parliament received between March and September 1993, 345 were referred to the Commission). At the same time, when the procedure involves the Commission this can frequently be seen as a specialised aspect of the Commission's role as guardian of the treaties, since many petitions involve everyday problems related to the implementation of Community law.

The parliamentary Ombudsman

Another important element in giving concrete substance to the concept of European citizenship was the Maastricht Treaty's provision for the creation of a parliamentary ombudsman. As was seen above (Chapter 2, Section 2.2), the Ombudsman is appointed by Parliament. The regulations and general conditions governing the performance of his (or her) duties are laid down by the Parliament (after seeking the Commission's opinion and with the Council's approval). The Ombudsman is empowered to receive complaints from any Union citizen or any person residing or having his or her registered office in a Member State concerning instances of maladministration in the activities of the Community institutions or bodies. Additionally, the Ombudsman may 'conduct inquiries for which he finds grounds, either on his own initiative or on the basis of complaints submitted to him direct or through a member of the European Parliament' and, once the inquiries are complete, the Ombudsman must forward a report to the European Parliament. In effect, the Ombudsman provides Parliament with an additional specialised form of scrutiny.

Parliament as litigant

The European Parliament now has an array of powers before the European Court of Justice. It can bring cases for failure to act, it can intervene in cases brought by others and (since the 1990 *Chernobyl* ruling, but consolidated by the entry into force of the Maastricht Treaty) it can bring cases for annulment in defence of its own prerogatives. Parliament's internal Rules of Procedure provide not only for automatic review of the legal basis chosen for draft legislation but also for automatic review of Community legislation to ensure that its rights have been fully respected. Parliament has given clear indication of its intention to exploit its legal powers and status to the full. For example, in July 1993 Parliament brought an action against the Commission for failure to act in relation to the abolition of frontiers and the free movement of people under the 1992 programme.

3.9 The power of expression and debate

Topical and urgent debates

Although its budgetary and legislative powers are limited, in one important sense the European Parliament is like any other: it has the right to debate and express itself on anything, regardless of whether a legislative proposal is on the table or not (and this right has been confirmed by the Court's jurisprudence — see Table 1). Parliament's rules provide that a political group, or at least twenty-three members, may request a debate to be held 'on a topical and urgent subject of major importance', linked to a motion for a resolution, and a half-day of Parliament's plenary sessions are set aside for debates on such motions. The Commission and the Council invariably take part in these debates and are frequently called upon to act in the resolutions adopted at the close of each debate. The procedure has become an important means for Parliament to let off steam on pressing matters — from flooding in a part of the Community to human rights' abuses or famine in some parts of the African continent — from an earthquake in Asia to a *coup d'état* in Latin America. The Conference of Presidents draws up a list of the subjects to be debated and always groups various related subjects together. (Thus, there are invariably two groups of related motions on natural disasters and human rights.) Parliament's power to express itself would be of no consequence if nobody listened but, as was explained above in relation to Parliament's external powers (Section 3.5), people do listen, whether in the Community institutions, the Member States or the world at large, and on occasion the representatives of the Community institutions do give undertakings or promise to follow up questions raised. At the very least, the procedure provides the possibility for constructive dialogue among the institutions on matters which are frequently of common concern.

Commission and Council statements

The treaties provide that 'members of the Commission may, . . . at their request, be heard on behalf of the Commission' and that 'the Council

181

shall be heard'. Parliament's Rules of Procedure provide that 'members of the Commission, Council and European Council may at any time ask the President for permission to make a statement', but in practice most Council and Commission statements are in response to parliamentary requests for such statements, rather than a spontaneous volunteering of information. The Parliament is sparing in its requests to the Council, and the Council quite frequently refuses to oblige. Political considerations undoubtedly come into play, but the principal reason is that the Council is conventionally represented by the Presidency, and the appropriate minister from the Presidency may not be available. Indeed, the Parliament generally tries to organise its debates around the availability of Presidency ministers.

Requests to the Commission, on the other hand, are very frequent and, because of the different nature of the relationship between the two institutions, the Commission very rarely refuses, the major obstacle typically being to find a spare 'slot' in Parliament's plenary agenda. Although the Parliament has tightened up its rules since the Maastricht Treaty came into force, a plenary week will typically see several such requests for Commission statements. The reason for this insistence on Commission statements, even where the Commission's responsibility for a particular matter is only tangential, is simple. If the Commission (or the Council or the European Council) makes a statement, then Parliament's rules provide for this to be followed by a debate; thus a committee, a political group, or at least twenty-three members may then table a motion for a resolution. In other words, the other institution's statement enables the Parliament to hold a debate and adopt a resolution. Frequently, that institution will have something of substance to say on the matter in question, and the Commission often gives undertakings in such debates, but Parliament will also have had its say.

Dialogue in committee

One of the most striking developments in Parliament's committee work is the increasing presence and participation of members of the Commission and of specialised ministers representing the Presidency. In the case of the Commission, this has been a consistent policy, dating back to an overall review of its relations with the Parliament in the light of the first direct elections in 1979 and reinforced by the entry into force of the Single European Act in 1987. Commissioners now appear frequently before the parliamentary committee shadowing their responsibilities (the commissioner responsible for budgetary affairs has a particularly close relationship with the Budgets Committee), and it has now become conventional for a ministerial representative of the

Presidency to appear at least once before each committee during its six-month period in office.

Dialogue in committee is far less formalised than in plenary. The need for simultaneous interpretation may still diminish the spontaneity of discussions and debates (although, in heated moments, the principle of speaking one's own language frequently evaporates and animated *ad hoc* exchanges can take place in passable French or English — some polyglot commissioners and ministers insist on answering questions in the language of the questioner). But these are also enlivened by the fact that there is no fixed time for speakers and no verbatim report of proceedings (though most meetings are public and journalists may be present). Commissioners and ministers are physically closer to their interlocutors, and questions are directly put and answered, rather than cushioned in speeches.

Public hearings

Another striking development in the European Parliament's activities is a great increase in the organisation of public hearings by its committees. Such hearings typically last a day or a half-day, and will consist of presentations by invited experts, followed by discussion. These hearings serve a number of purposes. They can help with the identification of, and familiarisation with, a particular problem or issue. They can reveal a need for legislation or other action. They can help a committee in its scrutiny of draft legislation, and they can help a committee make up its own mind on a particular issue. Where draft legislation is concerned, the organising committee will frequently invite representatives from the industries or interests that will be affected by the legislation and thus serve as an adjunct to the Commission's own broad, pre-legislative consultations. A recent example of successful use of the device was a public hearing organised jointly by Parliament's Foreign Affairs Committee, its Sub-Committee on Human Rights and its Committee on Legal Affairs and Citizens' Rights in January 1994 on the subject of torture and rehabilitation. The hearing brought together experts and officials from the United Nations, the Council of Europe and NGOs, together with a series of medical experts in the field of treatment and rehabilitation and was considered a great success in sensitising MEPs to the problems involved, particularly since many of the medical centres and NGOs are based within the European Union.

4
The politics of the European Parliament

4.1 Parliament's structure

The political groups

Oligopoly

Most Member State parliaments lay down rules governing the formation of political groups. These typically specify a minimum size (three in the Belgian *chambre*, five in the Spanish *congreso*, twenty in the French *assemblée*, 5 per cent membership in the German Bundestag) and a series of privileges. Typically, political groups have rights to staff, secretarial assistance, office space, membership of committees, speaking time, financial assistance and, in some systems, financial assistance for elections. In the parliaments where they exist, political groups within the Parliament generally correspond to political parties outside the Parliament.

Political groups within the European Parliament are like political groups in Member State parliaments in all but this last sense; for most of the European Parliament's life there have been no European political parties. Moreover, a political group within the European Parliament may have more than one political party from a Member State within its membership. For example, the primary condition for membership of the Group of the Party of European Socialists is membership of the Socialist International. Thus, in the 1989–94 period the Group contained three parties from Italy (Socialist Party, Italian Social Democratic Party and the new Social Democratic Party — the former Communist Party), two from Belgium (Flemish and Wallonian) and two from the United Kingdom (the Labour Party and John Hume's Social and Democratic Labour Party).

The members of the Common Assembly of the European Coal and Steel Community (and later the members of the EEC Parliamentary Assembly) sat in three groups, corresponding to the three traditional continental European political families: the Christian Democrats, the Socialists and the Liberals. Other political parties existed within the six Member States (the most obvious being the Communists), but as members were delegated by the governments of the Member States these were effectively excluded. The Christian Democrats were the largest group, sometimes coming close to achieving an absolute majority. The Socialists were generally second largest, although the Liberals overtook them in the 1959–62 period. Despite differences *within* these groups, they worked consensually together at the practical level, sharing out responsibilities on a proportional basis among themselves. The absence of anything other than the three main political families until 1965, combined with the strong consensual urge examined in Chapter 2, Section 2.11, has inculcated into the European Parliament a tradition of political group oligopoly which exists to this day.

A major factor undermining the cross-group consensus has been attitude to European integration. A first indication of this came in 1965, when the French Gaullists broke away from the Liberal Group to form their own political group which, as the European Democratic Alliance, still exists. The trend was further enhanced by the northern enlargements. The British Labour Party decided not to send a contingent to the European Parliament until after the 1975 referendum on continued EC membership, and as a consequence prevented the Socialist Group from becoming the largest group in the Parliament. The Irish Fianna Fail party joined the European Democratic Alliance (though more for the practical reason that Fine Gael had joined the Christian Democrats than out of opposition to European integration). Until 1992, the British Conservatives sat in their own group, together with an Ulster Unionist and two Danish Conservatives. The overall effect of this fragmentation was to consolidate the oligopoly of the three main political groupings. In 1973, the Christian Democrats, Socialists and Liberals between them held 123 (67 per cent) of the 183 sitting MEPs.

Again, the dual trends towards fragmentation and consolidation can still be discerned. The overall political variety in the European Parliament has been steadily increasing as a result of enlargements and the changing politics of the Member States. A Communist Group was formed in 1974, a European Right Group in 1984, and a Green Group in 1989. The arrival of various regional representatives (for example, a Scottish National Party MEP, a Basque, two Catalan representatives, MEPs from the Tyrol, Lombardy and Sardinia), the rise of smaller political parties (for example, the Dutch Democracy '66) and the rise of independents and single-issue parties (for example, two Irish independents, an Italian anti-drug MEP, a Danish anti-Market MEP, a Dutch Protestant Coalition MEP) have all contributed to the richness of the European Parliament's membership but have also contributed to its fragmentation and hence to the consolidation of the larger political groups' oligopoly.

Within this oligopoly, the position of the Liberals has steadily waned since the first direct elections in 1979, while that of the Christian Democrats and, above all, the Socialists has increased to a position where the largest two political groups between them command an overwhelming majority in the Parliament. In 1979, the position of the Liberals enabled them to get their candidate, Simone Veil, elected to the Presidency of the Parliament against a Socialist Group candidate (but with Christian Democratic backing). That experience, and the increasing need to muster majorities to exercise Parliament's budgetary powers (see the next section), led to an increasing awareness among the two largest political groups that more could be achieved through cooperation than opposition. The chairman of the Socialist Group between 1984 and 1989, the German SPD MEP Rudi Arndt (now retired) has recalled how:

> We learnt a lesson, because we started by setting off the two great political camps against each other. This was obvious with the election of the President, and in the initial period following the direct elections Parliament was largely a set piece display of pure ideology. We were not seeking a broad-based majority; broadly speaking, what we were endeavouring to do was to show the other political camp how clever our own ideas were and how wrong theirs were . . . Then there was the second legislative period of the directly elected Parliament. It started with the Brussels meeting of the two major groupings. It subsequently became known in many quarters as 'the meeting of the giants' at which it was agreed that there was no point in a mutual flexing of muscles; the only sensible strategy was to achieve the appropriate majorities. At that meeting in Brussels — I remember it well — both the Christian Democrats and the Socialists said: 'that's the right approach, let's try it' (Arndt, 1992, p.65).

The need to achieve majorities if Parliament were to exercise its powers was, as the next section will show, the key to this process. From 1984–9, the trend towards greater cooperation was happily helped on by the fact that Arndt's opposite number at the helm of the Christian Democrat group, Egon Klepsch, was a German politician from the same generation and a very similar school of non-demonstrative, consensus-building politics.

The Socialist–Christian Democrat oligopoly has since been consolidated, and its fruits are all about. Since 1989, the Presidency of the European Parliament, theoretically the result of popular election by Parliament's membership, has been determined by an arrangement agreed between the two groups. Thus, a Spanish Socialist and former minister, Enrique Baron Crespo, was president for the first half of the mandate, and the same Egon Klepsch was president for the second half. The September 1993 rules-change package which, through weighted voting, has greatly accentuated the powers of the leaders of the two larger groups, was the result of a similar consensual process. If not all matters are decided by the Socialist (Party of European Socialists) and Christian Democrat (European People's Party) groups, few can be decided without their tacit acceptance, and this 'iron law of oligopoly' has been further reinforced by the September 1993 rules-change package.

Such consolidated consensus has potential disadvantages. The greatest — a serious disadvantage in an institution where representativeness is an end in itself — is the potential exclusion of all groups, parties or views not rallying to the consensus or, at the least, not fitting easily into it. (The British Conservatives took this argument to its logical conclusion by dissolving their own group and joining the Christian Democrats. By contrast, when anti-Market arguments and members were in the ascendance in the British Labour contingent in the early 1980s, such considerations militated against arguments that it should withdraw from the Socialist Group.) As Arndt himself put it: 'I admit that this is not entirely above board. It has meant steamrolling the smaller factions in the Group and, of course, the smaller Groups who often got very annoyed' (Arndt, 1992, p.67).

At the same conference, Pierre Pflimlin, a former President of the Parliament at the time of Arndt's leadership, confirmed Arndt's recollections:

> It is perfectly true that owing to the agreement between the main groups — of which Mr Arndt himself, together with my fried Egon Klepsch, was the main architect — majorities and absolute majorities have been produced. It is also true, however, . . . that this has provoked reactions within the small groups. I have often had occasion to listen to such remonstrating, and many regarded Mr Arndt and Mr Klepsch as the European Parliament's two 'co-dictators', since they represented the two principal groups and very sensibly and very intelligently succeeded in getting along and managed to produce majorities, which, at the end of the day, was the main thing (Pflimlin, 1992, p.70).

The danger of frustration is mitigated to some extent by the fact that the oligopoly is a benign one. A seating plan of the Parliament shows how the Liberals and the members of the European Democratic Alliance sit beside (in the Liberals' case almost *within*) the European People's Party, and the same is true of the Greens and the Communists with regard to the Party of European Socialists. Parliament's consensual method runs deep, and great effort is made to take on board as many views as possible. The method is etched into Parliament's Rules of Procedure, which declare that Parliament's Conference of Presidents (where the political Groups' power is chiefly exercised — see below) 'shall endeavour to reach a consensus on matters referred to it'.

The danger is further mitigated by the fact that virtually everything within the Parliament is divided up on a proportional basis, from speaking time to number of members on a committee. The Socialist–Christian Democrat oligopoly is not absolute. And there are, as Arndt puts it, 'safety valves': 'We also have safety valves, of course, so that the individual political Groups can make known their ideological positions. These are the famous urgency resolutions when we spend the whole of every Thursday morning thrashing out the issue although the results of the votes are known long in advance since they are prearranged within the Groups' (Arndt, 1992, p.67).

However, the oligopoly can be deliberately exclusive where the views of a political group are considered to lie beyond the political pale. This has been particularly true for the Group of the European Right, which has been consistently excluded from hierarchical positions (including its proportional entitlement) and rapporteurships on important political reports.

Rules

A traditional form of exclusion from political group status is the setting of thresholds for minimum membership. The European Parliament had an early taste of the problems this can create in 1979, after the first direct elections, when an attempt was made to raise the threshold (which then stood at ten from three Member States) in line with the new Parliament's greatly increased membership (from 198 to 410). However, such an increase in the threshold would have prevented the formation of a proposed Group for the Technical Coordination and Defence of Independent Groups and Members, a heterogeneous mixture of anti-Market Danes, three Italian parties, including the Radical Party, an Irish independent and a Belgian Volksunie representative. The proposed group's members, led by Italian Radical Marco Pannella, successfully filibustered away the proposed change, and the group was subsequently formed.

The introduction of strict limits on speaking time and electronic voting machines mean that Pannella could not today launch a similar filibustering campaign, but, in large part because of that original campaign, Parliament's rules on the formation of political groups remain very liberal. As the rules now stand, 'the minimum number of Members required to form a political group shall be twenty-six if they come from one Member State, twenty-one if they come from two Member States, sixteen if they come from three Member States and thirteen if they come from four or more Member States'. Twenty-six members would represent a quarter of the German contingent, or 30 per cent of the French, Italian or United Kingdom contingents, and thirteen members would represent just 2.3 per cent of Parliament's total membership. The only other restriction in Parliament's rules is that 'a member may not belong to more than one group'.

Powers and structure

Parliament's rules grant its political groups considerable formal powers. They may table oral questions to the Council or the Commission and, where Commission, Council or European Council members make statements to Parliament, they may table resolutions and may agree joint resolutions among themselves. They may table proposals for recommendations under the second and third (Common Foreign and Security Policy, and Cooperation in the Fields of Justice and Home Affairs) pillars of the new Maastricht Treaty provisions. A political group may ask that a debate be held on a topical and urgent subject of major importance, and it may table an accompanying motion. Political groups submit nominations for membership of committees and inter-parliamentary delegations. Finally, they may propose amendments to Parliament's plenary agenda.

In addition, Parliament's political groups enjoy considerable financial and practical advantages. About a sixth of Parliament's internal budget is devoted to its political groups, with the amount granted to any particular group dependent on its numerical size. The sort of expenditure covered includes the salaries of staff, political advisers and secretaries, the purchase or hire of data processing and office equipment and other administrative expenditure. The groups additionally benefit from payments from a European Information Campaign fund, designed to increase awareness among the European electorate about the European Union and its Parliament.

The political groups, particularly the larger ones, are made up of distinct national delegations. Money and resources within political groups are divided among the national contingents on the basis of their numerical size, as are hierarchical positions. Political discipline within the political groups is primarily exercised at the level of the national contingents, which have their own officers and hierarchical structures. The larger component national delegations can be very influential. Nevertheless, the political groups' basic working method is consensual.

The Conference of Presidents

Until November 1993, political power within the European Parliament was principally exercised through a body known as the 'enlarged Bureau'. The Bureau, which still exists, consists of the president and the fourteen vice-presidents of Parliament, together with five quaestors acting in an advisory capacity. The 'enlarged Bureau' consisted of the Bureau together with the leaders of the political groups. Each member of the enlarged Bureau (with the exception of the five quaestors) had an equal vote. The president and vice-presidents are elected by Parliament's membership. Although in recent years, successful candidatures for the Presidency, together with a number of the vice-presidential positions, have arisen out of consensual agreements, turnout for their election is very high.

In September 1993, in an act symbolising the gradual concentration of political power within the Parliament in the political groups, the enlarged Bureau was abolished, and its political functions taken over by a new body called the 'Conference of Presidents'. The Conference of Presidents consists of the president of Parliament (who chairs the Conference but has no vote), and the chairmen of the political groups (or their representatives). As already pointed out, the Conference of Presidents is charged with endeavouring 'to reach a consensus on matters referred to it'. However, the rules provide that, 'where a consensus cannot be reached, the matter shall be put to a vote subject to a weighting based on the number of Members in each political group'. Given the pre-eminent numerical status of the Socialist and Christian Democrat Groups, it is clearly in the interests of all the other, smaller political groups to reach a consensual agreement on any matter, since they are bound to be outvoted, should any matter go to a vote. The result of this arrangement has been a further consolidation of the political power of the two largest political groups, the oligopoly described above.

At the same time, the arrangement has consolidated the overall power of the political groups. Parliament's rules now provide that the Conference of Presidents shall:

— take decisions on the organisation of Parliament's work and matters relating to legislative planning;
— be the authority responsible for matters relating to relations with the other institutions and bodies of the European Community and with the national parliaments of Member States;
— be the authority responsible for matters relating to relations with non-member countries and with non-Community institutions and organisations;
— draw up the draft agenda of Parliament's part-sessions;
— be the authority responsible for the composition and competence of committees and temporary committees of inquiry and joint parliamentary committees, standing delegations and *ad hoc* delegations;
— decide how seats in the Chamber are to be allocated;
— be the authority responsible for authorising the drawing up of own-initiative reports;
— submit proposals . . . concerning administrative and budgetary matters relating to the political groups.

Additional rules grant the Conference of Presidents particular powers in relation to motions for resolutions, the Annual Legislative Programme, the drawing up of the agenda and the fair representation of Member

States and political views. These are all fundamental, far-reaching and wide-ranging powers, establishing the Conference of Presidents and the largest political groups within it as the pre-eminent political power bases within the post-Maastricht Parliament.

The committees

If the political groups are the Parliament's life blood, then its nineteen committees and four sub-committees are its legislative backbone. Their competences are set out in an annex to Parliament's Rules of Procedure and together represent a particular hybrid mixture. Two committees, on Foreign Affairs and Security, and on Civil Liberties and Internal Affairs, follow the two new inter-governmental pillars created by the Maastricht Treaty, and a Sub-Committee on Monetary Affairs follows the monetary aspects of the economic and monetary union process established by the same treaty (its parent committee, the Committee on Economic and Monetary Policy and Industrial Affairs, follows the broader economic policy aspects). Two committees, on Budgets and Budgetary Control, assure Parliament's particular budgetary powers. A number of committees (for example, Agriculture, Transport, Energy, Environment, Development) follow particular policy sectors, and others (for example, Institutional Affairs, Rules, Women's Rights) have horizontal briefs. Parliament's committee structure does not correspond to any particular model. The Foreign Affairs Committee is clearly modelled on its equivalent in the United States' Senate, but disposes of far less power. Its Committee for Economic and Monetary Affairs and Industrial Policy corresponds far more closely to the German Arbeitsparlament model. Committees with sectoral briefs correspond closely to the House of Commons' Select Committees, shadowing Commission directorates general much as Westminster Select Committees shadow Whitehall ministerial departments. Perhaps more than in other parliaments, the European Parliament's committees have their own distinctive characters and styles, resulting from a combination of their functions, active members and chairmen.

Rules

Parliament's rules grant its committees many of the same formal powers enjoyed by the political groups. Committees can table oral questions to the Council and the Commission, they can table resolutions following statements by the other institutions and they can propose amendments to Parliament's plenary agenda. But most of the committees' formal powers are bound up with the legislative process. Parliamentary requests to the Commission for legislative initiatives must be based on own-initiative reports from a parliamentary committee. All legislative proposals and other legislative documents must be considered in committee and, indeed, the bulk of the legislative process under all of the legislative procedures, from the tabling of amendments to the scrutiny of the Council's common positions and, where appropriate, the Commission's modifications, takes place primarily in Parliament's specialised committees. Members of the responsible committees are also appointed to serve in the conciliation committees created by the new co-decision procedure. Finally, in certain circumstances, the plenary's powers of decision making may be delegated to committees.

Horizontal functions and specialised powers

In addition to the legislative function, certain committees have particular powers and specialised roles within Parliament's structure, generally combined with horizontal briefs. For example, the Committee on Legal Affairs is the Parliament's legal authority on 'the creation, interpretation and application of Community law, including the choice of legal basis for Community acts' and is responsible for decisions about Parliament's involvement in actions before the Court of Justice. All legal problems and disputes are referred to the Committee, and its role as arbiter on problems about legal bases is reinforced by Parliament's rules.

Parliament's Committee on the Rules of Procedure plays a similar role as arbiter on disputes involving the rules. Reference to the Committee for a ruling or opinion is, for example, a much-favoured device of Parliament's president and vice-presidents when confronted with prolonged disputes in plenary over points of order related to interpretation of the rules. But the primary role of the Committee (which is also responsible for the verification of the credentials of newly-elected members and all rulings on members' privileges and immunities) is the formulation of the Rules of Procedure and any amendments to them. The Committee is constantly involved in the drafting of minor reforms to the rules, but its workload is episodically swollen by the major rules-changes packages necessitated by changes to the treaties (the Single European Act, the Maastricht Treaty) or Court rulings (for example, the 'Isoglucose' case). Drafting rule changes is a quintessentially consensual exercise, since any change to the rules must be passed by an absolute majority (currently 284) of Parliament's membership so that, in this context, the Committee's primary power lies in forcing consensus and consistence.

Another committee with a broad horizontal brief and specialised powers is Parliament's Committee on Institutional Affairs. The rules grant it three specialised functions: the drawing up of a draft uniform electoral procedure, political considerations relating to the seat of the Community institutions and the development of European integration in the framework of the inter-governmental conferences. All three functions are episodic in importance. In addition, the Committee is more broadly responsible for general relations with the other institutions or bodies of the European Community, the institutional structures of the European Community within the framework of the treaties and the assessment of the implications of the Maastricht Treaty and its implementation. The Institutional Affairs Committee is Parliament's integrationist hot house and its strategic command centre. It is here that Parliament's constitutional blueprints are drafted, its strategy towards inter-governmental conferences decided, and the nature of its inter-institutional relations primarily determined. Again, the Committee's work is quintessentially consensual. The treaties require an absolute majority only for the adoption of the draft uniform electoral procedure, but in all other areas of its activities the Committee's recommendations must necessarily be reinforced through the gathering of large and broad majorities. In particular, small majorities, or the existence of sizeable dissenting minorities, may fatally undermine the authority of the Committee's recommendations.

The Budgetary Control Committee has the specialised occasional function of considering the Council's nominees for membership of the Court of Auditors (see Chapter 3, Section 3.2), and the annual function of granting the Commission discharge on the Community budget. But it plays a constant and wide-ranging role in scrutinising the implementation of the Community budget, exercised on the basis of periodic reports provided by the Commission.

By far the most powerful of Parliament's horizontal committees is its Committee on Budgets. The Committee is responsible for matters relating to the definition and exercise of the Parliament's budgetary powers, the budgets of the European Community, the multi-annual estimates of revenue and expenditure and the inter-institutional agreement, the Community's financial resources, the financial implications of Community acts, the preparation and coordination of the budgetary conciliation procedure, authorisation for transfers of expenditure and Parliament's own internal budget. Throughout the budgetary procedure the Committee exercises its power *vis-à-vis* the Council and the Commission, but also *vis-à-vis* Parliament's other spending committees. Because of this dual role, which was consolidated by the inter-institutional agreements, the Budgets Committee is undoubtedly *primus inter pares*. All spending proposals have to pass through the Committee, which does not hesitate to discipline the ambitions of other committees and obliges them to justify their proposed budgetary amendments. In so doing, the Committee has come to act as Parliament's star chamber. The source of the Committee's power is the requirement incumbent upon the Parliament to muster special majorities in order to be able to wield its budgetary powers (absolute majorities and, in some cases, three-fifths of the votes cast — see Table 5). The Budgets Committee has been wielding these powers with increasing dexterity and authority since 1975 and has developed the formation of budgetary majorities into a refined art. A clear proof of this refinement is the fact that there is now very little chance of overturning the Budgets Committee's majority in the plenary vote, either by voting down its amendments or introducing new ones.

The committee chairmen

In theory, committee chairmen are elected by their respective committees. In practice, their election is almost always a formality. Their selection lies within the gift of the political groups and primarily the national contingents within the political groups. The numerical distribution of committee chairmanships is decided on the basis of the proportional strength of the political groups and the choice of particular committee chairmanships on the basis of the strength of national contingents within political groups. For example, between 1989 and 1994, the Socialist Group was the largest group within the Parliament, and it was thus entitled (using the d'Hondt system of proportional representation) to eight committee chairmanships and two sub-committee chairmanships. The British Labour (European Parliamentary Labour Party) Members were the largest national contingent within the Socialist Group and thus had first choice of committee chairmanship. Their first choice was the Environment Committee, and the strongest candidate for that position within the Labour contingent was a highly experienced former chairman of the Committee, Ken Collins. His subsequent election to the Committee's chairmanship was a relative formality (see Westlake, 1994a).

The committee chairmen can be powerful individuals, both within their committees and within Parliament as a whole. This holds particularly true of those committees — for example, Foreign Affairs Budgets, Legal Affairs — with important inter-institutional functions and those — for example, Economic and Monetary Affairs, Environment — with heavy legislative loads or extensive legislative powers. The Parliament's September 1993 (post-Maastricht) rules-change package formalised their collective powers by establishing a Conference of Committee Chairmen. The formal function of the Conference of Committee Chairmen, which should not be confused with the Conference of [Political Group] Presidents, is to 'make recommendations to the Conference of Presidents about the work of committees and the drafting of the agenda of part-sessions'. This apparently weak power is in practice extensive. The Conference of Committee Chairmen has become essential to the good working of Parliament's legislative machinery. The committee chairmen have their collective finger on the Parliament's legislative pulse, and the Conference of Presidents depends heavily on them to realise its strategies in relation to legislative planning as well as, at a more practical level, the organisation of Parliament's plenary session agendas. The Conference elects a chairman from among its members and this (awkwardly named) Chairman of the Conference of Committee Chairmen wields considerable influence.

Parliament's hierarchy

The treaties mention just one parliamentary officer: its president. As the rules now stand, the president has considerable formal powers. He (or she) signs the Community's budget into existence. Together with the Council Presidency, he convokes (and may lead) the conciliation committee foreseen in, and co-signs acts adopted under, the co-decision procedure. He presides over the Conference of Presidents (in a non-voting capacity), the Bureau (where he has a casting vote) and the plenary itself (where he may open, suspend and close sittings and generally preside, including ultimately the expulsion of members causing disturbances). He represents his institution in international relations, on ceremonial occasions, in administrative, legal or financial matters and in dealing with the other institutions (although he may act under instructions from the Conference of Presidents).

The president is assisted by fourteen vice-presidents, to whom he may delegate his duties and functions. Together, the president and the vice-presidents make up Parliament's Bureau. The Bureau has a series of basically administrative functions. Parliament's rules state that it shall *inter alia* 'take financial, organizational and administrative decisions on matters concerning Members and the internal organization of Parliament, its Secretariat and its bodies', 'decide the establishment plan of the Secretariat and lay down regulations relating to the administrative and financial situation of officials and other servants', 'draw up Parliament's preliminary draft estimates' (of its own internal budget), and 'appoint the Secretary General'. In practice, although it wields considerable independence in administrative matters, the Bureau lives in the political shadow of the Conference of Presidents.

The Bureau lays down guidelines for five quaestors, who are directly elected by Parliament, take part in the Bureau's work in a non-voting capacity and are responsible for administrative and financial matters directly concerning members. The continental traditional of the quaestor, alien to Westminster, is intended to safeguard backbenchers' rights, and the five quaestors in the European Parliament act very much in this tradition. The president, the vice-presidents and the quaestors are elected for two-and-a-half-year mandates which may be renewed.

Each political group has its own hierarchical structure, typically consisting of a chairman or president, several vice-chairmen or vice-presidents, a treasurer and a number of other executive officers, together known as the bureau. Convention has it that each political party within a political group should have a place on the bureau and that the more numerous political parties should be represented by at least a vice-chairman/president.

In turn, each political party has its own hierarchical structure, with a bureau typically consisting of at least a leader, vice-leader and treasurer.

Each parliamentary committee is headed by a chairman and up to three vice-chairmen, together making up the committee's bureau.

Each inter-parliamentary delegation is headed by a chairman and two or three vice-chairmen, together making up the delegation's bureau.

Finally, Parliament's rules provide for a Conference of Delegation Chairmen made up of the Chairmen of inter-parliamentary delegations. The Conference's powers are largely advisory.

From all of the foregoing it will have become clear that the European Parliament has an extensive formal hierarchical structure. In the 1989–94 Parliament, which consisted of 518 members, there were 329 formal leadership positions, excluding hierarchical positions within the political party contingents and parliamentary intergroups. In other words, over six out of ten of these were chairmen or vice-chairmen or held other hierarchical office of some sort.

These statistics underline a simple fact: Parliament's extensive hierarchical structure is an integral part of its consensual and representational mechanisms or, to put it another way, a response to the obligation, written into its rules at several points, to ensure fair representation of Member States and of political views (see Westlake, 1994a).

Parliament's bureaucracy

Like the other Community institutions, the European Parliament is assisted by a Secretariat General, which is headed by a secretary general and made up of directly recruited civil servants and a number of seconded national officials. The Secretariat General is divided up into seven Directorates General dealing respectively with the organisation of the sessions, committees and delegations, information and public relations, research, personnel, budget and finance, administration and translation. The total number of civil servants in 1993 was 3,790 (3,243 permanent posts and 547 temporary posts). About one-third of these work in translation and interpretation or associated work.

The European Parliament's Secretariat, together with the officials working in the political groups, have been a significant though frequently unremarked factor in its recent development. The burst of activity after the first direct elections in 1979 was undoubtedly the result of the initial frustration of the first directly elected members of the Parliament. But political and budgetary independence, together with the practical needs of servicing a Parliament which had more than doubled in size (from 198 to 410 members), led to sustained recruitment drives (in 1979, Parliament's staff consisted of 1,995 officials, in 1984, 2,966, and in 1990, 3,482). These recruitment waves in turn led to the creation of a pool of young, talented and committed officials who thereafter devoted their talents to sustaining and extending the Parliament's role and powers.

As was remarked in Chapter 1, Section 1.1, Pryce and Wessels (1987) more generally described such committed officials, so important in the development of the Community, as 'propulsive elites'. Their future was bound up in the institution for which they worked (in many cases, it was the potential of the institution that had attracted them in the first place). Once recruited, their energies were devoted to a creative exploration of the Parliament's potential. This commitment led in turn to a creative tension between staff within the Parliament, but also between staff in the Parliament and in the other institutions. A good example of this tension is provided by the Parliament's legal activism, which has frequently led to battles before the Court. These activist officials have naturally tended to gravitate to the strategic sections of the political groups, the legal service and to the committees nearest the institutional cutting edge, particularly the Budgets, Institutional Affairs, Foreign Affairs and Rules Committees. But they have been of influence throughout Parliament's services.

4.2 Parliament's method

Reports

The European Parliament works in two basic modes: responsive and pro-active. Parliament's legislative and budgetary functions are, for example, basically responsive, with the Parliament reacting to the Commission's draft legislation or preliminary draft budget and, later in the procedures, the Council's drafts. On the other hand, Parliament may pro-actively call upon the Commission to draft legislation or the Council to act. In both responsive and pro-active modes, the Parliament's basic tool is the parliamentary *report*. A report generally consists of two sections, a *resolution* and an *explanatory memorandum*. The resolution is forwarded to the institutions addressed by it. The explanatory memorandum is, as its name suggests, a purely internal document designed to explain the position taken in the resolution. A resolution drafted in response to a legislative document is known as a *legislative resolution* and may contain amendments. A pro-active report on a particular subject is known as an *own-initiative report*.

Under a series of conventions, the Council and the Commission have agreed to consult Parliament on most proposals, even where consultation is not required by the treaties, and to forward other important documents to it. In these cases, too, Parliament will generally respond through the drafting of a report. Indeed, although there are exceptions (for example, topical and urgent debates usually result in the adoption of resolutions), the European Parliament's basic method is overwhelmingly characterised by the adoption of reports.

Committees and rapporteurs

Commission proposals and all other legislative documents are by convention addressed to Parliament's president, who refers them on to the responsible committee. In the pro-active mode, a committee may be authorised by the Conference of Presidents to draw up an own-initiative report on a particular subject. In both cases, one specific committee will be responsible for drafting the report. However, the subject matter may also be of interest to other committees, and these may be authorised (by the president or the Conference of Presidents respectively) to draft *opinions*. Authors of opinions are known as *draftsmen*. Opinions are submitted to the main committee, which may take them into account in drafting its report, but in general only the main committee may table amendments to a legislative report in plenary.

The committee responsible for a report will appoint a *rapporteur* who is thereafter responsible for drawing up the report. Rapporteurs are appointed consensually by the political groups. Rapporteurships on important reports, such as the budgets, or the Commission's annual economic report, are agreed among the political groups at a higher level. The 'ownership' and alternance of major annual reports is generally agreed at the outset of a legislature (this is particularly the case with the annual report on the budget). However, most rapporteurships are decided at committee level. Each political group has a 'kitty' of points, calculated on the basis of its numerical strength, which it may spend by buying rapporteurships or draftsmanships. The two largest political groups tend to predominate in the share-out of important reports, but they are at pains to maintain consensuality by leaving the smaller groups a fair share in qualitative as well as quantitative terms. Because of the increasing emphasis on legislative programming, the process of sharing out reports and opinions tends to be decided on a more rational and less *ad hoc* basis, since the overall legislative load of a committee can be gleaned from the annual legislative programme.

Once a political group has 'bought' the rights to a report or an opinion, it will appoint a rapporteur or a draftsman from among its membership of the responsible committee, generally on the basis of that person's expertise. Rapporteurships, particularly on important high-profile reports, bring the occupant status and privileges, as he/she will be expected to present the report to the other institutions (and will therefore be engaged in dialogue with the Commissioner and perhaps with the Council as well) and to the outside world (through press and television and radio interviews). The rapporteur shepherds the report throughout the adoption process, from drafting and voting in committee to presentation and adoption in plenary. Parliament's rules state only that the rapporteur 'shall be responsible for preparing the committee's report and for presenting it to Parliament on behalf of the committee', but there may be important informal duties, particularly where legislative reports are concerned, since Parliament will tend to trust in his/her judgement in deciding whether to accept or reject amendments or reject the Council's Common Positions. Above all, the unwritten code of the art of good rapporteurship is the gathering of maximum consensus through the building of majorities.

Majority building

The need for majority building within Parliament was first derived from the parliamentary majority requirements — absolute majorities, three-fifths or two-thirds of the votes cast — laid down by the budgets procedure. Parliament had to muster such requirements if it wanted to amend or modify (or reject) the draft budget, and yet, since 1975, no single political group has come close to commanding an absolute majority of its membership. The implication was clear: majorities had to be built across political groups. As the quotation from Rudi Arndt in Section 4.1 above revealed, the political groups' instincts to 'go it alone' after the first direct elections were soon curbed, and a tacit agreement reached between the two largest, the Socialists and the Christian Democrats. The smaller groups, he admitted, often got annoyed 'because they regarded Parliament as a forum for making known their views, whereas we regarded it as a forum for achieving majorities'. Arndt's recollections on the way this agreement worked are revealing:

> The agreement in Brussels was that the Socialist Group would be responsible for discussing details with the Left wing in Parliament and the Christian Democrats had the task of doing the same with the Right wing, to ensure that a majority could be created. We agreed that the working parties would keep in touch with each other on a permanent basis and that whenever there was an issue on which a joint approach was not possible in the working parties, there would be a coordinating meeting in Strasbourg. As far as I remember, these meetings, at which the chief spokesmen of the Christian Democrats would have talks with the main spokesmen of the Socialist Group after reaching an understanding with the other groups, took place on Tuesdays.

Experience showed that these meetings were very important since a result was almost always achieved, as prior agreement had normally already been reached in the committees (Arndt, 1992, p.66).

The 1986 Single European Act, with its absolute majority requirements, consolidated this agreement. Again, Arndt's recollections are revealing:

> When the united European ministerial bureaucracies prepared the Single European Act they obviously said to themselves: 'we will continue to control Europe. Our minister will only be putting across our views in the Council and we are the only people who can put it across. And if we write into the Single European Act that Parliament can only enforce its position with an absolute majority, we can safely say that no majority will be found, that the major groups will just snipe at each other until no progress is possible' — since we needed an absolute majority of the statutory number of members. This is why they included this formula in the Single European Act, on the assumption that Parliament would prove unable to create a majority. This, of course, simply encouraged MEPs to show that they could reach unity. From 1985 onwards these majorities have been regularly achieved . . . We had problems in our own Groups of course; there were plenty of people who objected to their policies being 'watered down'. I know for a fact that if the Chairman of the Christian Democratic Group wanted to introduce something he would say to his Group: 'if we don't do this, we won't get Arndt's support'. And I'd agreed with him beforehand that I would say to my Group: 'if we don't do this then we won't get the support of Klepsch. That, more or less, is how things operated' (Arndt, 1992, p.66).

The absolute majority requirements in the Maastricht Treaty have further consolidated this tradition, which the more fragmented political representation in the Parliament after the June 1994 elections has rendered more necessary. Indeed, as Table 5 shows, the Parliament's Rules of Procedure are peppered with majority requirements, whether imposed by the treaties or by its own volition.

However, the rapporteur's job of building majorities goes beyond mustering the various majorities necessitated by the rules. On the one hand, as has been remarked at several points in this study, the authority of a majority decision can be grievously undermined if the majority is small or if it is opposed by a sizeable minority. On the other hand, as was pointed out in Chapter 2, Section 2.11, a strong tradition of achieving the broadest possible consensus is inculcated in the Parliament and hence its working methods. This is represented in the rules' requirement that the rapporteur should present his committee's views rather than his own. In fact, it is almost impossible for an extreme, or extremely adversarial, report to get to Parliament's plenary, let alone be adopted by it.

The art of the rapporteur's job in committee is to take on board the views of his fellow committee members without sacrificing too many of his own views. Frequently, the knack is in finding a formula of words (not made easier, given translation and interpretation difficulties) that gives satisfaction to both, or all, sides. On legislative reports, particularly where Parliament has real legislative input, the rapporteur may also play a role as inter-institutional go-between, championing his committee's amendments to the other institutions but sometimes also, inevitably, defending or explaining the other institutions' positions on parliamentary amendments. A similar process occurs in Parliament's plenary sessions. The plenary will depend extensively on the rapporteur's guidance as to whether or not to accept amendments, and the extent of his/her consensual arts will be reflected in the size of the parliamentary majority the report wins. The co-decision procedure introduced by the Maastricht Treaty has created a new role and responsibility for rapporteurs, who may now have to shepherd such legislative reports through the complicated negotiations of the third-reading conciliation committee.

The formalism of the plenary

A commonly voiced criticism of the European Parliament is that its plenary sessions are, variously, chaotic, badly organised, boring and ill-attended (for a good example, see Engel, 1994). Debate is said to be flat and lacking in passion. Unfavourable comparisons are made with the 'cockpit' of the House of Commons (although most people have in mind the weekly pyrotechnics of Prime Minister's Question Time rather than the Commons' ordinary business). There are degrees of truth in all of these criticisms, but comparisons with the House of Commons are misleading. Above all, to judge the relevance and efficacy of the European Parliament by the appearance of its plenary sessions is to misunderstand the nature of the Parliament's working methods and role.

In the first place, at the formal level the treaties only recognise the Parliament (as a body) and its president, although at the political level most of its work is done in its specialised committees and political groups. A consequence of the plenary's formal pre-eminence is that parliamentary debates in plenary are faithfully recorded, translated and published in the *Official Journal*, whereas debates in committee are simply minuted and only distributed within the committee. Committees can exercise delegated powers but generally only in areas free of controversy. Even where committees (for example, the budgets and budgetary control committees) exercise substantial delegated powers, the results still have to pass through the formal imprimatur of the plenary. The formalism and official publication of plenary debates explains the popularity among backbenchers of such particularities as 'explanations of vote' (a one-minute speech or a two-hundred-word written explanation grafted into the minutes), 'personal statements' (a three-minute speech of rebuttal or clarification) and 'points of order' (one-minute points which tend to wander from the subject), all of which enable a member to put a concern or a point of view on the public record. The formalism of the plenary also explains why battles sometimes long since won in a committee room have to be orally refought for the record.

In the second place, final votes can only take place in Parliament's plenary sessions and, given the many different majority requirements imposed upon the Parliament and its traditionally low attendance rates (see Chapter 2, Section 2.11), these tend to be grouped together at certain times during the plenary sessions. In some specialised areas — the budget, or the annual fixing of agricultural prices, for example — there can be literally hundreds of amendments, each with a majority requirement, so that the Parliament has no choice but to vote them one-by-one (or grouped by category). This detachment from debate on the one hand, and grouping on the other, inevitably removes the climactic element from parliamentary debate and makes the Parliament seem like a voting machine, but the Parliament has no choice. As this study has shown, Parliament has to muster plenary majorities to exercise its powers, although the substantial political and legislative work has almost always been done elsewhere, in the committees and political groups.

A third important and frequently forgotten point is that the European Parliament does not have the luxury of meeting in lengthy sessions of several months' duration. The Parliament meets episodically and then just for four working days (Monday afternoon to Friday morning) in each month. A direct result of this is that the plenary sessions are the focus of hectic amounts of activity as lobbyists, intergroups, pressure groups, journalists, personalities and constituents descend on Strasbourg *en masse*. In addition, the political groups and many parliamentary committees have to meet during plenary sessions. Indeed, the Parliament's meetings in Strasbourg could be compared to a cross between a vast academic convention and an American-style party convention, with the 'action' simultaneously taking place in a large number of forums and meeting rooms. This concentrated and disparate activity inevitably leads to conflicting demands on parliamentarians' time. Sitting in the hemicycle to listen to a plenary debate may not seem the most productive way of spending precious Strasbourg time, particularly if a member has already heard all the political arguments several times over in committee and in political group. A perhaps inevitable consequence of these considerations is that attendance at most parliamentary debates tends to be restricted to those members with an immediate interest in the report under consideration (typically, the committee chairman, the rapporteur and any draftsmen, political group spokesmen on the subject and some interested members).

A fourth point is that, for a number of reasons, the European Parliament is not the (nor the primary) 'cockpit' of Europe, much as it would like to be. The Parliament is undeniably the only supranational parliamentary body within Europe but, as Chapter 1, Section 1.5 showed, it is not the only European parliamentary body. Moreover, within the European Union other bodies, above all the Council and the European Council, could lay at least partial claim to the role. But the Parliament is additionally crippled by a number of mechanical problems. A major problem is the episodic nature of its meetings. The European Parliament, at the formal level of its plenary, can only debate topical events and only interact with the other Community institutions when it is in session, yet for over 300 of the 365 days in the year the European Parliament is not in session. As a result, the Parliament cannot fulfil a number of traditional parliamentary roles: it cannot always react swiftly to events and it (as opposed to the media) cannot always be the first port of call for the Council or the Commission. Various suggestions have been made to overcome these problems, including the organisation of open-ended committee meetings, committees of the whole house and more supplementary sessions. Many members see the obligation to meet in Strasbourg as a further stumbling-block, although, whatever the nature of its obligations as to where it should meet, there is a clear trend for the European Parliament to meet more often. Between 1952 and 1958, the ECSC Common Assembly met for just ninety-four days (about fifteen days a year); between 1958 and 1972 (until the first enlargement), the Parliament met on average thirty-four days in each year; between 1973 and the first direct elections in 1979, the Parliament met on average fifty-five days a year; since then the Parliament has been meeting about sixty days a year, but in 1994, following the 1992 Edinburgh Council's decision, the Parliament will altogether hold eight days of supplementary plenary session in Brussels. Thus, as the European Parliament becomes more flexible on the one hand, and enlarging Europe's organisation and institutions are rationalised on the other, the Parliament may well become better placed to play the role of European 'cockpit'.

Fifth, and perhaps more academically, a mono-cultural insistence on the merits of any particular parliamentary system obscures the very different functions, and the varying emphases upon them, that different parliaments play. In seeking to analyse parliaments political scientists have established a series of typologies of legislatures and of parliamentary functions (see, for example, Norton, 1990b). What is clear from these analyses is that not all parliaments place emphasis on plenary sessions and the debating function; others, the American Congress and the German Bundestag among them, have powerful committee systems, and the European Parliament falls into a similar category. This is partly because of the technical nature of much of the draft legislation which it has to consider, but it is also bound up with the cultural differences which make the European Parliament such a unique institution.

Plenary debates take place in up to nine different languages (by contrast, the United Nations uses but six). These are simultaneously translated and relayed to other members through headphones. Oratory, rhetoric, invective, irony, sarcasm and humour all lose much in translation. Misunderstandings are common. Debates cannot be open-ended because the thirty-odd interpreters in the cabins ringing the hemicycle work, for health reasons, to strictly demarcated shifts. As a consequence of all these considerations, debating time is carefully divided up among the political group spokesmen and other participants in debates. Speaking time is necessarily strictly enforced by the president, since any over-runs will inevitably cut into other members' speaking time. This can frequently result in the reading out of speeches carefully drafted to take up precisely the allotted amount of time. The strict distribution of speaking time may discipline debates, but it can also hamper expression; a minute's speaking time is hardly enough, for example, to develop a reasoned argument. (Occasionally the interpreters have to beg the president to slow down a member intent on speed-reading as much political argument as possible within his allotted time!) At the same time, members accept the system as the fairest and most equitable possible. Discussions about the possible limitation of working languages have occasionally surfaced, particularly in the context of enlargement, but these touch on fundamental sensitivities and, in any case, nobody has ever suggested that languages should be limited in plenary debate.

Another cultural difference concerns the substantial nature of debate in the European Parliament. There is no 'government' and 'opposition' as such and certainly no adversarial culture in the chamber. As explained above, rapporteurs have to work with all sides of the house, and the general mode of the Parliament is consensual, although occasionally passions can be roused, particularly over matters of principal. The absence of an identifiable government removes another element familiar in Westminster debate. The Commission is frequently taken to task for the quality of its draft legislation, its timidity in Council or its management, but as Chapter 1, Section 1.3 made clear, the two institutions are on the same side and obliged to collaborate constructively. Council Presidencies-in-Office are sometimes treated as a substitute for an adversary, but, as Chapter 1, Section 1.3 also made clear, Parliament knows that the real 'adversary' is the Member States in the Council rather than the Presidency. Debates are further coloured by the technical and essentially positive and constructive nature of much of

Parliament's legislative work. As Chapter 3 explained, the Parliament has various sorts of weak and strong vetoes in its armoury, but its use of these is sparing. Most of its work is bound up in constructive attempts to improve draft legislation, so that legislative debates are frequently dominated by esoteric exchanges among the initiated. Lastly, the European Parliament is a very polite institution. Some cross-chamber heckling goes on, particularly in the *longeurs* of voting sessions, but is generally good-natured and always off-record. Shouting can occur but is frowned upon. For all of these reasons debates can seem stolid affairs.

From all of the foregoing it will have become clear that much of the business of Parliament's plenary sessions is formalistic and likely to remain so. Major, and animated, debates do sometimes take place, particularly when the Council Presidency is actively represented (but even then the importance of the occasion encourages large numbers of speakers to 'sign up' for the debate, so that the debate tends to peter out into a large number of one-minute-long speeches), but it must be assumed that enlargement, with new languages and parliamentary cultures and increased majority requirements, will accentuate the trends identified here.

Lobbyists and intergroups

The European Parliament is an open institution. The vast bulk of its functions, including its plenary sessions and most of its committee meetings, are open to the public. Its documentation is freely available, and it insists on a maximum degree of transparency in the legislative process. Simply because of this easy access to information and documentation, the Parliament has always been attractive to lobbyists and consultants.

The 1986 Single European Act brought a new dimension to the lobbyists' interest. Thereafter, Parliament could hope to oblige the Commission and the Council to take on board legislative amendments, and interest groups, who were excluded from any direct participation in the Council's deliberations, saw Parliament's legislative input as an additional point of entry into the legislative process (following on from the Commission's initial consultative processes during pre-legislative drafting). Lobbyists' and consultants' offices mushroomed in Brussels, and their representatives descended in large numbers on Parliament's committee meetings. MEPs themselves became the targets of sustained mail and telephone campaigns on political issues.

Another striking development in Parliament's working methods since direct elections has been the establishment of what are known as *intergroups* (see Jacobs and Corbett, 1990, pp.146–55). Few intergroups have any official status. They exist unofficially alongside Parliament's formal structures. They typically consist of a number of members from different political groups with a shared interest in a particular political theme. Some (for example, the Rugby Union or the Mountaineering intergroups) seem to cater to a shared passion. But most have a clear political objective, existing in order to provide constant monitoring of and input into the legislative and political processes. Some (for example, the Kangaroo Group, which lobbies in favour of the dismantlement of the Community's internal frontiers and counts several prime ministers among its membership) are eminently respectable. Some (for example, the Animal Welfare intergroup) are formidably influential. Many are extremely well organised, with their own secretariats. Many are financed by the political groups, or indirectly by the Commission or by private sector interests. There is no official register of intergroups, but their number is currently put at about fifty.

The increase in the number of lobbyists and consultants and of intergroups has led to a great deal of introspection within the Parliament. An annex to Parliament's Rules of Procedure obliges individual members to make a written declaration of their professional activities and to list their paid functions or activities. This register is open to the public. The annex also obliges a member speaking in Parliament to disclose any direct financial interest he may have in the subject under debate. Some members see these measures as sufficient, others as inadequate. Other members have engaged in a broader deontological debate about their role and behaviour in regard to lobbyists and the representatives of interest groups in general.

This introspection met its apogee in 1991–2, in the aftermath of the 'no' vote in the first, June 1992, Danish referendum on the Maastricht Treaty. (The Commission, in particular, became engaged in a broad exercise to render its consultation and drafting processes more transparent, including the drafting of guidelines to govern access to documentation and its relations with external interests. Many MEPs were in turn spurred on by the Commission's activity.) In 1991, the Rules Committee was asked to draw up a code of conduct and a public register of accredited lobbyists, and the Committee's preparatory work involved the organisation of a public hearing in January 1992. The Committee's emphasis was on regulation rather than exclusion, but it soon became clear that there was no underlying consensus on what form that regulation should take. Should MEPs be able to take over amendments drafted by lobbyists, asked some? Why not, argued others, particularly if the draft legislation is highly technical? The Committee drafted a report, but the matter was then passed on to the Bureau for guidance, and subsequently lapsed.

A major problem was in determining where, if anywhere, the distinction lay between lobbyists and representatives of interest groups. Parliament prides itself on its openness, and many of the secondary problems encountered were more practical (access to documents, the library, meeting rooms) than deontological. The lobbying process in Brussels and Strasbourg has not yet reached the intensity of Washington, but the trend is clearly in that direction. Lobbyists, consultants, interest groups and intergroups are now familiar parts of the legislative and political processes, and their activity can be expected to increase in line with that of the Community's institutions. However, there is one important difference between the lobbying processes in Brussels and Washington. As an American observer has put it, 'The EC's legislative process operates in a tradition of civility and accommodation that is the antithesis of the atmosphere of hostility and stalemate that has become increasingly characteristic of special-interest politics in the U.S. Congress' (Gardner, 1993, p.17). Gardner goes on to stress the low-key, consensual, insiders' approach of Brussels lobbying, a practice which has had to graft itself on to a quintessentially consensual process where compromise is both an art and a necessity.

For as long as the Parliament remains the most open and accessible of the Community's institutions, it will continue to attract large numbers of those seeking information and influence. And that, most agree, is and should continue to be an important part of its functions.

Parliament's 'weaknesses'

As this study has shown, the European Parliament is frequently hampered by poor attendance and majority requirements. In addition, it suffers from a number of understandable 'weaknesses', some of which will be briefly considered here.

A first could be dubbed the 'do good' factor. As a young institution growing very slowly in the consciousness of the European electorate, the European Parliament is extremely sensitive to criticism and potentially negative impressions. This sensitivity goes some way towards explaining Parliament's dislike for its veto powers under the cooperation and co-decision procedures (see Chapter 3, Section 3.4 — just four common positions rejected in seven years!). Rejecting a piece of legislation outright, which may sometimes be the only way for Parliament to exercise its prerogatives, could easily backfire in terms of public opinion. In practice, Parliament only pushes to procedural extremes where it not only has a good case but is fairly confident of being able to present that case positively. Above all, Parliament wishes to be seen as a 'responsible' actor in the Community's inter-institutional and legislative processes, since it knows that the key to future extensions of its powers lies in 'responsible' use of those it already has.

A second, linked, weakness is Parliament's concern for appearances, sometimes to the potential detriment of substance. A good, if somewhat obscure, example of this is related to the take-up of parliamentary amendments under the cooperation procedure. By convention, Community legislative proposals consist of a series of preambles, followed by a series of substantial articles, and each article must have a corresponding preambular clause. But it is the substantial article which is important. A group within the Council known as the 'jurists–linguists' is responsible for ensuring that legislative proposals are correctly drafted. Their duties include adding corresponding preambular clauses where they consider these necessary. But Parliament frequently insists on tabling amendments of substance and on creating a corresponding preambular clause. Some preambular clauses, or parts of them, are used palliatively to address concerns without any corresponding substantial article. Finally, some amendments are tabled which only affect preambular clauses. In all three cases, parliamentary practice is bound up in concern for statistics relating to the take-up of parliamentary amendments. According to a simple quantitative analysis, the more amendments the Council takes up, the greater Parliament's influence but, as Chapter 3, Section 3.4 pointed out, quantitative success reveals little about Parliament's qualitative influence on legislation. The problem from Parliament's point of view, given the technical detail of much of the draft legislation it amends, is the impossibility of measuring and consequently explaining qualitative influence in any easily accessible way.

A third weakness is that the Parliament is frequently prepared to sacrifice the full extent of its theoretical powers to short-term policy interests and, as has been the case with 'comitology' (see Chapter 3, Section 3.8), is sometimes prepared to contradict its own strategies. This latter tendency is bound up in the strong roles of Parliament's committees and political groups, which may have strong policy preferences that 'override' decisions of principle about tactics of strategy taken elsewhere in Parliament. A fourth, related weakness (frequently emphasised by parliamentary constitutionalists such as Sir Christopher Prout) is that the European Parliament fails to exploit the full extent of its current powers. This has been particularly the case with Parliament's lesser and relatively unglamorous control powers (question time, for example), which have been overshadowed by Parliament's attention to its growing budgetary and legislative powers and its overall constitutional strategy.

Lastly, and as a consequence of all the previous 'weaknesses', the European Parliament is instinctively, and sometimes against its better judgement, predisposed to forego the full extent of its prerogatives on historical occasions (for example, German unification, enlargement), and yet paradoxically its powers are frequently at their greatest on just such occasions. It is easy to see why this should be the case, for it would be unthinkable for the Parliament to behave in a way that would lay it open to accusations of blocking such great historical advances in the Union's evolution.

4.3 Parliament's political agenda

Since 1979, the directly elected European Parliament has developed its own, distinctive political agenda. Whatever its formal powers, Parliament has chosen persistently to emphasise particular policies or particular aspects of policies. This constant pressure, the power of persuasion, backed up wherever possible by real legislative and budgetary powers, has clearly had knock-on effects on the Community's policy-information processes and the attitudes of the other Community institutions. The development of Parliament's political agenda must count as one of the most encouraging aspects of the Parliament's evolution, since these constantly espoused themes have not been plucked from the air but are built on, and a direct response to, the views and concerns of the European electorate.

Human rights

Although objectively an academic distinction, Parliament's concerns about human rights can be divided into two areas: those within the Community and those outwith it.

Within the Community, human rights and citizens' rights intertwine. Citizens' rights are primarily monitored and safeguarded by the Committee on Legal Affairs and Citizens' Rights. Human rights within the Community fall primarily within the remit of the Committee on Civil Liberties and Internal Affairs. These distinctions are important only for determining which committee will be responsible for drafting a report on a particular issue or subject. In practice, human and citizens' rights within the Community extend far beyond the remits of these two committees. Many of the petitions before the Petitions Committee, for example, are bound up with citizens' and human rights, and Parliament's ombudsman is empowered to receive complaints from any citizen of the Union but also any person residing in a Member State. Many of the matters dealt with by Parliament's Social Affairs and Women's Rights Committees touch frequently on rights issues. The political groups are particularly sensitive to such issues, and in addition a number of specialised intergroups concentrate on specific interests (for example, the elderly, the handicapped).

Parliament's Foreign Affairs Committee is primarily responsible for human rights issues outside the Community and has established a Sub-Committee on Human Rights with constant scrutiny and monitoring functions. Once again, other committees have overlapping interests. For example, the Development Committee's work is frequently linked to human rights' considerations and, despite a theoretically distinct brief, Parliament's Committee on External Economic Relations often finds itself taking humanitarian aspects into account in its consideration of trade and commercial agreements (for example, it is currently championing the cause of 'social clauses' in trade agreements). Again, intergroups (for example, on Russian Jewry, on East Timor) play an active role in sensitising the Parliament and sustaining its interest.

Parliament's committees often organise public hearings on issues or areas of particular concern, and the topical and urgent debates procedure gives individual members and the political groups a regular possibility to draw attention to current areas of concern. The annual Sakharov prize for freedom of thought gives Parliament the capacity to recognise and reward groups or individuals for their commitment to that cause. In addition to bringing public pressure and the weight of its own opinions to bear, Parliament has a considerable procedural arsenal at its disposal and has become adept at exploiting its legislative and budgetary powers, to which the Single European Act added the assent power (since arguably weakened by the Maastricht Treaty — see Chapter 3, Section 3.5). Perhaps above all, Parliament constantly calls the Commission and the Council to account. Commissioners and ministers frequently appear before Parliament's committees and are invariably taken to task over violations or the negligence of human rights in Community policies somewhere in the globe. This constant monitoring and sensitising function has been given fresh substance through the Maastricht Treaty's provisions on the Common Foreign and Security Policy which grant Parliament the right to information and consultation, and to make recommendations.

The tangible fruits of Parliament's constant efforts are a sizeable *tranche* of the budget now expressly devoted to human rights' issues, greatly increased conditionality in the granting of Community aid, greatly increased sensitivity in the Council and the Commission and a growing realisation among third countries that the Parliament's human rights' concerns are a potential force to be reckoned with wherever the treaties grant Parliament budgetary or legislative powers.

Development

Development issues consistently figure high on Parliament's agenda. A specialised Development Committee constantly scrutinises and monitors the Community's policy with regard to the North–South dialogue, emergency aid and food aid, technical, financial and educational cooperation, the Community's generalised system of preferences, industrial, agricultural and rural development, the application of the ACP–EC Convention (known universally as the Lomé Convention), the application of cooperation agreements with the Maghreb and Mashreq countries, cooperation and association agreements with developing countries and relations with specialist international organisations. In addition, Parliament sends a sixty-nine member delegation to the ACP–EC Joint Parliamentary Assembly. As with human rights, the Parliament has an array of legislative, budgetary and occasionally assent powers at its disposal. Its budgetary influence has been particularly effective. Community expenditure on 'external action' (made up of food aid and development cooperation) amounted to 444 Mecus (£333m) in 1979 but is forecast at 3,394 Mecus (£2.545m) for 1994. This pales in comparison with the figures the Community will spend on the Common Agricultural Policy (37,465 Mecus — £28,098m) and the Community's structural funds (21,681 Mecus — £16,260m). It even amounts to less than the Community's envisaged administrative expenses for the year (3,579 Mecus). However, Community external action comes in addition to the aid paid directly from the Member States (much of it complementary), and the large-scale financial assistance of the European Development Fund (over which the Parliament has less budgetary control) and amounts to an objectively large sum for the recipient countries. Again, as with human rights, parliamentary scrutiny in committee, debate in plenary, the organisation of public hearings and the use of other traditional parliamentary tools such as the tabling of questions have consistently sensitised the Community and its institutions to development issues and development aspects of other Community policies.

The environment

Environmental matters have always been of concern to the directly elected Parliament, which has sometimes been spurred on by a number of active and high-profile intergroups (for example, an early parliamentary victory was a ban on the importation of baby seals' fur after a campaign which had been heavily inspired by an intergroup). Nevertheless, Parliament's environmental concerns were greatly boosted by two developments. The first was the entry into force of the 1986 Single European Act, which granted Parliament cooperation powers in various environment-related policy areas. The second was the strong showing made by Green and ecologist parties in the 1989 European elections (see Chapter 2, Section 2.8) and the growing popular concern about the environment which this reflected.

Parliament's environmental concerns are tightly focused through its Environmental Affairs Committee, which has adopted a pugnacious attitude towards the defence of Parliament's legislative powers and prerogatives, leading to several notable battles between the Parliament and the Commission and the Council, some of them ending up in Court. A spectacular victory in the use of Parliament's cooperation procedure powers led to a significant and early increase in emission standards for small cars, where the Council was obliged to prefer tighter legislation to no legislation at all. The Maastricht Treaty has further consolidated Parliament's powers in the field through the introduction of the co-decision procedure and the extension of the cooperation procedure. Parliament's formal powers are further reinforced by the popular nature of the issues it espouses: for example, legislation on food quality or colouring, waste transport and disposal, the quality of drinking water or holiday beaches.

Prior to the implementation of the Maastricht Treaty, the Parliament made use of its own *ad hoc* powers to organise several temporary Committees of Inquiry into high-profile environmental matters. Thus, it investigated the treatment of toxic and dangerous substances (post-Seveso), the handling of nuclear waste, and hormones in meat. In future, such Committees will have the authority of the treaties behind them and the legal muscle to extract information that the pre-1993 Committees lacked (see Chapter 3, Section 3.8).

Sexual equality and women's rights

One of the directly elected Parliament's earliest acts was to establish a Committee of Inquiry into the Situation of Women in the Community. This was soon transformed into a permanent standing committee. Parliament is far from having equal representation of the sexes among its membership. Female members currently represent about 25 per cent of total membership, which is nevertheless a better percentage than most Member State parliaments. The first president of the directly elected European Parliament was a woman — Simone Veil (now a French minister) — and women occupy many of the most important positions within the Parliament, from vice-presidencies through committee and delegation chairmanships to rapporteurships on major reports. Thus, despite the low percentage of female members, explicit sexual discrimination within the Parliament is virtually non-existent, and the presence of a Women's Rights Committee with a constant monitoring brief has surely contributed to this good record.

The Women's Rights Committee has no corresponding Commission 'department', or directorate general, although there are specialised units within some directorates general (particularly those dealing with social affairs, personnel and information), and it has few legislative powers or duties, most of its work being conducted through legislative opinions to other committees or own-initiative reports. Nevertheless, the Parliament has maintained women's rights as a primary concern and political objective, both within the Community (particularly through social affairs-related issues, such as leave for pregnant women and sexual discrimination in wages but also by constantly monitoring the Commission's internal employment policy) and in the wider world (particularly through development and trade agreements).

Women's rights, as with most other items on Parliament's political agenda, are a horizontal issue stretching far beyond the remit of one committee. Women's rights are a frequent aspect of social policy within the Community, for example, and a central element in development policy outside it. In addition to the Social Affairs and Development Committees, women's rights' issues can surface tangentially in connection with the Community's commercial relations with countries in, for example, Latin America and Asia.

In a debate on International Women's Day 1994, Pádraig Flynn, Commissioner responsible for social policy, handsomely praised Parliament and its committee:

> The political backing of the European Parliament in pushing equality legislation and programmes forward has been crucial and it is only fitting that I pay tribute to the contributions of the committee . . . to the improvement of European society as a whole through the furthering of equality matters. Looking back briefly at the equality initiatives which have been successfully adopted and implemented since 1984, we recall by way of example the directives on equality for the self-employed in 1986 and on the protection of pregnant workers, the second and third Community medium-term action programmes, the recommendations on positive action, vocational training, childcare and sexual harassment. The Commission acknowledges the extent to which the European Parliament's interest in equal opportunities has contributed to the promotion of these initiatives and to raising awareness about equality throughout Europe (*Verbatim Report of Proceedings*, 8 March 1994, p.104).

Drug abuse and drug trafficking

The European Parliament has twice organised temporary Committees of Inquiry to investigate the twin problems of drug abuse and drug trafficking, and these had considerable success in highlighting a growing problem and in mobilising political action and public opinion. Parliament's Committee on Civil Liberties and Internal Affairs has a permanent monitoring brief on the fight against international crime, drug trafficking and fraud as well as on police and legal cooperation to prevent and combat, *inter alia*, drug trafficking. Inter-governmental activities in these areas are growing within the new context of the third 'pillar' of the Maastricht Treaty, and the Committee has already given clear indications of its intent to hold ministers and the Council Presidency to account as well as pressuring the Commission to give full information on third-pillar activities. In addition, the competences of several parliamentary committees frequently touch upon potentially drugs-related issues. Thus, the Committee on Budgetary Control may touch on fraud and money-laundering (and Community legislation on this in the context of the internal market involved the Committee on Economic Monetary Affairs). The Committee on Youth and Culture deals with the problem of drug abuse among the young. The Development Committee may touch, for example, on the problem of cash crops in drug-producing countries.

Racism and xenophobia

The rise of racism and xenophobia has been a constant concern of the Parliament. In 1984 and 1990 it established Committees of Inquiry on the subject, and it has now charged its Committee on Civil Liberties and Internal Affairs with a constant monitoring brief. The 1984 Committee of Inquiry resulted in the adoption by the Council, the Commission and the Parliament of a Joint Declaration against Racism and Xenophobia (1986). Concerns about racism frequently surface in Parliament's debates.

Fraud and budgetary discipline

Chapter 3, Section, 3.3 described in some detail Parliament's budgetary scrutiny mechanisms. Parliament's Budgetary Control Committee is particularly determined to identify and root out fraud and to ensure 'budgetary discipline' (that is, respect for agreed amounts of expenditure). A major reason for this intense scrutiny is the knock-on effects fraud and a lack of budgetary discipline (particularly agricultural spending) can have on other Community policies. Parliament now receives three-monthly reports on the execution of expenditure related to the Common Agricultural Policy in addition to the Court of Auditors' annual and occasional reports. The Maastricht Treaty's provisions on the establishment of Committees of Inquiry have reinforced Parliament's powers of independent inquiry. The Budgetary Control Committee has recently resorted to the practice of sending out small fact-finding delegations to investigate how Community money is being spent in the field. Thus, following repeated expressions of misgiving about the way in which economic assistance programmes were being implemented in Central and Eastern European countries, the Committee has sent small teams out to those countries for on-the-spot investigations.

Democracy

The European Parliament is a staunch proponent of democracy, both within the Community and in the world at large. Rulings of the European Court of Justice and the repeated pronouncements of Europe's statesmen have confirmed the Parliament's status as the embodiment of the European tradition of parliamentary democracy. It sees its struggle for more powers and more equal standing with the Council not as self-aggrandisement but as a reassertion of that tradition. Outside the Community, the European Parliament plays a passive, symbolic role (democracy incarnated at European level) but also an active, proselytising role, deploring and discouraging anti-democratic practices and praising and supporting the process of democratisation wherever it occurs. Both passive and active roles were much in evidence in 1989–93 as the Central and Eastern European countries threw off their Cold War shackles and opted for democratic systems of government. As with other matters on its political agenda, Parliament brings all of its powers to bear wherever possible in the furtherance of its cherished ideals. For example, Parliament has used its budgetary powers to create a democracy fund which can be used to fund research into democratisation. The Parliament also seeks to carry the torches of parliamentarianism and democracy abroad and is eager to send parliamentary observers to elections held in newly democratising countries (for example, the 1993 elections in the Russian Federation).

European Union

The European Parliament's commitment to the cause of European Union is symbolised by its adoption on 10 February 1994 of a new suggested blueprint for a European constitution. As the historical account in Chapter 2, Section 2.2 emphasised, the European Parliament's federal vocation stretches back to the institution's beginnings in the 1950s, nor has its faith in the federalist argument ever wavered significantly. But a subtle difference has occurred in its militancy.

The federalist spirit of the Common Assembly of the European Coal and Steel Community has to be seen against the backdrop of the Second World War and its aftermath. Parliament's early federalism was ideological in that it was opposed to the nation-statism that had led to war. However, there is much less danger of a similar world war today and, because of the European Community, war between any of the

Member States is unthinkable. Further, the generations that lived through the war and its aftermath are much less well represented in political debate today, forty years on, than they were in the 1950s and 1960s. Yet Parliament's federalism remains strong.

The difference is that this federalism is far less ideological and far more pragmatic in content. On the one hand, the Parliament has long since learned to tolerate the existence of 'statist' organisations such as the Council, the European Council and Coreper and even to appreciate their worth. On the other, the nation-states have come to be recognised as not only inevitable but perhaps essential building blocks within the Union, with some arguing that the growth of the Community has actually reinforced the nation-state (for example, Hoffman, 1982; Milward, 1992). A good example of Parliament's pragmatic federalism is to be found in its 1984 *Draft Treaty Establishing the European Union,* the directly elected Parliament's first constitutional blueprint. The principle of subsidiarity, now on everybody's lips (and enshrined by the SEA and, more substantially by the Maastricht Treaty), was first introduced in Parliament's draft as a pragmatic mechanism for determining the boundaries between the competences of the states and the Union.

Another factor involved in Parliament's pragmatic federalism is the increasingly rapid and progressive evolution of the European Union. The current reality and Parliament's ideal are far less distant than they were in 1979, let alone 1962. As the ideal approaches, Parliament finds itself increasingly tackling problems of a practical, rather than a theoretical, nature, as the next section will show.

4.4   Parliament's future

Evolving conventions

It could be argued that the European Parliament is constantly fashioning its future. The creative way in which it interprets its powers and drafts its rules obliges the other Community institutions to respond, tying them more or less willingly into an evolving process of establishing custom and convention. (One commentator has described it as 'a dynamic institution within an evolutive organisation': Bieber, 1987, p.357.) The Parliament has increasingly called for such conventions between the institutions to be formalised in the form of inter-institutional agreements. So successful had previous inter-institutional agreements been, particularly the 1988 agreement in the budgetary field, that the Maastricht Treaty itself provided for an inter-institutional agreement to be negotiated (on Committees of Inquiry), and the

December 1992 Edinburgh European Council called for another two such agreements, one in the budgetary field (renewing the 1988 agreement) and another on the implementation of the principle of subsidiarity. Ultimately, the October 1993 Brussels European Council saw the conclusion of inter-institutional agreements on: the 1993–9 financial perspectives, the subsidiarity principle, the conciliation procedures within the co-decision procedure and the parliamentary Ombudsman, as well as an inter-institutional declaration on democracy, transparency and subsidiarity. (Negotiations continued on the agreement on parliamentary Committees of Inquiry.)

This spate of agreements flowed directly from the implementation of the Maastricht Treaty, just as earlier inter-institutional agreements (for example, on the budget or the 1990 code of conduct) had flowed from the implementation of the Single European Act. In fact, all three institutions have increasingly come to recognise that the treaty amendments, and particularly the new procedures created by them, can only be successfully implemented if fleshed out with agreements as to how they are to be put into practice. However, the Parliament, denied any pro-active role in the inter-governmental conference process, additionally sees the negotiation of such agreements as providing a possibility for the furtherance of its role and powers. Thus, in addition to the six inter-institutional agreements listed above, the European Parliament is calling for the negotiation of agreements to interpret and flesh out the Maastricht Treaty's provisions on Economic and Monetary Union, the Common Foreign and Security Policy, and Cooperation in the Fields of Justice and Home Affairs; all areas, it will be recalled from Chapter 3, where Parliament feels its powers are fundamentally insufficient.

In 'forcing the pace' in this way, the Parliament is perhaps driven by the consideration that today's conventions frequently become tomorrow's treaty amendments. Good examples of such a process are provided by the Maastricht Treaty's provisions on parliamentary Committees of Inquiry and petitions. In fact, both procedures already existed and had been extensively used. But previously they had been founded on unilateral provisions in Parliament's Rules of Procedure, consolidated by inter-institutional agreements. In effect, the Maastricht Treaty enshrined existing practice.

Enlargements, and the 1996 intergovernmental conference

Although its seems as though the Maastricht Treaty has only just been implemented, further treaty amendments are not far away. In the first place, negotiations with the four candidate States (Austria, Finland,

Norway and Sweden) have now been completed, and it is hoped, national referendums permitting, that the four will be able to accede to the European Union in early 1995. Accession necessarily involves adjustments to the treaties in such areas as the number of commissioners, the number of members of the European Parliament, the weighting of votes and the size of the qualified majority in the Council. As was seen above, the December 1993 European Council opted for a mechanical extension of these factors. But this was seen very much as a provisional and transitional arrangement, with a clear understanding that the 1996 IGC would engage in a more substantial review.

In the second place, an article in the Maastricht Treaty provides that 'a conference of representatives of the governments of the Member States shall be convened in 1996 to examine those provisions of the Treaty for which revision is provided', and an earlier article sets out as an objective of the European Union 'to maintain in full the *acquis communautaire* and build on it with a view to considering [through the 1996 IGC] to what extent the policies and forms of cooperation introduced by this Treaty may need to be revised with the aim of ensuring the effectiveness of the mechanisms and institutions of the Community'. Those provisions subject to review include the scope of the new co-decision procedure, the Common Foreign and Security Policy, defence, the classification and hierarchy of Community acts and the 'pillar' structure introduced by the Maastricht Treaty, although few suppose that the 1996 inter-governmental conference will restrict its considerations to those areas alone; the Maastricht inter-governmental conference was preceded and accompanied by a plethora of proposals (see Corbett, 1993). With a view to the 1996 inter-governmental conference, the Greek Presidency in the first half of 1994 successfully pushed for the creation of a preparatory committee, much like the 'Spaak' (Rome Treaty), 'Dooge' (Single European Act) and 'Delors' (Maastricht provisions on Economic and Monetary Union) Committees.

Before the ink had dried on the Maastricht Treaty, the European Parliament was compiling its 'shopping list' for the 1996 inter-governmental conference, but its demands are likely to be very different from those preceding the Maastricht Treaty. Writing in 1990, two parliamentary 'insiders' set out the European Parliament's main objectives as 'above all co-decision including a stronger conciliation procedure, a broader budgetary role, better scrutiny of secondary legislation, the right to go to Court for annulment, and a formal right to initiate legislative proposals', together with powers over the appointment of the President of the Commission, a vote of confidence in the Commission as a whole and the vetting of other appointments (Jacobs and Corbett, 1990, pp. 257–61). If this check-list is compared with the Maastricht Treaty, it is striking just how many of Parliament's demands were met wholly or in part, as Chapter 3 showed. Co-decision between the Council and the Parliament, including a strong conciliation procedure, now exists. Parliament may now go to the Court for annulment. It may request legislative initiatives. And it now has powers of consultation in relation to the nomination of the Commission President and a vote of confidence in the Commission as a whole.

Thus, in many of the areas that were of concern to Parliament during the inter-governmental process, important points of principle were won; subsequently, in those areas Parliament's 1996 'shopping list' is more likely to concern degree. For example, Parliament will probably seek extensions of the co-decision procedure to other legislative areas, particularly those currently covered by the cooperation procedure. It will probably seek extensions of the assent procedure, and in particular may try to gain assent and consultation powers over trade and commercial agreements. The Parliament is likely to repeat its demands that it should have appointment powers in regard to members of the Court of Auditors and judges of the European Court of Justice. But the sum of Parliament's demands in these areas will seem small in comparison with previous inter-governmental conferences.

Nevertheless, the Parliament has already given notice that it will try to bring five matters of principle to the conference table: the Union's budgetary mechanisms, Parliament's role in relation to Economic and Monetary Union, the Common Foreign and Security Policy, the 'third pillar' of Cooperation in the Fields of Justice and Home Affairs and the nature of treaty change itself.

On the budget, Parliament will have two chief demands: an end to the distinction between compulsory and non-compulsory expenditure (with a corresponding extension of Parliament's budgetary powers) and the creation of a distinct revenue side to the budget (which, in the shorter term, would probably consist of a 'new resource', directly levied and collected by the Community — see Chapter 3, Section 3.3).

Parliament's demands in relation to the Economic and Monetary Union will also be twofold: some substantial input into economic policy formation and a better say in appointments to such bodies as the Monetary Committee (see Chapter 3, Section 3.6).

On the Common Foreign and Security Policy, the European Parliament's chief demand is that the policy should be brought within the structure of the Community. Ideally, Parliament would like to see a seamless common external policy, running from trade and aid through to foreign and security policy. Within this vision, Parliament takes its demand for a greater say, if not assent powers, over trade and aid to their logical conclusion, calling for similar powers in relation to CFSP decisions. However, Parliament pragmatically recognises that the first step must be to get the CFSP up and working. (The Maastricht Treaty provides that the CFSP may be revised at the 1996 IGC but on the basis of a Council report to the European Council evaluating progress made and experience gained — see Chapter 3, Section 3.5).

As was seen in Chapter 3, Section 3.7, the third inter-governmental 'pillar' within the Maastricht Treaty, on Cooperation in the Fields of Justice and Home Affairs, includes a *passerelle*, enabling the Council to recommend (unanimously) that certain policy areas be brought within the remit of the Community. Such a Council recommendation would have to be submitted to ratification in the Member States, and an inter-governmental conference would therefore provide an ideal occasion. The European Parliament's chief demand will be to bring as much as possible of the inter-governmental 'pillar', with subjects ranging from asylum and immigration policy to combating drug addiction and fraud, into the Community system. A secondary demand will be to grant the European Parliament more influential powers in regard to policies that do cross over into the Community than the simple consultation currently provided for by the Maastricht Treaty.

All of these demands will have to be filtered through parliamentary reports, the Commission, the Council Presidency and the representatives of friendly Member State governments at the inter-governmental conference because, as was emphasised in Chapter 1, Section 1.4, the European Parliament itself is both excluded from the inter-governmental conference process and denied ratification powers over the results. Hence, the European Parliament's fifth demand will be to gain pro-active access to the treaty amendment process and to be granted assent powers over draft treaty amendments.

This predicted list of parliamentary demands is long, though the European Parliament would consider it modest and reasonable. The Parliament knows that it will never get everything that it asks for, and it knows that it may not get exactly what it asks for, but it also knows that the inter-governmental conference will result in fresh extensions of its powers, as all previous inter-governmental conferences have done. From Parliament's point of view, the tactical art is to make reasonable demands and couch them in ways which the Member States are less likely to refuse. Thus, whatever the scope and 'generosity' of the 1996 inter-governmental conference, it will inevitably result in further consolidation of the European Parliament's role and powers.

For the foreseeable future, the European Union is likely to remain in a process of constant evolution, both in terms of its composition and the roles and powers of its institutions. However, it is possible to imagine that, at some stage, the European Union will reach its full size and will achieve, whether gradually or suddenly, a final constitutional settlement. Such a settlement would necessarily involve a finalisation of the Parliament's status, role and powers. At that moment the Parliament would have to come to terms with what has been and continues to be one of its principal roles — that of militant federalist and institutional reformer.

The longer term

The next century and the new millennium are now too near to be confined to science-fiction stories. What does the twenty-first century hold in store for the European Parliament? Clearly, the Parliament's future is entirely linked to the future of the European Union and of the European Community within it. As the dust begins to settle after the collapse of the Soviet Union and its satellite Communist states, it has become clear that the European Union will be the central and pre-eminent European organisation of the next century. Other organisations — the Council of Europe, the European Free Trade Association — may continue to play important roles, but the European Union will be at their heart. Six EFTA states have signed up to a joint European Economic Area with the European Union. Four of those states are hoping to join the European Union in the very near future. The Nordic Council may subsequently find four (Denmark, Finland, Norway and Sweden) of its five Member States in the European Union. The Vysegrad countries (Poland, Hungary, and the Czech and Slovak Republics) all have Europe Agreements which foresee ultimate membership of the Union. Other Europe Agreements are in the pipeline. Turkey, Malta and Cyprus all have Association Agreements with the Union and applications for membership on the table. At the other extreme, Comecon (and the Warsaw Pact) no longer exist, and the European Union may well become a member of the Council of Europe (which hopes one day to see Russia as a Member State). As Chapter 1, Section 1.5 showed, the logic of the Maastricht Treaty and the relevant protocol to it imply strongly that the competences and institutions of the Western European Union will be absorbed into the European Union. Thus, the next century will see a consolidation of the European Union's central role but also a rationalisation of European organisations and institutions. In turn, the European Parliament will seek to consolidate its role within the European Union.

The European Parliament's vision of the Europe of the next century is succinctly contained in a report adopted on 20 January 1993. Parliament believes that external and internal pressures will force further consolidation of the European Union. The Parliament does not believe that all European states will become members of the European Union, but it is convinced that most European states will be joined by a web of links and alliances spread over and about the Union. Indeed, Parliament believes that the wider Europe will consist of any number of confederal structures (a belief shared by France's President Mitterrand), elliptical and concentric circles based about the European Union. But the Union will be pre-eminent and ultimately will form, together with the United States, the twin pillar of a Trans-Atlantic Treaty Organisation. Who can say how true this vision will prove?

What is already clear is that the European Union will continue to consolidate its central role and that the European Parliament will continue to be Europe's only supranational parliamentary body and hence the only body able and willing to exercise democratic control at the European Union level.

Annexes

Annex 1: The 1994 European Elections and the new Parliament

In June 1994, 269 million European voters went to the polls to elect 567 members of the European Parliament for the next five years. These were the fourth European elections. The elections were held on Thursday 9 June in the United Kingdom, Ireland, the Netherlands and Denmark, and on Sunday 12 June in the other Member States. Overall turnout (about 56%) was at its lowest since the first direct elections in 1979. Large decreases in turnout were recorded in Ireland (44%, down 24.3% from 1989) and Portugal (35.7%, down 15.5% from 1989). Turnout was also down in the Netherlands, Greece and Italy. On the other hand, turnout went up by about 5% in Denmark, Spain and France. Unified Germany recorded a respectable 60%, while in Belgium (90%), Luxembourg (86%) and the United Kingdom (36%) there was little appreciable difference from 1989. With the exception of Ireland, few European citizens abroad availed themselves of the right to vote in their Member State of residence. The principle explanation advanced for this was a general lack of publicity.

As with the previous three European elections, the emphasis in the 1994 elections was very much on national issues, with the fortunes of governing parties and coalitions depending largely on the position the European elections took within each Member State's national electoral cycle. And, as on previous occasions, the *domestic* consequences of the elections were considered to be at least as significant as any broader phenomenon. Thus, in the United Kingdom and Spain, the results were largely interpreted as a sanction on the incumbent governing parties (Conservative and Socialist respectively), whereas in Italy the results were generally seen as a positive plebiscite on Silvio Berlusconi's recently formed coalition government. However, in some Member States, France and Belgium for example, votes lost to the major parties did not necessarily go to the orthodox opposition but were dispersed among a series of smaller parties and lists.

Although pan-European Socialist, Christian Democrat and Liberal parties existed, they did not really figure in the campaigns, and the electoral performance of the three major European party traditions varied considerably. Again, these variations could be attributed to a large degree to differing electoral cycles. Thus, the Christian Democrats did well in Spain and Germany (something of a surprise), but poorly in Italy. The opposition Labour Party did very well in the UK, but the incumbent Spanish Socialists suffered. The Liberals did well in the Netherlands and Belgium (though less well than expected), but the German Free Democrats fell foul of the 5% threshold for the second time

223

since 1979. (On the other hand, the British Liberal Democrats returned European Parliamentarians for the first time.) The Greens lost their seats in France, but confirmed their advance in Germany and returned members in six other Member States. On the far right, the German Republikaners lost their six seats, but the French *Front National* gained a seat and in Belgium the *Vlaams Blok* and the *Front National* returned three members between them.

The new Parliament is very different to its predecessor for a number of reasons Over a quarter of its members are women (18.5% in 1989). As is fitting in a post-cold war Europe, a number of new political parties made their first appearances and had to find their places in the Parliament's political group structure or, in some cases, create new groups. The Danish and French anti-Maastricht parties were significant newcomers. Perhaps most importantly, there has been a much greater 'turnover' of membership than in 1989 or 1984; over 50% of the MEPs elected in 1994 were new to the Parliament. This did not just mean that there would be a longer 'running in' period for the new Parliament but represented a generational change, as the 'old hands' first elected in 1979 or 1984 gave way to fresh blood. Moreover, further change (up to two new languages) will occur and more new faces (up to 54) will appear as a result of the 1995 enlargements. In organisational terms, the three largest political groups all changed leader, and most committee chairmanships also changed. However, the largest change was constitutional for, as was pointed out in the introduction, the 1994 Parliament came into its full inheritance of post-Maastricht powers. Not only could the newly-legitimated Parliament now fully exploit its innovatory powers but, as the dust settled, thoughts were already turning to the 1996 inter-governmental conference.

Amid all the change there is some important continuity. In particular, the Group of the Party of European Socialists and the Group of the European People's Party have consolidated their oligopoly (see Chapter 4, Section 4.1.). Together, they now occupy some 61% of Parliament's seats. Their members jointly hold the key to the absolute majorities Parliament must find if it is to wield its legislative and budgetary powers. An early indication of this continued oligopoly came with the two groups' informal agreement to 'alternate' the Parliament's Presidency, as had previously occurred in the 1989–1994 Parliament.

Parliament's Political Groups*

Group of the Party of European Socialists (PES): 198 members, with representatives from 15 political parties and from all 12 Member States.
Leader: Pauline Green (Labour, United Kingdom)

Group of the European People's Party (EPP): 157 members, with representatives from 24 political parties and all 12 Member States.
Leader: Wilfried Martens (Christelijke Volkspartij, Belgium)

Group of the European Liberal Democratic and Reformist Party (ELDR): 43 members, with representatives from 14 political parties and 10 Member States.
Leader: Gijs de Vries (VVD, Netherlands)

Confederal Group of the United Left (GUE): 28 members, with representatives from 6 political parties and 5 Member States.
Leader: Alonso Puerta Gutierrez (Izquierda Unida – Iniciativa per Catalunya, Spain)

Forza Europa Group (FE): 27 members, with representatives from one political party in one Member State.
Leader: Giancarlo Ligabue (Forza Italia, Italy)

Group of the European Democratic Alliance (EDA): 26 members, with representatives from 4 political parties and 4 Member States.
Leader: Jean-Claude Pasty (RPR, France)

Green Group in the European Parliament (Green): 23 members, with representatives from 9 political parties in 7 Member States.
Leaders: Claudia Roth (Die Grünen, Germany) and Alexander Langer (Federazione dei Verdi, Italy)

Group of the European Radical Alliance (ERA): 19 members, with representatives from 5 political parties and 5 Member States.
Leader: Jean-François Hory (Liste Energie Radicale, France)

Europe of Nations Group (EN): 19 members, with representatives from 5 political parties and 3 Member States.
Leader: Jimmy Goldsmith (Majorité pour l'autre Europe, France)
Delegated leader: Jens-Peter Bonde (Junibevaegelsen, Denmark)

Non-attached members (NI): 27 members, with representatives from 6 political parties and 4 Member States.
No leader

* As of 19.7.94.
Source: EP Infomemo, 19.7.94.

The New Parliament
(The 1994–1999 European Parliament)*

President: Klaus Hänsch (SPD, Germany)
(from July 1994 to December 1996)

Grp Member State	Total	PES	EPP	ELDR	GUE	FE	EDA	GREEN	ERA	EN	NI
Belgium	25	6	7	6				2	1		3
Denmark	16	3	3	5				1		4	
Germany	99	40	47					12			
Greece	25	10	9		4		2				
Spain	64	22	30	2	9				1		
France	87	15	13	1	7		14		13	13	11
Ireland	15	1	4	1			7	2			
Italy	87	18	12	7	5	27		4	2		12
Luxembourg	6	2	2	1				1			
Netherlands	31	8	10	10				1	2		
Portugal	25	10	1	8	3		3				
United Kingdom	87	63	19	2					2		1
Total	567	198	157	43	28	27	26	23	19	19	

* As of 19.7.94.
Source: EP Infomemo, 19.7.94.

Parliament's Committees*

I. **Committee on Foreign Affairs, Security and Defence Policy** (52 members)
    Chairman: Abel Matutes, EPP (Partido Popular, Spain)

II. **Committee on Agriculture and Rural Development** (45 members)
    Chairman: Christian Jacob, EDA (RPR, France)

III. **Committee on Budgets** (33 members)
    Chairman: Detlev Samland, PES (SPD, Germany)

IV. **Committee on Economic and Monetary Affairs and Industrial Policy** (50 members)
    Chairman: Karl von Wogau, EPP (CDU, Germany)

V. **Committee on Research, Technological Development and Energy** (26 members)
    Chairman: Claude Desama, PES (PS, Belgium) – to be confirmed

VI. **Committee on External Economic Relations** (25 members)
    Chairman: Willy De Clercq, ELDR (VLD, Belgium)

VII. **Committee on Legal Affairs and Citizens' Rights** (25 members)
    Chairman: Carlo Casini, EPP (PPI, Italy)

VIII. **Committee on Social Affairs and Employment** (40 members)
    Chairman: Stephen Hughes, PES (Labour, United Kingdom)

IX. **Committee on Regional Policy** (37 members)
    Chairman: Roberto Speciale, PES (PDS, Italy)

X. **Committee on Transport and Tourism** (28 members)
    Chairman: Petrus Cornelissen, EPP (CDA, Netherlands)

XI. **Committee on the Environment, Public Health and Consumer Protection** (44 members)
    Chairman: Ken Collins, PES (Labour, United Kingdom)

XII. **Committee on Culture, Youth, Education and the Media** (36 members)
    Chairwoman: Luciana Castellina, GUE (RC, Italy)

XIII. **Committee on Development and Cooperation** (36 members)
    Chairman: Bernard Kouchner, PES (l'Europe Solidaire, France)

XIV. **Committee on Civil Liberties and Internal Affairs** (31 members)
    Chairman: Antonio Vitorino, PES (PS, Portugal)

XV. **Committee on Budgetary Control** (18 members)
    Chairwoman: Diemut Theato, EPP (CDU, Germany)

XVI. **Committee on Institutional Affairs** (40 members)
    Chairman: Fernando Moran Lopez, PES (PSOE, Spain)

XVII. **Committee on Fisheries** (22 members)
    Chairman: Miguel Arias Canete, EPP (Partido Popular, Spain)

XVIII. **Committee on the Rules of Procedure, the Verification of Credentials and Immunities** (23 members)
    Chairman: Ben Fayot, PES (PSE, Luxembourg)

XIX. **Committee on Women's Rights** (36 members)
    Chairwoman: Nel van Dijk, Green (Groen Links, Netherlands)

XX. **Committee on Petitions** (27 members)
    Chairman: Eddie Newman, PES (Labour, United Kingdom)

In addition, Parliament has established three sub-committees (on Security and Disarmament, on Human Rights, and on Monetary Affairs), and a temporary committee on employment.

* As of 22.7.94.
Source: EP Minutes of the Sitting of 21.7.94, and author's notes on constitutive meetings held on 21.7.94.

Annex 2: A short note on the European Parliament's seat

Article 77 of the ECSC Treaty provided that the seat of the Community institutions should be decided unanimously ('by common accord') of the Member States' governments. The same provision was reiterated by Article 216 of the EEC Treaty and Article 189 of the Euratom Treaty. The ECSC Parliamentary Assembly first met in Strasbourg, which later became the provisional site for the European Parliament's plenary sessions. However, most of the Parliament's staff were permanently based in Luxembourg, and its parliamentary committees preferred to meet in Brussels, near to the Commission and the Council. In conjunction with the 1965 Merger Treaty, the heads of state and government took a 'provisional decision on the location of certain institutions'. The decision confirmed Luxembourg, Brussels and Strasbourg as the provisional places of work of the institutions of the Community, and went on to state that the General Secretariat of the European Parliament and its departments should remain in Luxembourg. In the late 1960s, and of its own initiative, the Parliament began to meet in Luxembourg, near to its secretariat, though it continued to meet in Strasbourg as well.

Direct elections increased the size of the Parliament from 198 to 410 members. Initially, only Strasbourg had a large enough hemicycle to house the Parliament, which resumed meeting there only. (Strasbourg had the attractive advantage of office space for all the MEPs.) Parliamentary committee meetings became far more frequent, and new premises were erected in Brussels to house these. The 1980s were characterised by a series of Court cases as the Luxembourg government contested, with some success (see Table 1), the Parliament's right to move elements of its Secretariat General to Brussels and by internal debates within the Parliament about the various merits of the different locations. The December 1992 European Council definitively decided, in fulfilment of the various treaty requirements, that 'the European Parliament shall have its seat in Strasbourg where the twelve periods of monthly plenary sessions, including the budget session, shall be held. The periods of additional plenary sessions shall be held in Brussels. The Committees of the European Parliament shall meet in Brussels. The General Secretariat of the European Parliament and its departments shall remain in Luxembourg.'

Parliament contested the legality of this decision but, once a large enough building had been constructed in Brussels, began to hold plenary sessions there. In 1994, four additional plenary sessions were held in Brussels. The Brussels hemicycle has been constructed to be large enough to house the Parliament of a Union enlarged by the accession of the four applicant states. By contrast, the French government and the authorities of the city of Strasbourg decided that the current Palais could not be 'stretched' further (the hemicycle had already been 'stretched' once), and plans were drawn up to build a new hemicycle complex in Strasbourg. There was some friction between the Parliament and the French government, as the latter sought guarantees that the Parliament would respect the conditions of the 1992 decision. However, on 31 March 1994, President

Klepsch signed a contract with the Mayor of Strasbourg committing the Parliament to renting a new hemicycle for twenty years. Construction work immediately began, and the new building is expected to be ready by October 1997.

Annex 3: The cost of the European Parliament

In December 1993, Lord Stoddart of Swindon asked the British government: 'What is the total cost of running (a) the House of Commons; (b) the House of Lords; (c) the European Parliament: and how much (sic) this cost represents per active member in each case?' The Earl of Caithness replied that: 'The total voted costs of the House of Commons this year are some £170 million. This represents £261,000 for each Member of Parliament. The corresponding costs for the House of Lords are £39.5 million, or some £38,000 for each active member of the House. Equivalent costs for the European Parliament are some £476 million; £919,000 for each MEP' (*Hansard*, WA Col.155, 17 December 1993). This reply was briefly reported in *The Daily Telegraph*. A sitting Conservative MEP, Richard Simmonds, wrote to the paper as follows:

> Your bald statement reporting the cost of each MEP to the tax payer is inadequate without explanation and comparison. A Euro-MP costs each of his or her constituent electors £1.58. 25% of this cost is accounted for by the use of nine official languages, because each Member State refuses to consider draft laws in anything other than its national language(s). A further 25% is taken up in the rent of buildings in Brussels, Luxembourg and Strasbourg ... However, the decision on a single seat for the Parliament lies with the Heads of State to whom the appropriate lobby should be made by concerned taxpayers. A British MP in the Westminster Parliament, which uses only one language and pays no rent for its buildings, costs each constituent elector £3.73.

The Daily Telegraph did not publish Mr Simmonds' letter, and I am grateful to him for permission to reproduce it, and his calculations, here.

Annex 4: Glossary of parliamentary terms and jargon

Note: The United Kingdom was absent in the early years of the Community's development, while France played a fundamental and formative role in the development of the ECSC and the EEC. As a result, many of the Parliament's jargon words are French or francophone in origin.

Additional session: see *supplementary session*.

Admissibility: Parliament's Rules lay down detailed conditions for the admissibility of amendments and compromise amendments (q.v.), and these conditions have proved to be of great worth in the cooperation procedure (q.v.) (see Chapter 3, Section 3.4). Parliament's president (q.v.) is ultimately responsible for interpreting these conditions. In addition, members may propose, by way of a procedural motion (q.v.), that a specific item on the agenda (q.v.) be ruled inadmissible. Such proposals are immediately put to the vote and, if carried, Parliament proceeds to the next item on its agenda (q.v.). An annex to Parliament's Rules lays down detailed conditions for the admissibility of questions under the question time (q.v.) procedure. Again, the president is ultimately responsible for deciding on admissibility.

Agenda: Parliament's plenary agenda is formally adopted by Parliament at the beginning of each part-session (q.v.). However, apart from minor changes, the agenda is largely the result of prior consultations among the political groups meeting in the Conference of Presidents (q.v.), with legislative work coordinated by the Conference of Committee Chairmen (q.v.) and the Neunreither Group (q.v.). Despite this, the adoption of Parliament's agenda generally takes up to an hour of parliamentary time (see also minutes of proceedings). By convention, this period is used to raise points of order (q.v.) and make personal statements (q.v.) relating to topical issues (for example, terrorist attacks or natural disasters). A favoured device is to call on the Commission to make a statement on a particular matter. British and Irish members are particularly assiduous in using this period to raise matters of concern to their constituencies.

Amendments: Any member may table amendments in committee, but only the responsible committee (q.v.), a political group or at least twenty-three members may table an amendment to plenary (q.v.). Additional conditions filter down amendments at the second reading stage in the cooperation and co-decision procedures (q.v.). Deadlines (q.v.) are laid down for the tabling of amendments. Amendments withdrawn by their authors may be taken over (with or without the authors' assent) by another member. In general, amendments can only be voted if they have been printed and distributed in all nine official languages, unless Parliament decides otherwise. However, if ten members object, such amendments cannot be voted.

Appropriations, commitment and payment: The European Union's budget is strictly annual, running from 1 January to 31 December of each year. However, multi-annual programmes (such as research) represent a growing proportion within the budget. To allow for this contradiction, the budgetary procedure distinguishes between commitment appropriations, which cover the total contractual cost of actions extending over more than one budgetary year, and payment appropriations, which authorise and therefore set a ceiling on expenditure in a given year.

Adjournment of debate: A political group or at least twenty-three members may move that a debate be adjourned to a specific date and time. Such motions are voted immediately. If they are carried, Parliament proceeds to the next item on its agenda.

'Arc-en-ciel': Officially entitled the *Verbatim Report of the Proceedings*. The *arc-en-ciel* ('rainbow'), so called because it consists of a record of proceedings in the original languages of the speakers, is generally published on the day following the proceedings in question. Once translated, debates are published in uniform editions in all of the working languages as an annex to the *Official Journal* (q.v.).

Assent: A procedure first introduced by the Single European Act (1987). Parliament grants assent in a straightforward yes/no vote. The Maastricht Treaty mostly relaxed what had previously been an absolute majority requirement for the granting of assent. An absolute majority is still required for the accession of new Member States and approval of a uniform electoral system (see Chapter 3, Section 3.5).

Bars: With its work divided up between three different complexes of buildings in three different cities, the European Parliament necessarily boasts a large number of bars and restaurants for its staff and members. In Strasbourg, the most important bars include the members' bar, which is in the Palais, close to the hemicycle, and the chauffeurs' bar and the bar *des cygnes*, both in the IPE 1 building. In Brussels, there are members' bars on the sixth floor of the Belliard building, on the first floor of the Van Maelant building, and (two) on the top floor of the Espace Leopold. It may seem spurious to list bars and restaurants in such a work but, particularly in Strasbourg, where most people are away from home and family, they provide important contexts for much of Parliament's informal work (much like Annie's bar and the tearoom at Westminster).

'Bilaterals': Jargon for informal negotiations between two sides, in this context most frequently between a parliamentary rapporteur (q.v.) and Commission officials on a technical dossier.

Buildings: The European Parliament's work is divided among three different cities: Strasbourg, Luxembourg and Brussels. In Strasbourg, the Parliament meets in plenary (q.v.) in the Palais de l'Europe, a building which actually belongs to the Council of Europe. The Palais was too small to provide office space for all members, and a separate building was built alongside the Palais and connected to it by a *passerelle* (bridge). This building, universally known as the IPE 1 building (from the French *'immeuble des parlementaires européens'*), sports the two largest meeting rooms in the whole complex. The largest, named after the late Willy Brandt, houses meetings of the Party of European Socialists (Socialist Group). The second largest, named after Robert Schuman, houses meetings of the European People's Party (Christian Democratic Group). The IPE 1 building was later extended by the construction of an almost identical building, imaginatively dubbed the IPE 2 building. The Parliament lets offices and a meeting room in the IPE 2 building to the European Commission (the Commission holds its weekly meeting in Strasbourg when the Parliament is in session there). The Strasbourg building complex was recently completed by the construction of a modernistic, high-tech press centre (IPE 3). (Other buildings in the Strasbourg complex which have nothing to do with the Parliament include an old, and a handsome new, building for the Council of Europe's Court of Human Rights.) Parliament's buildings in Luxembourg occupy sites in the Centre Européen on the windswept Plateau de Kirschberg. These include a largely deserted hemicycle, now too small for the enlarged European Parliament, the Schuman building and, most distinctive of all, the Tour building which, as its name suggests, is a high-rise building offering views out over the city. (The Luxembourg-based Court of Justice, Court of Auditors, and European Investment Bank all occupy nearby sites.) In Brussels, Parliament's main committee meeting rooms are in the Belliard building on the *rue* Belliard. A number of other buildings on the same side of the *rue* Belliard were gradually taken over and connected up by *passerelles* and passageways, and these now house some parts of the political groups' and committees' (q.v.) secretariats. The complement of members' offices and committee meeting rooms was extended by the construction of the new Van Maelant building on the opposite side of the *rue* Belliard, connected to the Belliard building by a double-decker bridge. More recently, a large building project has seen the construction of the Espace Leopold, which houses a new hemicycle and a number of new office buildings.

Bureau: *'Bureau'* is a widespread French term used to describe management bodies. Parliament's Bureau consists of the president and fourteen vice-presidents, together with the five quaestors acting in a non-voting capacity. The Bureau has broad duties relating to financial, organisational and administrative matters but lives very much in the political shadow of the political groups, meeting together in the Conference of Presidents (q.v.). Parliament's political groups also have bureaux, typically composed of the president, vice-presidents, treasurer and other representative members (by convention, each national political contingent is represented on the bureau). Lastly, Parliament's Rules provide for committees and inter-parliamentary delegations to have bureaux, composed of the chairmen and vice-chairmen.

Canteens: The large, distinctive, brightly-coloured metal trunks used to transport Parliament's documents to and from Brussels, Luxembourg and Strasbourg. Wherever it meets, Parliament's corridors are littered with canteens. Parliament has overcome its itinerancy with some ingenuity. Offices are furnished with mobile furniture, including mobile work stations, with shutters which can be quickly closed, locked and wheeled into the waiting lorries which ply the motorways criss-crossing the plateaux of Lorraine, the Vosges and the Ardennes.

'Caprice des dieux': Literally, 'whim of the Gods'. This is the nickname given by the long-suffering inhabitants of the Quartier Leopold in Brussels, rapidly dwindling in number, to the Parliament's new building, the Espace Leopold, and the surrounding complex. The Espace Leopold now towers uncompromisingly above what was previously a sleepy and slightly down-at-heel area of uptown Brussels. The whole neighbourhood is gradually succumbing to creeping development, most of it related, directly or indirectly, to the extension of the Community's institutions.

Censure motion: Parliament's (so far unused) 'nuclear weapon' for sacking the Commission. A censure motion can only be tabled by a tenth or more of Parliament's membership and must be passed by an absolute majority (see Chapter 3, Section 3.1).

CERT: see *committee acronyms.*

Chamber: The formal term used in Parliament's Rules to describe the hemicycle (q.v.).

'Check!': Most votes in plenary are taken by a simple show of hands. The president is best placed to gauge the result but may, at his/her discretion, verify the result by electronic vote (q.v.). In practice, if a member feels the president's judgement may have been mistaken, the president will readily check the result, using the voting machine (q.v.). Members, of whatever nationality, traditionally make their desire for verification known by shouting 'check!'.

Clocks: Like all functional buildings, clocks abound in those housing the European Parliament. But Parliament's hemicycles sport specialised timing devices, operated by the president or the sessional services (q.v.) assisting the president, used to indicate speaking time (q.v.). When a member's speaking time (q.v.) is exhausted, a warning light flashes; see *gavel waving* (q.v.).

Closure of a debate: Parliament's Rules provide that any debate may be closed, if Parliament so decides, at the request of a political group or twenty-three members. If a debate is so closed, Parliament moves immediately to the vote, except where the vote is scheduled to take place at another time.

Closure of the sitting: Parliament's Rules provide that a sitting (q.v.) may be closed during a debate or vote if Parliament so decides on a proposal from the president or at the request of a political group or at least twenty-three members. To date, no sitting has ever been closed in such a way.

Cocobu: see *committee acronyms.*

Co-decision: The legislative power Parliament would like to enjoy with the Council, thus embodying a classic states–people federal structure. As matters currently stand, the states, represented in the Council, very much have the legislative upper hand. The Maastricht Treaty introduced a new legislative procedure which provides for up to three readings, conciliation procedures between the Council and the Parliament and, ultimately, a parliamentary veto. Although the treaty gave the procedure no name, it is universally referred to as the 'co-decision' procedure (see Chapter 3, Section 3.4) — its prosaic formal title is the 'Article 189b procedure'.

Code of Conduct (1990): Running-in problems over the implementation of the Single European Act led the Commission and the Parliament to give a number of mutual undertakings about their conduct, principally in relation to the new legislative process of the cooperation procedure. These were grouped together in a code of conduct (see Westlake, 1994b, pp.65 and 125).

Comitology: The term was probably first coined in English by C. Northcote Parkinson (see Parkinson, 1959, p.39), albeit in a slightly different context. In the European Union context, comitology is a short-hand term for the process by which certain implementing powers are delegated to the Commission by the Council (and now, under the co-decision procedure, by the Parliament). The Council retains varying degrees of control through its representatives sitting in committees, hence comitology.

Committee acronyms: Most of the Parliament's standing committees are known by abbreviations of their full titles, but a few are commonly known by acronyms. Hence, *Cocobu*, the French acronym for the Budgetary Control Committee; *CERT*, for the Committee on Energy, Research and Technology; *EMAC*, the English acronym for the Economic and Monetary Affairs Committee (which is now also responsible for Industrial Affairs); and *REX*, the French acronym for the Committee on External Economic Affairs.

Committees: Parliament's Rules provide for the establishment of four sorts of committee. There are currently nineteen *standing committees*. Virtually all of Parliament's work, and certainly all of its legislative work, is processed through these committees (see Chapter 4, Section 4.1). They are assisted by four *sub-committees*, whose work must be filtered back through the parent committee. The Rules provide for the establishment of *temporary committees*, with limited terms of office, to examine particular problems (for example, German unification — see Westlake, 1991). Finally, the Maastricht Treaty introduced provisions allowing for the establishment of *committees of inquiry* to investigate alleged contraventions of Community law or maladministration (see Chapter 3, Section 3.8).

Committee secretariat: All of Parliament's committees are assisted by specialised secretariats, the number of officials depending on the size of the committee (the larger committees have five or six permanent officials). In addition to the organisation of committee meetings and the coordination of the translation (q.v.) and distribution (q.v.) of all necessary documentation, these officials play important roles in assisting members in the drafting of reports and opinions (q.v.), in conducting associated research and, vitally, in ensuring procedural follow-up.

Common position: The term can mean one of three different things. Under the cooperation and co-decision procedures, the Council's second-reading text is technically referred to as its common position (see Chapter 3, Section 3.4). Under the new Common Foreign and Security Policy provisions introduced by the

Maastricht Treaty, the European Parliament may adopt common positions on any matter of common foreign and security policy (see Chapter 3, Section 3.5). Finally, the Member States must adopt common positions on different chapters when negotiating the accession of a new Member State.

Compromise amendment: Parliament's Rules provide that amendments may exceptionally be tabled after a debate, their admissibility decided by the president, if they are compromise amendments, that is, they seek to bring opposing views close enough together for Parliament to be able to adopt a unified stance (particularly important where, as under the later stages of the cooperation and co-decision procedures, amendments have to satisfy absolute majority requirements). Parliament has to agree that such amendments may be put to the vote. They are generally tabled by political groups, committee chairmen, rapporteurs or draftsmen (q.v.), on the understanding that the original amendments they seek to replace or reconcile be withdrawn.

Compromise resolution: Parliament's Rules provide that, where more than one motion for a resolution has been tabled on the same subject, these may be replaced by a compromise resolution. A compromise resolution replaces those motions previously tabled by the same signatories but not those tabled by other committees, political groups or members. Compromise resolutions, jointly negotiated by the larger political groups, are frequently used to wind up topical and urgent debates (q.v.) and debates following Commission or Council statements. In particular, the larger political groups use their oligopolistic powers (see Chapter 4, Section 4.1) to ensure that Parliament speaks with a single, consistent and consensual voice.

Compulsory/non-compulsory expenditure: Compulsory expenditure can be loosely defined as all expenditure necessarily arising from the treaties or international agreements, and non-compulsory expenditure as all the rest. Compulsory expenditure includes expenditure related to the Common Agricultural Policy, which takes the lion's share of the Union's budget. The Parliament has only weak powers in relation to compulsory expenditure (see Chapter 3, Section 3.3).

Conciliation: Literally, reconciliation, as between the Council and the Parliament. There are several formal and informal varieties of conciliation procedure (see Chapter 3, Section 3.4).

Conference of Committee Chairmen: The body with its finger on Parliament's legislative pulse and hence an indispensable and powerful factor in legislative planning exercises and the drafting of Parliament's agenda (see Chapter 4, Section 4.1).

Conference of Delegation Chairmen: The delegation chairmen may make recommendations about the delegations' work to the Conference of Presidents. The body is of only occasional importance (see Chapter 4, Section 4.1).

Conference of Presidents: Composed of the chairmen of the political groups, with votes weighted according to the size of the groups' membership, the Conference of Presidents is the nucleus of Parliament's managerial and political power and the embodiment of the oligopoly described in Chapter 4, Section 4.1.

Consultation: The short-hand term for the procedure, described in Chapter 3, Section 3.4, whereby the Council is obliged to consult the Parliament on certain legislative proposals.

Cooperation procedure: A legislative procedure, introduced by the Single European Act, which provides for two parliamentary readings and constructive legislative input for the Parliament. The Maastricht Treaty has extended the scope of the procedure (see Chapter 3, Section 3.4).

Coordinators, political group: The political groups appoint one of their number within each standing committee's membership to act as coordinator. Between them, a committee's political group coordinators will generally decide on the division of work and reports between the political groups within that committee. Coordinators may also act as whips (q.v.) on important votes in committee.

Crocodile: One of two exotic animals in Parliament's vocabulary (the other being the Kangaroo (q.v.)). The crocodile group was a small group of MEPs in the first, 1979–84, elected Parliament who believed Parliament itself should take a more active part in forcing the pace of integration. The crocodile initiative (also known as the Spinelli initiative) ultimately resulted in the adoption by Parliament of a Draft Treaty on European Union (1984) which in turn contributed to the momentum resulting in the adoption of the Single European Act. The crocodile group took its name from the Strasbourg restaurant where it first met. The group, now of much broader and more numerous membership, publishes a widely-circulated newsletter.

Deadline for amendments: Committees and Parliament's plenary impose deadlines for amendments. These are of great practical importance in a Parliament where all documents have to be translated before they can be distributed to members.

Delegated powers (to committee): A simplified procedure (procedure without report) enables uncontroversial proposals to be dealt with in committee. The Budgets Committee also enjoys considerable *de facto* delegated powers.

Discharge: Parliament grants the Commission *discharge* on its implementation of the annual budget (see Chapter 3, Section 3.3).

Distribution: The name given to the counters in Brussels (in the Belliard building) and Strasbourg (in the Palais building during plenary sessions) where all parliamentary documents are available.

Doyenne d'age (oldest member): The sole duty of the *doyenne d'age* is to take the chair in Parliament's first sitting after European elections until the president has been elected.

Draft report: A report, generally consisting of a resolution (q.v.) and an explanatory memorandum (q.v.), is termed a draft report until it has been adopted by the Parliament.

Draftsman/woman: Committees requested to give an opinion on a draft report appoint (via the political group coordinators) a draftsman/woman to prepare that opinion. The draftsmen/women generally speak after the rapporteur in plenary debates.

Electronic vote: A vote taken using the voting machine (q.v.).

EMAC: see *committee acronyms.*

Explanation of vote: Parliament's Rules provide that, once a debate has been concluded, any member may give an oral explanation of vote of not longer than one minute, or submit a written explanation of vote of not more than 200 words. A political group may give an oral explanation of vote of not longer than two minutes. Explanations of vote are entered in the verbatim report of proceedings (q.v.). Together with points of order (q.v.), personal statements (q.v.), recommendations (q.v.) and declarations, and written questions and Question Time, explanations of vote are one of the few rights remaining to the backbencher in the Parliament and can be used as a valuable adjunct to speaking time (q.v.). Explanations of vote are traditionally taken before the final vote and can therefore greatly extend voting sessions (q.v.). Where votes are running late, members can come under a great deal of pressure to save voting time by submitting their explanations in writing. Hence it is common to hear the impatient heckler's phrase 'in writing!' during voting sessions.

Explanatory memorandum: A parliamentary report generally consists of a draft resolution and an explanatory memorandum. Only the resolution is voted on by Parliament (and/or the responsible committee), hence the explanatory memorandum has no official status (see Chapter 4, Section 4.2).

Filibustering: Is now virtually non-existent in Parliament. The voting machine has made lengthy roll-call votes (q.v.) a thing of the past. All the traditional weapons of the filibusterer — long speeches, points of order (q.v.), personal statements, explanations of vote — are disarmed by strict and strictly enforced limits on speaking time. Enforcement is facilitated by the president's control of the microphones; a speaker exceeding the allotted time can simply be 'switched off' (see also *clocks*). Parliament's idiosyncratic quorum (q.v.) rules also restrict the filibusterer's scope for action. Voting machines do not exist in committee, and requests for roll-call votes could therefore still prove disruptive yet are so uncommon an occurrence as to be almost non-existent. Repeated requests for secret ballots (q.v.) could slow down the plenary/voting sessions, but such requests must be made by at least one-fifth of Parliament's members.

Footnote: An oral question to the Commission or the Council (see Chapter 3, Section 3.8) may be submitted as a footnote to a debate on another, related, topic or report. Committees and political groups use such footnotes to elicit specific responses to particular questions from the institution concerned and to flesh out the framework of a debate.

Formal sittings: Formal sittings are generally held during normal plenary sittings but formally apart from them. They are held solely to hear addresses by distinguished visitors (who would not otherwise be able to address the Parliament). The verbatim report of the proceedings of formal sittings is appended to the normal verbatim report.

Gavel waving: The president or vice-president presiding over Parliament's plenary sessions is equipped with a wooden gavel and block. The gavel is used to open, suspend and close sittings, but it is also frequently used to enforce the limits on speaking time. When a speaker's time is exhausted, the president will first wave the gavel and then, if the speaker looks likely to continue, tap the block with increasing force until, ultimately, the speaker's microphone is cut off. Experienced members are adept both at translating the language of the gavel and at playing the president along with conciliatory or apologetic phrases (which must be translated), thus extending their speaking time considerably.

Group spokesmen: Parliament's political groups traditionally appoint group spokesmen on particular issues (for example, economics, finance, agriculture). Group spokesmen are generally members of the standing committee covering their specialisation. They traditionally have a prior claim to a share of their groups' allocation of speaking time, and an early place on the speakers' list (q.v.), during debates related to their specialisation.

Hearings, public: Parliament's standing committees increasingly resort to the organisation of public hearings to elucidate matters of particular concern or interest to the committee concerned (see Chapter 3, Section 3.9).

Hemicycle: All of the chambers in which the Parliament has met or continues to meet (at the moment Strasbourg and Brussels) are semi-circular in shape and are thus universally referred to as hemicycles.

Huis clos: Parliament's Rules provide that standing committees should decide at the outset of their mandate whether their meetings will normally be held in public. Most committees so decide. However, committees may also divide their agendas into items open to the public and items closed to the public. When a committee meeting is closed to the public, it is said to be meeting *huis clos*. The committees that most frequently meet *huis clos* are those (budgets, legal affairs, institutional affairs) with influential roles in deciding Parliament's external strategy, and the 'public' they have in mind is most often representatives of the other Community institutions. On the other hand, inquiry committees may well decide to close their meetings to the public in order to guarantee the confidentiality of their sources or any sensitive documentation under consideration.

Intergroups: Informal groupings bringing members of different political groups together with interest group representatives. Some are highly organised, well funded and widely respected (see *kangaroo*). Some are occasional and single issue (see Chapter 4, Section 4.2).

Initiative report: An initiative report, or own-initiative report, is one which a committee is authorised, by the Conference of Presidents, to produce at its own initiative (in the absence of a request for an opinion or a motion for a resolution). As Parliament's legislative load has steadily increased, the number of initiative reports has declined. Pressure on plenary time has also made initiative reports unpopular with Parliament's hard-pressed sessional services (q.v.), and authorisation for the preparation of such reports is now tightly circumscribed by Parliament's Rules. Own-initiative reports may take on fresh importance in the context of Parliament's new-found right to request initiatives (see Chapter 3, Section 3.4).

Interim report: On rare occasions, a developing issue may seem to warrant more than one report (for example, the unfolding deliberations within an inter-governmental conference) and Parliament may then decide to authorise one or more interim reports on the same issue before the adoption of a final, definitive report.

Inter-institutional agreements: Pseudo-constitutional agreements between two or more Community institutions. These are of increasing importance to the Community's inter-institutional relations (see Westlake, 1994b, pp.34 and 102).

Inter-institutional conference: Formalised conferences among the Parliament, the Commission and the Council, the latter normally represented by the Presidency. Such conferences are favoured by the Parliament as a way of influencing the work of Inter-governmental Conferences, from which the Parliament is excluded (see Chapter 1, Section 1.4).

Interpretation: All of the Parliament's official work — plenary sessions, committee meetings, political group meetings — is simultaneously translated into the Union's nine working languages. The interpreters sit in glass-walled cabins at the back of the hemicycle and the committee meeting rooms. They accompany committees and political groups on trips away from the usual working places and are generally well known to the members of their own nationality. For health reasons, the interpreters work strictly observed shifts and therefore impose unavoidable time limits on Parliament's meetings. Presidents and committee chairmen can frequently be heard pleading with the interpreters for a few minutes' more time to finish off business.

In the margin(s): European Union/Community jargon for 'in the sidelines of'.

Immunity: Elected members of the Parliament enjoy privileges and immunities in accordance with the 1965 protocol. Requests for the waiver of immunity are decided by Parliament on the basis of a recommendation from its Rules Committee.

Joint debate: To save plenary time, Parliament frequently merges the debates on reports on closely related subjects. These omnibus debates sometimes result in curiously mixed affairs in which, also because of the strict rules on speaking time, speeches may have little to do with one another and can thus be extremely bewildering for any uninformed audience.

Joint parliamentary committee: Joint parliamentary committees are set up with the parliaments of states enjoying association agreements with the Community or states with which accession negotiations have been initiated.

Joint text: The co-decision procedure provides for a conciliation committee at the third-reading stage. The conciliation negotiations between the representatives of the Council and the Parliament may result in a mutually acceptable joint text. If subsequently approved by both sides, the joint text may ultimately become law.

Jurisconsult: Another term for the head of Parliament's legal service. The jurisconsult is Parliament's chief legal adviser.

Kangaroo: The Kangaroo Group, otherwise known as 'the Movement for Free Movement', is a long-standing and highly respectable inter-group militating in favour of a frontier-free Europe.

Legal base/basis: Each piece of Community legislation is necessarily based on, and refers to, one or more treaty articles. These articles are referred to as the legal base or legal basis of a proposal. The legal basis determines the nature and extent (one or more readings) of the Parliament's role in the legislative process. Parliament's Legal Affairs Committee has a standing brief to monitor the appropriateness of the legal bases of all draft legislation on which Parliament is consulted. Differences of opinion occasionally arise, particularly if the Council decides to change the legal basis proposed by the Commission, and may ultimately result in Parliament bringing cases before the Court of Justice (see Table 1).

Legal service: The specialised service within Parliament's secretariat general (q.v.) responsible for advising Parliament, chiefly through its Legal Affairs Committee, on all legal matters. The legal service represents and acts on behalf of Parliament before the Court of Justice.

Legislative programme: An annual programme in which the Commission sets out its scheduled legislative activities for the forthcoming year, in consultation with the Parliament and, increasingly, the Council. Legislative planning originated in the vast raft of legislation necessary for the realisation of the internal market, which was tied to the '1992' deadline. The exercise is becoming increasingly formalised (see Westlake, 1994b, pp.22 and 99).

Legislative resolution: That part of a parliamentary report which formally discharges Parliament's legislative obligation. Legislative resolutions were first conceived of in the wake of the Court of Justice's 'Isoglucose' ruling (see Table 1) as a way of creating pressure for concessions on the part of the Commission under the consultation procedure. Parliament would first adopt its proposed amendments and then, before adopting the accompanying legislative resolution, ask the Commission its attitude in regard to the amendments. If unhappy with the Commission's response, Parliament could postpone voting on the legislative resolution by referral back to committee (q.v.), and thus postpone the formal adoption of its opinion.

Luns–Westerterp procedures: Named after two former Dutch ministers of foreign affairs and resulting from a series of Council and Commission undertakings, the Luns–Westerterp procedures provide for the information of Parliament's specialised committees on the state of play in commercial negotiations and the negotiations of association agreements.

Maximum rate (of increase): An important reference point in the annual budgetary procedure and an important determinant of the extent of Parliament's budgetary powers, the maximum rate is calculated by the Commission on a statistical basis (see Chapter 3, Section 3.3).

'Micro!': A cry frequently heard in both plenary and committee when speakers begin talking with their microphone off. Others of the same tongue may understand what is being said, but the interpreters in the fastness of their cabins can only interpret and relay the speaker's words if the microphone is on.

Minutes of the proceedings: Parliament's Rules provide that the minutes of each sitting shall be distributed 'at least half an hour before the opening of the next sitting'. The minutes are approved by the plenary at the beginning of each sitting. The minutes of proceedings are very summary affairs, containing the decisions of Parliament (including votes and amendments and all documents adopted) and the names of speakers. The approval of the minutes at the beginning of each sitting traditionally provides an opportunity for the raising of many points of order (q.v.).

Navette: Literally, 'shuttle'. The term is sometimes used to describe the movement of legislative proposals back and forth between the Council and the Parliament under the cooperation procedure (see Chapter 3, Section 3.4). In Strasbourg, the term is also used to describe the free shuttle bus service between the city centre and the Palais building laid on by the city administration, and the similarly free bus service between the Parliament and the airport. The term is also used to describe the internal mailing system between the Community institutions.

Neunreither Group: Named after the high-ranking official in Parliament's secretariat general who established the group as a reaction to the procedural requirements and deadlines resulting from the provisions of the Single European Act. The Neunreither Group regularly assembles representatives from the secretariats of the Parliament, the Commission and the Council with a view to coordinating such complicated legislative procedures as the cooperation and co-decision procedures.

Non-attached members: Members who do not belong to an established political group. Parliament's Rules allow for such non-attached members to have a secretariat, but they are largely marginalised in such matters as, for example, the share out of rapporteurships and committee chairmanships.

'Non-paper': This is a jargon term, more generally associated with the Council but increasingly borrowed by the other institutions, to denote a draft potential compromise with no formal status. 'Non-papers' in the Council usually emanate from the Presidency or the secretariat general.

Notenboom procedure: Named after a former Dutch MEP, Harry Notenboom, the procedure was initially an annual scrutiny exercise of how the current year's budget had been implemented (that is, whether and how appropriations had been spent). The Notenboom procedure is now an all-year-round monitoring exercise, with the Commission obliged to provide monthly indications on the implementation of the budget (see Chapter 3, Section 3.3).

Observers: Unlike the Council of Europe and its parliamentary assembly, the European Union and its Parliament do not allow for observer status. However, an exception was made between 1990 and 1994 for eighteen observers from the five new German *Länder* to attend Parliament's proceedings in a non-voting capacity. All-Germany European elections were held in June 1994, and the observers, together with the temporary rule which had allowed for their presence, were then disbanded.

Official Journal (OJ): The European Community's official gazette. Parliament's definitive minutes of sittings are published in the *Official Journal* ('C series'), and the definitive verbatim report of proceedings, translated into the nine working languages, in annexes to the *Official Journal*. These annexes are the European Parliament's equivalent of Hansard.

Opinion: The term has two meanings. First, Parliament must give its opinion under the consultation procedure (q.v.). Second, more than one standing committee might be requested/authorised to draft opinions on a report for the responsible committee (q.v.).

Oral amendments: In theory, oral amendments are outlawed in plenary because the Rules provide that all amendments should be tabled in writing and, unless compromise amendments, in respect of a previously established deadline (so that they might be translated and distributed in good time). However, on rare occasions typically linguistic problems may be ironed out through oral amendments. In committee, on the other hand, oral amendments are put to the vote unless a member objects.

Own-initiative report: see *initiative report.*

Own-resources: Those budgetary resources (currently composed of customs duties, agricultural levies and a percentage of the VAT base) accruing directly to the Community (see Chapter 3, Section 3.3).

Parliamentary assistant: MEPs receive an allowance designed to enable them to hire research and secretarial assistance. Parliamentary assistants are increasing in number but their total number is far from matching the generous staffing levels of US Congressmen.

Passerelle: Literally, a bridge between two buildings. Because of the *ad hoc* way in which Parliament's buildings have mushroomed in Brussels and Strasbourg, *passerelles* are much in evidence. In Strasbourg, a three-tiered *passerelle* connects the Palais building (containing the hemicycle) to the IPE buildings (housing most MEPs' offices). This *passerelle* gets particularly crowded before and after voting sessions, as members flood into and out of the hemicycle. In Brussels, a double-decker *passerelle* connects the original Belliard building to the buildings housing the committee and political group secretariats. Another, far more elegant, double-decker bridge arches over the *rue* Belliard, connecting the Belliard and Van Maelant buildings. Although not strictly speaking a *passerelle*, a long, broad, sculpture-lined passageway links the new Espace Leopold building with the Belliard complex. To confuse matters, since the implementation of the Maastricht Treaty the term *passerelle* has had a new, political connotation. Under Article K9 of the Treaty, certain aspects of inter-governmental cooperation in the fields of justice and home affairs may, by unanimous decision of the Member States, be transferred to the 'Community method' (see Chapter 3, Section 3.7). Article K9 is universally referred to as the *passerelle*.

Per diem: Daily payments for expenses (hotels, meals, etc.) made to members when on parliamentary business in Brussels or Strasbourg.

Personal statements: Parliament's Rules provide for members to make personal statements. These are confined to 'rebutting any remarks that have been made about his/her person in the course of ... debate or opinions that have been attributed to him/her, or to correcting observations that the Member has made'.

Petitions: Previously a unilateral provision in Parliament's Rules and now a treaty-based right, any citizen of the European Union and any natural or legal person residing in a Member State has the right to address a petition to the Parliament (see Chapter 3, Section 3.8).

Plenary: A short-hand term used to describe the (entire) Parliament or one of its part-sessions, sometimes also referred to as plenary sessions.

Points of order: Parliament's Rules provide that 'a Member may be allowed to speak to draw the attention of the President to any failure to respect Parliament's Rules of Procedure. The Member shall first specify to which Rule he/she is referring. A request to raise a point of order shall take precedence over all other requests to speak. Speaking time shall not exceed one minute.' In practice, Parliament's plenary sessions are peppered with such requests, particularly during voting sessions. Few of them are true points of order, many members fail to specify the Rule to which they are supposed to be referring, and some speak for well over a minute. Presidents are so relaxed about enforcing the Rule because, in reality, it provides a safety valve and an additional, if minimal, vehicle of expression for backbenchers. The sign language (q.v.) for points of order is distinctive. Most members cross their hands or arms above their heads, sometimes accompanying the signal with slaps or cries. Should the president fail to see them, members stand, and their gestures become more pronounced.

Preambles: see *recitals.*

Pre-copy: Before Commission documents enter the public domain they have to be formally adopted by the college of Commissioners. This is frequently done by an accelerated written procedure involving no further debate or amendment. On occasion, Commission officials may forward unofficial copies of Commission documents to parliamentary rapporteurs before they are formally adopted by the college so as to enable rapporteurs to begin their work as soon as possible. In the jargon, such unofficial copies are sometimes referred to as pre-copies.

President: The only parliamentary office specifically provided for by the treaties. The president has a number of ceremonial and symbolic duties (such as signing the budget) and a number of procedural powers, now largely circumscribed by the Rules and the Conference of Presidents. The president signs the budget (see Chapter 3, Section 3.3) and, together with the Council, acts adopted under the co-decision procedure (see Chapter 3, Section 3.4), into being.

Procedural motions: Parliament's Rules provide for five sorts of procedural motion: on the inadmissibility of a matter; on referral back to committee; on the closure of a debate; on the adjournment of a debate; on the suspension or closure of a sitting. Such motions take precedence over other requests to speak.

Procedure without debate: Parliament's Rules provide that, where a committee requests that its report be adopted without debate, or where the committee has delivered its views on a legislative proposal without report, the report or proposal in question is put on the next plenary agenda and, unless twenty-three members lodge a protest in advance, is put to the vote.

Procedure without report: Parliament's Rules provide that, on the recommendation of the president, and unless four committee members object within a set time limit, uncontroversial proposals may be dealt with in committee through the adoption of a brief report. In such cases, the draft legislative resolution is put to the vote in plenary under the procedure without debate but, to all intents and purposes, the procedure amounts to a delegated power of decision to committees.

Public gallery: Both the Strasbourg and Brussels hemicycles are surrounded by public galleries, where members of the public and visiting groups (q.v.) may sit and listen to debates.

Quaestor: A common office in continental parliaments, the quaestors are 'responsible for administrative and financial matters directly concerning Members'. However, they have to act in accordance with guidelines laid down by the Bureau, and in practice work in the shadow of the Conference of

Presidents. The five quaestors are popularly elected from among Parliament's membership.

Question time: A hybrid, currently late night, ill-attended and much-misunderstood version of the Westminster procedure (see Chapter 3, Section 3.8 and Westlake, 1990).

Quorum: The European Parliament's quorum rules are idiosyncratic. The plenary may deliberate, settle its agenda and approve the minutes of proceedings whatever the number of members present. However, the Rules also provide that 'if fewer than twenty-three Members are present, the President may rule that there is no quorum'. In practice, although there are frequently lesser numbers in the hemicycle, the president never uses this discretionary power. A quorum exists when one-third or more of Parliament's component members are present. However, the quorum is not ascertained unless there is a specific request that it should be so ascertained before a vote, and the Rules explicitly provide that otherwise 'all votes shall be valid whatever the number of voters'. A request to check whether a quorum is present must come from at least twenty-three members. The number of members is physically counted (the voting machine cannot be used). The Rules provide that 'the doors of the Chamber may not be closed' (implicitly, therefore, other members may be whipped (q.v.) into the Chamber during the count). If the president ascertains that a quorum is not present, the vote in question shall be placed on the agenda of the next sitting, and by implication the Parliament moves on to the next item of business. These rules have been carefully designed to overcome the twin problems of low levels of participation and the risk of filibustering, particularly by smaller political groups. The quorum provisions in committee are similarly idiosyncratic, if stricter. A committee may only validly vote if one-quarter of its members are present. However, if so requested by one-sixth of its members before voting begins, the vote shall be valid only if an absolute majority of the committee's membership has taken part in it.

Rapporteur: The author of a parliamentary report (the authors of opinions to the responsible committee are known as draftsmen and draftswomen). Reports and rapporteurs play vital roles in Parliament's work (see Chapter 4, Section 4.2). On rare occasions, particularly where a cross-group consensual approach is considered necessary, a committee may appoint two co-rapporteurs. Some political groups have adopted the informal practice of appointing shadow rapporteurs.

Recitals: Also known as whereas clauses, or preambles. Parliamentary motions for resolutions consist of two parts. A first, introductory, part is composed of preambular clauses — recitals — which typically recall Parliament's and/or the other institutions' previous pronouncements on an issue, set the general context within which the resolution is being adopted and establish the reasoning for the recommendations made in the second part, the resolution itself.

Recommendations: Parliament typically makes recommendations in its motions for resolutions, but since the implementation of the Maastricht Treaty the term has taken on a more formal meaning. Parliament may now make recommendations to the Council in the context of the Common Foreign and Security Policy (see Chapter 3, Section 3.5) and Cooperation in the Fields of Justice and Home Affairs (see Chapter 3, Section 3.7).

Re-consultation: Where Parliament has been consulted on a legislative proposal, it has the right to re-consultation (that is, the right to adopt a new opinion relating to the new text of the proposal) where it is adjudged that the substance of the proposal has been changed. Until recently, Parliament's right to re-consultation arose weakly out of Council undertakings and the implications of the Court's jurisprudence (see Table 1). However, in 1992 the Court explicitly ruled that Parliament must be re-consulted under such circumstances. In Parliament's eyes, the lateness of such a case and ruling arose directly from the fact that, until the 1990 'Chernobyl' ruling, Parliament was unable to bring cases to protect its own prerogatives.

Referral back to committee: A procedural legerdemain, the result of creative rules-drafting, designed to enable Parliament to capitalise on a *de facto* power of delay under the consultation procedure, arising out of a 1980 Court ruling (see Table 1). If Parliament is unhappy with the position of the Commission with regard to its amendments, its rules enable it to refer its legislative resolution back to committee (ostensibly for further consideration on the substance of the proposal), thus delaying the adoption of its opinion, without which the Council cannot formally adopt the legislation in question.

Resolution: The Parliament's chief form of (written) expression. Parliamentary reports always contain a resolution. In the case of legislative reports, this is a legislative resolution. A resolution will typically consist of a number of different, numbered paragraphs, each containing a separate statement or recommendation. Parliament's Rules provide that any member may table a motion for a resolution, of not more than 200 words, on a matter falling within the sphere of activities of the European Union. Such motions are referred to the responsible committee, which must decide what follow-up (to draft an opinion or a letter, or request permission to draft a report) to give the motion.

Responsible committee: Each report is prepared in a particular standing committee, known as the responsible committee. The decision as to which committee will be responsible for any particular report is taken by the Conference of Presidents.

Restaurants: These are of more importance in the hothouse atmosphere of the Strasbourg plenaries. There are two restaurants in the Palais building; the more expensive *Salle Bleu* with an *à la carte* menu, and the Council of Europe's self-service canteen. The IPE 1 building contains a similarly expensive members' restaurant, also with an *à la carte* menu. This restaurant is renowned for its cold buffet and is particularly popular among members waiting on Wednesday evenings for their questions to be taken in the Question Time procedure. Lastly, there is a large self-service restaurant on the ground floor of the IPE 2 building. In Brussels, the institutions' restaurants are of far less importance.

Rights of initiative: The Maastricht Treaty introduced the right for Parliament to request initiatives of the Commission. Parliament must muster an absolute majority and the Commission accepts no automaticity (see Chapter 3, Section 3.4).

Roll-call vote: Parliament's Rules make roll-call votes mandatory for the nomination of the Commission president, the approval of the Commission as a whole, and on a motion of censure. A political group or twenty-three members may at any time request for a roll-call vote (on an amendment, on a resolution). If the voting machine (q.v.) is used, the only difference between a roll-call vote and an electronic vote is that the names and positions of members voting are recorded in the minutes and, eventually, in the official record of proceedings in the *Official Journal*. If the voting machine is not used, the Rules provide for the roll to be called in alphabetical order, beginning with the name of a member drawn by lot. This time-consuming procedure was much favoured for filibustering in pre-voting machine days, but is now practically extinct. Political groups use roll-call voting as a form of whipping and also to embarrass their political opponents into taking public positions on potentially controversial issues. Voting in committee is by show of hands unless a quarter of the committee's members request a vote by roll-call.

Sakharov prize: Parliament has instituted an annual Sakharov prize for freedom of thought. Previous winners have included Nelson Mandela and Alexander Dubcek.

Seat: Parliament's place of work. In fact, Parliament has several seats: Strasbourg, Luxembourg and Brussels (see Annex 1).

Seating arrangements: The allocation of seats in the Chamber is decided by the Conference of Presidents. In practice, the exact layout depends mostly on the views of the benign oligopoly of the two largest political groups (described in Chapter 4, Section 4.1). The two largest groups sit in broad wedges on the left and the right of the Chamber (as seen from the president's podium). By its own choice, the Liberal Group sits on the middle-right-hand side of the Chamber. Smaller groups are deployed towards, or at the back of, the Chamber, and they are further marginalised by the fact that their chairmen cannot speak from the front benches, which are entirely taken up by the chairmen and vice-chairmen of the three largest groups. A not unimportant socio-political aspect of the seating arrangements is related to the position of the Council and Commission benches in the Chamber. The Council, which is only occasionally represented, sits on the front left of the Chamber (from the president's point of view). The Commission, which is almost always represented, sits on the front right of the Chamber. This means that, in most debates, the largest political group (the Party of European Socialists) talks across the Chamber to the Commission, which sits beside the European People's Party. The sociological, if not the political, relationship would surely be different if the Commission sat alongside the Group of the Party of European Socialists.

Seating plan: Fold-out seating plans of the seating arrangements in the Chamber are available from distribution (q.v.). The seating plans are regularly updated to take account of changes in membership and in the Council's Presidency-in-Office.

Secretariat general: The approximately 3,800-strong administration, headed by the secretary general and mostly based in Luxembourg and Brussels, which assists the Parliament in its work. About a third of these are involved in translation and interpretation (see Chapter 4, Section 4.1).

Secretary general: The head of Parliament's secretariat general.

Secret ballots: All of Parliament's internal appointments — the president, vice-presidents, and the quaestors — are by secret ballot. In addition, any vote may be by secret ballot if requested by at least one-fifth of the component members of Parliament.

Session: The treaties laconically provide that 'the European Parliament shall hold an annual session', yet from its earliest days the Parliament has met more than once a year. Thus, each separate meeting is officially termed a part-session, with the various part-sessions held in one year together constituting the session.

Sessional services (the 'greffe'): Parliament's plenary sessions are assisted by a specialised branch of its secretariat general, broadly similar to the Office of the Clerk in the House of Commons. The sessional services are, among other things, responsible for the calculation of speaking time and the management of speakers' lists and, vitally, the organisation of voting sessions.

'Shevardnaze formula': The Parliament has experimented with a number of different forums which enable it to meet representatively outside the plenary sessions and/or to receive distinguished visitors outside the formal sitting formula. One durable formula, first used to receive the then Soviet foreign minister, involved a combination of Parliament's political management body (now the Conference of Presidents) and the relevant specialised standing committee. The term 'Shevardnaze formula' is now more loosely used to describe any such combination of the Conference of Presidents and standing committees.

Sign language: Parliament's work is facilitated by a number (perhaps surprisingly few) of universally recognised signs. One of these concerns points of order (q.v.). Another is the president's gavel waving (q.v.). Another is used in voting. Those responsible for whipping their political group's vote sit in the front benches in the hemicycle and signal that group's position on individual votes: thumbs up for a positive vote; thumbs down for a negative vote; and waving the flat hand from left to right for abstention.

Sitting: Each separate day of Parliament's plenary sessions is termed a sitting.

Speakers' list: The sessional services prepare a speakers' list before each plenary debate. The list which is prepared in the language of the presiding president or vice-president, lists all those who have requested to speak, their position in the speaking order, their role (if rapporteur or speaking on behalf of the political group) and the amount of speaking time they have been allotted.

Speaking time: Parliament has established a complex formula for the allocation of speaking time in order to assure the most equitable and representative distribution of contributions in debate. The Conference of Presidents effectively decides on the allocation of overall speaking time for any particular debate (in consultation with the sessional services). A first fraction of the overall speaking time is divided equally among all the political groups and a further fraction is divided among the political groups in proportion to the total number of their members. Rapporteurs and group spokesmen traditionally receive a larger proportion of their groups' overall allocation.

Split vote: Parliament's Rules provide that where a text to be put to the vote contains 'two or more provisions or references to two or more points or lends itself to division into two or more parts each with a distinct logical meaning and normative value, a split vote may be requested'. However, such requests must be made at least one hour before the beginning of the relevant voting session.

Substitute members: In addition to the full members of parliamentary committees, the political groups may appoint a number of permanent substitutes for each committee equal to their allocation of full members. Substitutes enjoy exactly the same rights and privileges as full members except that, where a political group's full complement of full members is present, the substitute may not vote. Substitutes were introduced as a way of overcoming the poor general attendance in committees, but they also create a broader net of patronage for the political groups (see Westlake, 1994a).

Suites données: A currently obscure but potentially important procedure whereby, on the basis of a detailed Commission communication, the Commission is interrogated by members on the follow-up it has given to Parliament's resolutions and amendments. The procedure is basically a device to ensure that the Commission does what it has said it is going to do.

Supplementary session: The December 1992 Edinburgh European Council decided that the Parliament should 'have its seat in Strasbourg where the twelve periods of monthly plenary sessions ... shall be held. The periods of additional plenary sessions shall be held in Brussels.' Such additional sessions are commonly referred to as supplementary sessions.

Suspension of sitting: Parliament's Rules provide that a sitting may be suspended, whether during a debate or a vote, if Parliament so decides on a proposal from the president or at the request of a political group or at least twenty-three members. In addition to this rarely used formal procedure, the president frequently suspends sittings for a few minutes: for example, in order to prepare the Chamber for a formal sitting or if a few minutes remain between a debate and a vote.

Topical and urgent debate: Parliament traditionally puts aside the whole of the Thursday morning of its plenary sessions in Strasbourg to debate topical and urgent subjects of major importance (see Chapter 3, Section 3.9).

Translation: The equitable provision that all parliamentary documents should be available in all working languages imposes practical constraints on Parliament's work. In particular, early deadlines have to be set for the tabling of amendments.

Trilogue (or 'Trialogue'): A jargon term, probably originating from the budgetary procedure, to describe a meeting between representatives of the Council (usually the Presidency), the Commission and the Parliament.

Urgency: The Community's legislative procedures are generally beholden to Parliament's monthly cycle of political group meetings' week, committee meetings' week and plenary. However, Parliament's Rules enable the Council and the Commission to request the treatment of urgent legislative proposals by an accelerated procedure, universally referred to as urgency (as in 'the Commission has requested urgency').

Verbatim report of proceedings: see *arc-en-ciel*.

Verification of credentials: Parliament's Rules provide that the credentials of all new members should be verified (to ensure compliance with the 1976 Act establishing direct elections, for example). Credentials are verified by the Rules Committee.

Visitors' group: Parliament's buildings in Brussels and Strasbourg are awash with groups of visitors. They visit the hemicycle, may be smuggled into a public committee meeting and will typically be addressed by a number of officials on what the Parliament does, how it works etc. Many visitors' groups come to Brussels and Strasbourg at the invitation of members, who generally see such visits as an effective way of educating the public to the ways and role of the Parliament.

Voting card: see *voting machine*.

Voting list: Parliament's sessional services prepare voting lists for the president so that he or she can effectively preside over votes. A typical voting list sets out the order of the vote on amendments and the paragraphs of the draft resolution, indicating where requests have been made for split votes or roll-call votes and the position on amendments of the rapporteur. The political groups prepare their own voting lists, based on the voting list prepared by the sessional services, setting out the group's position on the various clauses and amendments. These voting lists are an integral part of the whipping process in the European Parliament.

Voting machine: The key to electronic voting. Each member is issued with a personalised voting card, about the size and thickness of a credit card. In front of each member's seat in the hemicycle there is a bench with a slot into which the voting card is inserted. When an electronic vote or a roll-call vote is announced by the president, members must vote by using the voting machine, which will have been activated by the insertion of the voting card. The member places a hand in a shielded box containing three buttons, one for a positive vote, one for a negative vote and one for abstention. Outside the box, a row of four coloured lights tells the member whether the vote is open (blue) and which way the member has voted (red for 'no', green for 'yes', yellow for 'abstention'). A common scene at lengthy voting sessions is a sudden scramble for the voting machines, as members who have wandered from their seats race back to register their vote before the vote is closed and the voting machine turned off. The results of electronic votes are displayed on large electronic 'scoreboards' placed around the hemicycle.

Voting session(s): Primarily as a response to the absolute majority requirements imposed upon it by the Single European Act, and as a safeguard against the low levels of participation it has traditionally suffered, the Parliament habitually gathers together all votes on legislative proposals into voting sessions (SEA voting sessions in Strasbourg habitually take place on Wednesday evenings). Special majority requirements were first imposed on the Parliament by the 1970s' budgets treaties, and the techniques later adapted to the procedural circumstances of the SEA were first developed and implemented in the context of the annual budgetary cycle (see Chapter 4, Section 4.2).

Whip/whipping: The European Parliament's whipping practices are a far cry from the Westminster model (see Westlake, 1994a). Whipping is as likely to be done by political group officials as by influential members, and there are few sanctions beyond moral pressure. The strongest pressure is intellectual: members are collectively well aware that their institution cannot wield legislative and budgetary power unless it meets the majority requirements imposed by the treaties.

Working document: A frequent first stage in the drafting of reports. A rapporteur may first submit an outline of his/her intended report or of the subject matter with which it deals. Committee secretariats may also on occasion help a committee in its deliberations through the preparation of a working document. Not all working documents ultimately result in reports.

Written declaration: Parliament's Rules provide that any member may submit a written declaration of not more than 200 words 'on a matter falling within the sphere of activities of the European Union', which is translated, distributed to members and entered in a register to which any member may add his or her signature. Written declarations attracting the signatures of an absolute majority of Parliament's membership are forwarded to the institutions to which they are addressed, announced to a sitting and annexed to the minutes of the sitting. Written declarations which do not attract a sufficient number of signatures within two months lapse.

Tables

Table 1: The evolution of the European Parliament and its powers through the jurisprudence of the Court of Justice

Year	Case	Rulings and consequences
1963	Fohrmann and Krier (1964) ECR 195 Case 101/63 *Parliamentary involvement in the Court's proceedings (definition of the duration of parliamentary sessions)*	Only occasion, prior to direct elections, when the Parliament participated in legal proceedings (apart from administrative cases) and then at the invitation of the Court. (The Court had to rule on when the immunity of a parliamentarian no longer applied and in so doing on when the Parliament could be considered to be in session or not.)
1969	Chemiefarma v. European Commission ECR 661 Case 41/69 *Implicitly, Parliament should be reconsulted where the substance of a proposal has been altered*	The Court ruled that where the Council, having obligatorily consulted the Parliament on a draft regulation proposed by the Commission, modified the text, it was not obliged to reconsult the Parliament if the modification did not alter the substance of the proposal.
1979	('Isoglucose') SA Roquette Frères v. Council (1980) ECR 3333 Case 138/79 Maizena GmbH v. Council (1980) ECR 3393 Case 139/79 *Obligation to consult Parliament where so provided*	The European Parliament may intervene in cases considered by the Court (the Council had claimed that it could not). Consultation of Parliament in the cases provided for by the treaties constitutes an essential formality, disregard of which means that the measure concerned is void. (The Court ruled that the Council had not exhausted all possibilities for obtaining the Parliament's opinion prior to acting — the Parliament subsequently redrafted its rules of procedure so as to create, through the mechanism of referral back to committee, a *de facto* suspensive veto. The Court left open the matter of what would happen if,

the Council having exhausted all the possibilities open to it, Parliament still failed to deliver its opinion. Hence it remains unclear whether the *de facto* suspensive veto is of limited, or indefinite, duration.)
The Court declared that the Parliament's part in the legislative process 'reflects at Community level the fundamental democratic principle that the peoples should take part in the exercise of power through the intermediary of a representative assembly'.

1979	Battaglia v. Commission (1982) ECR 297 Case 1253/79 *Modified proposals and reconsultation*	'Regular consultation with the Parliament before the adoption of a regulation . . . constitutes . . . an essential procedural requirement . . . that requirement may be regarded as having been met when the regulation finally adopted conforms to the proposal submitted to the Parliament, so long as changes made are of method rather than substance.' (The Court had to rule on a retired civil servant's claim that Parliament had not been duly consulted on a modified proposal concerning the exchange rates used in calculating the civil servant's pension — the Court ultimately ruled against his claim.)
1980	Lord Bruce of Donnington v. Aspden (1981) ECR 2205 Case 208/80 *Parliament's internal autonomy*	MEPs' travel and subsistence allowances are not a hidden salary supplement and are therefore not taxable (the Inland Revenue had claimed that they were taxable). Implicitly, Parliament's rules on reimbursement of expenses are in conformity with the treaties. The Court declared that member states are under an obligation not to take 'measures which are likely to interfere with the internal functioning of the institutions of the Community'.
1981	Luxembourg v. European Parliament (1983) ECR 255 Case 230/81 *Parliament's freedom of expression and organisation*	'The powers of the governments of the Member States in the matter [of the seat of the European Parliament] do not affect the right inherent in the Parliament to discuss any question concerning the Communities, to adopt resolutions on such questions and to

invite the Governments to act.'
(Parliament had adopted a resolution setting out its preferred views on the seat of the Parliament.)
Parliament has the right to determine its own internal organisation and to adopt 'appropriate measures to ensure the due functioning and conduct of its proceedings'.
The Court declared that 'in the absence of a seat or even a single place of work, the Parliament must be in a position to maintain in the various places of work outside the place where its secretariat is established the infrastructure essential for ensuring that it may fulfil in all those places the tasks which are entrusted to it by the Treaties'. (Parliament interpreted this judgment as authorisation to locate parts of its secretariat in Brussels.)

1983	Luxembourg v. European Parliament (1984) ECR 1945 Case 108/83 *Parliamentary acts with legal effect are subject to review*	'A resolution of the Parliament which is of a specific and precise decision-making character, producing legal effects, may be the subject of an application for a declaration that it is void.' Resolutions which do not respect the provisions (of Article 4) of the 8 April 1965 decision [on the seat] are void. (Parliament had adopted a resolution resolving to divide the staff of its secretariat between Strasbourg and Brussels.)
1983	('Transport') Parliament v. Council (1985) ECR 1513 Case 13/83 *Parliament's right to bring actions for failure to act*	Parliament has the right of action under Article 175 of the treaty to bring actions against the Council or the Commission for failure to act. (The Court went on to find in the Parliament's favour that the Council had failed to adopt a common transport policy; the Commission supported the Parliament's case.)
1983	Les Verts v. European Parliament (1986) ECR 1339 Case 294/83 *Annulment actions may lie against Parliament's acts*	Payments for the reimbursement of election campaign expenses *per se* are within the sole competence of the member states. (Parliament could not justify, through its power of internal organisation, a scheme for the dissemination of information

concerning the European Parliament and its political groupings.) Annulment actions may lie against acts of the European Parliament. 'Neither . . . Member States nor . . . institutions can avoid a review of the question whether the measures adopted by them are in conformity with the basic constitutional charter, the Treaty.'

1985, 1990	Group of the European Right v. European Parliament (1986) ECR 1753 Case 78/85 Yvan Blot and Front National v. European Parliament (1990) ECR I-2101 Case 68/90 *Parliament's internal organisational autonomy*	A parliamentary decision to set up a committee of inquiry is a measure of internal organisation which cannot be the subject of annulment proceedings. Measures which relate only to the internal organisation of Parliament's work cannot be the subject of review by the Court. Measures relating to the appointment of the members and the election of the chairmen of inter-parliamentary delegations concern only the internal organisation of the Parliament's work. (In the first case, the European Right contested Parliament's right to establish a committee of inquiry into the rise of Fascism and racism in Europe. In the second case, the plaintiffs contested Parliament's internal mechanisms for the election of delegation chairmen.)
1986	('Budget') Council v. European Parliament ECR 2189 Case 34/86 *Limits to Parliament's budgetary powers*	Parliament must respect the provisions of Article 203(9). (The Parliament's president's declaration that the budgetary procedure for the 1986 financial year was completed was ruled to be illegal.) (Implicitly) the Court refused to become a third arm of the budgetary authority and urged the two sides, in respect of their treaty-based powers, to reach political agreement, rather than resorting to the Court, in particular with regard to the fixing of the maximum rate of increase. (Parliament could no longer simply exceed the maximum rate at second reading and challenge the Council to call its bluff or not before the Court. The ruling made it clear that an increase in the maximum rate required an explicit positive decision; 'agreement may not

be inferred on the basis of the presumed intention of one or other of those institutions'.)

1987	('Comitology') European Parliament v. Council (1988) ECR 5615 Case 302/87 *Parliament cannot bring actions for annulment*	The Court did not examine the substance of the case but ruled that the Parliament's case was inadmissible in that particular context, as the Court could not recognise 'the capacity of the European Parliament to bring an action for annulment'. 'Intervention and the action for failure to act which are available to the Parliament . . . are wholly separate from the action for annulment.' However, the Court pointed out that 'Art 155 of the Treaty confers more specifically on the Commission the responsibility for ensuring that the Parliament's prerogatives are respected'.
1988	('Chernobyl') European Parliament v. Council (1990) ECRI-2067 Case C-70/88 *Parliament can bring actions for annulment to safeguard its prerogatives*	'An action for annulment brought by the Parliament against an act of the Council or the Commission is admissible provided that the action seeks only to safeguard its prerogatives and that it is founded only on submissions alleging their infringement.' (The Court ruled against the substance of the Parliament's case; the Commission supported Parliament's right to bring the case, while disagreeing on the substance.) 'It is the Court's duty to ensure that the provisions of the Treaties concerning the institutional balance are fully applied and to see to it that the Parliament's prerogatives, like those of the other institutions, cannot be breached without it having a legal remedy, among those laid down in the Treaties, which may be exercised in a certain and effective manner.'
1989	('Titanium Dioxyde') Commission v. Council (1991) ECR I-2895 Case C300/89 *Correct choice of legal basis (parliamentary participation in legislative process)*	The Court annulled a Council directive, ruling that the legal base should be different (as argued by the Commission and the Parliament), thus giving the European Parliament two readings. In its ruling, the Court underlined the Parliament's participation in the legislative process as the reflection

		of a fundamental democratic principle.
1990	('Cabotage') European Parliament v. Council (1992) *Parliament's innate right to reconsultation where a proposal is substantially altered*	The Court annulled a Council regulation, ruling that 'it follows from the case law of the Court that the requirement that the European Parliament should be consulted in the course of the legislative procedure implies that a new consultation is implied each time that the text finally adopted, considered as a whole, differs in substance from the one on which the Parliament has already been consulted'. The Court's jurisprudence in the *Chemiefarma* and *Battaglia* cases strongly implied that the Parliament had such rights, but the 1992 'cabotage' ruling was the first explicitly to confirm Parliament's right to reconsultation.
1991	Weber v. European Parliament (23 March 1993) Case C-314/91 *Definition of categories of parliamentary acts subject to review*	The Court held that only two categories of acts of Parliament could escape review: those which produce no legal effects, and those which only produce legal effects within Parliament and which can be reviewed under procedures laid down in its rules of procedure.

Table 2: Seats, population per MEP and constituencies/voting system in the Member States

State	Seats		Total population (millions)	Population per MEP		Constituencies/ voting system
	(pre-1994)	1994		(pre-1994)	1994	
Belgium	(24)	25	10.0	(416,667)	400,000	Proportional representation in 3 regional constituencies/ electoral colleges (regional lists)
Denmark	(16)	16	5.1	(318,750)	318,750	Proportional representation in single constituency (national list)
France	(81)	87	56.8	(701,235)	652,874	Proportional representation in single constituency (national list)
Germany	(81)	99	79.4	(980,247)	802,020	Proportional representation in 15 *Länder* constituencies (regional and national lists)
Greece	(24)	25	10.0	(416,667)	400,000	Proportional representation in single constituency (national list)
Ireland	(15)	15	3.6	(240,000)	240,000	Proportional representation (Single Transferable Vote) in 4 multi-member constituencies
Italy	(81)	87	57.4	(708,642)	659,770	Proportional representation in 5 regional constituencies (regional lists)
Luxembourg	(6)	6	0.4	(66,667)	66,667	Proportional representation in single constituency (national list)
Netherlands	(25)	31	14.7	(588,000)	474,194	Proportional representation in single constituency (national list)

Portugal	(24)	25	10.2	(425,000)	408,000	Proportional representation in single constituency (national list)
Spain	(60)	64	38.8	(646,667)	606,250	Proportional representation in single constituency (national list)
United Kingdom	(81)	87	56.9	(702,469)	654,023	Simple majority in 84 single-member constituencies in England, Wales and Scotland; proportional representation (Single Transferable Vote) in one three-member constituency in Northern Ireland

Sources: HC Deb 19/3/93 c429-30W; *EP Infomemo 1994*

Table 3: The different numbers of members of the European Parliament, proposed and decided, 1951–95

Member State	ECSC Common Assembly Monnet's original proposal (1951)	Paris Treaty (1952)	European Assembly Rome Treaties (1957)	European Parliament EP's First Convention – Dehousse Report (1960)	First enlargement (1973)	EP's Second Convention Patijn Report (1975)	1976 Act (1979)	Second enlargement (1981)	Third enlargement (1986)	1992 Edinburgh Council Agreement (1994)	1993 Brussels Council Agreement (1995?)
(Total)	62	78	142	426	198	355	410	434	518	567	639
Germany	18	18	36	108	36	71	81	81	81	99	99
France	18	18	36	108	36	65	81	81	81	87	87
Italy	18	18	36	108	36	66	81	81	81	87	87
Netherlands	18 for the	14	14	42	14	27	25	25	25	31	31
Belgium	three states	14	14	42	14	23	24	24	24	25	25
Luxembourg	together	6	6	18	6	6	6	6	6	6	6
United Kingdom					36	67	81	81	81	87	87
Denmark					10	17	16	16	16	16	16
Ireland					10	13	15	15	15	15	15
Greece								24	24	25	25
Spain									60	64	64
Portugal									24	25	25
Sweden											21
Austria											20
Finland											16
Norway											15

Sources: Monnet, 1976; Scalingi, 1980; Edinburgh and Brussels European Council Conclusions (*EC Bulletin* December 1992 and December 1993)

Table 4: Turnout in European elections to 1989

Member State	1979	1981	1984	1987	1989
Belgium	91.4		92.1		90.7
France	60.7		56.7		48.7
Germany	65.7		56.8		62.3
Italy	84.9		83.4		81.0
Luxembourg	88.9		88.8		87.4
Netherlands	57.8		50.6		47.2
Average 6	**74.9**		**71.4**		**69.6**
Denmark	47.8		52.4		46.2
Ireland	63.6		47.6		68.3
United Kingdom	32.3		32.6		36.2
(Northern Ireland)	(56.9)		(65.4)		(48.8)
Average 9	**63.0**		**62.3**		**63.1**
Greece		78.6	77.2		79.9
Average 10			**61.0**		**64.8**
Portugal				72.6	51.2
Spain				68.9	54.6
Average 12					**58.5**

Source: Euroinfomemo, 14.6.94.

Table 5: Required parliamentary majorities

Subject	Rule	Majority Requirement	Basis
Convene Parliament	10.5	absolute	rules
Convene Parliament with the approval of the Conference of Presidents	10.5	one-third	rules
Election of president of Parliament (first three ballots)	14.1	absolute	rules
Election of president (fourth and final ballot)	14.1	simple	rules
Election of vice-presidents (first two ballots)	15	absolute	rules
Election of vice-presidents (third ballot)	15	simple	rules
Election of quaestors (first two ballots)	16	absolute	rules
Election of quaestors (third ballot)	16	simple	rules
Motion of censure on the Commission	34	absolute, and two-thirds of the votes cast	treaty

Table 5: *continued*

Subject	Rule	Majority Requirement	Basis
Written declarations by individual members	48	only forwarded to institution concerned if the declaration is signed by at least one-half of Parliament's component members	rules
Request for a legislative initiative	50.1	absolute	treaty
Referral back to plenary of a committee's power of decision	52.2	one-third	rules
Referral back to plenary of a committee report under the delegated procedure	52.5	one-tenth, belonging to at least three political groups	rules
Request for the Commission to withdraw a proposal	59	Parliament's president must automatically request withdrawal where a proposal fails to secure a simple majority of the votes cast	rules
Amendment of the Council Common Position (cooperation or co-decision procedure)	67.2 72.3	absolute	treaty
Intention to reject the Council's Common Position (co-decision)	69.1	absolute	treaty
Confirmation of intention to reject the Council's Common Position (co-decision procedure)	70.1	absolute	treaty
Rejection of the Common Position (cooperation or co-decision procedure)	71.7	absolute	treaty
Request to Commission to withdraw its proposal (cooperation procedure)	73.2	absolute	rules
Approval of the conciliation committee's joint text (co-decision procedure)	77	simple	treaty
Rejection of the Council text (co-decision third reading)	78.4	absolute	treaty
Assent on accession	80.1 89.6	absolute	treaty
Assent on uniform electoral system	80.1	absolute	treaty

Table 5: *continued*

Subject	Rule	Majority Requirement	Basis
The Budget			
Proposals on fixing the maximum rate	Annex IV 2.5	absolute and three-fifths of the votes cast	treaty
Draft amendments to the draft budget	3.8	absolute	treaty
Draft modifications to the draft budget	3.8	simple	treaty
Second-reading amendments	5.6	absolute and three-fifths of votes cast	treaty
Rejection of the budget	6.2	absolute and two-thirds of votes cast	treaty
Authorisation of expenditure in excess of 'provisional twelfths'	7.4	absolute and three-fifths of votes cast	treaty
Refusal of discharge	Annex V 5.2	absolute	rules
ECSC Treaty amendments	88.2	three-quarters majority of votes cast, representing a two-thirds' majority of the component members of the Parliament	treaty
Quorum	112.2	one-third of component members	rules
Request for secret ballot	121.2	one-fifth of component members	rules
Establishment of temporary committees of inquiry	136	at request of one-quarter of its members	treaty
Request for dismissal of ombudsman	160.1	one-tenth	rules
Vote on request to dismiss ombudsman	160.3	at least half of members must be present	rules
Amending rules of procedure	163.2	absolute	rules

Table 6: The evolution of compulsory and non-compulsory expenditure as proportions of overall expenditure

Year	Compulsory expenditure (in m ECU)	Non-Compulsory expenditure (in m ECU)	Compulsory expenditure (%)
1980	13.25	2.93	81.9
1981	14.92	3.51	81.0
1982	17.58	4.40	80.0
1983	18.94	6.12	75.6
1984	20.42	6.83	74.9
1985	22.30	6.13	78.4
1986	26.64	8.54	75.7
1987	27.07	9.25	74.5
1988	33.65	10.13	76.9
1989	31.79	13.05	70.9
1990	31.22	15.49	66.8
1991	35.23	20.33	63.4

Source: EP resolution on the classification of expenditure in the budget (adopted 24 October 1991).

Table 7: Take-up of parliamentary amendments under the cooperation procedure (of the 322 proposals dealt with under the cooperation procedure up to 30 December 1993)

	First reading			Second reading		
European Parliament amendments	tabled		4,572	tabled		1,074
European Commission	taken up	2,499 (54.65%)		taken up	475 (44.22%)	
Council	accepted	1,966 (43%)		accepted	253 (23.55%)	

Table 8: 1993: a year's parliamentary activity in figures

(Part) Session	Normal consultations (one reading)	Cooperation procedure (first readings)	Cooperation procedure (second readings)	Assent	Co-decision procedure (first readings)	Other opinions and recommendations	Own-initiative reports and resolutions		Budget questions	Miscellaneous decisions and resolutions
							Committee own initiative reports	Topical and urgent debates		
January	6	7	3			4	23	17	1	1
February	13	4	6			3	8	24	1	4
March	19	5	2	1		3	14	13	3	
April	51	1	11			4	10	24	6	
May	14	7	4			2	5	16	1	1
June	14	7	1	1		1	7	20	1	2
July	17	4	5			4	12	18	1	
September (I)	4						7	27		1
September (II)							1	2		
October (I)								1		
October (II)	18	7	12	4		2	6	22	8	1
November	23	4			1	4	11	19	1	1
December (I)	1		2	1		2	1	1		
December (II)	19	4		1	4	7	15	21	3	2
Total	199	50	46	8	5	36	25	120	225	13

Source: EC Commission, 1994, *XXVIIth General Report on the Activities of the European Communities*, Brussels, p.360.

Bibliography

NB The Bibliography lists only those works referred to in the text or consulted by the author and is in no way intended as a comprehensive guide to the extensive literature on the Parliament.

Arndt, Rudi, 1992, 'The Political Groups in the European Parliament', in European Parliament, 1992d.

Arter, David, 'The Swedish Riksdag: The Case of a Strong Policy-Influencing Assembly', in Norton, 1990c.

Barav, A., and Wyatt, D.A. (eds), 1989, *Yearbook of European Law 8 1988*, Clarendon Press, Oxford.

Barav, A., and Wyatt, D.A. (eds), 1991, *Yearbook of European Law 10 1990*, Clarendon Press, Oxford.

Bebr, Gerhard, 1990, 'The Standing of the European Parliament in the Community System of Legal Remedies: A Thorny Jurisprudential Development', in Barav and Wyatt, 1991.

Belgian Sénat and Chambre des Représentants, 1993, *Activités parlementaires dans le cadre de la presidence Belge de la Communauté européenne* (1 July–31 December 1993), Brussels.

Bieber, Roland, 1986, 'Legal Developments in the European Parliament', in Jacobs (ed.).

Bieber, Roland, 1987, 'Legal Developments in the European Parliament', in Jacobs, 1987.

Boyce, Brigitte, 1993, 'The Democratic Deficit of the European Community', *Parliamentary Affairs*, **46**, 4, October.

Bradley, Kieran St Clair, 1987, 'Maintaining the Balance: The Role of the Court of Justice in Defining the Institutional Position of the European Parliament', *Common Market Law Review*, **24**.

Bradley, Kieran St Clair, 1989, 'The Variable Evolution of the Standing of the European Parliament in Proceedings Before the Court of Justice, in Barav and Wyatt, 1989.

Bradley, Kieran St Clair, 1989, 'Legal Developments in the European Parliament', in Barav and Wyatt, 1989.

Bradley, Kieran St Clair, 1992, 'Comitology and the Law: Through a Glass Darkly', *Common Market Law Review*, **29**.

Bradley, Kieran St Clair, 1993, '"Better Rusty Than Missin"?: Institutional Reforms of the Maastricht Treaty and the European Parliament', in O'Keefe and Twomey, 1993.

Brittan, Sir Leon, 1994, *Europe: The Europe We Need*, Hamish Hamilton, London.

Butler, David, and Marquand, David, 1981, *European Elections and British Politics*, Longman, London.

Butler, David, and Jowett, Paul, 1985, *Party Strategies in Britain. A Study of the 1984 European Elections*, Macmillan, London.

Caravelis, Georges, 1994, *European Monetary Union. An Application of the Fundamental Principles of Monetary Theory*, Avebury, Aldershot.

Closa, Carlos, 1993, 'National Parliaments and the Maastricht Treaty', Centre for Legislative Studies, Hull University (unpublished paper).

Commission of the European Communities, 1985, *The Relaunching of Europe: From the Messina Conference to the Treaties of Rome, 1955–1957* (Catalogue of an exhibition compiled by the General Archives of the Commission), Office for Official Publications of the European Communities, Luxembourg.

Commission of the European Communities, 1993, *Vade mecum budgétaire*, Brussels.

Constituency Committees for England and Wales, 1993 and 1994, Various publications and announcements related to their work.

Coombes, David, 1979, *The Future of the European Parliament*, Policy Studies Institute, London.

Coombes, David, 1988, 'The European Parliamentary Tradition and its Significance for European Integration', unpublished paper delivered at the international symposium, 'Beyond Traditional Parliamentarism: The European Parliament in the Community System', Strasbourg, 17–18 November 1988.

Coppé, Albert, 1992, 'The Common Assembly as seen from the High Authority', in European Parliament, 1992d.

Corbett, Richard, 1989, 'Testing the New Procedures: The European Parliament's First Experiences with its New "Single Act" Powers', *Journal of Common Market Studies*, 4, June.

Corbett, Richard, 1992, 'The Intergovernmental Conference on Political Union', *Journal of Common Market Studies*, XXX, 3, September.

Corbett, Richard, 1993a, 'Governance and Institutional Developments', *Journal of Common Market Studies*, XXXI, August.

Corbett, Richard, 1993b, *The Treaty of Maastricht. From Conception to Ratification: A Comprehensive Reference Guide*, Longman, Harlow.

Council of Europe, 1973, *The Consultative Assembly, Procedure and Practice (seventh edition)*, Council of Europe, Strasbourg.

Council of Europe, 1994, *Cooperation entre les commissions de l'assemblée parlementaire et du parlement Européen (janvier 1993–janvier 1994)*, internal, unpublished document, Strasbourg.

Council of the European Communities, 1992, *Treaty on European Union*, Office for Official Publications of the European Communities, Luxembourg.

Earnshaw, David, and Judge, David, 1993, 'The European Parliament and the Sweeteners Directive: From Footnote to Inter-Institutional Conflict', *Journal of Common Market Studies*, 31, 1, March.

Ellwood, David W., 1992, *Rebuilding Europe: Western Europe, America and Postwar Reconstruction*, Longman, Harlow.

Engel, Matthew, 1994, 'Parliament of Snoozers', *The Guardian*, 25 January.

European Constitutional Group (European Policy Forum), 1993, *A European Constitutional Settlement*, London.

European Parliament, 1982, *Forging Ahead* (1st edition), Office for Official Publications of the European Communities, Luxembourg.

European Parliament, 1989, *Forging Ahead* (3rd edition), Office for Official Publications of the European Communities, Luxembourg.

European Parliament, 1990, *Texts of an institutional nature adopted by the European Parliament from January 1988 to July 1990, forwarded to the national parliaments*, Office for Official Publications of the European Communities, Luxembourg.

European Parliament, 1991, *The Funding of Political Parties in European Community Member States*, Research and Documentation Papers, Political Series 12, Luxembourg.

European Parliament, 1992a, *National Parliamentary Election Procedures in Members States of the European Communities*, Research and Documentation Papers, Political Series W-16 (2-1992), Luxembourg.

European Parliament, 1992b, *An Enlarged Community: Institutional Adaptations*, Research and Documentation Papers, Political Series 17, Brussels.

European Parliament, 1992c, *Texts of an institutional nature adopted by the European Parliament from July 1990 to December 1991, forwarded to the national parliaments*, Office for Official Publications of the European Communities, Luxembourg.

European Parliament, 1992d, *The European Community in the Historical Context of its Parliament*, Strasbourg.

European Parliament, 1993a, *Rules of Procedure* (8th edition; Provisional Edition), Luxembourg, October.

European Parliament, 1993b (April), 'Les commissions parlementaires d'enquête dans la Communauté européenne', *Les Echos du Parlement Européen*, No. 83, Paris.

European Parliament, 1993c (July/August), 'L'immunité parlementaire dans les Etats membres de la Communauté et au Parlement européen', *Les Echos du Parlement Européen*, No. 86, Paris.

European Parliament, 1994a, *Info Memo 'Special Elections' No 1: Le PE sortant et les premières listes de candidats*, Brussels.

European Parliament, 1994b, *Le Parlement européen et les droits de l'homme*, Office for Official Publications of the European Community, Luxembourg.

Fitzmaurice, John, 1979, 'The Danish System of Parliamentary Control over the EC', in Herman and van Schendelen, 1979.

Fitzmaurice, John, 1988, 'An Analysis of the European Community's Co-operation Procedure', *Journal of Common Market Studies*, **XXVI**, 4, June.

Fitzmaurice, John, 1994, 'The Commission and the Parliament', speech delivered at the Centre for European Studies, Brussels, 12 January.

Ford, Glyn, 1992, *Fascist Europe. The Rise of Racism and Xenophobia*, Pluto Press, London.

Frears, John, 1990, 'The French Parliament: Loyal Workhorse, Poor Watchdog', in Norton, 1990c.

Furlong, Paul, 1990, 'Parliament in Italian Politics', in Norton, 1990c.

Gardner, James N., 1993, 'The Dynamics of Political Decision-Making in the European Community and the United States', unpublished paper delivered to the Transatlantic Forum, The Aspen Institute's Wye Centre, Maryland, 17–19 October.

George, Stephen, 1990, *Politics and Policy in the European Community*, Clarendon Press, Oxford.

Gerbet, Pierre, 1986, 'Les origines du plan Schuman: le choix de la méthode communautaire par le gouvernement français', in Poidevin, 1986.

Gerbet, Pierre, 1987, 'In Search of Political Union: The Fouchet Plan Negotiations (1960–62)', in Pryce, 1987.

Gladdish, Ken, 1990, 'Parliamentary Activism and Legitimacy in the Netherlands', in Norton, 1990c.

Gosalbo Bono, Ricardo, 'Maastricht et les Citoyens: Le Mediateur Européen', *Revue française d'administration publique*, octobre–decembre 1992, No. 64.

Harris, Geoffrey, 1992, 'Europe in Crisis? A Personal View', Mellon Scholar Paper (unpublished), delivered 20 November, Cornell University.

Harris, Geoffrey, 1993, *The Dark Side of Europe. The Extreme Right Today* (2nd edition), Edinburgh University Press, Edinburgh.

Herman, Valentine, and van Schendelen, Rinus (eds), 1979, *The European Parliament and the National Parliaments*, Saxon House, Farnborough.

Herman, Valentine, and Hagger, Mark (eds), 1980, *The Legislation of Direct Elections to the European Parliament*, Gower, Farnborough.

Herman, Valentine, and Lodge, Juliet, 1978, 'Is the European Parliament a Parliament?', *European Journal of Political Research*, 6.

Herman, Valentine, and Lodge, Juliet, 1978, *The European Parliament and the European Community*, Macmillan, London.

Heseltine, Michael, 1989, *The Challenge of Europe. Can Britain Win?*, Weidenfeld and Nicolson, London.

Hirst, Paul, 1994, *Associative Democracy. New Forms of Economic and Social Governance*, Polity Press, Oxford.

Hoffman, Stanley, 1982, 'Reflections on the Nation-State in Europe Today', *Journal of Common Market Studies*, **XXI**, 1 and 2.

House of Commons Library, 1993, *UK Elections to the European Parliament*, Research Paper 93/70, London.

House of Commons, 1993, Select Committee on European Legislation, *First Report, Session 1993–4*, HC 48-i, HMSO, London.

House of Lords, 1993, Select Committee on the European Communities, *EC Aid and Trade Policy*, Session 1992–3, 27th Report, HL Paper 123, HMSO, London.

House of Lords, 1993, Select Committee on the European Communities, *House of Lords Scrutiny of the Inter-Governmental Pillars of the European Union*, Session 1992–3, 28th Report, HL Paper 124, HMSO, London.

Hurwitz, L., and Lesquesne, C. (eds), 1993, *The State of the European Community*, Longman, Harlow.

Institut d'études européennes, 1986, *l'acte unique européen*, Université Libre de Bruxelles.

Ionescu, Ghita (ed.), 1972, *The New Politics of European Integration*, Macmillan, London.

Jackson, Robert, and Fitzmaurice, John, 1979, *The European Parliament: A Guide to Direct Elections*, Penguin, Harmondsworth.

Jacobs, Francis G. (ed.), 1986, *Yearbook of European Law 5 1985*, Clarendon Press, Oxford.

Jacobs, Francis G. (ed.), 1987, *Yearbook of European Law 6 1986*, Clarendon Press, Oxford.

Jacobs, Francis, and Corbett, Richard, 1990, *The European Parliament*, Longman, Harlow.

Jacobs, Francis Brendan, 1991, 'The European Parliament and Economic and Monetary Union', *Common Market Law Review*, **28**.

Judge, David, 1993, *The Parliamentary State*, Sage, London.

Kapteyn, Paul J.G., 1962, *L'Assemblée commune de la Communauté Européenne du charbon et de l'acier; un essai de parlementarisme européen*, A.W. Sythoff, Leiden.

Laprat, Gérard, 1991, 'Les Parlements nationaux et l'élaboration de la norme communautaire', *Revue du Marché Commun*, October 1991.

Laundy, Philip, 1989, *Parliaments in the Modern World*, Dartmouth, Aldershot.

Lenman, Bruce P., 1993, *The Eclipse of Parliament: Appearance and Reality in British Politics since 1914*, Edward Arnold, London.

Louis, Jean-Victor, and Waelbroek, Denis (eds), 1989, *Le parlement Européen dans l'évolution institutionnelle*, Editions de l'Université de Bruxelles, Brussels.

MacDougall, Sir D., 1975, *The Role of Public Finances in European Integration* (two volumes), Commission of the European Communities, Luxembourg.

Majone, Giandomenico, 1993, 'The European Community: An "Independent Fourth Branch of Government"?', EUI Working Paper in Political and Social Sciences 93/9, EUI, Florence.

Marquand, David, 1979, *Parliament for Europe*, Jonathan Cape, London.

Martin, David, 1993, *European Union: The Shattered Dream?*, John Wheatley Centre, West Lothian.

Meehan, Elizabeth, 1993, 'Citizenship and the European Community', *Political Quarterly*, **64**, 2, April–June.

Milward, Alan S., 1992, *The European Rescue of the Nation State*, Routledge, London.

Monnet, Jean, 1976, *Mémoires*, Fayard, Paris.

Morgan, Roger, 1992, 'The European Parliament and the National Parliaments', in European Parliament, 1992d.

Mowat, R., 1973, *Creating the European Community*, Blandford Press, London.

Noël, Emile, 1989, 'Le Parlement face à la Commission', in Louis and Waelbroek, 1989.

Noël, Emile, 1992, 'Reflections on the Maastricht Treaty', *Government and Opposition*, **27**, 2.

North Atlantic Assembly, 1993, *North Atlantic Assembly (Information Document)*, Brussels, May.

Norton, Philip, 1983, *Does Parliament Matter?*, Simon and Schuster, Hemel Hempstead.

Norton, Philip, 1990a, 'Parliament in the United Kingdom: Balancing Effectiveness and Consent?', *West European Politics*, **13**, 3, July.

Norton, Philip, 1990b, 'Parliaments: A Framework for Analysis', in Norton, 1990c.

Norton, Philip (ed.), 1990c, *Parliaments in Western Europe*, Frank Cass, London.

Neunreither, Karlheinz, 1994a, 'The Syndrome of democratic deficit in the European Community', in Parry, 1994.

Neunreither, Karlheinz, 1994b, 'The Democratic Deficit of the European Union: Will closer cooperation between the European Parliament and the national parliaments fill the gap?', unpublished paper delivered to the 5–6 May 1994 World Conference of the European Community Studies Association.

Nugent, Neill, 1991, *The Government and Politics of the European Community* (2nd edition), Macmillan, London.

O'Keefe, David, and Twomey, Patrick (eds), 1993, *Legal Issues of the Maastricht Treaty*, Chancery, Chichester.

Ollerenshaw, Steve, 1993, 'The European Parliament. More Democracy or More Rhetoric?', Occasional Papers in European Studies 2, Centre for European Studies, University of Essex.

O'Neill, Aidan, 1993, 'The Government of Judges, The Impact of the European Court of Justice on the Constitutional Order of the United Kingdom', EUI Working Paper in Law 93/3, EUI, Florence.

Parkinson, Cyril Northcote, 1959, *Parkinson's Law*, John Murray, London.

Parry, Geraint (ed.), 1994, *Politics in an Interdependent World*, Edward Elgar, Hants.

Pasetti Bombardella, Francesco, 1989, 'Le Parlement face au Conseil', in Louis and Waelbroek, 1989.

Pescatore, Pierre, 1989, 'Le Parlement face à la Cour', in Louis and Waelbroek, 1989.

Peterson, John, 1994, 'Understanding Decision-Making in the European Community. Towards a Framework for Analysis', draft York Working Paper in Politics.

Pflimlin, Pierre, 1991, *Mémoires d'un Européen de la IVe à la Ve République*, Fayard, Paris.

Pflimlin, Pierre, 1992, 'Comments', in European Parliament, 1992d.

Plant, Lord Raymond, 1993, *The Report of the Working Party on Electoral Systems 1993* (Plant Report), published 19 May 1993, Walworth Road, London.

Poidevin, Raymond (ed.), 1986, *Histoire des debuts de la construction Européenne*, Bruylant, Brussels.

Prout, Sir Christopher, 1989, 'Problèmes d'actualité pour le Parlement', in Louis and Waelbroek, 1989.

Pryce, Roy (ed.), 1987, *The Dynamics of European Union*, Routledge, London.

Pryce, Roy, and Wessels, Wolfgang, 1987, 'The Search for an Ever Closer Union: A Framework for Analysis', in Pryce, 1987.

Racine, Raymond, 1954, *Vers une Europe Nouvelle par le Plan Schuman*, Editions de la Baconnière, Neuchâtel.

Rasmussen, Hjalte, 1992, 'The Institutional Relationship between Parliament and the Court of Justice: The Problem of an Alliance between them', in European Parliament, 1992d.

Reif, Karlheinz, 1985, *Ten European Elections*, Gower, Aldershot.

Reif, Karlheinz, and Schmitt, Hermann, 1980, 'Nine Second Order National Elections: A Conceptual Framework for the Analysis of European Election Results', *European Journal of Political Research*, **8**, 1.

Reuter, Paul, 1953, *La Communauté Européenne du Charbon et de l'Acier*, Librairie Générale de Droit et de Jurisprudence, R. Pichon et R. Durand-Auzias, Paris.

Reuter, Paul, 1980, *La naissance de l'Europe Communautaire*, Fondation Jean Monnet pour l'Europe, Centre de Recherches Européennes, Lausanne.

Robertson, Arthur Henry, *Le Conseil de l'Europe, sa structure, ses fonctions et ses réalisations*, Sythoff, Paris.

Rosenzweig, Luc, 1993, '1994: une année électorale en Europe', *Le Monde*, 31 December.

Saalfield, Thomas, 1990, 'The West German Bundestag after 40 Years: The Role of Parliament in a "Party Democracy"', in Norton, 1990c.

Scalingi, Paula, 1980, *The European Parliament: The Three-Decade Search for a United Europe*, Aldwych Press, London.

Shackleton, Michael, 1990, *Financing the European Community*, Pinter, London.

Shackleton, Michael, 1993a, 'Budgetary Policy in Transition', in Hurwitz and Lesquesne, 1993.

Shackleton, Michael, 1993b, 'The Democratic Deficit in the European Community', unpublished paper, Brussels.

Shonfield, Andrew, 1973, *Europe: Journey to an Unknown Destination*, Penguin, Harmondsworth.

Smith, Julie, 1994, 'Citizens' Europe? The European Elections and the Role of the European Parliament', The Royal Institute of International Affairs, Chatham House, London.

Spaak, Paul-Henri, 1969, *Combats Inachevés: de l'espoir aux déceptions*, Fayard, Paris.

Spierenburg, Dirk, and Poidevin, Raymond, 1993, *Histoire de la Haute Autorité de la Communauté européenne du charbon et de l'acier; une experience supranational*, Bruylant, Brussels.

Steed, Michael, 1972, 'The Significance of Direct Elections', in Ionescu, 1972.

Strasser, Daniel, 1990, *Les finances de l'Europe* (6th edition), Librairie Générale de Droit et de Jurisprudence, Paris.

Sutherland, Peter, 1989, 'La Commission et le Parlement européen. Partenaires ou protagonistes?', in Louis and Waelbroek, 1989.

Teasdale, Anthony, L., 1993, 'Subsidiarity in Post-Maastricht Europe', *Political Quarterly*, **64**, 2, April–June.

Teasdale, Anthony, L., 1993, 'The Life and Death of the Luxembourg Compromise', *Journal of Common Market Studies*, **XXXI**, 4, December.

Urwin, Derek, W., 1991, *The Community of Europe; A History of European Integration since 1945*, Longman, Harlow.

Vallance, Elizabeth, and Davies, Elizabeth, 1986, *Women of Europe, Women MEPs and Equality Policy*, Cambridge University Press, Cambridge.

Welsh, Jennifer M., 1993, 'A People's Europe? European Citizenship and European Identity', EUI Working Paper in European Cultural Studies 93/2, EUI, Florence.

Westlake, Martin, 1990, 'The Origin and Development of the Question Time Procedure in the European Parliament', EUI Working Paper 90/4, European University Institute, Florence.

Westlake, Martin, 1991, 'The Community Express Service: The Rapid Passage of Emergency Legislation on German Unification', *Common Market Law Review*, 28.

Westlake, Martin, 1994a, *Britain's Emerging Euro-Elite? The British in the European Parliament, 1979–1992*, Dartmouth, Aldershot.

Westlake, Martin, 1994b, *The Parliament and the Commission: Partners and Rivals in the European Policy-Making Process*, Butterworths, London.

Wood, David, and Wood, Alan (eds), 1979, *The Times Guide to the European Parliament*, Times Books, London.

Wood, Alan (ed.), 1984, *The Times Guide to the European Parliament 1984*, Times Books, London.

Wood, Alan (ed.), 1989, *The Times Guide to the European Parliament 1989*, Times Books, London.

Zuleeg, Manfred, 1989, 'Le Parlement face à la Cour', in Louis and Waelbroek, 1989.

Parliamentary resolutions

Resolution on the role of the European Parliament in its relations with the European Council, adopted 18.12.81, OJ N° C 11, 18.1.82, p.191.

Resolution on relations between the European Parliament and the Economic and Social Committee, adopted 9.7.81, OJ N° C 234, 14.9.81, p.60.

Written Declaration on the European Parliament's powers and the convening of the 'European States General', adopted 16.5.88, OJ N° C 167, 27.6.88, p.19.

Written Declaration on the holding of a plebiscite on the political Union of Europe and the constituent, adopted 16.6.88, OJ N° C 187, 18.7.88, p.200.

Resolution on the democratic deficit in the European Community, adopted 17.6.88, OJ N° C 187, 18.7.88, p.230.

Resolution on the procedures for consulting European citizens on European political union, adopted 17.6.88, OJ N° C 187, 18.7.88, p.231.

Resolution on the results obtained from the implementation of the Single Act, adopted 27.10.88, OJ N° C 309, 5.12.88, p.93.

Resolution on the strategy of the European Parliament for achieving European Union, adopted 16.2.89, OJ N° C 69, 20.3.89, p.145.

Resolution on relations between the national parliaments and the European Parliament, adopted 16.2.89, OJ N° C 69, 20.3.89, p.149.

Resolution on the Presidency of the European Community, adopted 26.5.89, OJ N° C 158, 26.6.89, p.368.

Resolution on the intergovernmental conference decided on at the European Council in Madrid, adopted 23.11.89, OJ N° C 323, 27.12.89, p.111.

Resolution on the Strasbourg European Council, adopted 14.12.89, OJ N° C 15, 22.1.90, p.319.

Resolution on the Intergovernmental Conference in the context of Parliament's strategy for European Union, adopted 14.3.90, OJ N° C 96, 17.4.90, p.114.

Resolution on the Temporary Committee to study the impact on the European Community of the German unification process, adopted 4.4.90, OJ N° C 113, 7.5.90, p.97.

Resolution on the Dublin European Council, adopted 17.5.90, OJ N° C 149, 18.6.90, p.170.

Resolution on the conclusions of the special meeting of the European Council in Dublin on 18 April 1990, adopted 17.5.90, OJ N° C 149, 18.6.90, p.172.

Resolution on the institutional guidelines for the second Dublin Summit, adopted 14.6.90, OJ N° C 231, 17.9.90, p.91.

Resolution on the European Parliament's guidelines for a draft constitution for the European Union, adopted 11.7.90, OJ N° C 231, 17.9.90, p.91.

Resolution on the Intergovernmental Conference in the context of Parliament's strategy for European Union, adopted 11.7.90, OJ N° C 231, 17.9.90, p.97.

Resolution on the preparation of the meeting with the national parliaments to discuss the future of the Community (the 'Assises'), adopted 12.7.90, OJ N° C 231, 17.9.90, p.165.

Resolution on the implications of German unification for the European Community, adopted 12.7.90, OJ N° C 231, 17.9.90, p.154.

Resolution on the principle of subsidiarity, adopted 12.7.90, OJ N° C 231, 17.9.90, p.163.

Resolution on the Dublin European Council, adopted 13.7.90, OJ N° C 231, 17.9.90, p.212.

Resolution on the Conference on Security and Cooperation in Europe (Helsinki II Conference), adopted 9.10.90, OJ N° C 284, 12.11.90, p.36.

Resolution on Relations between the European Parliament and the Council, adopted 10.10.90, OJ N° C 284, 12.11.90, p.59.

Resolution on Economic and Monetary Union, adopted 10.10.90, OJ N° C 284, 12.11.90, p.58.

Resolution on Parliamentary assent: practice, procedure and prospects for the future, adopted 25.10.90, OJ N° C 295, p.208.

Resolution on the principle of subsidiarity, adopted 21.11.90, OJ N° C 324, 24.12.90, p.168.

Resolution on the Intergovernmental Conferences in the context of the European Parliament's strategy for European Union, adopted 22.11.90, OJ N° C 324, p.220.

Resolution embodying Parliament's opinion on the convening of the Intergovernmental Conferences on Economic and Monetary Union and on Political Union, adopted 22.11.90, OJ N° C 324, p.235.

Resolution on strengthening Parliament's powers of budgetary control in the context of Parliament's strategy for European Union, adopted 22.11.90, OJ N° C 324, p.241.

Resolution on the constitutional basis of European Union, adopted 12.12.90, OJ N° C 19, 28.1.91, p.65.

Resolution on the executive powers of the Commission (comitology) and the role of the Commission in the Community's external relations, adopted 13.12.90, OJ N° C 19, 28.1.91, p.273.

Resolution on the Rome Summit, adopted 24.1.91, OJ N° C 48, 25.2.91, p.163.

Resolution on the enhancement of democratic legitimacy in the context of the Intergovernmental Conference on Political Union, adopted 18.4.91, OJ N° C 129, 20.5.91, p.134.

Resolution on Community enlargement and relations with other European countries, adopted 15.5.91, OJ N° C 158, 17.6.91, p.54.

Resolution on the outlook for a European security policy: the significance of a European security policy and its institutional implications for European Political Union, adopted 10.6.91, OJ N° C 183, 15.7.91, p.18.

Resolution on economic and monetary union in the context of the Intergovernmental Conference, adopted 14.6.91, OJ N° C 183, 15.7.91, p.361.

Resolution on the Intergovernmental Conference on Political Union, adopted 14.6.91, OJ N° C 183, 15.7.91, p.363.

Resolution on Union citizenship, adopted 14.6.91, OJ N° C 183, 15.7.91, p. 473.

Resolution on the Conference on Security and Cooperation in Europe, adopted 11.7.91, OJ N° C 240, 16.9.91, p.187.

Resolution on the classification of expenditure in the budget, adopted 24.10.91, OJ N° C 305, 25.11.91, p.93.

Resolution on democratic representation in the European Parliament of the 16 million new German EC citizens, adopted 9.10.91, OJ N° C 280, 28.10.91, p.94.

Resolution on the European Parliament's guidelines for the draft uniform electoral procedure, adopted 10.10.91, OJ N° C 280, 28.10.91, p.141.

Resolution on relations between the European Parliament and the national parliaments after the Conference of Parliaments of the European Community, adopted 10.10.91, OJ N° C 280, p.144.

Resolution on the Intergovernmental Conference on Political Union, adopted 10.10.91, OJ N° C 280, p.148.

Resolution on the Intergovernmental Conference on a common foreign and security policy, adopted 24.10.91, OJ N° C 305, 25.11.91, p.98.

Resolution on the proposal of the Netherlands Presidency of the Council to the Intergovernmental Conference on Economic and Monetary Union, adopted 24.10.91, OJ N° C 305, p.102.

Resolution on strengthening the European Parliament's powers of budgetary control in the context of its strategy for European Union, adopted 24.10.91, OJ N° C 305, 25.11.91, p.104.

Resolution on the institutional role of the Economic and Social Committee, adopted 21.11.91, OJ N° C 326, 16.12.91, p.203.

Resolution on Union citizenship, adopted 21.11.91, OJ N° C 326, 16.12.91, p.205.

Resolution on the results of the Intergovernmental Conferences, adopted 7.4.92, OJ N° C 125, 18.5.92, p.81.

Resolution on a uniform electoral procedure: a scheme for allocating the seats of Members of the European Parliament, adopted 10.6.92, OJ N° C 176, 13.7.92, p.72.

Resolution on the Commission communication 'From the Single Act to Maastricht and beyond: the means to match our ambitions', adopted 10.6.92, OJ N° C 176, 13.7.92, p.74.

Resolution on the procedure for consulting the European Parliament on the appointment of members of the Court of Auditors, adopted 17.11.92, OJ N° C 337, 21.12.92, p.51.

Resolution on the extraordinary European Council meeting in Birmingham on 16 October 1992, adopted 28.10.92, OJ N° C 305, 23.11.92, p.57.

Resolution on the Decision on the conclusion of the agreement on the European Economic Area between the European Communities and their Member States and the Republic of Austria, the Republic of Finland, the Republic of Iceland, the Principality of Liechtenstein, the Kingdom of Norway, the Kingdom of Sweden and the Swiss Confederation, adopted 28.10.92, OJ N° C 305, 23.11.92, p.66.

Resolution on the conclusions of the European Council meeting in Edinburgh on 11 and 12 December 1992, adopted 16.12.92, OJ N° C 21, 25.1.93, p.105.

Resolution on the establishment of the European Community's common foreign policy, adopted 18.12.92, OJ N° C 21, 25.1.93, p.503.

Resolution on the structure and strategy for the European Union with regard to its enlargement and the creation of a Europe-wide order, adopted 20.1.93, OJ N° C 42, 15.2.93, p.124.

Resolution on the draft uniform electoral procedure for the election of Members of the European Parliament, adopted 10.3.93, OJ N° C 115, 26.4.93, p.121.

Resolution on the enlargement of the Community, adopted 10.2.93, OJ N° C 72, 15.3.93, p.69.

Resolution on respect for human rights in the European Community, adopted 11.3.93, OJ N° C 115, 26.4.93, p.178.

Resolution on the resurgence of racism and xenophobia in Europe and the danger of right-wing extremist violence, adopted 21.4.93, OJ N° C 150, 31.5.93, p.127.

Resolution on development in East–West relations in Europe and their impact on European security, adopted 27.5.93, OJ N° C 172, 28.6.93, p.185.

Resolution on the Decision on the conclusion of the agreement on the European Economic Area as adjusted by the Protocol adjusting the Agreement on the European Economic Area between the European Community, its Member States and the Republic of Austria, the Republic of Finland, the Republic of Iceland, the Principality of Liechtenstein, the Kingdom of Norway and the Kingdom of Sweden, adopted 23.6.93, OJ N° C 194, 19.7.93, p.143.

Resolution on the outcome of the Copenhagen European Council meeting of 21/22 June 1993, adopted 24.6.93, OJ N° C 194, 19.7.93, p.216.

Resolution on cooperation in the fields of justice and home affairs under the Treaty on European Union (Title VI and other provisions), adopted 15.7.93, OJ N° C 255, 20.9.93, p.168.

Resolution on enlargement, adopted 15.7.93, OJ N° C 255, 20.9.93, p.207.

Resolution on the role of the Court of Justice in the development of the European Community's constitutional system, adopted 16.9.93, OJ N° C 268, 4.11.93, p.156.

Opinion of the Committee on Foreign Affairs and Security for the Committee on Institutional Affairs on the report on future relations between the European Community, the WEU and the Atlantic Alliance (draftsman: Mr Hans-Gert Poettering) dated 7.10.93.

Resolution on the Commission proposal for a Council regulation establishing a Guarantee Fund, adopted 28.10.93, European Parliament Minutes of the Sitting of 28.10.93, p.48.

Resolution on the Commission proposal for a Council decision granting a Community guarantee to the European Investment Bank against losses under loans for projects in Central and Eastern European countries (Poland, Hungary, the Czech Republic, the Slovak Republic, Romanian, Bulgaria, Latvia, Estonia, Lithuania and Albania), adopted 28.10.93, European Parliament Minutes of the Sitting of 28.10.93, p.51.

Resolution on the participation and representation of the regions in the process of European integration: the Committee of the Regions, adopted 18.11.93, European Parliament Minutes of the Sitting of 18.11.93, p.19.

Resolution on the Commission proposal for a Council directive laying down detailed arrangements for the exercise of the right to vote and to stand as a candidate in elections to the European Parliament in the Member State of residence, adopted 17.11.93, European Parliament Minutes of the Sitting of 17.11.93, p.46.

Resolution on relations between the Union and the Council of Europe, adopted 15.12.93, European Parliament Minutes of the Sitting of 15.12.93, p.2.

Resolution on the role of national experts and the Commission's right of initiative, adopted 15.12.93, European Parliament Minutes of the Sitting of 15.12.93, p.22.

Resolution on questions of comitology relating to the entry into force of the Treaty on European Union, adopted 15.12.93, European Parliament Minutes of the Sitting of 15.12.93, p.24.

European Parliament, Resolution on the conclusions of the Brussels European Council of 10 and 11 December 1993, adopted 15.12.93, European Parliament Minutes of the Sitting of 15.12.93, p.78.

Resolution on the independence of the national central banks in the context of the second and third stages of Economic and Monetary Union, adopted 15.12.93, European Parliament Minutes of the Sitting of 15.12.93, p.82.

Resolution on Community accession to the European Convention on Human Rights, adopted 18.1.94, European Parliament Minutes of the Sitting of 18.1.94, p.1.

Resolution on voting rights for citizens of the Union in the European elections, adopted 20.1.94, European Parliament Minutes of the Sitting of 20.1.94, p.5.

Resolution on NATO, adopted 20.1.94, European Parliament Minutes of the Sitting of 20.1.94, p.26.

Resolution on participation by the European Parliament in international agreements by the Member States and the Union on cooperation in the fields of justice and home affairs, adopted 20.1.94, European Parliament Minutes of the Sitting of 20.1.94, p.35.

Resolution on the role of the Union within the UN and the problems of reforming the UN, adopted 8.2.94, European Parliament Minutes of the Sitting of 8.2.94, p.18.

Resolution on the results of the deliberations of the ACP–EEC Joint Assembly in 1993, adopted 9.2.94, European Parliament Minutes of the Sitting of 9.2.94, p.60.

Resolution on the state of enlargement negotiations with Austria, Sweden, Finland and Norway, adopted 9.2.94, European Parliament Minutes of the Sitting of 9.2.94, p.83.

Resolution on the appointment of members of the Court of Justice, adopted 9.2.94, European Parliament Minutes of the Sitting of 9.2.94, p.86.

Resolution on the Constitution of the European Union, adopted 10.2.94, European Parliament Minutes of the Sitting of 10.2.94, p.1.

Resolution on future relations between the European Union, the WEU and the Atlantic Alliance, adopted 24.2.94, European Parliament Minutes of the Sitting of 24.2.94, p.2.

Decision of the European Parliament on the regulations and general conditions governing the performance of the Ombudsman's duties, adopted 9.3.94, European Parliament Minutes of the Sitting of 9.3.94, p.18.

Resolution on the situation of women in the European Union, adopted 10.3.94, European Parliament Minutes of the Sitting of 10.3.94, p.48.

Resolution on the democratic control of the financial policy of the European Investment Bank (EIB) and the European Bank for Reconstruction and Development (EBRD), adopted 11.3.94, European Parliament Minutes of the Sitting of 11.3.94, p.72.

Resolution on relations between bodies responsible for control of the Community budget, adopted 11.3.94, European Parliament Minutes of the Sitting of 11.3.94, p.66.

Resolution on the Conference on Security and Cooperation in Europe, adopted 24.3.94, European Parliament Minutes of the Sitting of 24.3.94, p.1.

Resolution on relations between the European Union and the United States of America, adopted 24.3.94, European Parliament Minutes of the Sitting of 24.3.94, p.4.

Resolution on the development of a common security and defence policy for the European Union — objectives, instruments and procedures, adopted 24.3.94, European Parliament Minutes of the Sitting of 24.3.94, p.7.

Resolution on the adaptation of Community legislation to the subsidiarity principle, adopted 20.4.94, European Parliament Minutes of the Sitting of 20.4.94, p.82.

Resolution to inform the Commission of the reasons why the discharge cannot at present be given in respect of the implementation of the general budget of the European Communities for the 1992 financial year, adopted 21.4.94, European Parliament Minutes of the Sitting of 21.4.94, p.100.

Resolution on the investiture of the Commission, adopted 21.4.94, European Parliament Minutes of the Sitting of 21.4.94, p.154.

Resolution on a new system of own resources for the European Union, adopted 21.4.94, European Parliament Minutes of the Sitting of 21.4.94, p.161.

Resolution on the future of the ECSC Treaty, adopted 21.4.94, European Parliament Minutes of the Sitting of 21.4.94, p.170.

Resolution on human rights in the European Union's foreign policy, adopted 21.4.94, European Parliament Minutes of the Sitting of 21.4.94, p.173.

Other documentation

Final Declaration of the Conference of Parliaments of the European Community, adopted 30.11.90, *EP Bulletin* 4/S-90.

European Parliament, 19.5.93, Division for Relations with the Parliaments of the Member States, Information Note, 'The Second Report on "Europe after Maastricht" of the Foreign Affairs Committee of the House of Commons' (internal document).

European Parliament, undated, Division for Relations with the Parliaments of the Member States, Information Note, 'Recent changes in parliamentary scrutiny by national parliaments of the Community activities of their governments' (internal document).

European Parliament, 15.6.93, Committee on the Rules of Procedure, the Verification of Credentials and Immunities, Notice to Members, *Rules for setting up political groups* (internal document).

European Parliament, 15.8.93, Committee on Budgets, Working Document on a New Interinstitutional Agreement; the Agreement reached at the Trialogue of 9.9.93 (internal document).

European Parliament, 29.9.93, Subcommittee on Human Rights, 'Follow-up to initiative resolutions concerning foreign policy, human rights and security adopted by Parliament, July 1989 to July 1993' (Notice to Members).

European Parliament, 31.1.94, Information document submitted to the Conference of Committee Chairmen on the co-decision procedure (internal document).

Index

(NB Index does not include annexes and tables.)